International Kierkegaard
Commentary

International Kierkegaard Commentary

Concluding Unscientific Postscript to "Philosophical Fragments"

edited by
Robert L. Perkins

MERCER UNIVERSITY PRESS

ISBN 0-86554-575-8   MUP/H430

International Kierkegaard Commentary
Concluding Unscientific Postscript
to "Philosophical Fragments"
Copyright ©1997
Mercer University Press, Macon, Georgia 31210-3960 USA
Printed in the United States of America

The paper used in this publication meets the minimum requirements
of American National Standard for Information Sciences—
Permanence of Paper for Printed Library Materials, ANSI Z39.48-1984.

Library of Congress Cataloging-in-Publication Data

Concluding unscientific postscript to "Philosophical Fragments" /
edited by Robert L. Perkins
xii+356pp. 6x9" (15x22cm.)—(International Kierkegaard Commentary ; 12)
Includes bibliographical references and index.
ISBN 0-86554-575-8 (alk. paper).
1. Kierkegaard, Søren, 1813–1855. Afsluttende uvidenskabelig efterskrift.
2. Christianity—Philosophy. 3. Apologetics.
I. Perkins, Robert L., 1930– .   II. Series.
B4376.I58   1984 Vol. 12
[B4373.A4723]
201—dc21   97-31039

CIP

Contents

Acknowledgments

All the contributors to this volume would desire to make acknowledgments, but it is a privilege reserved for the editor. Those whom the contributors would have named will be content to have served their friends and colleagues.

I have the privilege of thanking a number of persons at Stetson University who have supported my work in general and the *International Kierkegaard Commentary* in particular: H. Douglas Lee, president; Eugene S. Lubot, provost; Ann Y. Graham, vice-president for Business and Finance; and Gary Maris, dean of the College of Arts and Sciences. Special acknowledgement is also due to Ms. Joyce Eubank, secretary of the Philosophy Department.

The advisory board and the volume consultant read all the contributions, offered valuable insights into the articles, and also made recommendations for some changes. Dr. Julia Watkin of the University of Tasmania was particularly helpful in suggesting possible authors and tracking down obscure allusions in the text. The interest of Mercer University Press and especially the efforts of Senior Editor Edmon L. Rowell, Jr. are deeply appreciated. Princeton University Press gave permission to quote from *Concluding Unscientific Postscript to "Philosophical Fragments"* and the other translations to which they hold copyright.

The several contributors and I also thank our families for the lost evenings and other scattered hours while we pursued these tasks. Finally, I wish to thank my wife Sylvia Walsh for assistance at every stage of this project and for making our life together an unutterable joy.

Robert L. Perkins

Sigla

AN   *Armed Neutrality* and *An Open Letter*. Trans. Howard V. Hong and Edna H. Hong. Bloomington and London: Indiana Univ. Press, 1968. (*Den bevæbnede Neutralitet*, written 1848–1849, publ. 1965; "Foranledigt ved en Yttring af Dr. Rudelbach mig betræffende," *Fædrelandet*, no. 26 [31 January 1851].)

C   *The Crisis [and a Crisis] in the life of an Actress*. Trans. Stephen Crites. New York: Harper & Row, 1967. (*Krisen og en Krise i en Skuespillerindes Liv*, by Inter et Inter. *Fædrelandet* 188–191 [24–27 July 1848].)

CA   *The Concept of Anxiety*. Kierkegaard's Writings 8. Trans. Reidar Thomte, in collaboration with Albert B. Anderson. Princeton: Princeton Univ. Press, 1980. (*Begrebet Angest*, by Vigilius Haufniensis, ed. S. Kierkegaard, 1844.)

CD   *Christian Discourses*, including *The Lilies of the Field and the Birds of the Air* and *Three Discourses at the Communion on Fridays*. Trans. Walter Lowrie. London and New York: Oxford Univ. Press, 1940. (*Christelige Taler*, by S. Kierkegaard, 1848; *Lilien paa Marken og Fuglen under Himlen*, by S. Kierkegaard, 1849; *Tre Taler ved Altergangen om Fredagen*, by S. Kierkegaard, 1849.)

CI   *The Concept of Irony*; "Notes on Schelling's Berlin Lectures." Kierke-
NSBL   gaard's Writings 2. Trans. Howard V. Hong and Edna H. Hong. Princeton: Princeton Univ. Press, 1989. (*Om Begrebet Ironi*, by S. A. Kierkegaard, 1841.)

COR   *The Corsair Affair*. Kierkegaard's Writings 13. Trans. Howard V. Hong and Edna H. Hong. Princeton: Princeton Univ. Press, 1982.

CUP,1   *Concluding Unscientific Postscript*. Two volumes. Kierkegaard's Writings
CUP,2   12:1-2. Trans. Howard V. Hong and Edna H. Hong. Princeton: Princeton Univ. Press, 1992. (*Afsluttende uvidenskabelig Efterskrift*, by Johannes Climacus, ed. S. Kierkegaard, 1846.)

EO,1   *Either/Or*. Two volumes. Kierkegaard's Writings 3 and 4. Trans.
EO,2   Howard V. Hong and Edna H. Hong. Princeton: Princeton Univ. Press, 1987. (*Enten/Eller* I-II, ed. Victor Eremita, 1843.)

EPW *Early Polemical Writings*. Kierkegaard's Writings 1. Trans. Julia Watkin. Princeton: Princeton Univ. Press, 1990.

EUD *Eighteen Upbuilding Discourses*. Kierkegaard's Writings 5. Trans. Howard V. Hong and Edna H. Hong. Princeton: Princeton Univ. Press, 1990. (*Atten opbyggelige taler*, by S. Kierkegaard, 1843–1845.)

FPOSL *From the Papers of One Still Living*. See EPW.

FSE *For Self-Examination* and *Judge for Yourself!* Kierkegaard's Writings 21.
JFY Trans. Howard V. Hong and Edna H. Hong. Princeton: Princeton Univ. Press, 1990. (*Til Selvprøvelse*, by S. Kierkegaard, 1851, and *Dømmer Selv!* by S. Kierkegaard, 1852.)

FT *Fear and Trembling* and *Repetition*. Kierkegaard's Writings 6. Trans.
R Howard V. Hong and Edna H. Hong. Princeton: Princeton Univ. Press, 1983. (*Frygt og Bæven*, by Johannes de Silentio, 1843, and *Gjentagelsen*, by Constantin Constantius, 1843.)

JC "Johannes Climacus or *De omnibus dubitandum est*." See PF JC.

JFY *Judge for Yourself!* See FSE.

JP *Søren Kierkegaard's Journals and Papers*. Ed. and trans. Howard V. Hong and Edna H. Hong, assisted by Gregor Malantschuk. Bloomington and London: Indiana Univ. Press, (1) 1967; (2) 1970; (3-4) 1975; (5-7) 1978. (From *Søren Kierkegaards Papier* I-XI³ and XII-XIII, 2nd ed., and *Breve og Akstykker vedrørende Søren Kierkegaard*, ed. Niels Thulstrup, I-II, 1953–1954.)

JSK *The Journals of Søren Kierkegaard*. Trans. Alexander Dru. London and New York: Oxford Univ. Press, 1938. (From *Søren Kierkegaards Papier* I-XI³ in 18 volumes, 1909–1936.)

KAUC *Kierkegaard's Attack upon "Christendom,"* 1854–1855. Trans. Walter Lowrie. Princeton: Princeton Univ. Press, 1944. (*Bladartikler* I-XXI, by S. Kierkegaard, *Fædrelandet*, 1854–1855; *Dette skal siges; saa være det da sagt*, by S. Kierkegaard, 1855; *Øieblikket*, by S. Kierkegaard, 1-9, 1855; 10, 1881; *Hvad Christus dømmer om officiel Christendom*, by S. Kierkegaard, 1855.)

LD *Letters and Documents*. Kierkegaard's Writings 25. Trans. Hendrik Rosenmeier. Princeton: Princeton Univ. Press, 1978.

LY *The Last Years*. Trans. Ronald C. Smith. New York: Harper & Row, 1965. (From *Søren Kierkegaards Papier* XI¹-XI².)

NSBL "Notes on Schilling's Berlin Lectures." See CI.

OAR *On Authority and Revelation, The Book on Adler.* Trans. Walter Lowrie. Princeton: Princeton Univ. Press, 1955. (*Bogen om Adler*, written 1846–1847, unpublished, Søren Kierkegaards *Papirer* VII^2 235; VIII^2 B 1-27.)

P *Prefaces: Light Reading for Certain Classes as the Occasion May Require.* Trans. William McDonald. Tallahassee: Florida State University Press, 1989. (*Forord: Morskabslæsning for Enkelte Stænder efter Tid or Leilighed*, by Nicolaus Notabene, 1844.)

PC *Practice in Christianity.* Kierkegaard's Writings 20. Trans. Howard V. Hong and Edna H. Hong. Princeton: Princeton Univ. Press, 1991. (*Indøvelse i Christendom*, by Anti-Climacus, ed. S. Kierkegaard, 1850.)

PF *Philosophical Fragments* and *Johannes Climacus.* Kierkegaard's Writings
JC 7. Trans. Howard V. Hong and Edna H. Hong. Princeton: Princeton Univ. Press, 1985. (*Philosophiske Smuler*, by Johannes Climacus, ed. S. Kierkegaard, 1844. "Johannes Climacus eller *De omnibus dubitandum est*," written 1842–1843, unpublished, *Søren Kierkegaards Papirer* IV C 1.)

PV *The Point of View Etc., including The Point of View for My Work as an Author, Two Notes about "The Individual," and On My Work as an Author.* Trans. Walter Lowrie. London/New York/Toronto: Oxford University Press, 1939. (*Synspunktet for min Forfatter-Virksomhed*, by S. Kierkegaard, posthumously publ. 1859; *Om min Forfatter-Virksomhed*, by S. Kierkegaard, 1851.)

R *Repetition.* See FT, R.

SLW *Stages on Life's Way.* Kierkegaard's Writings 11. Trans. Howard V. Hong and Edna H. Hong. Princeton: Princeton Univ. Press, 1988. (*Stadier paa Livets Vej*, ed. Hilarius Bogbinder 1845.)

SUD *The Sickness unto Death.* Kierkegaard's Writings 19. Trans. Howard V. Hong and Edna H. Hong. Princeton: Princeton Univ. Press, 1980. (*Sygdommen til Døden*, by Anti-Climacus, ed. S. Kierkegaard, 1849.)

TA *Two Ages: The Present Age and the Age of Revolution. A Literary Review.* Kierkegaard's Writings 14. Trans. Howard V. and Edna H. Hong. Princeton: Princeton Univ. Press, 1978. (*En literair Anmeldelse. To Tidsaldre*, by S. Kierkegaard, 1846.)

TDIO *Three Discourses on Imagined Occasions.* Kierkegaard's Writings 10. Trans. Howard V. Hong and Edna H. Hong. Princeton: Princeton University Press, 1993. (*Tre Taler ved tænkte Leiligheder*, by S. Kierkegaard, 1845.)

UDVS *Upbuilding Discourses in Various Spirits*. Kierkegaard's Writings 15. Trans. Howard V. Hong and Edna H. Hong. Princeton: Princeton University Press, 1993. (*Obyggelige Taler i forskjellig Aand*, 1847.)

WL *Works of Love*. Trans. Howard V. and Edna H. Hong. New York: Harper & Row, 1962. (*Kjerlighedens Gjerninger*, 1847.)

Introduction

Concluding Unscientific Postscript to "Philosophical Fragments" was published 28 February 1846, and this collection of essays, all written for the sesquicentennial, is offered in celebration of this singular event in the history of philosophy. Not since Hume's *Treatise* has a philosophic work of such singular merit fallen so near stillborn from the press. Hume attempted to be his own publicist and recast his revolutionary new arguments in his *Inquiries* and the *Abstract*. Kierkegaard, by contrast, made the best of the silence, doggedly pursuing his philosophic task, at least as he Socratically understood it: "once again to read through solo, if possible in a more inward way, the original text of individual human existence relationships, the old familiar text handed down from the fathers" (CUP, 1:629-30).

Philosophical Fragments and *Concluding Unscientific Postscript to "Philosophical Fragments"*[1] are the two works Kierkegaard published under the pseudonym Johannes Climacus.[2] Taken together as the collected works of "John the Climber," they constitute the most contentious contribution to the philosophy of religion in the nineteenth century. Although Climacus responds positively to much of the modernist philosophic enterprize, his originality and perennial importance lies in the fact that his effort more critically and decisively than any other major treatment from that age undercuts key features of the modernist project in the philosophical approach to religion. Both Marx and Nietzsche may be thought to offer more radical treatments of the modern philosophy of religion, but both are more deeply involved with and committed to the common assumptions of the modern age than Climacus: Marx grants priority to materialist considerations in configuring the human

---

[1]For a brief discussion of the ironic relations of the two works and inside jokes Kierkegaard plays on his readers, see Howard V. Hong's introduction to the *Postscript*, CUP, 2:vii-ix.

[2]Kierkegaard attempted to write an intellectual biography of Johannes Climacus, but it remained unfinished. See JC, 113-72.

telos, and his confidence in scientific development and historical progress, though critical, is unquestioned; while Nietzsche's secularism, Darwinism, subjectivism and relativism (perspectivism), and atheism brand him as a rather traditional modernist. By contrast, Climacus's wrestling with the concept of the divine accounts for the continued interest in his thought.

One of the most fetching characteristics of the works of Johannes Climacus is the light touch of his literary style. *Philosophical Fragments* is one of the most aesthetically pleasing philosophic texts since the middle dialogues of Plato. Climacus's style is not at all didactic, but rather he raises philosophical problems as a "thought project" (PF, 9) or as a "poetical venture" (PF, 23). It is, however, the unhappy fate of philosophic works of high literary quality to be commented upon didactically, and the works of Johannes Climacus are no exception.

Climacus confronts modern persons with the question of the divine in the two forms which we in the West have most pointedly raised it: Greek and modern rationalism and the revelation claimed first by the children of Abraham and radically revised by those who found in Jesus of Nazareth the fulfilled promises of God. Without reprising the history of the relations of these two vital understandings or experiences of the divine, or its absence, to each other, Climacus causes us to examine afresh the dialectic that drew them together while at the same time keeping them in so great a tension that neither could finally reduce the other to itself.

Philosophical Fragments focuses on the relation of contingent and necessary truths, the first referring to the historical elements of the Judeo-Christian revelation and the latter to the forms of idealism that identify thought and being with the result that historical events become subordinated in some fashion to the concept of necessity.[3] Climacus rejects all such reductionism of historical contingency to the logic of necessity—playing out again, apparently unbeknownst to himself and in an entirely different intellectual milieu, the medieval arguments about the relation of the freedom of God to the freedom of persons.

---

[3]This qualification puts the idealism of Bishop Berkeley, for instance, outside Climacus's concerns.

Fragments is written "algebraically" (PF, 91), but Part One of *Concluding Unscientific Postscript* "call[s] the matter by its proper name and clothe[s] the issue in its historical costume" (PF, 109; CUP, 1:15). There the historical arguments for the truth of Christianity are laid out and decisively rebutted (CUP, 1:21-49). The speculative, that is, loosely Hegelian, view of Christianity is presented and shown to be utterly different in form, content, and purpose from Christianity itself (CUP, 1:50-57).

Part Two of the *Postscript* undertakes an entirely new project: the examination of human subjectivity in its ethical and religious dimensions. Most of modern philosophy is so out of touch with subjectivity that this part of Climacus's work is frequently radically misunderstood. All too many philosophers take the term "subjectivity" to be the equivalent of "subjectivism" and as a result they simply do not examine his arguments at all. If we substitute the more modern but conceptually thinner jargon of "becoming a person" for his "task of becoming subjective," then some of the prejudice against Climacus may disappear. As he expresses himself:

> But with regard to actually becoming subjective, it is again a matter of what reflective presuppositions the subject must penetrate, what ballast of objectivity he must dispose of, and what infinite conception he has of the significance of this turning, its responsibility and its *discrimen* (distinctive mark).   (CUP, 1:66)

Whatever is the case of modern emotivism and/or subjectivism, Climacus asks us to undertake the intellectual and logical task of analyzing our reflective presuppositions, of distinguishing the relative spheres of objectivity and subjectivity, of understanding the responsibility each person has toward his or her own self, and of comprehending the responsibilities implied in becoming a subject, and also the logical confines and moral implications of the concept of subjectivity and the task of becoming subjective. Such is a complex *philosophic* program, both in terms of logical analysis and moral formation. And it is the antithesis of subjectivism, at least as commonly understood.

Continuing the arguments and analyses of a previous volume of *International Kierkegaard Commentary* dedicated to *Philosophical*

Fragments,[4] this collection of essays focuses on the *Postscript* and undertakes to examine a number of Climacus's arguments and views of classical and contemporary issues in philosophy.

The first five essays discuss issues provoked by developments in recent philosophy. Perspectives from feminist epistemology (Walsh), philosophy of politics (Perkins), postmodernism (Westphal), speculative physics (Watkin), and virtue theory (Roberts) have recently been used to uncover fresh insights in Climacus's thought.

Although critical of sexist elements in Climacus's own thought—for example, his concept of subjectivity—Walsh finds the pseudonym a ready ally in the feminist critique of traditional Western epistemology with its emphasis upon objectivity and disinterestedness, and its single-minded preference for value-free and verifiable truth claims. Distinguishing Climacus's concept of subjectivity from subjectivism, on the one hand, and from a "chummy" form of intersubjectivity, on the other, she identifies several ways in which his thought may aid feminist epistemology in its effort to reformulate the concepts of subjectivity and objectivity in a nonandrocentric fashion.

Perkins, using Plato's *Republic* as a foil, addresses the hoary yet contemporary charges that Kierkegaard's thought is apolitical and quietistic, or, if political implications can be read out of it at all, they are decisionistic. Perkins is emboldened in his effort to reverse these judgments by the presence of numerous overt (and perhaps ironic) political statements in the text. He also notes that Climacus's view of the difficulties of politics expresses the same existential conundrum that finally caused Plato to admit that the education of the philosophic ruler was impossible: how is ideality related to existence, to the individual human being? A third line of Perkins's argument is found in Climacus's treatment of baptism, which frames the *Postscript* and which underlies the sociopolitical arrangements of Golden age Denmark—a cozy form of social control that Kierkegaard is soon to criticize even more explicitly.

Westphal claims that Climacus is as much a postmodernist as Nietzsche and that this recognition forces one to admit that a

---

[4]*International Kierkegaard Commentary: Philosophical Fragments and Johannes Climacus*, ed. Robert L. Perkins (Macon GA: Mercer University Press, 1994).

robust religious postmodernism is possible. His essay is thus programmatic in that it calls for a reexamination of the very definition of postmodernism itself. It "is not necessary to strip Kierkegaard's writings of their [religious] core in order to include them in contemporary postmodernist conversations." To illustrate and demonstrate this assertion, Westphal first compares and contrasts Climacus's thought with Heidegger's critique of ontotheology and then with Derrida's critique of the metaphysics of presence. Westphal claims that the critique of the theology of presence is inherent in orthodox Christianity itself, a disconcerting thought to many, atheists and orthodox alike.

Roberts exploits recent work in philosophical psychology to discuss Climacus's concept of faith as a virtue, which he finds to be more like the virtue of friendship, as Aristotle understands it, than any of the other virtues. Having characterized faith as a "happy passion" in *Fragments*, Climacus in the *Postscript* elaborates it through such concepts as subjectivity, inwardness, existence, eternal happiness, existential pathos, and dialectical pathos. According to Roberts, Climacus shares the common assumption of all value theorists that the task of personal formation is largely a matter of proper passional development of the proper interests, enthusiasms, and concerns, and of the various emotions that arise from them. Roberts then applies what Climacus says about these matters to exegete certain passages in Anti-Climacus's *Practice in Christianity* and the New Testament.

Watkin examines some of the arguments and disputes in the unified field theories of David Atkins and Stephen Hawking and finds there many of the same philosophic problems that challenged Climacus: the privileging of subjectivity over objectivity, the subjugation of the particular to the concept of totality, the approximate nature of empirical knowledge as opposed to the ideal nature of system, and the questionable identity of thought and being in an ideal system. Whatever the differences between Atkins and Hawking, and Watkin points out several, they both share philosophical characteristics that are reminiscent of Hegelianism, whatever its differences from modern field theory.

The next three essays (Jansen, Mooney, and Pyper) address various approaches to Kierkegaard's and Climacus's views of communication.

Jansen utilizes Kierkegaard's lecture notes from the journals on ethicoreligious communication to approach Climacus's views of communication in *Postscript*. According to Climacus and Kierkegaard, the most important issue for communication in modern societies is the disappearance of the personal dimension, the powerlessness of the communication to elicit interest and faith in the message, whether in philosophy or in religious orthodoxy. The question is how a speaker/writer can restore in modern media, which focuses on "information," the existential provocation to Socratic inwardness and/or Christianity. Jansen addresses these issues in order to relate Kierkegaard's lecture notes and discussion to contemporary issues in communication theory.

Continuing in line with Jansen's argument, Mooney demonstrates how philosophy, religion, and ethics are ways of life, forms of life founded upon a set of beliefs that motivate and shape the personality rather than matters of mere information or objective knowledge. The question for the philosopher, the ethicist, or the religious teacher is how one can evoke a personal response to the truth-claims in these disciplines: How can the objective knowledge, say, about an exemplar such as Socrates or Abraham, be appropriated to the task of personal becoming? How does one engage the subject? Mooney discusses some of the literary techniques Climacus uses as well as some of the exemplars which both Climacus and other pseudonyms use to motivate and elicit response.

Pyper picks up on Westphal's claim that postmodernism does not exclude a "robust" examination of religious issues and on Jansen's and Mooney's concern with texts as communicative instruments. Treating *Postscript* as a communicative instrument, he examines irony, humor, and the comic as literary modes which are used by Climacus to elicit an existential response to the ethicoreligious and to the religious strictly understood (Christianity). Appealing to Gérard Genette's literary study, *Seuils*, Pyper also discusses the significance of some of the paratextual literary structures of the *Postscript* such as the fact that it is a postscript and has two "postscripts" itself in the "appendix," both an "An Understanding with the Reader" and "A First and Last Explanation."

The next two essays concentrate on contentious issues in metaphysics and epistemology (Piety and Anderson) and are also conceptually related to Walsh's essay which opens this volume.

Piety's paper attempts to "debunk" the charge made by Louis Mackey that the *Postscript* is, in a few unguarded passages, anti-realist or "acosmic." Piety argues that Mackey's view is based, first, in his confusion of ontological and epistemological issues and, second, in his false assumption that Kierkegaard's view of freedom is identical with some forms of the existentialist view, that is, that the individual's freedom is absolute. Also implicit in Mackey's view is his lack of appreciation of the distinction of the very different concepts of *Realitet* and *Virkelighed* in the Danish language and in Kierkegaard's thought. Kierkegaard never denies or defends the reality of the world, for such an effort on his part would be superfluous from his philosophic standpoint. He is a realist through and through.

Clearly complementing Piety's critique of Climacus's supposed acosmism, Anderson addresses the widely held view that his epistemology finally resolves itself into skepticism. Anderson carefully analyzes Climacus's treatment of empirical knowledge as approximate knowledge and notes that Climacus is well aware of the difficulties internal to skepticism, indeed, that he addressed them as objections to epistemological skepticism! In contrast to the skeptical reading of *Postscript*, Anderson highlights for us the "rationalist" view of knowledge held by Climacus in contrast to which empirical knowledge is indeed approximate.

The next two essays (Hannay and McDonald) focus on Kierkegaard's relations to philosophers of his recent past: the critical historical epistemology of Lessing (which relates this essay to the two previous ones) and the system of Hegel (which relates especially to the essay by Anderson).

Hannay attempts to sort out the benefits and liabilities of having Lessing on one's side. By appealing to Lessing as a subjective thinker, a claim Climacus needs to establish in order to place his own effort in the immediate cultural discussion of the meaning of faith, Climacus is able to distinguish his critical position from others current at the time. The appeal to Lessing also provides a stance from which the limits of reason come into view without having to bear the weight of Kant's *Critique of Pure Reason*. So well worked out is the portrait of Lessing that Climacus can arguably attribute the distinction between the objective and the subjective as well as tie the discussions of pathos and the comic to him. These inventions on Climacus's part enable him to add another figure to his cast of philosophic heroes, which to this point has focused primarily upon Socrates.

McDonald's essay examines the possible relations of Kierkegaard's *Postscript* to the preface of Hegel's *Phenomenology of Spirit* from a postmodernist and literary point of view. McDonald reads the *Phenomenology* as a preface to the whole system as presented in Hegel's *Encyclopedia of the Philosophical Sciences*. The *Postscript*, by contrast, ends with a revocation of all said in it, including the review of the authorship. Thus the idea of a preface and a postface stand in tension with each other, and McDonald finds the rhetorical structures of Hegel's *Encyclopedia* and Kierkegaard's authorship stand in inverse relation to each other. The result is that there are important differences between their philosophic rhetorics and what can be communicated within them.

The next four essays (Glenn, Law, Barrett, Keeley) discuss major themes internal to the *Postscript* itself.

Glenn notes that Climacus does not discuss the nature of eternal happiness, that is, what that state would be like, but rather what is the proper relation an individual should and can have to such an end if there be one. Interestingly, however, Glenn infers some aspects of Climacus's concept of an eternal happiness from what he says about one's proper relation to it. To bring out the issues, Glenn analyzes Aristotle's and Kant's concepts of a highest good and finds certain differences between Climacus and both, but with more affinity to Kant than Aristotle. When Glenn compares what Climacus says of the matter with the New Testament, a serious omission and difference is noted, and that difference is also apparent between Climacus's idea of eternal happiness and what Kierkegaard published under his own name, especially in *Works of Love*.

Founding his analysis upon a brief statement of Climacus's psychology, Law exegetes three of the thickest, and most widely misunderstood, concepts in the *Postscript*: resignation, suffering, and guilt. The three categories are stages on subjectivity's way to the establishment and maintenance of an absolute relation to the absolute and a relative relation to the relative. The three stages raise difficult questions about the intellectualist content of Climacus's view of Religion B (Christianity), the charge of elitism, and the social import of these concepts, if any, expressing a view quite different from that of Perkins.

Barrett addresses the relation of the apparently contradictory propositions found on the very same page in the *Postscript*, "Subjectivity is truth" and "Subjectivity is untruth." His analysis of these texts suggests there are two uses of the term "subjectivity" in the *Postscript* and that the recognition of this enables one to resolve the apparent contradiction. The first use is an expression of the passionate concern that qualifies any and all religion. The second use draws attention to the insufficiency of inwardness to redeem itself and points the subject to another, to such phenomena as the incarnation.

Keeley supplies important detail to Law's and Barrett's studies in her examination of the concept of spiritual trial by raising the question whether the religious individual can take a trip to Deer Park: Can the religiously serious person take such an entertaining and trivial diversion in view of the necessity to relate all of existence to the serious matter of religious formation, of relating to the absolute absolutely and to the relative relatively? If such a trip is permitted, what arguments support such a frivolous waste of time?

The final essay (Burgess) analyzes certain structural features of the *Postscript* that experienced readers have always puzzled over, what he calls the "postscriptness of the *Postscript*." Experienced readers of the *Postscript* have wondered why Climacus seems to linger in some places, and then the reader has wondered more why some of the most important issues are dealt with almost cryptically. Most of us have wished there had been an editor with a red pencil in the publishing house. Burgess finds a bilateral, though rather lopsided, symmetry within three envelopes which enclose the text, and so has specified the map of the structural difficulties readers experience. He also offers interesting philosophic and literary suggestions why Climacus proceeded as he did. The reason, in twenty-five words or less, for this lay-out is found in Climacus's own "outsider" appraisal of Christianity (he being no Christian himself).

This volume of essays is offered to our readers, who by criticism and better thinking we invite to become our teachers.

1

Subjectivity versus Objectivity:
Kierkegaard's Postscript and Feminist Epistemology

Sylvia Walsh

One of the main targets of the feminist critique of the Western philosophic/scientific epistemological tradition has been its objectivist emphasis on dispassionate inquiry in the search for value-free, universalizable truths. In this paper I shall argue that Kierkegaard's *Concluding Unscientific Postscript* (1846) may be regarded as a philosophical precursor of and ally in this critique, as well as an important resource for rethinking the concept of subjectivity in a manner that does not collapse into an isolated subjectivism, on the one hand, or into a "chummy" form of intersubjectivity that compromises the integrity of the individual, on the other.

This is not to claim that the position of Johannes Climacus, the pseudonymous "author" of this text, is not also subject to feminist critique on various aspects of his understanding of objectivity and subjectivity.[1] On the contrary, from a feminist perspective there are

---

[1] In a "A First and Last Explanation" appended to the text of *Concluding Unscientific Postscript*, to which Kierkegaard affixed his name only as "editor" of the published version, the claim is put forth that in his pseudonymous works "there is not a single word by me" and that he is responsible for these works only "in a legal and in a literary sense" (CUP, 1:626-27). Therefore, one cannot unequivocally equate the views expressed in this work with those of Kierkegaard himself, although there is undoubtedly much in it with which Kierkegaard agrees inasmuch as it constitutes the central philosophical statement of his authorship. On the purpose and role of pseudonymity in Kierkegaard's writings, see my discussion in *Living Poetically: Kierkegaard's Existential Aesthetics* (University Park PA: Penn State University Press, 1994) 10-15; C. Stephen Evans, *Kierkegaard's "Fragments" and "Postscript": The Religious Philosophy of Johannes Climacus* (Atlantic Highlands NJ: Humanities Press, 1983) 6-16; and M. Holmes Hartshorne, *Kierkegaard, Godly Deceiver: The Nature and Meaning of His Pseudonymous Writings* (New

some serious deficiencies in Climacus's thought that need to be pointed out. It should be noted at the outset, however, that feminist philosophy is not monolithic in its critique and rethinking of the concepts of objectivity and subjectivity. Before turning to a consideration of these concepts in the *Postscript*, therefore, I shall briefly characterize the conventional understanding of objectivity and the knowing subject that has provoked feminist critique, indicate the main objections feminists have raised to it, and sketch several feminist epistemological approaches that have emerged in the process of assessing and reformulating these concepts from a feminist perspective. We should then be in a position to determine more precisely the similarities and differences between Climacus and feminist epistemologists on these issues.

I. Feminist Criticisms of and Responses to the Conventional Understanding of Objectivity and the Knowing Subject

The conventional concept of objectivity in Western philosophy is variously analyzed by feminist philosophers as having its inception in Plato (e.g., Duran, Keller, Irigaray), Descartes (Bordo, Hodge), and the empiricist as well as rationalist epistemologies of the Englightenment that gave birth to modern science (Code, Hekman, Harding).[2] This concept is typically characterized by

---

York: Columbia University Press, 1990).

[2]For a concise differentiation between four senses of objectivity (absolute, disciplinary, dialectical, and procedural) in current discussions, see Allan Megill, "Introduction: Four Senses of Objectivity," in *Rethinking Objectivity*, ed. Allan Megill (Durham: Duke University Press, 1994) 1-20. It is primarily the absolute sense of objectivity that corresponds to the concept of objectivity attacked by feminist epistemologists, although the disciplinary and procedural senses of the term also involve elements of the absolute sense. On the sources of the conventional concept of objectivity, see Jane Duran, *Toward a Feminist Epistemology* (Savage MD: Rowman and Littlefield, 1991) 5-8; Evelyn Fox Keller, "Gender and Science," in *Discovering Reality: Feminist Perspectives on Epistemology, Metaphysics, Methodology, and Philosophy of Science*, ed. Sandra Harding and Merill B. Hintikka (Dordrecht: D. Reidel Publishing Co., 1983) 187-205, and idem., *Reflections on Gender and Science* (New Haven: Yale University Press, 1985); Luce Irigaray, *Speculum of the Other Woman*, trans. Gillian C. Gill (Ithaca NY: Cornell University Press, 1985); Susan R. Bordo, *The Flight to Objectivity: Essays on Cartesianism & Culture* (Albany: State University of New York Press, 1987); Joanna Hodge,

feminists as one that assumes a separation between subject and object, fact and value, and requires the rendering of an impartial, dispassionate, value-free, empirically verifiable, and rationally coherent account of the objective world. The concept of the knowing subject corresponding to this view of objectivity is that of an autonomous, detached, dispassionate individual who has the capacity to adopt the stance of an independent, neutral observer in relation to the external world and to suppress or eliminate personal, or merely subjective, feelings, interests, and values in coming to know and describe that world.[3]

In the view of some feminist critics, this understanding of objectivity and subjectivity, exemplified in modern scientific method, with physics serving as its paradigm,[4] reflects a typically masculine way of relating to the world and thus actually represents an androcentric, male-biased, and male-constructed perspec-

---

"Subject, Body, and the Exclusion of Women from Philosophy," in *Feminist Perspectives in Philosophy*, ed. Morwenna Griffiths and Margaret Whitford (Bloomington: Indiana University Press, 1988) 152-68; Lorraine Code, *What Can She Know? Feminist Theory and the Construction of Knowledge* (Ithaca: Cornell University Press, 1991) 27-70; Susan J. Hekman, *Gender and Knowledge: Elements of a Postmodern Feminism* (Boston: Northeastern University Press, 1990) 1-10; Sandra Harding, *The Science Question in Feminism* (Ithaca: Cornell University Press, 1986) 36-57.

[3]Hodge, "Subject, Body, and the Exclusion of Women from Philosophy," 154-66; Code, *What Can She Know?*, 46-52; Mary E. Hawkesworth, "Knowers, Knowing, Known: Feminist Theory and Claims of Truth," *Signs: Journal of Women in Culture and Society* 14/3 (1989): 533-57.

[4]For a critique of physics as a paradigm of scientific knowledge-seeking, see Harding, *The Science Question in Feminism*, 43-48, and *Whose Science? Whose Knowledge?* (Ithaca and New York: Cornell University Press, 1991) 77-102. In place of physics, which in her view is atypical of scientific inquiry and anachronistic in its exclusion of values or social influences in explaining reality, Harding recommends that the social sciences be regarded as the model for all science. See also Code, *What Can She Know?*, 40-41, and Ruth Hubbard, "Some Thoughts about the Masculinity of Science," in *Feminist Thought and the Structure of Knowledge*, ed. Mary McCanney Gergen (New York and London: New York University Press, 1988) 1-15, who concur with Harding's recommendation. Hubbard points out, however, that even physicists recognized early in this century that experimenters influence the outcome of their experiments, an insight expressed in Heisenberg's "uncertainty principle" (11).

tive rather than a gender-neutral stance toward reality.[5] This means that the so-called value free descriptions of modern science and epistemology are not value free but rather reflect the social values and interests of a specific gender. A particularly objectionable feature of this androcentric viewpoint for many feminists is the fact that it is predicated on and perpetuates a fundamentally dichotomous form of thought in which one term is privileged, the other negated or suppressed, in the affirmation of reason against passion, mind over body, objectivity over subjective interests and values.[6] Since women traditionally have been associated with the devalued terms of these dichotomies, the effect has been an exclusion of women from participation in philosophic and scientific endeavors or else a denial of their female nature (assuming there is one) in the requirement that they become more like men by developing the kind of detached subjectivity or objective stance necessary for acquiring a true knowledge of the world. Another objection voiced by some feminists is that the "male gaze," or the indifferent, disinterested, and nonreciprocal objective stance associated with the conventional understanding of objectivity, results in the objectification or reification and dehumanization of women into things or objects.[7]

---

[5]Kenneth Gergen, "Feminist Critique of Science and the Challenge of Social Epistemology," in *Feminist Thought and the Structure of Knowledge*, ed. Gergen, 27-48; Code, *What Can She Know?*, 35, 117-19; Genevieve Lloyd, *The Man of Reason* (London: Methuen, 1984); Duran, 5-14, 44; Harding, *Whose Science? Whose Knowledge?*, 39-50; Lynn Hankinson Nelson, *Who Knows? From Quine to a Feminist Empiricism* (Philadelphia: Temple University Press, 1990) 189-90; Catharine MacKinnon, *Feminism Unmodified* (Cambridge: Harvard University Press, 1987) 50, 54-55.

[6]Code, *What Can She Know?*, 27-55; Hekman, *Gender and Knowledge*, passim; Jennifer Ring, *Modern Political Theory and Contemporary Feminism: A Dialectical Analysis* (Albany: State University of New York Press, 1991) 17-25.

[7]See MacKinnon and the discussion of her position by Sally Haslanger, "On Being Objective and Being Objectified," in *A Mind of One's Own: Feminist Essays on Reason & Objectivity*, ed. Louise M. Antony and Charlotte Witt (Boulder CO: Westview Press, 1993) 85-125. See also Mary E. Hawkesworth, "From Objectivity to Objectification: Feminist Objections," in *Rethinking Objectivity*, ed. Megill, 151-77, and relevant references cited therein. Although Hawkesworth finds "no inherent link between objectivity and objectification," she thinks feminist critiques making this objection offer "important insights about the nature and limits of dominant conceptions of objectivity" and may serve as a corrective (151).

Feminist responses to this understanding of objectivity and the knowing subject are varied but may be grouped into four major approaches: feminist empiricism, feminist standpoint theory, post-modern feminism, and a mediating, integrationist understanding of objectivity and subjectivity.[8]

1. Feminist Empiricism

Orienting their positions in the naturalized, contextualized epistemologies of contemporary theorists in philosophy of science, cognitive science, and analytic philosophy, feminist empiricists argue that there is no need to abandon an empirical and scientific approach to knowledge.[9] Rather, what is needed, in their view, is a new empirical approach to epistemology that is anti- or post-individualist in its recognition of the communal, contextual, socially constructed, nonfoundational, descriptive rather than normative character of knowledge and that incorporates, rather than excludes, social, political, moral, and gender values in a self-conscious and self-critical fashion in its understanding of objectivity.[10] By becoming more inclusive of the experiences and participation of women in the scientific enterprise, it is believed that empirical science will be able to give a less androcentric, more complete, and therefore more objective account of the world.

2. Feminist Standpoint Theory

Feminist standpoint theorists, like feminist empiricists, acknowledge the social situatedness of knowledge and advocate the use of women's experiences as a basis for scientific research in the

---

[8]For more extended discussions of the first three approaches, see Harding, *Whose Science? Whose Knowledge?*, 111-87, and *The Science Question in Feminism*, 36-57; 136-62; and Hekman, *Gender and Knowledge*, 128-35.

[9]Nelson, *Who Knows? From Quine to a Feminist Empiricism*, 5-7, 85; Duran, *Toward a Feminist Epistemology*, 3-5, 105-10. See also Louise M. Antony, "Quine as Feminist: The Radical Import of Naturalized Epistemology," in *A Mind of One's Own*, ed. Antony and Witt, 185-225.

[10]Nelson, *Who Knows? From Quine to a Feminist Empiricism*, 5, 7, 14; Duran, *Toward a Feminist Epistemology*, 3-5, 13-14, 43-69, 110-15; Antony, "Quine as Feminist," 213. See also Helen E. Longino, *Science as Social Knowledge: Values and Objectivity in Scientific Inquiry* (Princeton: Princeton University Press, 1990) 62-85, 215-25.

belief that they will yield a greater objectivity, or "strong objectivity," in contrast to the "weak objectivity" of objectivism or the conventional perspective.[11] Having its theoretical basis in post-Freudian object relations theory and in a post-Marxist historical-materialist analysis of female oppression as resulting from the sexual division of labor, this position claims that "women's lives differ structurally from those of men" and provide "a particular and privileged vantage point" that is less partial and distorted than that of men.[12] In other words, the feminist standpoint, oriented as it is in the historical development of personality structures and modes of reasoning that foster contextual understanding, psychosomatic unity, and a sense of connectedness with other persons and nature, not only provides *greater* objectivity but also a *better* objective basis for making observations about nature, social relations, and the social order.[13] Because women are "strangers" or

---

[11]Harding, *Whose Science? Whose Knowledge?*, 138-63. While objectivists advocate the elimination of all social values and interests in the pursuit of objective knowledge, Harding claims they fail to recognize and critically examine the historical, social position of their own background assumptions and beliefs, thus providing only a limited, partial, distorted view of reality. Strong objectivity, by contrast, "requires causal analyses not just of the micro processes in the laboratory but also of the macro tendencies in the social order, which shape scientific practices" (144, 147).

[12]Nancy C. M. Hartsock, "The Feminist Standpoint: Developing the Ground for a Specifically Feminist Historical Materialism" (284) and Sandra Harding, "Why Has the Sex/Gender System Become Visible Only Now?" (321) in *Discovering Reality*, ed. Harding and Hintikka. As Harding points out in her discussion of feminist standpoint theory in *Whose Science? Whose Knowledge?*, this position is not based on biological differences between men and women or upon essentialist claims of a distinctive "female nature," although it is often misunderstood as doing so. Rather, it is based on gender differences, or differences rooted in women's social situation and experiences, which provide an objective location from which to conduct feminist research and to criticize knowledge claims, although not an epistemological foundation for grounding knowledge claims as such, since "experience itself is shaped by social relations" (120-21 and n. 19; 123, 132-34, 137n.39). On object relations theory, which accounts for the development of gender differences between males and females on the basis of how their oedipal relation to the mother is resolved, see Nancy Chodorow, *The Reproduction of Mothering* (Berkeley: University of California Press, 1978).

[13]Harding, *Whose Science? Whose Knowledge?*, 124-33; Hartsock, "The Feminist Standpoint," 298-304; Hilary Rose, "Hand, Brain, and Heart: A Feminist

"outsiders" both to and within the established order, women's experiences provide a fresh, more distant perspective from which to test and evaluate conventional knowledge claims.[14]

3. Postmodern Feminist Epistemology

Rejecting the notion of a univocal and universal feminist standpoint, or a "women's way of knowing," as well as the masculinist, unitary conception of truth fostered by the Englightenment tradition, postmodern feminists recognize a plurality of women's voices and interpretations of truth, none of which, in their view, is epistemologically privileged. Thus they seek to abandon the conventional concepts of objectivity and subjectivity altogether, finding them a perpetuation of the masculinist, dichotomous thinking inherent in Enlightenment epistemology.[15] In their view, both knowledge and the knowing subject are socially constituted through language or forms of discourse. The focus of their attack thus falls upon the humanist ideal of the autonomous, self-constituting subject, which they find to be inherently masculinist, and thus hopelessly phallocentric, in spite of the fact that feminism historically has appealed to humanist values such as natural rights, dignity, and autonomy in its fight against female oppression.[16] From the viewpoint of postmodern feminists, therefore, it will not do to argue—as Simone de Beauvoir does in *The Second Sex*, for example—that women should become independent subjects like

---

Epistemology for the Natural Sciences," *Signs* 9/1 (1983): 73-90.

[14]Harding, *Whose Science? Whose Knowledge?*, 124-26, 128-32, and other works cited by Harding therein.

[15]Hekman, *Gender and Knowledge*, 9-16. Hekman thus opposes the notion of a "feminist epistemology," if that means one which privileges the feminine over against the masculine. As Kenneth Gergen points out in "Feminist Critique of Science and the Challenge of Social Epistemology," the problem with the feminist standpoint theory is that it is difficult, if not impossible, to locate a common perspective on knowledge among women since there are a variety of schools of feminist interpretation. Which among these, he asks, should be granted epistemological privilege as the feminist standpoint, and on what grounds (32)? On the abandonment of the concept of objectivity, see also MacKinnon, although her critique of objectivity proceeds from a Marxist rather than postmodernist perspective.

[16]Hekman, *Gender and Knowledge*, 63, 79; Alice Jardine, *Gynesis: Configurations of Women and Modernity* (Ithaca: Cornell University Press, 1985) 44.

men in order to realize their self-identity, because all the qualities that characterize the humanist/existentialist subject are associated with the masculine.[17] Postmodern feminists opt instead to view woman as a process whose self-identity is multiple, decentered, nonpersonal, and/or constantly deferred.[18]

Although the female subject is a construct of discourse, and thus socially determined rather than self-constituting, she nevertheless has the power, they claim, to resist those modes of discourse which historically have constituted her in oppressive ways, opening up the possibility of fashioning new modes of female subjectivity that transgress the traditionally sharp boundaries between subject and object, self and other.[19]

4. Integrationist Approach

Many feminist thinkers, however, are unwilling to embrace postmodernism as well as some forms of feminist standpoint theory because, in their interpretation, these positions endorse not only cultural relativism but also an epistemological relativism that lapses into subjectivism or a denial of objective knowledge altogether.[20] As Sandra Harding succinctly states their objection: "One cannot afford to 'just say no' to objectivity."[21] Along with postmod-

---

[17]Hekman, *Gender and Knowledge*, 77. Cf. Simone de Beauvoir, *The Second Sex*, trans. and ed. H. M. Parshley (New York: Vintage Books, 1989).

[18]For a discussion of French postmodern feminist concepts of self-identity, see my *Living Poetically*, 251-57, and other works cited therein.

[19]Hekman, 68, 73, 87, 189. Hekman appeals to Foucault's view of the constituted subject as "the subject that resists" and to Julia Kristeva's claim that the subject in process is one that has revolutionary potential, although it is not clear from either of these analyses how the subject who is constituted by discourse has the power to resist that constitution.

[20]For an example of feminist standpoint theory that advocates subjectivism, see Mary Field Belenky et al., *Women's Ways of Knowing: The Development of Self, Voice, and Mind* (New York: Basic Books, Inc., 1986) 10, 52-75. For a critique of this position see Code, *What Can She Know?*, 253-64. Harding argues that feminist standpoint theory advocates cultural or historical relativism but not an epistemological or judgmental relativism, since critical evaluation based on a scientific account is required "to determine which social situations tend to generate the most objective knowledge claims" (142). Hekman counters the charge of relativism in postmodernist thought by arguing that "all knowledge is contextual and historical, thus rendering the opposition between absolute and relative obselete" (153).

[21]Harding, *Whose Science, Whose Knowledge?*, 160.

ern feminists and feminist theorists from the other feminist epistemological approaches, this group recognizes the fundamentally
communal or contextual character of knowledge and thus denies
the possibility of a pure or value-free objectivity, but not the
"independent integrity" of the objective world and the possibility
of gaining an objective knowledge of it.[22] Consequently, these
feminist epistemologists seek to articulate a mediating position that
involves an integration, interpenetration, or dialectical interplay of
objectivity and subjectivity rather than a negation of them.[23] In line
with the postmodernist critique of dichotomizing forms of thought,
this approach envisions at least a momentary dissolution of the
boundaries between subjectivity and objectivity in a mutuality of
influence or intersubjectivity that affirms both separation and
unity, a merging and differentiation of subject from object.[24] What
is needed, then, in the view of this group, is a recasting or recon-
ceptualization of objectivity and subjectivity in a nondichotomous,
more harmonious relationship.[25]

---

[22]Keller, *Reflections on Gender and Science*, 117. See also Longino, *Science as Social Knowledge*.

[23]See Ring, *Modern Political Theory and Contemporary Feminism*, who espouses a "minimalist dialectics" in line with the positions of Harding and Keller but places greater emphasis on the element of conflict than they do (27). On dialectical objectivity generally, see Megill, "Four Senses of Objectivity," 7-10. See also Code, *What Can She Know?*, who advocates a "mitigated relativism" that is constrained by objectivity but takes subjectivity into account (251).

[24]For an account of scientific practice involving such an interaction, see Evelyn Fox Keller, *A Feeling for the Organism: The Life and Work of Barbara McClintock* (New York: W. H. Freeman, 1983). See also Code, who argues with regard to knowing subjects "that there is no stark dichotomy between interdependence and autonomy, that they are neither oppositional nor mutually exclusive" (74).

[25]Feminists taking this approach do not entirely agree, however, in their rein-scription of these terms. While Keller, for example, calls for a "dynamic objectiv-ity" that includes a sense of connectedness to the objective world, thus redefining it in a feminine sense that downplays (masculine) separation or autonomy (*Reflec-tions on Gender and Science*, 115-26), Ring retains the traditional association of this term with distance, detachment, and isolation but is unwilling to concede that these elements are specifically male or entirely bad (*Modern Political Theory and Contemporary Feminism*, 54). Indeed, feminist standpoint epistemologists appeal precisely to women's outsider or isolated status in relation to the established order as enabling them to give a better and more objective account of the world because they are distanced from it.

II. Objectivity and Subjectivity
in Concluding Unscientific Postscript

In light of these developments in feminist epistemology, let us now examine the critique of objectivity and the concept of subjectivity offered in *Concluding Unscientific Postscript*. Although the central problem for the pseudonymous author, Johannes Climacus, is a religious one concerning the individual's relation to Christianity, the text addresses this issue in the context of a wide-ranging discussion of historical, scientific, and speculative modes of inquiry as ways of determining objective truth and knowledge. Climacus frames his critique of objectivity primarily around an analysis of two issues: (1) the presumed certainty of objective knowledge and (2) the indifferent or disinterested stance of the objective knower. He begins by making a fundamental distinction between two kinds of truth and, in correspondence with these, two modes of knowing: (1) objective truth, which is known through a rational and/or empirical mode of inquiry; and (2) subjective truth, the truth of appropriating or making something one's own (*Tilegnelse*), which is known by existing in a particular state (CUP, 1:21, 53-54; 2:185n.2). Objective truth is further subdivided by Climacus into two forms: historical and philosophical. The former, he states, is determined empirically by the historical-critical method of examining and assessing various historical reports, while the latter is established rationally by showing how doctrines that have been "historically given and verified" are related to eternal truth. (Climacus does not address here the status of *nonhistorical* objective truths such as logic and mathematics.) From Climacus's perspective, both forms of objective truth may be regarded as "scientific," in the broad sense in which this term was understood in the nineteenth century, inasmuch as they are purported to provide an absolute certainty of knowledge.

Far from yielding such absolute certainty, however, all objective knowledge relating to history or actuality is really uncertain and only an approximation, Climacus charges (CUP, 1:38). Historical knowledge in particular, he points out, is incomplete and always subject to doubt and revision on the basis of further observation and research (CUP, 1:30, 42, 150). But the charge is expanded to include sense certainty and speculative philosophical truths as well as the claim that "objectively there is no truth for existing beings, but only approximations" (CUP, 1:38, 44, 218). All "positive" knowledge is therefore declared to be untrue by Climacus, and sense certainty, historical knowledge, and speculative results are branded a delusion, illusion, and phantom respectively (CUP, 1:81, 314, 316).[26]

As Climacus sees it, the only certainty lies in the infinite and the eternal, which speculative thought in particular claims to have grasped but has not, since the knowing subject does not exist *sub specie aeterni* but is continually in the process of arriving at truth (CUP, 1:82). "Whatever is known is known in the mode of the knower"—an old saying to which Climacus appeals in his discussion—may be taken as stating a fundamental principle of his epistemology (CUP, 1:52). Thus the fact that the knowing subject is an existing subject, for whom everything historical—except one's own existence, which we shall consider in a moment—is uncertain, must be expressed in all of our knowing; otherwise, Climacus maintains, that knowledge does not pertain to the state of the knowing subject *in existence* but to a fictive "objective subject" who does not exist (CUP, 1:81).

---

[26]Cf. *Philosophical Fragments*, 79-84 and n. 53, where Climacus shows that, in a very fundamental way, every historical event requires an element of belief in its having come into existence, since events are always known after the fact, that is, after they have come into existence. The illusive quality of every historical event, to which we are not privy through immediate sensation and cognition, is that transition moment of coming into existence, by which the occurrence of that event is rendered uncertain. In this work Climacus also points out—in conformity, he claims, with Greek skepticism as well as with Plato and Aristotle—that immediate sensation and cognition are not in themselves deceptive; rather, the possibility of deception arises in the *conclusions* one draws on the basis of immediate sensation and cognition. But, whereas the Greek skeptics engaged in a suspension of judgment in order to avoid error, Climacus calls for a decision or resolution (*Beslutning*), in the form of belief, that involves risk or the possibility of error, in contrast to a conclusion (*Slutning*), whose claims are those of positive or certain knowledge. Belief, like doubt, he further points out, is not a cognitive act or form of knowledge; rather, these existential modes are opposite passions— belief constituting "a sense for coming into existence," while "doubt is a protest against any conclusion that wants to go beyond immediate sensation and immediate knowledge" (PF, 84).

Climacus further points out that all objective knowledge about actuality is an abstraction from existence that gives a false rendition of actuality, which must be annulled or transposed into possibility in order to be grasped conceptually (CUP, 1:314-18). The only actuality to which one has more than a cognitive relation, or "knowledge about," Climacus claims, is one's own existence, which constitutes the only *actuality* for an existing person; every other actuality is known only in the form of possibility (CUP, 1:316-17). This means that the only certain historical knowledge to be had by an existing individual is self-knowledge or subjective truth—not in the Cartesian sense of being certain of one's own existence on the basis of thought, which in Climacus's view is an abstraction from existence rather than a demonstration of it, but in the Socratic sense of being infinitely interested in relating oneself to the truth, so as to exist in it (CUP, 1:37, 82, 152, 153-54, 204-205, 316-17).

It is this relation of the knowing subject to the truth that constitutes the chief concern and "knotty difficulty" for Climacus (CUP, 1:37). Like feminists, Climacus describes the posture of the inquiring, knowing subject in objective modes of knowledge as that of a disinterested observer: "Let the scientific researcher labor with restless zeal, let him even shorten his life in the enthusiastic service of science and scholarship; let the speculative thinker spare neither time nor effort—they are nevertheless not infinitely, personally, impassionedly interested" (CUP, 1:21-22). Nor should they be, Climacus thinks, since in objective modes of knowledge it is the truth itself that is important, not the individual's relation to the truth, which must be placed in parenthesis (CUP, 1:27-29, 47, 75). Thus, whereas feminists fault objective modes of knowledge for failing to recognize the masculine subjective agendas that currently drive them and for neglecting to incorporate the subjective interests and values of women as well as men, Climacus accepts the essentially disinterested character of objective modes of inquiry, although he admits that in those endeavors "where one should be objective, in strict scholarship, objectivity is rare" (CUP, 1:43, 76n).

But Climacus also proceeds to fault objective modes of knowledge, in company with feminists, precisely because one is required to move away from and abandon oneself in objectivity, thereby becoming indifferent to one's own existence and relation to the truth and ultimately disappearing from oneself altogether in becoming the "gazing power" of speculative thought (CUP, 1:56, 75, 116).[27] In Climacus's view, every human being has, or should have, an infinite interest or passionate concern about his or her own existence and eternal happiness. This passionate self-interest is understood in an ethical, not an egotistical, sense by Climacus; that is, it has to do with the cultivation of subjectivity or inward-ness in the human personality, which in his view is the highest task assigned to every human being, thus constituting the univer-sal ethical requirement (CUP, 1:134, 151, 158, 163, 346). The adop-tion of an objective posture, especially in relation to ethical or exis-tential matters, not only is incongruous with this self-interest but also renders the individual who adopts it *comic* inasmuch as it requires one to move away from, rather than toward, oneself in in-finite interest (CUP, 1:43, 54-56, 120, 124, 353). Thus, while Climacus recognizes that there are legitimate objective disciplines, such as logic and mathematics, that bear no relation to existence or else require one to abstract from existence, in general he regards the objective tendency as "a venture in the comic" because it en-courages human beings to forget what they are, what it means to exist, and what inwardness is (CUP, 1:110-11, 124; cf. also 249, 259, 263, 269, 275n, 287, 289). "Even if a man his whole life through occupies himself exclusively with logic, he still does not become logic; he himself therefore exists in other categories," Climacus points out (CUP, 1:93), and if that fact is ignored or neglected, "existence mocks the one who keeps on wanting to become purely objective," he warns (CUP, 1:93). Over against a disinterested pur-suit of objective truth, therefore, Climacus recommends striving for subjective truth and propounds the thesis that "[the] subjectivity, inwardness, is [the] truth" (*Subjektiviteten, Inderligheden er Sand-heden*) as the central tenet of his thought (CUP, 1:278).[28]

---

[27]On this point see also Robert L. Perkins, "Kierkegaard's Epistemological Preferences," *International Journal for Philosophy of Religion* 4/4 (Winter 1973): 197-217. Perkins states: "The ultimate limit of the objective way of knowing is to for-get the subjective aspect, the knower, entirely and arrive at some type of fantastic knowledge without a knower. . . . Objective knowledge can and does with profit exclude the subjective, but it cannot exclude the knower" (213).

[28]Although the definite article may be used enclitically to form abstract nouns in Danish, I have amended the Hong translation of this passage to emphasize its

From a feminist perspective, however, it is important to determine exactly what subjectivity is and is not for Climacus. Subjectivity is defined as inwardness and passion—maximally a passion
for one's eternal happiness—by Kierkegaard's pseudonym, but he
does not consider it equivalent to any and every form of inwardness and passion (CUP, 1:33, 131, 203). In fact, he takes pains to distinguish true inwardness or subjectivity from two forms of
inwardness in particular: (1) "feminine inwardness" or the
momentary inwardness of a "woman's infatuation" that corresponds, in his view, to the "feminine nature" and "to what is ordinarily understood by inwardness" (CUP, 1:236); and (2) the
"chummy inwardness" of friends (CUP, 1:249). Let us examine
each of these a bit more closely.

Associating "the feminine" in stereotypical fashion with the
expression of momentary, emotional outbursts of feeling, which he
characterizes elsewhere in the text as "feminine screaming,"
"blather," and "momentary feminine squealing" (CUP, 1:266, 430,
443), Climacus rejects feminine inwardness as an expression of true
inwardness because in his opinion the latter is hidden and cannot
be given expression in any direct or external form (CUP, 1:236-37,
260). Externally, the person who possesses true inwardness relates
to it as a dead person: "He does not gesticulate, he does not protest, he does not flare up in a moment of inwardness, but, silent as
the grave and quiet as a dead person, he maintains his inwardness
and stands by his word" (CUP, 1:236). It is not out of mere
conformity to traditional grammatical convention that Climacus
uses the third person masculine pronoun to describe such a
person, for he explicitly states that: "Such a person is a man (*en
Mand*)" (CUP, 1:236). It would seem, then, that in his view only

---

reference to the truth of subjectivity in the concrete individual rather than to the
subjective nature of truth. The construal of Climacus's statement in terms of the
latter meaning leaves him open to the charge of subjectivism, which is entirely
unjustified. For the Danish phrase see *Søren Kierkegaards Samlede Værker*, 1st ed.,
14 vols., ed. A. B. Drachmann, J. L. Heiberg, and H. O. Lange (Copenhagen: Gyl-
dendalske Boghandels Forlag, 1902) 7:237. On the need for amending the standard
translation of this phrase, see Robert L. Perkins, "Kierkegaard's Epistemological
Preferences," 211. For an interpretation of Kierkegaard's understanding of subjectivity in terms of the concept of upbuilding, see also Perkins' article, "Kierkegaard, a Kind of Epistemologist," *History of European Ideas* 12/1 (1990): 7-18.

men are capable of manifesting true inwardness, while women are given to momentary excitement and external outbursts of feeling which, although "not unlovely" in them, nevertheless fall short of being true inwardness and are "always dangerous" because they frequently result in lethargy (CUP, 1:236, 239-40). Even more enduring expressions of feminine inwardness in the form of devotedness to others are relegated to the level of "less inwardness" by Climacus because "the direction is obviously outward," whereas true inwardness is directed inward to the contrast or comic discrepancy between the individual's existence and the eternal, to which he stands related via inwardness (CUP, 1:291).

It is unfortunate that Climacus's negative opinion of women leads him here to compromise universal human claims made elsewhere in the text, such as his statement that "[e]very human being is by nature designed to become a thinker" (CUP, 1:47) and the often repeated claim that the ethical, or the task of becoming subjective, "is the highest task assigned to every human being" (CUP, 1:151, 158, 163; cf. also 134). On the basis of his derogatory remarks about women and "the feminine nature" in relation to the expression of true inwardness, one must conclude either that women are excluded from the category of "human being" or else that they are constitutionally incapable of assuming the highest task assigned to them as human beings. Consequently, they must be regarded as unethical creatures who, ironically, lack subjectivity—the very quality with which they traditionally have been associated, although that quality is to be understood here quite differently from its conventional acceptation.

Climacus's relegation of feminine devotedness to the status of "less inwardness" is particularly problematic when considered in relation to *Works of Love*, a collection of deliberations published only a year after the *Postscript* under Kierkegaard's own name and therefore unequivocally reflecting the philosopher's own views as opposed to those of a pseudonym. While recognizing that there are forms of devotion which are really expressions of self-love, or a "devoted self-love," in the "enormous self-willfulness" with which one other person is loved exclusively in an "unlimited devotion" that ought to be given up (WL, 55), Kierkegaard sets forth in this book a Christian understanding of love based on the biblical commandment to love the neighbor, or all human beings, as oneself.[29] Although hidden in its inmost depths, having its ground in the mysterious love of God, neighbor love seeks outward expression and is made known or recognizable by its "fruits" or works of love for others (WL, 8-16). Optimally, the Christian view of love, as Kierkegaard understands it, is one in which one's life is "completely squandered . . . on the existence of others" (WL, 279). Such a view of love, however, does not square with the "hidden inwardness" of Johannes Climacus, who can find no satisfactory external expression for subjectivity or inwardness and thus cloaks it in humor as the incognito for the incongruity between the internal and the external in the religious individual's life (CUP, 1:461-62, 472-75, 492, 499-500).[30] In equating true inwardness with hidden inwardness, therefore, Climacus does not reflect Kierkegaard's own viewpoint, or at least not his view of inwardness as

---

[29]For more extended treatments of this work see my articles "Forming the Heart: The Role of Love in Kierkegaard's Thought," in *The Grammar of the Heart: New Essays in Moral Philosophy & Theology*, ed. Richard H. Bell (San Francisco: Harper & Row, 1988) 234-56, and "Kierkegaard's Philosophy of Love," in *The Nature and Pursuit of Love*, ed. David Goicoechea (Amherst NY: Prometheus Books, 1995) 167-79. See also *The Sickness unto Death*, where Kierkegaard's pseudonymous Christian author, Anti-Climacus, also associates the feminine nature with devotedness and, like Climacus, regards femininity as constituting a "lower synthesis" than does masculinity, which he thinks "essentially belongs within the qualification of spirit" (50n, 67). But Anti-Climacus nevertheless claims that in relation to God it holds for both men and women that "devotion is the self" and that "in the giving of oneself the self is gained" (50n). This suggests that while devotedness in woman is a natural phenomenon which may serve as a mode of despair, or failure to become a self, because of a misplaced identification of the self with the object of her devotion, it is essential to the definition of a self and to becoming such in relation to God. For a more detailed discussion of devotedness as a mode of despair, see my article "On 'Feminine' and 'Masculine' Forms of Despair," *International Kierkegaard Commentary: The Sickness unto Death*, ed. Robert L. Perkins (Macon GA: Mercer University Press, 1987) 121-34.

[30]For a more extended discussion of the role of humor in the *Postscript*, see my book *Living Poetically*, 212-17. On hidden inwardness see also *Practice in Christianity*, 212-20, where Kierkegaard, in the persona of his Christian pseudonym Anti-Climacus, explicitly rejects the notion of hidden inwardness because it too easily may serve in established Christendom as a ploy for claiming that all are true Christians. Instead, Anti-Climacus insists upon an "inverted recognizability" of the Christian life in voluntary suffering as a result of opposition from the world.

given expression in Christianity, which for him constitutes the highest form of subjectivity.

The second form of inwardness from which Climacus seeks to distinguish true inwardness is "chummy inwardness" or what I take to be a form of intersubjectivity that compromises the integrity of the individual. In contrast to the anti-individualist stance of some feminist epistemologists, Climacus emphasizes the distinctiveness and importance of the single individual or the individual subject, which every human being is and has as his or her task to become (CUP, 1:49, 131, 149, 355). In his view, "subjective individuals must be held devoutly apart from one another and must not run coagulatingly together in objectivity" (CUP, 1:79). We have already seen that, for Climacus, every actuality outside oneself can be grasped only through thought, or in the form of possibility. To know another person as an actuality would require one to make oneself into the other, or vice versa, to make the actuality of the other into one's own personal actuality, which in Climacus's view is clearly impossible (CUP, 1:321). Even if one were able to do that, he says, the new actuality would belong to oneself as distinct from the other (CUP, 1:321). Ethically considered, then, "there is no direct relation between subject and subject" (CUP, 1:321).

This does not mean, however, that there is no communication or commonality between subjects. Like Socrates and Lessing, who closed themselves off in the isolation of subjectivity, or what Climacus calls "inclosed reserve," the subjective individual is solitary in relation to God, where "the meddling busyness of a third person" signifies "a lack of inwardness" (CUP, 1:65, 69, 77, 80).[31] But the subjective individual does sustain, like Socrates, a maieutic relation to others, seeking to help them acquire the same understanding he (or she) possesses through the practice of

---

[31] Although the phenomenon of inclosing reserve is analyzed in *The Concept of Anxiety* as a demonic attempt to close oneself off from others in anxiety about the good or the possibility of freedom, Vigilius Haufniensis, the pseudonymous author of this book, also identifies a "lofty inclosing reserve," exemplified by Socrates, which he associates with earnestness and true (as opposed to spurious) religious inwardness. For a discussion of this form of inclosed reserve, which is what Johannes Climacus has in mind when he speaks of it in the *Postscript*, see my book, *Living Poetically*, 159-63.

indirect communication, or the communication of subjective truth in such a way as to leave the other free to appropriate that which constitutes the essentially human (CUP, 1:73-79). As Climacus sees it, "[e]very human being must be assumed to possess essentially what belongs essentially to being a human being. The subjective thinker's task is to transform himself [or herself] into an instrument that clearly and definitely expresses in existence the essentially human" (CUP, 1:356). But Climacus goes on to point out that "[t]o depend upon differences in this regard is a misunderstanding," for "[to] will to be an individual human being (which one unquestionably is) with the help of and by virtue of one's difference is flabbiness; but to will to be an individual existing human being (which one unquestionably is) in the same sense as everyone else is capable of being—that is the ethical victory over life and over every mirage" (CUP, 1:356). For Climacus, therefore, the art of subjectivity is to become what one essentially is, an individual human being or subject in common with others, not merely a "so-called subject of sorts," in whom "the accidental, the angular, the selfish, the eccentric, etc." are accentuated in distinction from others (CUP, 1:130-31). True subjectivity is rooted in our commonality as human beings, not in our individual differences, although paradoxically individuality is affirmed and cultivated precisely in and through a recognition of our common humanity in striving personally to appropriate that which constitutes the essentially human and to communicate it to others. At the most fundamental level, then, all essential knowledge, or that knowledge which pertains essentially to human existence (CUP, 1:197-98), is communally shared in the sense that it pertains essentially to every human being, but it is known and appropriated subjectively by each distinctive individual.

III. Conclusions

From this brief account of Johannes Climacus's views on objectivity and subjectivity several conclusions vis-à-vis recent developments in feminist epistemology may be proposed. First of all, Climacan subjectivity clearly is not subjectivism, as Climacus does not deny the reality of objective truth or our ability to acquire a limited or approximate knowledge of it by objective means.

Although he shares the postmodernist suspicion of the positivity or certainty of objective knowledge, he avoids epistemological relativism by recognizing that objective knowledge is approximate and for that reason, none other, is uncertain.

Second, we have seen that, while feminists fault the conventional view of objectivity because of its androcentric orientation, which purports to be disinterested but is not, Climacus accepts the essentially disinterested character of objective knowledge but faults it precisely because subjectivity is abandoned in objective modes of inquiry. Whereas feminist epistemologists view objectivity itself as including subjective factors, either surreptitiously (as in the masculinist concept of objectivity) or self-consciously (as in a feminist perspective), Climacus clearly separates the objective and subjective spheres. However, some forms of knowledge that currently fall under the sphere of objectivity, such as the social sciences, might qualify as essential knowledge for him if one is able to detect and appropriate an existential significance behind the numerical, quantitative analysis to which such knowledge is subjected.

Third, while Climacus clearly rejects the anti-individualist stance of feminist epistemologists in emphasizing the single individual whose task first and foremost is to develop subjectivity or inwardness, he nevertheless affirms the concrete, contextual, and communal character of subjective truth or essential knowledge inasmuch as it pertains equally to all human beings with respect to the existential task of realizing in oneself and communicating to others that which constitutes the essentially human. Climacus would deny the communal character of such knowledge, however, if that means we learn and communicate truth through a form of intersubjectivity that blurs the distinction between self and others, as in some postmodernist and integrationist feminist epistemologies. He does not deny that individual subjects are socially constituted through relations to others, but in his view they are able to transcend human relations in the relation to God. Part of the task of subjectivity, therefore, is to assert oneself as an individual over against the determining forces of society such as family, church, and state. In this feminists may find an emancipatory pulse in Climacan subjectivity which, unlike the social determinism of some feminist positions, is able to explain why and how women are

capable of resisting the social forces that historically have op-
pressed them.

Fourth, in emphasizing the cultivation of passion and subjectivity, which are capacities traditionally associated with women,
Climacus can be said to be calling for the incorporation of "the
feminine" into epistemology as a way of knowing. But insofar as
he associates a particular form of subjectivity—momentary inwardness or emotional enthusiasm—stereotypically with women and
distinguishes true inwardness from it, he compromises the feminist
thrust of his insight and appears to be antiwomen. Essentially,
however, existential pathos is nongendered for him inasmuch as
it constitutes "the pathos for everyone" (CUP, 1:394). Stripped of
its sexist associations and narrow conception as hidden inwardness, his understanding of subjectivity or pathos could form the
basis for a feminist rethinking of subjectivity in a manner that
gives greater depth to the concept as it relates to women and that
serves to distinguish female subjectivity precisely from the stereo-
typed, sexist view of feminine inwardness perpetuated by
Climacus.

Fifth, while Climacus agrees with feminists in criticizing the
epistemological privileging of objectivity over subjectivity, his
failure to recognize the masculinist character of objectivity and his
own reverse privileging of subjectivity over against objectivity
would lead some feminists to conclude that he was not radical
enough in his critique of the speculative-scientific mentality of his
time and that his thought continues to reflect and perpetuate the
very structures of the dualistic or dichotomous thinking they are
intent on displacing. Inasmuch as Climacus does not question the
validity of objective thought in itself, however, it would perhaps
be more accurate to characterize his understanding of the relation
between objectivity and subjectivity, in the manner of some integrationist feminists, as dialectical rather than dualistic or dichotomous, but dialectical in such a way as not to blur the distinction
between these terms.

These conclusions suggest that Kierkegaard's *Concluding Unscientific Postscript*, often ignored by the philosophical community
because of its emphasis on subjectivity, deserves a sympathetic as
well as critical rereading by feminist epistemologists. They will

undoubtedly find some viewpoints in it to reject, but also much to support and advance their own attempts to rethink and reformulate the concepts of objectivity and subjectivity in the context of this present age.

2

Climacan Politics:
Person and Polis in Kierkegaard's Postscript

Robert L. Perkins

Until quite recently Kierkegaard has been thought of as at least apolitical, if not antipolitical. Though political matters were far from the center of his concerns, his first publication was an ironic essay on women's emancipation, and he died in the midst of an attack on the established church. These facts embolden one to think there may be a political reading of the authorship. The crucial test of such a reading would be an examination of *Concluding Unscientific Postscript*, the centerpiece of Kierkegaard's study of ethicoreligious subjectivity, the pseudonymous author of which is Johannes Climacus. Climacus himself, perhaps ironically, invites such a reading when he overstates what is not obviously the case for many of his first readers nor for us: "Of all forms of government, the monarchical is the best" (CUP, 1:620). This paper offers such a political reading. After an initial section comparing Climacus's and Plato's views of the relation of the individual to ideality and politics, I shall briefly indicate the sociopolitical critique implied in "Part One" of *Postscript* and show how Climacus frames this work with a critique of the political/religious practice that assures the continuation of the religious nonchalance of bourgeois Christianity: infant baptism. This framing shows that *Postscript* contains an important political and sociological subtext to the principal issue of the book: human subjectivity.

Plato and Climacus on Ideality and Politics

The normativity of the Platonic Socrates in the Climacan writings, as well as in the complete authorship, suggests that Plato's thought may serve as a foil against which to demarcate

Climacus's political views. Plato, it will be recalled, focuses a set of virtues that have the same essential nature in the society and in the person[1] and argues that it will be easier to see these virtues in the polis, that is, on the larger scale, than in the individual. After determining how justice, for instance, appears in the state, we can then determine how it will appear in the individual. Plato thinks that political and social life is a product of the persons who govern and are governed, that is, the state and society will finally be no different, neither better nor worse, than the persons composing it. To adapt a term from biology, we may say that, for Plato, there is an isomorphism between the appearance of a virtue in the state and in the individual. This does not mean that justice is the same in the polis and in the individual, but only that it has the same nature wherever it does appear.[2]

From a Platonic point of view, Climacus's effort would appear to be quite the opposite, for he begins with what Plato thinks is hardest to understand, the individual, whom he does not focus within a comprehensive political and social theory. Contrary to Plato, Climacus thinks the understanding of any of our human endeavors must begin with the individual (CUP, 1:189). Insofar as Climacus discusses political and social arrangements, he does so in a way that subordinates these interests to the existential striving of the individual. The existential thinker could well be puzzled that Plato begins as he does, for he could have begun his analysis of justice with an extraordinary individual, the living and remembered presence of Socrates, the best and most just man of the times.[3] No doubt Plato realizes, as does Climacus, how difficult it is to present the inwardness of the individual in language. However, and this is important, Climacus as much as Plato thinks that, ideally and empirically, the moral structure of the political and of the individual are isomorphic.

---

[1]Plato, *Republic*, 368d-69a.

[2]See the old but still useful *Lectures on the Republic of Plato* by Richard Lewis Nettleship (repr.: London: Macmillan, 1951; [2]1901; [1]1897) 69. See Seth Benardete's interesting treatment of the theme in *Socrates' Second Sailing: on Plato's "Republic"* (Chicago: University of Chicago Press, 1989) 44-46, which emphasizes the distinction between "writ large" and "writ small."

[3]Plato, *Apology*, 118.

The most remarkable difference between Plato's and Kierke-gaard's views of the person is that Kierkegaard does not speak of the *nature* of the person in the fashion that emerges from Plato into Aristotle's definition of the person as a rational animal. As a postnominalist, Climacus discusses, only and always, the individu-al. As a philosopher with a touch of the poet,[4] he like Plato invents literary types, such as "Judge William," but even as he presents his view of any problem, he does so always as the issue relates to the existing individual. The modern shift from the discussion of persons as exemplars of a genus and species to the individual, who in modern parlance bears, at best, a "family resemblance" to other individuals, means that Kierkegaard's view of state and society will also be different from that of Plato. The absolutely first fact of Kierkegaard's view of the state and society is that they are both "denatured," that is, the state and society are founded in the individual who, though he or she may have distinctive properties, is not essentially defined. Each person must, within the context of the given, define himself or herself as the person he/she is and would be (SUD, 29-42).[5] The isomorphism of the person and the state and society, then, must take a radically different turn in Kierkegaard from the view of Plato.

Plato focuses the fundamental paradox of his ideal state with the question: How is the philosophic ruler possible? This question wrecks his whole project as expressed in *The Republic*. The failure of his project is based upon his model of ideality represented through the appearance of the virtues in the individual and the state. Climacus, in an important discovery in the logic of sub-jectivity, affirms the paradox of subjectivity exactly where Plato discovered the paradox that wrecked his political ideal: the relation of the individual to the eternal truth. "Nevertheless," Climacus writes, "the eternal, essential truth is itself not at all a paradox, but

---

[4]On Kierkegaard's aesthetics see, Sylvia Walsh, *Living Poetically: Kierkegaard's Existential Aesthetics* (University Park: Pennsylvania State University Press: 1994).

[5]Due cognizance must be taken of the fact that we must not read the work of Anti-Climacus, the author of *The Sickness unto Death*, back into the work of Climacus. Climacus emphasizes that one become a self in such a way as to express the "universally human" while Anti-Climcus writes that one can become a self only in a relation with God (SUD, 30).

it is a paradox by being related to an existing person" (CUP, 1:205). Both Climacus and Plato find the paradoxicality of ideality and the empirical-existential in the relations between them, not in the ideality itself. In a fresh way Climacus attempts the task of relating the eternal truth, first and foremost, to the existence of an individual, leaving to his readers the task of thinking through the issues of political philosophy in the light of his vision of essential truth. We must see if he succeeds where Plato fails. Kierkegaard's question, had he put it so, would have been, "How is the subjective existing thinker possible?" Beginning thus with the individual, Kierkegaard reverses Plato's analytic and constructive program.

The common ground between Plato and Climacus is the importance of ideality. A major difference between them is the ontological and epistemological status of this ideality. Plato pursues the objectivity of the idea through Socratic questioning in an attempt to gain access to an ideal and universal definition, a ruled concept. But that creates a problem for him: how is the ruled concept, considered as a universal, related to existence, which is always particular? Plato appealed to at least two analogies or myths in his attempt to explain how the individual, be it person or object, relates or is related to the objective idea: participation and recollection. The presence of these two myths suggests that Plato and Climacus address the same problem. Distinguishing between Plato and Socrates, Climacus urges that Socrates was interested in existing in the truth, in appropriating it, and so turned away from the myth of recollection (CUP, 1:204-205).[6] Climacus also argues for a change in the ontological locus of ideality from an objective realm of eternal ideas to human subjectivity or inwardness, and he also renegotiates Plato's view of the separation of the ideal from the empirical appearances which can never embody it. Climacus, by contrast, argues for an inward or subjective view of ideality that one strives to appropriate existentially (CUP, 1:199, 278).

Climacus's focus on subjectivity or inwardness occasionally provokes a critique that is unwarranted. Subjectivity, for Climacus,

---

[6]Climacus, the other pseudonyms, and Kierkegaard do not discuss the analogy of participation. Also, since Kierkegaard is not interested in the relation of an object to the ideal form, I shall discuss only the relation of the form to a person.

is not subjectivism, irrationality, arbitrariness, or eccentricity (CUP, 1:131). Rather subjectivity is, perhaps paradoxically, Climacus's language for the universal. If I may be permitted a rhetorical flourish, it is not too much to say that for Climacus the task of becoming an individual is the universal. As frightfully as any medieval thinker, Climacus relates Hebrew creationism and Greek rationality and finds universality in the combination: "Every human being is by nature designed to become a thinker (all honor and praise to the God who created man in his image)" (CUP, 1:47). At the same time, the subject's task is to become a subject and, "to intensify passion to its highest, [for] passion is subjectivity" (CUP, 1:131). Climacus, then, does not see the passions and rational capacities necessarily in conflict. Moreover, ethics involves both Socratic self-knowledge and passion. Climacus writes,

> Yet ethics and the ethical, by being the essential stronghold of individual existence, have an irrefutable claim upon every existing individual, an irrefutable claim of such a nature that whatever a person achieves in the world, even the most amazing thing, is nevertheless dubious if he himself has not been ethically clear when he chose and has not made his choice ethically clear to himself.   (CUP, 1:134)

So these three—reason, passion, and the ethical—are combined in Climacus's view of becoming a person, that is, becoming subjective, the first two being understood as universal properties inherent in each person, and the last, the ethical, as "the highest task assigned to every human being" (CUP, 1:151, 158). Climacus equates the task of becoming ethical with the task of becoming subjective; "the highest reward, and eternal happiness" exists only for those who become subjective (CUP, 1:163).

Yet the critic may not be finished with poor Plato and Climacus. The critic, having no obligation to be consistent but only critical, may reverse his first critique and urge that if the concept of becoming subjective does not include subjectivism, arbitrariness, willfulness, and eccentricity, then it is actually elitist—like Plato is an elitist. This is a serious charge. The philosophic ruler, the critic could continue, is the only one who has access to the truth of things, the key to the understanding of the myths, etc. Further, only the philosopher ruler has an artisan's skill, a warrior's courage, a ruler's wisdom, and the fullest measure of the temperance that harmonizes the strata of the society. A very brief response must suffice. It must be admitted that wisdom and courage are class specific, but this criticism of Plato does not address the concepts of justice and temperance, both of which must be possessed, in varying degrees to be sure, by each and every member of the society.[7] Finally, against the critic of Plato, it would require near total blindness not to recognize an obvious fact that Plato attempted to address: there are many persons who could not endure the rigorous philosophic education and who would not undergo the moral development necessary to become a just and effective philosophic ruler.

These differences in talents, intellectual gifts, and tenacity are simply not at all pertinent in Climacus's thought, which is egalitarian. Climacus could reply to the critic by noting that there is indeed a difference between the simple person and the wise: the simple person knows the essential, while the wise person knows that he does or does not know it, but "what they know is the same" (CUP, 1:160). Books like *Postscript* are not for the simple, whom God will mercifully preserve in their simplicity, but for the wise who can be tempted to think that cleverness is more important than simplicity—a temptation which Climacus admitted to struggling with (CUP, 1:170).[8] The difference between the wise and the simple is "evanescent" (CUP, 1:160) and "ludicrous" (CUP, 1:182).

Climacus is not an elitist; rather, his thought is through and through egalitarian in a sense far deeper and different from political equality. The concept of political equality has its roots in theological and ethical egalitarianism. Climacus bases his view of equality upon the concept of the individual human being, each of which has all the marks of humanity. Thus moral sense requires that we assume that "every human being possesses essentially what belongs essentially to being a human being. The subjective thinker's task is to transform himself into an instrument that clearly and definitely expresses in existence the essentially

---

[7]Plato, *Republic*, 430-434.

[8]To be sure there is a complete Platonic-Christian doctrine of "simplicity" involved here. It is more fully expressed, with Kantian overtones, in UDVS, 3-154, traditionally known as *Purity of Heart*.

human." It is an unremarkable but important fact, that so far as becoming subjective is concerned, "no difference makes any difference" (CUP, 1:356).

> To will to be an individual human being (which one unquestionably is) with the help of and by virtue of one's difference is flabbiness; but to will to be an individual existing human being (which one unquestionably is) in the same sense as everyone else is capable of being—that is the ethical victory over life and every mirage, the victory that is perhaps most difficult of all.
>
> (CUP, 1:356)

Shifting the focus to an egalitarian inwardness enables Climacus to present a view of subjectivity charged with political import but devoid of the hierarchical political structures evident in Plato's *Republic*. Just as Plato thinks that the empirical world can never fully express the ideal, Climacus also thinks that no political or social form can fully express the dialectics of human inwardness. The result, for Climacus, is that no particular social arrangement is fully, finally, or ultimately legitimized, the implication of which is a radical undermining of authoritarian political, religious, and social privilege in Climacus's philosophy.

Climacus's egalitarianism also calls into question the traditional privileged positions of the state church, the remnants of the feudal order, and, interestingly, the class structures of modern societies. Climacus does not draw revolutionary political proposals from his egalitarianism, and he certainly does not endorse either the liberal or communist line. Becoming subjective is the object of his investigation, but the conceptual basis of a radical critique of traditional and modern religion, society, and politics is present in his profound egalitarianism.

Climacus rejects the modern progressivist view, known to him through Lessing and Hegel, that legitimizes the present over against the past. However, and it must be emphasized, Climacus in no way legitimates the past against the present. No reactionary, Climacus does not urge the restoration of any "golden age" of the past. Politics is, then, between the times. Political arrangements are *ad hoc*, temporary, nonauthoritarian, and subject to revision as circumstances change. Political arrangements have only the necessity of the temporal or circumstantial and fill only a narrow space of the whole context within which we attempt to find and express our humanity.

The subjective individual in Climacus's thought would be an open personality, ironic, urbane, and ethical. Such a person is as positive as negative, has as much humor as pathos and is always in the process of becoming (CUP, 1:80). Such a person is never finished, complete, but is always striving to become what he or she is.[9] Existential striving is such a complex task that it will require a lifetime (CUP, 1:170n.**).

It is at this point that the personality profile becomes the basis of social and political structure. The subjective existing thinker has neither the time nor the necessary wisdom, much less the political or ecclesiastical authority, and still less the desire, to oversee the religious, social, and political dimensions of other persons' lives and beliefs. No more than Plato's philosopher king/queen does the subjective existing thinker desire to rule. Praise of the monarchy is the praise of an ideal type, and his preference for it is based solely upon the fact that it permits more privacy than democracy (CUP, 1:620). This is a very weak reason, and Climacus offers it only ironically, but it is fully consistent with Plato's philosophic ruler's preference not to govern. Still, this privacy would enhance the development of a subject's own understanding of the truth, even if what one is related to is the untruth (CUP, 1:199). Such a view of truth and of the person's becoming subjective suggests the political right to religious freedom, so that legal strictures against those who have differing religious views or even no religious views would have no legitimacy in his thought. The subjective appropriation of the eternal does not guarantee the being of the religious object or the truth of the assertions in a religion, but it does guarantee the social and political freedom of all to experience what they perceive as the eternal just as it forbids religious authoritarianism.

---

[9]This strange expression does not suggest that there is an essence which we are to express. Rather, we are like the football player who is such by past decisions and effort, but who still strives to be what he already is in a more complete fashion. Human activity is teleological, but, so far as we know, the telos is not given, part of the nature of things.

The Climacan individual rejects dogmatic religious views and also totalizing, absolute, systems. He or she accepts the ironic skepticism of Lessing toward supposed "systems" of assertions about religious truth. The subjective thinker's epistemological stance is naively empirical and his or her metaphysics is basically, though unsophisticatedly, realistic.[10] The subjective thinker rejects the idealist identity of thought and being (CUP, 1:109-25), although he or she understands that one should appropriate in one's life what one understands to be the "essential truth," which is the same as edifying truth (CUP, 1:189-251, 256-61). The subjective thinker is a radically modified edition of a modern individual, neither a revival of some ancient philosophical or medieval religious model, nor the consumer, capitalist, or worker so necessary in capitalism,[11] and certainly not the nonsubject focused by postmodernism.[12] The modern subjective existing thinker is more like Socrates than any of our other cultural heroes. The ideality of Climacus is focused in the ethical as expressed through and in ethical subjectivity.

Though Plato's thought is more explicitly and subversively political, Climacus's view of the existing subjective thinker also carries with it serious political implications that challenge the status quo. As the individual must strive to express his or her inwardness in the world ethically, he or she comes to inhabit a social and political world where one "gain[s] a history" (CUP, 1:254). The person is both a citizen and also one who may have to challenge the local mores, politics, and divinities for solid moral, political, and religious reasons.[13]

---

[10]Robert L. Perkins, "Kierkegaard's Epistemological Preferences," *International Journal for Philosophy of Religion* 4 (1973): 197-217.

[11]C.B. McPherson's magisterial work, *The Political Theory of Possessive Individualism* (London: Oxford University Press, 1975), analyses the phenomena to which I refer in the context of the emergence of early English capitalism, but the application of his categories to a study of modernization in Denmark would, no doubt, suggest some interesting insights in Kierkegaard's political and social thought.

[12]Sylvia Walsh, "Kierkegaard and Postmodernism," *International Journal for Philosophy of Religion* 29 (1991): 113-22.

[13]A point well put by Merold Westphal in his *Kierkegaard's Critique of Reason and Society* (Macon GA: Mercer University Press, 1987) 35.

Although it is not Climacus's intention to present a political philosophy in *Postscript*, at least some of the values of a Climacan state and politics can be ascertained, particularly if we continue to think of issues raised by Plato. Such an interface will suggest numerous likenesses and differences. Primarily, a Climacan state would be an open society, emphasizing personal moral and social development in policies and structures.[14] Communication regarding public affairs would be direct and nonmanipulative; clarity and honesty would be its end.[15] Just as the individual is constantly in the process of becoming, the political dimensions of life would be open to revision. Climacan politics, like those of Plato's *Republic*, would respect individual differences, and the variety of human gifts would determine the educational structures and social policies of the state. The end of the state would be to enable each person to develop his or her potentialities to the fullest extent possible, limited only by the dominance of existential need over aesthetic desire. Neither "need" nor "desire" are eternal forms, but both would undergo constant renegotiation because of changing historical circumstances. Climacus would no doubt agree with Plato that the state can be more intelligently governed by the learned and those with moral discernment than by the ignorant and those in whom vagrant passions run riot. Because of the disordered egoism evident in the success of the sophists and the obvious class conflicts in politics and society at the end of Golden age Denmark, and in spite of the vast historical differences between Athens and Copenhagen, the similarities of their political and social views are as remarkable as their differences.[16]

Like Plato's ideal state in *Republic*, a Climacan state would be impossible. In Plato, the difficulty was the paradox of beginning,

---

[14]R.B. Levinson, *In Defence of Plato* (Cambridge MA: Harvard University Press, 1953). This controversial volume is a reply to the charge that Plato advocated a closed society.

[15]Simply because political communication is public and addresses the universal, understood in an Hegelian sense, there should be no confusion between it and indirect communication which must be used when addressing inwardness (CUP, 1:274-77).

[16]Climacus's respect for historical specificity can be gathered from his reflections on Lessing (CUP, 1:59-127).

a point not missed by Climacus: How can one have a just state before one has just persons? The problem for Plato is the inherent unruliness, based upon ignorance, of the inclinations and passions. But how can the ignorance be remedied by persons whose inclinations and passions are already corrupt? For Climacus, the problem of politics is more difficult, for not only are all the problems of the beginning that Plato found present, but apparently there is also a desire present in the human psyche to be less than one can ideally be, i.e., to choose the lesser of goods.[17] Climacus discovers that the eros upon which Plato depended to lead us to intellectual truth and to moral integrity is corrupt and incurable by philosophy. This difference between Plato and Climacus is suggestive of the Christian view of original sin (CUP, 1:208, 583-86), a distinction that would require Climacus to revise his view of the subjective existing thinker.[18] Climacus recognizes the displacement of reason from the center of the modern concept of the person and its replacement by the same unruly passions which Plato attempted to order in his moral and political theory. For Climacus the problem of the person and the political order is not ignorance which produces unruly passions and then a corrupt state, but, rather, the authority of the erotically decentered passions which in turn produces various forms of egoistic self-destruction in the aesthetic life and a moral complacency in the practices of the "righteous."[19] In the Climacan state reason is reduced to serving the passions, be they ever so base or upbuilding.[20] When Climacus

---

[17]The optimism of Platonic intellectualism is remarkable, confronted as it was by the sophists, their students, and the intellectual giant and moral monstrosity by the name of Alcibiades.

[18]When sin enters Climacus's conceptual scheme, the project of the subjective existing thinker is qualified away from the Socratic.

[19]It is indeed a marvel that Plato did not develop the issue of the corruption of eros more accurately than he did. In the *Symposium* itself, Plato presents persona who show the smugness of the conventional aesthete in the figures of Phaedrus, Pausanius, and Agathon, the smugness of the righteous in the figure of Eryximachus, and the corruption of the passions that has led to a severe case of the weakness of the will in the figure of Alcibiades.

[20]Kierkegaard's view of the passions is quite complex. For a brief statement see Sylvia Walsh, *Living Poetically: Kierkegaard's Existential Aesthetics*, 200-202. See also Robert C Roberts's article in this volume for a more extensive study.

does not tell us how the subjective existing thinker is related to the objective state, he does no less and no more than Plato when he does not tell us how a just state is possible.

Intellectualist Support of the Status Quo
Masquerading as Orthodox Apologetics

Just as Plato's elaboration of a just person and state implied many criticisms of Athenian society in whole and in part, so Climacus's view of the subjective existing thinker and the political import of this concept imply a many sided critique of Golden Age Denmark. I shall now look at certain features of the then current religious apologetic to show how they support the political and social status quo. This religious apologetic, as Climacus presents it, subverts subjective, ethical religion and, being conservative, is opposed to political and social change. I shall support that claim by a brief examination of "Part One" of *Postscript*, where he places the subjective religious interest of the individual against the objective and positive religious dogmas of the established institutions.

Climacus examines the then current assumption of religious apologetic that theological questions can be objectively examined and that rationally authoritative answers can be given. The theological establishment, the clergy, and the theological faculty, present a rationalistic apologetic that, though Protestant in form and content, is as rationalistic as any ever seen. Moreover, the apologetic arguments Climacus examines assume a broad social consensus with the result that the terms and issues are, by and large, socially agreed to. Thus it is assumed, with rare exceptions such as Lessing and Climacus, that apologetic arguments defending the Bible, the church, and its apologetic are decisive for the defence of the religion of the state and society. I shall briefly indicate the content of Climacus's extensive and perceptive arguments.

Climacus urges that the arguments supporting the authority, authenticity, and inspiration of the Bible are logically confused, for they disguise the subjectivity inherent in religion with an appeal to an objective authority without addressing the question why the subject should accept this authority. Moreover, suggesting that the Bible is an objective authority one can trust for one's eternal salvation is to play directly into the hands of the Bible critics who think their activities have some religious value. The religious issue about the Bible, for Climacus, is inspiration, not historical or objective evidence about this or that claim in, for, or about the Bible (CUP, 1:24-34). Apologetic arguments that appeal to the church, considered as an objectively present institution, are also circular, because they require a prior faith in the arguments that support faith in the church which can then validate the subjective faith of the individual (CUP, 1:34-46). Apologetic arguments that consider the church as a survivor of the historic ravages that have changed, if not destroyed, other institutions are as logically flawed as any other historical arguments and for the same reason: historical arguments are objective, about matters of fact, and uncertain (CUP, 1:46-49, 93-106). Needless to say, the reliance on the church and the proof of the centuries is a claim on behalf of the established church. Hard questions about whether the present church is the same as the founder's persecuted church are suppressed—an exercise in intellectual dishonesty.

Climacus also questions the speculative justification of religion. The speculative defence of religion assumes a broad intellectual consensus, with the result that religious faith is considered an immature form of philosophic knowledge. Speculation also demands disinterest while faith is the most important interest of the individual (CUP, 1:50-57).

Climacus characterizes both of these approaches, the historical and the speculative, as objective, and criticizes both as neglecting the question of the subjective appropriation of the religious truth into the personal life for determining life-policy decisions. A comfortable delusion about religious authority is substituted for the passion of faith.

Climacus's approach to issues of religious authority is existential. Religious authority, in the fundamental sense, lies in the domain of personal reflection, appropriation, and decision rather than in the official authorization of some organization or doctrine to determine the content, form, and communal expression of the religious life. More damaging still, the apologetic arguments based in church history (the proof of the centuries) are at best rhetorical and are not logically persuasive, being only a shoddy form of the fallacy of authority or what Bentham happily called the fallacy of "the wisdom of our fathers."

The most radical political and social implication of "Part One" is the challenge Climacus offers the identity of religious and political modes, so characteristic of societies which maintain official religious establishments or where one particular religious expression has near complete cultural dominance. Such ecclesiotheological hegemony is authoritarian, even in Protestantism.

All of Climacus's objections to the scriptural, historical, and ecclesiological proofs of the Christian religion are based upon Lessing's theological views, which Climacus previously discussed in *Philosophical Fragments*. In *Postscript*, Climacus hones the critique of religious "knowledge" by developing the uncertainties found in historical knowledge. Climacus, no more than Lessing, is an historical skeptic, but just as firmly as Lessing, he denies that an eternal happiness can be built upon the deliverances of historical knowledge.[21]

Climacus's destructive analysis of the apologetic stances offered by and on behalf of the officially approved and governmentally sponsored religious institutions places his position in the tradition of religious liberty as a chosen life-view and commitment. Moreover, perhaps unaware of the implication, Climacus's emphasis upon subjectivity implies a modern associational or sectarian view of religious institutions.[22] In the modern period, according to Climacus's analysis, the intellectual vision of an ecclesiotheocentric society has simply vanished, but certain of its forms and formula remain. Modern societies that succeeded medieval feudalism and the various forms of absolutism have modified certain "theological" claims and practices so they can be used to support modern political and social arrangements.

---

[21]See *Lessing's Theological Writings*, Translated and introduction by Henry Chadwick (Stanford CA: Stanford University Press, 1957) 51-56. Valuable recent work on Lessing includes: Henry F. Allison, *Lessing and the Enlightenment* (Ann Arbor MI: University of Michigan Press, 1966) and Gordon E. Michalson, *Lessing's "Ugly Ditch": A Study of Theology and History* (University Park: Pennsylvania State University Press, 1985). See also Hannay's article in this volume.

[22]For a close reading of the issue of Kierkegaard's ecclesiology and his relation to the sectarian movements see Vernard Eller's *Kierkegaard and Radical Discipleship* (Princeton: Princeton University Press, 1968).

Infant Baptism: A Legitimating Mechanism of the Absolute
and Bourgeois State Masquerading as a Religious Practice

The ambiguity of Climacus's effort to avoid discussing the social import of the subjective appropriation of faith is nowhere more apparent than in his consideration of the practice of baptism, a subject he treats from time to time throughout *Postscript*. Aware that the practice of infant baptism is the ecclesiotheological glue that binds the society together, Climacus never recommends the end of the practice. I shall review some of the issues he raises regarding the practice before concluding with a suggestion of the reason he resisted its end.

In "Book One" Climacus argues that baptism cannot be the basis for one's eternal happiness (CUP, 1:43-45). His first argument is that one's own baptism is not witnessed by the subject, who is an infant, and, as a result, the person has only historical information of the event. Unfortunately, though the event is well attested, it is still an historical event of which the subject has no direct or personal knowledge. If one has "passion enough to grasp the meaning of his own eternal happiness, and then let him tie it to his having been baptized—he will despair. Along this path, the Church theory would have to lead to the Baptist movement or to a repetition of Baptism" (CUP, 1:44). Although the logical implication of the rejection of the Church theory would be to accept adult (or believer's) baptism, it is precisely this next step to the Baptist movement that Climacus refuses to take. His reason is that appeal to the fact that one is baptized, no matter whether as an infant or as a believer, may equally stop the dialectic of religious reflection and dry up the inwardness. The possibility that the Baptists and Anabaptists could make adult baptism an external sign led Climacus to reject both of their protests against infant baptism.[23] However, infant baptism becomes "magic" (CUP, 1:44) and assures that one is a Christian just as one is a Dane. For a solid citizen, a good Dane, and a civil servant to make a fuss about whether one

---

[23]Climacus, like most Europeans then and now, could not distinguish the Baptists from the Anabaptists, for he uses both words interchangeably to establish similar arguments (CUP, 1:44, 365, 477).

is a Christian or not is "really boring" and "makes so much ado about nothing" (CUP, 1:50). The lynch pin that makes the objective and the speculative approaches to religion work is the social consensus that "we are all Christians," and in Denmark that consensus is founded solidly upon the practice of infant baptism. The result is the naturalization of Christianity, the view that to be a Christian and to be a person and citizen are identical (CUP, 1:367n).

Climacus notes that in the beginning Christianity was not preached to infants and children, but to adults. In the practice of infant baptism belief and inwardness have no significance (CUP, 1:293). However, since Christianity is inwardness (CUP, 1:215), the baptism of infants has befuddled the whole problem of becoming a Christian. Becoming a Christian is now a different sort of problem than it first was. In the beginning, becoming a Christian was more obvious, for no one was a Christian. An explicit confession was necessary. Now the first move is that one must recognize that being a baptized member of the official church does not make one a Christian. Once one recognizes that one is not a Christian, one may possibly become a Christian. Because of all this backpedaling, Climacus is forced to the ironic conclusion that "it is easier to become a Christian when I am not Christian than to become a Christian when I am one" (CUP, 1:366).

The issue of baptism was hotly debated in Copenhagen in Climacus's time, for Bishop Mynster attempted to force the baptism of the children of the few Danish Baptists, most of whom were peasants. He was successful in compelling the baptism of the children of the very few Baptists in Copenhagen, but he lost this struggle outside the city. Kierkegaard's brother, Peter, an aspiring cleric in the Grundtvigian wing of the state church, refused to compel the Baptists in his parish to submit, though he was twice instructed to do so by the bishop. Mynster's reason for desiring to baptize the hapless infants is revealing. He rejected the right of persons to decide their own religious fate, and he coupled this declaration of independence from the state church with a claim of political disloyalty to the crown—in spite of the fact that the peasants were among the king's most loyal subjects.[24] Mynster transforms religious dissent into the mold of political disloyalty, an accusation still known among reactionary and conservative religionists.[25]

Climacus, in spite of his criticism of infant baptism, urges that any change must occur quietly, within the inwardness of the individual, lest it "become an Anabaptist heresy" (CUP, 1:365). This appeal to a quiet inwardness is in stark contrast with the militancy of Bishop Mynster's pursuit of the Baptists. Bishop Mynster, because of the false accusation of disloyalty to the crown, has a political agenda.[26] He thinks the emergence of the Grundtvigians, the Methodists, the Mormons, the revivalist movement, and the Baptists, with their insistence on believer's baptism, is an open invitation to a pluralism that will undermine the present state of affairs in which the power and cultural elite in Copenhagen enjoy a privileged status. Moreover, Mynster's persecution of the economically poor and politically powerless Baptists, who have been hounded and slain by every established church in western Europe,[27] suggests that he has a blind spot on the relation of power, suffering, and Christianity. Mynster is quite willing to use the power of a

---

[24]Kirmmse, *Kierkegaard in Golden Age Denmark*, 43-44, 130-31, 186, 233. Niels Thulstrup, *Commentary on Kierkegaard's "Concluding Unscientific Postscript,"* trans. Robert J. Widenmann (Princeton: Princeton University Press, 1984) 191-93. Kirmmse's book contains several (damning) quotations from Mynster.

[25]Merold Westphal reminded me that it is important to note that neither the critique of objectivist apologetics nor infant baptism is addressed directly to the issue of the form of the state. Although Climacus's concern is directed primarily to the delineation of religious inwardness, he clearly saw, like Marx, that the official religion served a vital role in legitimating the political, economic, and cultural life of Denmark and, more widely, modernity generally. Climacus and Marx both recognize that the critique of the social forms and the legitimating principles are opposite sides of the same coin. A one-sided coin is a logical impossibility.

[26]This point is vigorously argued by Kirmmse in his *Kierkegaard in Golden Age Denmark*, 130-31.

[27]Philip of Hesse was the only ruler in the sixteenth century who did not use the death penalty against the Anabaptists. See Franklin H. Littell, "The Radical Reformation and Revolution" in *Marxism and Radical Religion, Essays Toward a Revolutionary Humanism*, ed. John C. Raines and Thomas Dean (Philadelphia: Temple University Press, 1970) 86.

Constantinian church against an underprivileged minority in order to secure the privileged interests of his social and economic class.[28] Of course, the stated agenda is religious uniformity, but the unstated agenda is security of the present powers that be.

The persecution of the Baptists was over when Climacus wrote *Postscript*, but one thinks it was instructive for him. One can sense the irony and humor of some of his remarks. For instance, he thinks that to have one's eternal happiness decided "two weeks after one's birth" in "five minutes still seems to be almost a little too much of the paradox" (CUP, 1:368). One wonders how one can add the quantitative qualification, "a little too much," in a body of discourse where an absolute paradox is the fundamental term.

Climacus also uses this ironic thrust to develop a doubt concerning hidden inwardness. He suggests that the highest intensification of inwardness is possible when a person who was baptized when a child appropriates the truth of Christianity inwardly as an adult. But he turns this into an ironic critique of "hidden inwardness." His ironic qualification suggests that "it is also the case that the less externality, the greater the possibility that the inwardness will entirely fail to appear." Outwardness may serve as the "watchman that awakens the sleeper," and the lack of outwardness may also mean that the individual may not possess an inwardness (CUP, 1:382). It turns out, then, that outwardness does have a use in the development of inwardness, be it ever so slight. Climacus adapts the oft stated position that the inner is not the outer and the outer is not the inner to a new situation (EO, 1:3; FT, 68-69). Climacus's concept of subjectivity leads him, in this single instance, to see that both poles of the dialectic, the inner and the outer, need the other and that each is finally incomplete without the other. His views about baptism do not in any way infringe upon the priority of inwardness, but they do indicate that the outer must be revisioned in some way.

This discussion concerning a nearly forgotten controversy about baptism suggests an important dimension of Climacus's

---

[28]This reading of the untoward remark about the Anabaptists is supported by Kierkegaard's correspondence with his brother during this period. See *Letters and Documents*, letters 116-18.

views of the relation of religion and society. The remark about the Anabaptists notwithstanding, Climacus realizes that in the nationalistic and cultural expression of Christianity in Denmark, ethnic values that stress social conformity prevail and that Christianity, understood as inwardness, is jeopardized by the practices of the official church itself. As a result, the "orthodoxy" of the cultural and religious elite is not an expression of hidden inwardness, but rather of a hidden emptiness. The dispute over baptism shows the division within the official church and also that it is powerless in the face of the changes being forced upon Denmark and its state religion. The church no longer leads; it reacts socially and politically to preserve its interests. Climacus, along with several other authors he mentions (CUP, 1:251-300), attempts to revive the inward reality of religion by questioning and undermining the aesthetic, ethical, and religious assumptions of the political and cultural elite.

In this paper I have shown how Climacus, if not Kierkegaard, criticized the dominant features of the intellectual and religious life of his times. His critique of the official religious apologetic shows it to be an ideological defence of the social forms and political structures of the times. The continued practice of infant baptism assures that "we are all Christians," with the result that religious inwardness and its ethical passion cannot even be conceived, much less deemed necessary for the full flowering of the person. The surprising result of his critique of the official religious ideology and ecclesiastical practice, a critique based on purely religious and philosophical grounds, turns out to be quite political in its implications. About this time it became clear to Kierkegaard that he would not be successful in calling persons to the challenge of recovering themselves as ethicoreligious persons on the Socratic and/or Christian models he presented in *Fragments* and in *Postscript*. The *Postscript* itself fell dead from the press; its challenge to Danish and modern European bourgeois society remained unknown for decades. The conflict with the *Corsair* instructed Kierkegaard how little ethicoreligious insight the public possessed, and how little it understood about the possible connections between a demoralized aesthetic and the common life. The publication of *Two Ages* is the first fruits of the growing insight that the whole of the common life must be more directly challenged, although Kierkegaard continued to address the issues using an aesthetic device, a book review, remaining a writer rather than becoming a political revolutionary.

In the meantime, life simply went on. Or, rather, it continued in the direction that Kierkegaard most opposed: the triumph of the aesthetic, even in the religious realms of life. The political and social consequences of this triumph were enormous: the continued empowerment of the old or a new regime based solidly in aesthetic values. Religiously, the result was disastrous, for religion became "boring" or irrelevant (CUP, 1:50).

Kierkegaard's failure to turn his society from aesthetic values to his or her own ethical subjectivity is similar to the failure of Socrates to overcome the self-destructive aestheticism and sophism of the Athenians. Socrates questioned the politicians, the poets, and the artisans, and found none knew anything "really worth knowing." Kierkegaard challenged the poets and the priests, and found both in the grip of a powerful aestheticism that titillated their passions or served their economic and political interests. Both Socrates and Kierkegaard failed in their respective undertakings, and though there may be some comfort in the company, there is none in the failure.

3

Kierkegaard's Climacus—a Kind of Postmodernist

Merold Westphal

When Kierkegaard and Nietzsche were the founding fathers of existentialism, even Sartre knew that there were both religious and atheistic existentialisms. Now that Nietzsche has become the (un)-founding (un)father of philosophical postmodernism, it is widely assumed that postmodernism is inherently secular or compatible only with a/theistic religion. But Kierkegaard's Johannes Climacus is as much a postmodernist as he is an existentialist, and to recognize this is to recognize the possibility of a robustly religious postmodernism. This possibility suggests it is not necessary to strip Kierkegaard's writings of the religious concerns at their core in order to include them in contemporary postmodern conversations.

Perhaps there is no deeper continuity between postmodernism and the modernity it seeks to transcend than in the conception of philosophy as critique. Postmodernism is critique in the Kantian sense; it is the critique of metaphysics. Whether we are dealing with Heidegger's analysis of the onto-theological constitution of metaphysics or with Derrida's analysis of the metaphysics of presence—to mention only the two versions that will concern us in this essay—we are on Kantian ground.[1] Each of these represents a variation on a familiar theme, or, if you prefer, a deepening of that reflection in which Reason, the pride and joy of modernity, having criticized everything else, finally turns its critical gaze upon itself.

---

[1] These two themes are not the whole story about philosophical postmodernism, nor even the whole story about Heidegger and Derrida, respectively. I focus on them here because (1) they are central postmodernist themes, (2) they have powerful parallels in the Climacus writings, and (3) they are, for those reasons, especially helpful in discussing the possibility of what I have just called a "robustly religious postmodernism." In this essay, my thesis about a possible religious appropriation of postmodernism is restricted to these two themes.

But postmodernism is also critique in the Marxian sense; it is ideology critique. It recognizes that the theories spun by speculative reason are not innocent but serve to legitimize social practices that welcome such legitimation precisely because they are so questionable—precisely by the standards of modernity, whether these be construed as liberty, equality, and fraternity or as the equal and inalienable right to life, liberty, and the pursuit of happiness. If this sounds more obviously true of Derrida and his French partners, we must not forget that Heidegger's project of overcoming metaphysics is at the same time a critique of technology as the dominant social formation of modernity.

Like the writings of Kierkegaard as a whole, the part of those writings that is Johannes Climacus's *Concluding Unscientific Postscript* is critique in this double sense. As a critique of the speculative project that is shared by Plato and Hegel, it is a critique of metaphysics; and as an attack upon Christendom, both in its bourgeois everydayness and in its Sunday childishness, it is ideology critique. First pantheistic Hegelianism is presented as all too harmonious with the orthodoxy of the churches (not by virtue of the what, but by virtue of the how); then both theories about God (or Absolute Spirit) are presented as mirroring and ratifying the complacent practices of a society that thinks of itself as Christian.

Does this mean that Climacus is as much a postmodernist as an existentialist? Perhaps, but a yes or no answer doesn't get us very far because neither the critique of metaphysics nor ideology critique are uniquely postmodern. Both are the offspring of modernity but at the same time its Achilles' heels; for they are an open invitation to the internal critique of modernity (including Kant and Marx themselves) that is postmodernism. The question, however, invites us to explore the affinities of the double critique of Climacus with those of postmodernism. There will be real differences, of course, just as there already are between Heidegger and Derrida. (Postmodernism is more than a pluralizing challenge to totalizing cultures; it is a pluralistic phenomenon in its own right.) But the continuities may prove to be as deep as the differences.

Negativity is one of the similarities. As critique of both the conceptual and social systems of the modern world, postmodernism is negative thinking. As early as his dissertation, Kierkegaard focused on irony as infinite negativity and on Socrates as the paradigmatic negative thinker. In *Postscript* Climacus, a great admirer of Socrates,[2] identifies himself as a negative thinker. In his discussion of Lessing he says "*the existing subjective thinker is just as negative as positive, has just as much of the comic as he essentially has of pathos*" (CUP, 1:80). This apposition of the comic with the negative is important in view of Climacus's repeated self-identification of himself as a humorist.

Irony and humor, the two species of the comic that he discusses are the incognitos, respectively, of ethical and religious subjectivity. By contrast with Johannes de Silentio, Climacus tends to collapse the difference between the ethical and the religious in order to emphasize the subjectivity they share; so the difference between irony and humor is not very important here. As the incognitos of subjectivity, they are the disguises, the masks in which hidden inwardness becomes public without really showing itself. Irony and humor are hints of something whose presence they cannot guarantee. Just as someone wearing a Santa Claus suit may not be Santa Claus, so Climacus insists that he is only a humorist and not a religious person.

The mere comedians and the knights of hidden inwardness share important insights. They juxtapose human life in its everydayness with "the absolute requirement" (irony) or "the conception of God" (humor); the contradiction (incongruity, discrepancy) is the source of the negative thinking that takes comical form, including the delicious satires of Climacus. An ironist would be truly ethical "only by relating himself within himself to the absolute requirement." But from his jokes we cannot tell whether Woody Allen is a knight of hidden inwardness who does this. Similarly, the mere humorist "joins the conception of God together with something else and brings out the contradiction—but he does not relate himself to God in religious passion" (CUP, 1:502-505).

Who are these mere comedians? They might be, like Climacus, seriously interested in the religious life and zealous to protect it, less from refutation than from domestication. But they might also

---

[2]In *Fragments* Socrates simply stands for the Platonic speculative project. But in *Postscript* his irony and ignorance come to the fore and he stands over against that project as a skeptical gadfly. Whereas before he was the alternative to Christian faith, now he is its analogue.

be cynics and nihilists, allergic to both ethics and religion. The negative thinking that accompanies the moral passion of Socrates can easily turn into sophistry.[3] This has an important bearing on any attempt to introduce Kierkegaard into postmodern conversations. The insights of Kierkegaard (and his pseudonyms) are never safely removed from cynicism and nihilism. But by the same token, the insights of the most thoroughly secular contemporary postmodernist are never safely removed from ethical and religious subjectivity. The wall dividing Socrates from the sophists is thin and porous *in both directions*. Everything depends on the reader's appropriation, which is even further removed from the author's control than the reader's interpretation.[4] Kierkegaard and postmodernism agree that authors have no decisive privilege among the readers of their texts and that the *mens auctoris* cannot fix the meaning as, say, religious or secular.[5] This is part of that ineluctable riskiness of postmetaphysical existence that Climacus keeps stressing.

---

[3]Thus, in his dissertation Kierkegaard distinguishes two kinds of negativity. "Irony [as infinite negativity] is a healthiness insofar as it rescues the soul from the snares of relativity; it is a sickness insofar as it cannot bear the absolute except in the form of nothing . . . " (CI, 77). One might say the same thing about deconstruction, which is not so different from irony. I often hear the complaint that my reading of postmodernism in essays such as this one is "too charitable." The problem, so far as I can tell, is that I focus on the potential healthiness of postmodern negativity rather than identifying it with the sophistic sickness Kierkegaard describes. But the texts do not support such an identification. Postmodern critique can (and has) become an excuse for cynical nihilism, just as biblical faith can (and has) become an excuse for racism of various sorts. But in both cases there are better possibilities to be found by attending closely to the texts.

[4]If Gadamer is right in collapsing the difference between appropriation and interpretation, this does not bring appropriation closer to the author's control, but removes interpretation further.

[5]For a comparison of Kierkegaard on this "death of the author" with Barthes, Foucault, and Derrida, along with Gadamer, see my "Kierkegaard and the Anxiety of Authorship," *International Philosophical Quarterly* 34 (1994): 5-22. For Heidegger's ambivalent renunciation of *mens auctoris* authority, see chap. 1 of John van Buren, *The Young Heidegger: Rumor of a Hidden King* (Bloomington: Indiana University Press, 1994).

Climacus, Heidegger, and Onto-theo-logy

So let us venture to bring Climacus's assault on speculation and the system into dialogue with Heidegger's project of overcoming metaphysics. Heidegger began his academic career as very much a metaphysician and as late as *What Is Metaphysics?* (1930), when his attempt to develop a phenomenological neo-scholasticism was far behind him, he was willing to call his own thinking of being (as a meditation on nothing) by the name of metaphysics. But as he came to see his task as going deeper by finding "The Way Back into the Ground of Metaphysics," he became increasingly critical of "The Onto-Theo-Logical Constitution of Metaphysics" and described his path as "Overcoming Metaphysics."[6]

For Heidegger the highest task (to use the language of Climacus) is to think being. It is through the forgetting of being that metaphysics goes astray, loses touch with its ground, and needs to be overcome. This happens when ontology is teleologically suspended in theology, when the question of the meaning of being as such becomes the question of the highest being.[7] This is the onto-theo-logical constitution of metaphysics, whose *locus classicus* is Aristotle's *Metaphysics*.[8]

Heidegger views this piety of philosophy with Nietzschean suspicion. Philosophy takes God into account, but "the deity can come into philosophy only insofar as philosophy, of its own accord and by its own nature, requires and determines that and how the

---

[6]These three essays are to be found, respectively, in *Existentialism from Dostoevsky to Sartre*, ed. Walter Kaufmann (New York: New American Library, 1975); Martin Heidegger, *Identity and Difference*, trans. Joan Stambaugh (New York: Harper & Row, 1969); and Martin Heidegger, *The End of Philosophy*, trans. Joan Stambaugh (New York: Harper & Row, 1973).

[7]The thrust of this objection is unchanged by Heidegger's shifts to talking about the truth of being and the place of being and, eventually, to a gradual replacement of being talk with talk about *Ereignis* and so forth.

[8]See especially book VI, chap. 1. In *The Young Heidegger*, John van Buren describes Heidegger's complaint this way: "The *terminus a quo* [the world] and *ad quem* [God] of the questioning is beings. Being is used to explain beings without itself having been interrogated regarding how it comes about" (31).

deity enters into it."[9] The task it assigns to God, who thus becomes a means to human ends, is to gather all beings into a totality intelligible to human thought. In assigning this task to God philosophy turns away from its own highest task and embarks on the path that leads to modern technology.

Climacus is equally suspicious of the piety of Hegelian speculation. In both of the versions he considers, it is ontotheological to the core, introducing God (the Idea, Absolute Spirit) for the sake of rendering the whole of reality intelligible to human thought. The logic, which Hegel describes as showing God's nature before the creation of the world, does this synchronically and structurally. The philosophy of world history, which Hegel describes as a theory of divine providence, does this diachronically and concretely.[10]

Climacus and Heidegger are in agreement that the onto-theological project cannot be fulfilled. The temporal finitude of human understanding precludes the possibility that it can render the world wholly intelligible. Both are Kantians for whom the urge toward the unconditioned and totality is as futile as it is fascinating. Both would be sympathetic with Marion's claim that "the unthinkable enters into the field of our thought only by rendering itself unthinkable there by excess, that is, by criticizing our thought."[11] For Heidegger unconcealment is never separable from concealment; and for Climacus existence is dialectical and paradoxical long before Christianity enters the scene. The latter is "dialectical in the second place" (CUP, 1:556-559); it rests on the *absolute* paradox, the paradox *sensu strictissimo* or *sensu eminenti* (CUP, 1:217, 558). When Heidegger says that "theology is not speculative knowledge of God," Climacus agrees heartily.[12]

---

[9]Heidegger, *Identity and Difference*, 56.

[10]See *Hegel's Science of Logic*, trans. A. V. Miller (New York: Humanities, 1969) 50, and Hegel, *Lectures on the Philosophy of World History: Introduction*, trans. H. B. Nisbet (Cambridge: Cambridge University Press, 1975) 27. Cf. *The Encyclopaedia Logic*, trans. T. F. Geraets et al., (Indianapolis: Hackett, 1991) ¶¶1 and 85.

[11]Jean-Luc Marion, *God without Being*, trans. Thomas A. Carlson (Chicago: University of Chicago Press, 1991) 46.

[12]Martin Heidegger, *The Piety of Thinking*, trans. James G. Hart and John C. Maraldo (Bloomington: Indiana University Press, 1976) 15.

It is on the far side of this Kantian futility that the interesting part of the dialogue between Climacus and Heidegger comes, namely, in their accounts of how this project, which they see as dominating the cultures in which they live, is a deadly danger, far deeper than the danger of paralogism and antinomy, which merely manifest the futility. For Climacus the danger lies in forgetting that we are human beings (CUP, 1:117, 120). "Let us be human beings," he pleads, but in vain. "To be a human being has been abolished, and every speculative thinker confuses himself with humankind" (CUP, 1:114, 124).

For Heidegger the danger lies in forgetting being, the question of being, the thinking of being. This forgetting would seem to be different from forgetting that we are human beings. By now we could beat Climacus to the satirical punch with a story about the professor who was so afraid he would forget to think being that he forgot to pick up his paycheck. In relation to himself, if not in relation to the Jews, whose humanity he also seemed to forget at times, he is at least as comical as the man who mistook his wife for a hat. Perhaps he could set his watch to beep every fifteen minutes so that he could say loudly three times, "Boom! I am a human being." In this way he could prove that he had not jumped out of the frying pan of *Seinsvergessenheit* into the fire of *Daseinsvergessenheit*.

When Climacus could get in a word he would remind us that in *Being and Time* it is the essence of *Dasein* to exist and that the being of *Dasein* is in each case mine. This sounds promising, but (1) the analytic of Dasein is already only a means to getting at the meaning of being, and (2) almost immediately Heidegger abandons the "existentialism" of *Being and Time* in order to overcome the excessive subjectivity of that path to thinking being. The *terminus a quo* and *ad quem* of Heidegger's questioning is being. *Dasein* is used to explain being without itself having been interrogated with regard to its highest task.[13]

But the objectivity in which ontological speculation takes place stems from a disastrous category mistake since it is not our highest task to be an observer of being (as in Hegel's logic) or of the world

---

[13]I am here reversing van Buren's account of metaphysics (as seen by Heidegger). See n. 8 above.

historical epochs of being (as in Hegel's philosophy of history). The highest task for the being that is in each case mine is precisely subjectivity, my total self-transformation before the infinite requirement of the eternal, or, speaking religiously, before God.

This is all good fun, assimilating Heidegger to Hegel and making him the butt of Johannine satires. But perhaps we are going a bit too fast. After all, Heidegger's critique of metaphysics describes it not only as the forgetting of being but also as the loss of the human.[14] In itself this does not mean that Heidegger does not himself remain trapped in metaphysics. After all, he himself has argued that Nietzsche is more nearly the fulfillment of metaphysics than its overcoming; Levinas has argued that Heidegger, too, belongs to the ontological tradition that reduces the other to the same; and no one would be admitted to any postmodernist party who thought that Kantian transcendentalism was not the continuation of metaphysics by other means.

Still, we might do well to take a closer look. Climacus often puts the issue in terms of whether objectivity or the ethical is the highest task. But *Being and Time* is already a move away from the theoretical objectivism of Heidegger's dissertations toward an understanding of understanding grounded in praxis and affect. Thus, for example, the primacy of *Zuhandenheit* over *Vorhandenheit* and the revelatory significance of mood. His later critique of the excessive subjectivity of *Being and Time* can be read (1) as the repudiation of a transcendental approach that remains too theoretical, methodologically at odds with its own discoveries, and (2) as the repudiation of a questioning of the highest task of Dasein only in relation to itself (authenticity, resoluteness) and not in relation to its other. Finally, the critique of calculative thinking is surely a step back out of objectivism.

But isn't a meditative thinking of being as much embedded in the spectator posture as the calculative thinking of beings? Not if Heidegger is right when he writes that "the thinking that thinks the truth of being as the primordial element of man, as one who

---

[14]See, e.g., *The Question Concerning Technology*, trans. William Lovitt (New York: Harper & Row, 1977) 27, and *Basic Writings*, ed. David Farrell Krell (New York: Harper & Row, 1977) 193, 235-36.

eksists, is in itself the original ethics."[15] Is it possible that the thinking of being is not only compatible with but even an expression of the claim that the ethical (or more generally, subjectivity) is the highest task for an existing human being?

Let us try to get clear about what "original ethics" might be. It clearly does not provide concrete prescriptions for daily life. We should not look for instruction about adultery, lying, cheating on our income tax, or how to treat the Jews. Original ethics is a matter of basic posture, one's fundamental project vis-à-vis that which is ultimate (which I am not—so this is not a Sartrean fundamental project nor, since We are not ultimate either, a posture at ease in modern technology) and to which I am essentially related.

We might call this an ethical formalism even emptier than Kantian formalism. But that would be to miss the point, and it is Climacus who can help us see why. Kantian formalism occurs in the attempt to spell out the content of my duty. It concerns the *what* and not the *how* of the ethical life. But the ethical which Climacus contrasts with the world historical and the more general ethicoreligious subjectivity he contrasts with the speculative in general are regularly presented as the *how* and not the *what* of the spiritual life.[16] They do not entail, nor do they try to ground the specific content. When Climacus presents the highest task as learning simultaneously to be absolutely related to the absolute and relatively related to the relative (CUP, 1:387, 407, 414, 422, 431), he does not even try to tell us who or what is absolute or what form our relative relationships should take. His adverbial formalism is not a species of Kantian formalism. But it is at least a close cousin of what Heidegger means by original ethics.[17]

---

[15]*Basic Writings*, 235.

[16]Most famously in the chapter on truth as subjectivity, but throughout *Postscript*, beginning with the contrast between approximation and appropriation.

[17]In a gloss on Jesus' command "Seek ye first God's kingdom and his righteousness," Kierkegaard points to the *how* that must precede every *what* in Christian ethics. "Shall I try to get a job suitable to my talents and powers in order thereby to exert an influence? No, thou shalt *first* seek God's Kingdom. Shall I then give all my fortune to the poor? No, thou shalt *first* seek God's kingdom. . . . But then in a certain sense it is nothing I shall do. Yes, certainly, in a certain sense it is nothing; thou shalt in the deepest sense make thyself nothing, become nothing before God, learn to keep silent; in this silence is the beginning,

This original ethics can also be called adverbial humanism. For it would seem that the critique of onto-theo-logy in both Climacus and Heidegger has an ethical humanism in the mode of adverbial formalism as its flip side. Go easy on metaphysics, they tell us. Not only is it a task that cannot be accomplished; your humanity calls you to a higher task that does not presuppose its accomplishment and might well be forgotten in the attempt. That task is learning to live the whole of life out of a proper posture toward your most ultimate other.

Having pulled Climacus and Heidegger together as closely as possible, I want to explore three differences. They involve the *what* that accompanies the *how* of any adverbial humanism. Climacus assumes (1) that some *what* accompanies every *how*, (2) that these will differ from one case to another just as the hows differ, and (3) that we have every right to speak of a given *what* as true or false, even if we do not have the final certainty of absolute knowledge (CUP, 1:201, 226). Metaphysically speaking, the *what* concerns the way we construe our most ultimate other. So we are reminded, in the first place, of the far from trivial difference between designating our most ultimate other as being, or *es gibt*, or *Ereignis* and designating it ethically as the infinite requirement, religiously as God, or (in Religiousness B) as God in Christ.

The enormous significance of this difference is deepened by a second difference, a meta-difference about this difference. Climacus makes it clear, as Heidegger does not, that the critique of onto-theo-logy is adverbial and not substantive. It concerns the *how* of our relation to our most ultimate other without excluding any answers to *what* (or *who*) that other might be.

Climacus calls attention to the fact that nothing in his argument precludes the possibility that the world as a whole may be intelligible in the way that Plato, or Hegel, or orthodox Christianity says it is. Most conspicuously he leaves open the possibility that the doubly dialectical and eminently paradoxical metaphysical claims of orthodox Christianity might be true. Our most ultimate

---

which is, *first* to seek God's kingdom" (CD, 322). In the following paragraphs Kierkegaard equates this silence with fear and trembling before God. Climacus would recognize in it his own "self-annihilation" before God in hidden inwardness that constitutes religious suffering. See CUP, 1:461, 488-89.

other might indeed be God in Christ. What the critique of onto-theo-logy precludes is not that these claims may be true but that they, or any analogous claims of, say, Plato or Hegel can become a first principle in terms of which we can possess and embody the total intelligibility we seek. That intelligibility is there, on each hypothesis, but not to be found by us, who are here and not there. The Kantian distinction between what is there and what is available to us returns.

But it would be dogmatic to assume that whatever is not available to us is simply not there. It would be to suppose that our present understanding is the touchstone of reality, an assumption—let us put this gently—more nearly Hegelian than postmodern. To expose the futility and the danger of putting God to work on philosophy's terms is one thing; to show that there is no God whose work is our highest task is quite another. Heidegger does not follow Climacus in making this distinction in his critique of onto-theo-logy. Perhaps this helps to explain why so much contemporary postmodernism bandies the term "onto-theo-logy" about as if it signified a successful attempt to make the world safe for atheism, to separate the question of freedom from the questions of God and immortality, and to free time completely from eternity. A postmodern Climacus stands as a challenge to this non sequitur.

The third difference concerns the ethical *what* rather than the metaphysical *what*. Adverbial humanism may be an ethos, but it is no *Sittlichkeit*. It contains no positive teaching about the duties and virtues that give goodness to daily life. But it is no substitute for concrete moral instruction either. The questions about cheating on my income tax and how to treat the Jews don't disappear. In practice, if not in theory, I will answer them one way or another.

When Heidegger has been charged with having no ethics, the force of his original ethics has been overlooked. But when he responds by pointing to his adverbial humanism, he neglects to acknowledge the absence of a concrete ethics of daily life in his thought, which is what the critics meant in the first place. If there is a difference between Climacus and Heidegger on this point, it is not because Climacus has such a concrete ethics but because of the penultimate role he plays in the writings of Kierkegaard. Like Heidegger, he does not himself go beyond an adverbial humanism devoid of concrete moral substance. But by relating himself so strongly to Socrates and to Christianity, his writing cries out for completion in keeping with the mundane moral passion they exhibit.

Kierkegaard responds. In *Works of Love* he develops a positive ethic of neighbor love. In *Practice in Christianity* he has Anti-Climacus develop a positive ethic of *imitatio Christi*, an ethic that clearly moves the ethic of neighbor love out of the private sphere and makes it a challenge to the class privilege (and disadvantage) of bourgeois society.[18] The verbal ethics built around the verbs to love (the neighbor) and to follow or to imitate (Christ in his reckless compassion) is a dangerous supplement to the adverbial ethics of being absolutely related to the absolute. It makes the tasks of hidden inwardness even more difficult by requiring their completion in the messy world of daily life. It is hard enough to wrestle with God, who loves me and always fights fairly; it is harder still to deal with other humans, who so often do not.

No one open to the moral instruction of Kierkegaard's verbal ethics could be an anti-Semite.

Climacus, Derrida, and the Metaphysics of Presence

Death seems to be contagious in postmodernism. The death of God reproduces itself as the death of man (both as the end of humanism and as the end of patriarchy). This death in turn becomes, not surprisingly, the death of the subject, and, surprisingly, the death of the author. Almost simultaneously with Barthes's announcement of the death of the author (1968) and Derrida's proclamation of the end of the book (1967), Foucault asks the question they were answering, "What Is an Author?" (1969)[19]

---

[18]I call this Religiousness C. It is also developed under Kierkegaard's own name in *For Self-Examination* and *Judge for Yourself!*. See "Kierkegaard's Teleological Suspension of Religiousness B" in *The Foundations of Kierkegaard's Vision of Community*, ed. George B. Connell and C. Stephen Evans (Atlantic Highlands NJ: Humanities Press, 1992). Kierkegaard continues to develop the formal, adverbial dimension in such subsequent works as *Upbuilding Discourses in Various Spirits* and *Christian Discourses*.

[19]See Roland Barthes, "The Death of the Author," *Image, Music, Text*, trans. Stephen Heath (New York: Noon Day Press, 1977); Michel Foucault, "What Is an Author?" *The Foucault Reader*, ed. Paul Rabinow (New York: Pantheon Books,

This trio is taking up where Gadamer left off. He writes: "Not occasionally but always, the meaning of a text goes beyond its author. That is why understanding is not merely a reproductive but always a productive activity as well. . . . It is enough to say that we understand in a *different* way, *if we understand at all.*"[20] Among the younger, prodigal sons of Heidegger, there is an agreement with this elder brother on a number of important points.

(1) The intention of the author (*mens auctoris*) does not determine the meaning of the text.

(2) This kind of control exceeds the author's grasp because the process of expression is internal to the meaning of the text. The author does not inwardly possess a clear and complete meaning which is subsequently transferred to the public domain without being affected in the process.

(3) The death of the author (as lord and master of the text) is the birth of the reader as coproducer of the text's meaning. A kind of semantic democracy replaces a dictatorship of meaning.

But while for Gadamer the basic issue here is whether hermeneutics and with it the *Geisteswissenschaften* can have an objectivity analogous to that of the natural sciences, our postmodern trio sees the issue largely in theological terms. According to the view they reject, the author's relation to the text is like that of God to the world, pure origin and sovereign lord. But God is dead, and the death of God entails the death of the author.[21] No one has that kind of absolute control over meaning. The death of the author is the demise of one of the ways human beings arrogate to themselves the powers and privileges of deity.

If this were an essay about authorship, it would be time to trace the surprisingly extensive agreement between this death of

---

1984); and Jacques Derrida, *Of Grammatology*, trans. Gayatri Chakrovorty Spivak (Baltimore: Johns Hopkins University Press, 1976).

[20]Hans-Georg Gadamer, *Truth and Method*, trans. Joel Weinsheimer and Donald G. Marshall (New York: Crossroad, 1991) 296-97.

[21]It is worth noting, as our postmodern trio tends not to do, that the converse entailment is entirely dubious. So far from showing the absence of God, the fact that we always begin *in medias res* and do not have total control over the worlds we create is just what one would expect if we were created by a God who is both pure origin and sovereign lord.

the author tradition and the views of Kierkegaard and his pseudo-nyms. But I have done that elsewhere,[22] and here wish to explore the deeper grounds of that agreement and the accompanying dis-agreement. Because of its concreteness and accessibility, the death of the author motif is a good introduction to Derrida's critique of metaphysics. Drawing extensively on Heidegger, he interprets metaphysics as a quest for presence that regularly lapses into wish-fulfilling presumptions of success. Like Heidegger he has in mind a tradition (tendency) that includes Plato and Hegel among its proudest moments, along with various scholastic versions of the-ism.[23] In other words, we are looking at what Heidegger calls onto-theo-logy from a different angle.

Like onto-theo-logy, the metaphysics of presence is actually a theory of knowledge. The onto-theo-logical claim is that we can render the whole of reality intelligible to ourselves with the help of the idea of God (or various surrogates for God). The claim of the metaphysics of presence is that we can obtain absolute knowledge by rendering the object of knowledge totally present to our cognition. In a phenomenological and structuralist context, that object, the signified, is often the sense, the essential meaning, the noematic content of our discourse. At other times, more in keeping with common sense, the signified is the fact or world of facts described and referred to by those meanings. Derrida's claim is that we can never experience sheer presence, not in the empirical world of facts or even in the semantic world of meanings.

What motivates the contrary assumption is the quest for certainty, for fixed and final knowledge. To be present is to be both here and now. I need not go elsewhere in either space (conceptual or physical) or time (inner time consciousness or world history) for what is present.[24] Absent the need for either journey,

---

[22]See n. 5 above. The essay cited there also pursues the theological dimension of the postmodern critique.

[23]I use the term "scholastic" ecumenically. Protestant theology, especially in the seventeenth century, has often been so designated.

[24]Derrida's claim is that my knowledge always refers me elsewhere, both in space and in time. That is why he coins the term *différance* to signify both spatial difference and temporal deferral. See "Différance" in *Margins of Philosophy*, trans. Alan Bass (Chicago: University of Chicago Press, 1982).

I have immediate access to the object. The Cartesian strategy for achieving absolute knowledge is fulfilled. But meanings and facts are not atomic; they are interrelated and I can have immediate access to some only if I have complete access to all. The demand for presence becomes the presumption that the totality of meanings and the totality of facts (or at least the totality of their categoreal structure) is simply here and now before me. In this holism the Hegelian strategy for achieving absolute knowledge is fulfilled.

In the immediacy that is made possible by totality we have an interesting analogue to God's eternity as classically defined by Boethius "Eternity is the whole, perfect, and simultaneous possession of endless life."[25] Everything is present to God at once: semantically speaking, the totality of the divine ideas, and empirically speaking, the totality of the world's history. Standing at the Alpha point, God is the pure origin of thoughts and actions that are unmediated, conditioned by no other.[26] Standing at the Omega point, God's thoughts and actions are fulfillments that need await no further developments. In the *totum simul* all is at once unconditioned and completed. That Climacus's critique of speculation is directed first at Hegel's logic as the totality of the divine ideas and then to his philosophy of world history as the totality of the unfolding of spirit suggests that Climacus will appreciate the critique of the metaphysics of presence.

But before turning to the specifics of that appreciation, we should cash in on the death of the author motif. According to the "metaphysical" view of authorship, the author is a kind of Boethian God in relation to the world of the text. Prior to history, that is, to the temporal process of inscription, the world that is to come forth is present in the mind of its creator, a "subject who supposedly would be the absolute origin of his own discourse and supposedly would construct it 'out of nothing,' 'out of whole cloth,' would be the creator of the verb, the verb itself." The idea of the author's intention "as simply anterior to a work which would

---

[25] . . . *interminabilis vitae tota simul et perfecta possessio. The Consolation of Philosophy*, 5, 6.

[26] Hegel writes that "mediation consists in having already left a first behind, to go on to a second," which means that in immediacy "we have as yet no other." *The Encyclopaedia Logic*, ¶86 and addition 1.

supposedly be the expression of it" is an instance of "Divine creativity . . . reappropriated by a hypocritical humanism."[27]

According to the metaphysics of presence, the philosopher can achieve the same author's eye view of the real world that the author has been alleged to have of the textual world s/he "creates." Instead of inhabiting the world *in medias res*, the philosopher occupies a point outside its temporal flux, a now unmediated by any past or future, since every past and future are already contained within it. It is this epistemological-anthropological claim that Derrida's critique seeks to deconstruct. For example, against the Husserlian semantics of a world of essences fixed in the inwardness of thought prior to and only contingently related to their linguistic expression (a generalization of the "metaphysical" author-text relation), Derrida poses Husserl's own phenomenology of internal time consciousness, according to which the retention of past meaning and the protention or anticipation of future meaning is internally related to every "present" moment of signification.[28] Finality of meaning is never present, since it awaits future completion. In this unfinished condition meaning is, strictly speaking, undecidable, and every interpretation is a decision, in the language of Climacus, a leap, an objective uncertainty.[29]

By now it should be obvious that Climacus's critique of the speculative, both as Platonic recollection and as Hegelian system, is a critique of the metaphysics of presence. Like Heidegger and Derrida, he seeks to radicalize the Kantian realization that the essential temporality of human knowing is the Achilles' heel of the metaphysical project. Since the presence that project requires is a kind of eternity, Climacus carries on a sustained assault on specu-

---

[27]Jacques Derrida, *Writing and Difference*, trans. Alan Bass (Chicago: University of Chicago Press, 1978) 285, 11-12.

[28]See Derrida's *Speech and Phenomena*, trans. David B. Allison (Evanston: Northwestern University Press, 1973).

[29]The correlativity of undecidability and decision in Derrida leaves open the possibility of an ethics of belief which discusses what makes decisions of this sort responsible, or even reasonable. But such an ethics will itself be without absolute foundation. Hence the inescapable element of violence in the law giving that founds any human social order. See Derrida's "Force of Law: The 'Mystical Foundation of Authority'," in *Deconstruction and the Possibility of Justice*, ed. Drucilla Cornell et al. (New York: Routledge, 1992).

lation as the attempt to see the world *sub specie aeterni*. To occupy such a standpoint, it has to presuppose a "fictive objective subject" and an "illusory termination" of the cognitive process (CUP, 1:81; cf. 189-93, 197-98, 217, 305-308, 361-62; SUD, 97-98; PC, 123-27).[30]

The Platonic version of this move is recollection. While the sophists flee eternity for a purely temporal flux, Plato backs out of time into eternity (CUP, 1:207-209, 217, 226, 270-73, 291). The Hegelian version of the same flight is the *aufhebung* of the dialectical in the speculative.[31] All forms of objectivity, of which speculation is a species, want "to have something really firm and fixed that can exclude the dialectical." Such projects express the need "for something firm with which the dialectical can be held at bay. But such a need is simply a need for a superstitious fixed point" (CUP, 1:35n, 44). This "superstitious fixed point" is the "fictive objective subject" and the "illusory termination" of which we just read. The dialectical is the second half of the *Critique of Pure Reason*, the realm of paralogism, antinomy, opposition, tension. The speculative overcomes the dialectical; it is the relaxing of the tension, the resolution of the dissonance, the repose of the eternal.

These flights from time to eternity and from the dialectical to the speculative are flights from existence, since "to exist does not mean to be *sub specie aeterni*" (CUP, 1:362). For this reason the Christian does not demand a demonstration of the eternal happiness for which s/he hopes, since "it is actually too much to demand that something that is in store shall be definite and certain, because the future and the present do have a little moment between them, which makes it possible to expect the future but impossible *in praesenti* to have certainty and definiteness . . . a present relation to a future is *eo ipso* one of uncertainty" (CUP,

---

[30]The fictive subjects include Plato's divine, recollecting soul and Hegel's Absolute Spirit as the subject of Absolute Knowledge. The "pure I = I" whom Climacus satirizes, is the Fichtean transcendental ego who has transcended the thing in itself and become, like the speculative subjects of Plato and Hegel, the identity of thought and being. It was Spinoza who overtly identified metaphysics with thinking *sub specie aeternitatis*.

[31]See ¶¶ 79-82 of *The Encyclopaedia Logic*.

1:424).[32] The Christian knows that "faith is abolished in eternity" (CUP, 1:30) and the philosopher should know that existence itself "must be annulled in the eternal before the system concludes itself" (CUP, 1:122). It is Climacus's existentialism that makes him a postmodernist.

" . . . before the system concludes itself." But what if the system isn't quite finished? Wouldn't that be a sliding back out of the *in praesenti* of the *sub specie aeterni* into human, all too human, time? Or perhaps the realization that we had never quite escaped time in the first place? Climacus first makes the point with reference to empirical knowledge such as ordinary historical knowledge. It never more than approximates finality and thus is never finished (CUP, 1:26-44). The idea of a last history of the Civil War or of the Renaissance doesn't really make sense. (Even when public relations people speak of a "definitive" study, they don't really think the topic has been laid to rest.) But the same thing is true of the speculative system, both in its logical and its world historical forms. Over and above the serious problems relating to the beginning of the logic, neither the formal nor the material version of the system can ever be finished (CUP, 1:13, 76-77, 106-112, 118-24, 145, 150, 150n.).

In everyday life there is a strongly felt need to have results, to be finished with one's essential tasks so as to live happily ever after. Climacus satirizes this aspect of our everydayness, not to be cruel to ordinary people, but to show how comical the system looks when placed beside its pre-theoretical, quotidian equivalent. For ordinary people and for the intellectual elite, "the urge to have something finished . . . is of evil and must be renounced" because the only one who "really has style [is the one] who is never finished" (CUP, 1:85-86; cf. 92). Existence is made too easy when its essential tasks are completed too quickly (CUP, 1:526). Needless to say, these completions are as fictitious (and as comical) as the bourgeois and speculative subjects who presume to have accomplished them.

---

[32]Derrida would say that we do not even possess our meanings *in praesenti* and that a present related to a future is one of undecidability.

Finally, the metaphysics of presence is as much a theological issue for Climacus as it is for Derrida. It involves a spurious humanism in which human knowers presume for themselves divine prerogatives. Because speculation arises from the "sorry error literally to want to be like God," theology in its speculative mode becomes anthropology (CUP, 1:565, 579); Feuerbach lets the Hegelian cat out of the bag. Aristotle had unfortunately assimilated the philosopher to the gods, blissful in their contemplation, oblivious to the tasks of existence (CUP, 1:56). Far wiser was Lessing, who knew that pure truth was for God alone (CUP, 1:106). Climacus rings the changes on this theme: a system of existence is for God alone (CUP, 1:118-19); to be the spectator of world history so that *die Weltgeschichte ist das Weltgericht* is for God alone (CUP, 1:141, 158); the identity of thought and being (subject and object) is for God alone (CUP, 1:190, 196); to have the explanation of the paradox so that it ceases to be paradoxical is for God alone (CUP, 1:212, 562).

Are there then no interesting differences between Derrida's critique of the metaphysics of presence and Climacus's? Hardly. For my money the most interesting is this. Climacus could hardly have enthusiastic readers who thought the critique, seen as a radicalizing of the Kantian critique, was the exclusive possession of secular or a/theistic thought. He makes it overtly clear, not simply that it might be appropriated by religious subjectivity in general (immanent, universal, Socratic), but that it is an essential, negative component of a properly orthodox Christianity that has, to recall *Philosophical Fragments*, gone beyond Socrates. This may be disconcerting to secular postmodernists who like to see the deconstruction of the metaphysics of presence as providing them with just the kind of theoretical-existential security it is designed to deny; and it may be disconcerting to Christians who like to see the deconstruction of the metaphysics of presence as a work of the devil, or at least of rampant nihilism. But Climacus was never out to win a popularity contest.

4

Dialectical Emotions and the Virtue of Faith[1]

Robert C. Roberts

Introduction

The central serious[2] project of *Philosophical Fragments* was to limn the logical contours of Christian faith, thought of as a condition or state of the individual—what in a traditional vocabulary would be called the *virtue* of faith. Johannes Climacus approaches the clarification with a sustained contrast, between the relationship that a Socrates bears to someone he undertakes to nurture morally and religiously, and the relationship that the incarnate God of the New Testament bears to any true disciple. While faith is a personal trait, and thus analogous to generosity, courage, or truthfulness, it is also a relationship with a particular other person, and thus is a special kind of virtue, in some respects more like friendship, as Aristotle understands it, than like the other virtues.[3] *Concluding Unscientific Postscript* is a continuation of the project of *Fragments*, but with a much more strongly psychological emphasis. In *Fragments,* Climacus passingly characterized faith as a "happy passion" [*lykkelige Lidenskab*] (PF, 54), but this description is now elaborated by way of such concepts as *subjectivity, inwardness, existence, eternal happiness, existential pathos,* and *dialectical pathos.* Like traditional

[1]I am very grateful to the Pew Charitable Trusts for financial support that enabled me to write this essay, and to Steve Evans, Gordon Marino, and Robert Perkins for suggestions that led to improvements of it.

[2]For an effort to sort out the serious from the unserious in *Fragments,* see my *Faith, Reason, and History: Rethinking Kierkegaard's Philosophical Fragments* (Macon GA: Mercer University Press, 1986).

[3]Regarding friendship Aristotle says it is "a virtue, or implies virtue" (*Nicomachean Ethics* 8.1).

virtue-oriented thinkers about the moral and spiritual life[4], Climacus thinks of proper personal formation as in large part a matter of proper *passional* formation—the proper formation of interests, enthusiasms and concerns, and of the various emotions that arise from these. In a virtue like friendship, the concerns and patterns of emotional response will take as their primary object the particular other person in the relationship—the friend. Similarly, Christian faith as Climacus envisages it in the *Postscript* is in large part a disposition to a set of emotional responses to the "object" of faith, the incarnate god. The emotions characteristic of this particular relationship or virtue are of a special type, which it is the business of the present paper to explain. Climacus speaks of the emotions characteristic of Christian faith as "dialectical in second place" (CUP, 1:556).

I shall begin with some general remarks about the nature of emotion and then introduce Climacus's concepts through a study of ways he uses some of the central terms of his vocabulary of pathos in *Postscript*. Then, because the *Postscript* remains rather abstract in its discussion of the dialectical emotions, I shall interpret it by reference to a more concretely exegetical work (*Practice in Christianity*) and by discussing some New Testament passages in which emotions that are "dialectical in second place" are taken to exemplify Christian and nonChristian character.

The Nature of Emotion

It is an insight of classical discussions that virtues are as typically exemplified in emotional states as they are by actions. Thus Aristotle defines the virtues as mean states with respect to actions *and passions* (πάθη).[5] Emotions have this power of exemplifying virtues or the lack thereof because of what they "say" about

---

[4]For more argument that Kierkegaard and several of his personæ are "virtue ethicists," see my "Kierkegaard, Wittgenstein, and a Method of 'Virtue Ethics'" in *Kierkegaard in Post/Modernity*, ed. Martin J. Matuštík and Merold Westphal (Bloomington: Indiana University Press, 1995); and "Existence, Emotion, and Virtue: Classical Themes in Kierkegaard" in *The Cambridge Companion to Kierkegaard*, ed. Alastair Hannay and Gordon Marino (Cambridge UK and New York: Cambridge University Press, 1997).

[5]*Nicomachean Ethics* 2.6.

what the individual cares about and how the individual "sees" the world in which he dwells. Aristotle makes it a mark of the just person that he or she "rejoices" (χαίρειν)[6] in performing just actions, and a plausible explanation of this fact (though not the one characteristic of Aristotle) is that the just person is *concerned* about justice. The unjust person, by contrast, experiences no such joy because he is not "interested" in justice, does not care about it, is indifferent to it. Joy in doing justice or seeing it done is not the only emotion that arises out of the concern for justice. The just person regrets the injustices in his own nation's past, feels contrition about the ones he himself has committed, is angered at culpable perpetrators of injustice, feels hopeful when prospects of justice are looking up and anxious or fearful when prospects of injustice are high, admires conspicuous doers of justice, is grateful to those who help in the cause of justice, and so forth. This whole range of emotional responses, which vary with the perceived circumstances and vicissitudes of justice, arise out of the concern for justice. Thus a certain class of virtues, of which justice is a prime example—virtues which are constituted of some moral concern or other—are exemplified not only in actions, but in a range of emotions.

Another virtue in this class is friendship, which is worth a brief examination here, inasmuch as Climacus construes faith as a personal relationship with a particular individual, the God-man Jesus of Nazareth. Friends care about one another. Each is concerned about the well-being of the other, about his or her own well-being in relation to the other, and about the well-being of the relationship. These concerns show up in actions of spending time together, sharing activities, seeking one another's aid and coming to one another's aid. But it is also essential to friendship that the concerns show up in various emotions: Rejoicing in one another's company, especially after an absence, feeling grateful for one another's aid, feeling relief when the friend has survived a close call; if one of the friends is threatened or in trouble, the other will feel anxiety or sorrow; if the friend is culpably harmed by someone, the other will feel anger; if the relationship is threatened by strife, the friends will feel anxious until the strife is resolved or the friendship ends;

---

[6]*Nicomachean Ethics* 1.8.

if a third party intervenes to help the friend out of trouble, the other friend will be grateful to the third party. Such emotions are not merely indicative of the friends' attachment to one another; they are partially constitutive of the relationship. The friends' mutually recognized emotions often bind the two together even more strongly than actions can do. So friendship, like the virtue of justice, is made up in large part of concerns and displayed in large part in emotions.

These facts of moral psychology are instances of a more general fact about emotions: they are based on concerns. Essential to the explanation of any emotion will be reference to what its subject cares about. If Suzy is embarrassed about the mistakes in her presentation to the last board meeting, it will be because she is concerned to make a good impression (another outcome would have yielded a different emotion based on the same concern). By knowing that Herb is afraid of losing his job, we know that under some description Herb cares about keeping his job. But emotions not only indicate what a person cares about, but also how he or she sees his present circumstances: the embarrassed person sees herself as looking bad in the sight of others; the fearful person sees himself as under some threat or other; and so forth for every type of emotion. Thus emotions are circumstantial instantiations of the concerns on which they are based: Some circumstance of the subject is perceived (though not necessarily *sense* perceived) in such a way as to impinge on and activate the concern. In earlier work I have called emotions "concern-based construals," since they are gestalt-like perceptions (cases of "seeing-as," "hearing-as," "thinking of-as," etc.) that activate and transfigure concerns.[7] Just as a person's concerns are constitutive of character, so are his "perceptual" habits, the "terms" in which he is characteristically disposed to view his world.

The distinction between emotions and concerns, and the connection of both of these with character, are present in the *Postscript*, though the distinction between emotions and concerns is not marked by a distinction of vocabulary. The two chief general words of Climacus's emotion-vocabulary are *Pathos* (almost always

---

[7]"What an Emotion Is: A Sketch," *The Philosophical Review* 97 (1988): 183-209.

translated "pathos" in English), and *Lidenskab* (almost always translated "passion"), and their cognates. While discussion of emotion-related topics pervades the *Postscript*, it remains rather generic, as compared with other places in the works of Kierkegaard, where particular emotion types, such as anxiety, envy, admiration, hope, despair, and joy get discussed at some length. This generic character of Climacus's discussion tends to obscure the distinction I am interested in drawing out. Let us begin with Climacus's word "passion" (*Lidenskab*).

Passion

Sometimes Climacus uses the word "interest" (*Interesse*) or "interested" (*interesseret*) in connection with "passion," in such phrases as "the subject's personal, infinite, impassioned interestedness" (*personlige, uendelige Interesserethed i Lidenskab*) (CUP, 1:27), or even as an apparent synonym of "passion" as when he says that "faith is precisely the infinite interest (*uendelige Interesse*) in Christianity and any other interest (*Interesse*) easily becomes a temptation" (CUP, 1:21). In such passages it seems to me that "passion" refers to the concern for an eternal happiness, on the basis of which the particular emotions of the daily life of faith are erected. Passion as interest or concern is one fundamental concept expressed by *Lidenskab* in the *Postscript*. In this sense *Lidenskab* will be a dispositional term, as in the phrase, "Socrates had a passion for truth." Let us say that during his entire adulthood Socrates had a passion for truth." This does not imply that at every given moment—say, when he was sleeping, or when he was admiring Xanthippe's fine figure—he was feeling something with respect to truth; it implies, instead, that he was *disposed* to do so, and so, consequently, often did.

But sometimes *Lidenskab* refers to what in this paper I am calling emotions—those particular, situation-picturing states of passion that come and go with changes of thought and situation. In some passages we find both senses of *Lidenskab* occurring side by side. Commenting on the parable of the wise and foolish virgins (Matthew 25.1-12), Climacus says,

> The five foolish maidens had indeed lost the infinite passion [*Lidenskab*] of expectancy [*Forventning*]. So the lamp went out.

> Then a cry arose that the bridegroom was coming. Then they rushed to the dealer and bought new oil and wanted to start afresh and let everything be forgotten. And, of course, everything was indeed forgotten. The door was shut and they were shut out, and when they knocked at the door, the bridegroom said to them: I do not know you. This was not just a quip by the bridegroom but a truth, for in a spiritual sense they had become unrecognizable through having lost the infinite passion [*Lidenskab*].
> (CUP, 1:16-17)

Eager expectancy is a particular situational determination of an interest in the bridegroom's coming. It is what I am calling an emotion. Other emotions might be based on the concern for the bridegroom's coming, and be just as characteristic of the infinite interest as expectancy. For example, one who is intensely concerned that he come, yet convinced that he will *not* come (news has arrived that he was killed in an accident on the way to the wedding) will not be in a state of expectation, but of regret, disappointment, or grief that equally shows the character of the subject's "subjectivity." Or again, one who is passionately concerned that he come, but sees that he has already arrived, will not be in expectation, but in a state of joy; etc.

A passage that nicely illustrates the dual sense of *Lidenskab* comes later in the *Postscript*:

> I have often thought about how one might bring a person into passion (*Lidenskab*). So I have considered the possibility of getting him astride a horse and then frightening the horse into the wildest gallop, or even better, in order to draw out the passion (*Lidenskaben*) properly, the possibility of getting a man who wants to go somewhere as quickly as possible (and therefore was already in something of a passion [*Lidenskab*]) astride a horse that can hardly walk—and yet existing is like that if one is conscious of it.   (CUP, 1:311)

It seems clear that the "passion" in the first experiment is the emotion of fear, indeed fear for one's life, and it is "drawn out" by putting the person in a situation of kinesthetically impressive danger. It presupposes the latent and dispositional interest in (passion for) staying alive and uninjured. In the second experiment, the passion that is drawn out is a form of frustration or impatience, again created by manipulating the individual's particular situation, and again based on an interest that is already there—the interest in getting somewhere expeditiously. It is clear that passion in the sense of frustration or impatience cannot be drawn out of just anybody by this particular manipulation, since not everybody wants to get somewhere in a hurry. Some people would be quite content to sit on the old nag and daydream.

Given the distinction between passion as interest and passion as emotion, we can offer an interpretation of Climacus's description of faith as a "happy passion" (*lykkelige Lidenskab*). An infinite passionate interest in an eternal happiness is not necessarily happy. This is clear from the latter half of the *Postscript*, where such unhappy emotions as the ones that Climacus gathers under the rubrics of suffering, guilt, and offense are discussed. In these emotions the infinite passionate interest is, in one way or another, *frustrated*. Faith, then, is neither just the infinite passionate interest nor any single emotion that is based on it, but a *range* of *happy* emotions based in the infinite passionate interest in an eternal happiness. The person of faith is one who is related to his or her divine Friend by such emotions as joy in his presence, hope (expectancy) of his coming, and gratitude for his friendship.

I have found one parenthetical remark in the *Postscript* that seems to suggest that passion as interest may not, in Climacus's view, always be the basis for passion as emotion. He says, "the existence of the believer is even more passionate [*lidenskabelig*] than that of the Greek philosopher (who to a high degree needed passion [*Lidenskab*] even in connection with his ataraxia) ... " (CUP, 1:354). For the skeptic, ataraxy is absence of emotion; so, if the skeptical project makes any sense at all, the skeptic's passionate commitment to the project of becoming ataractic cannot be a groundwork for emotion. It is indeed questionable whether the skeptical project can be carried out in the radical way that the skeptics envision. Climacus admires the Greek skeptics, not because he thinks the skeptical life-ideal is healthy or even possible, but because of their seriousness in applying their philosophy to their personal lives, in contrast to most modern philosophers. If pressed on the topic, Climacus would probably predict for the intense and thoroughly honest development of the skeptical project the kind of "contradictions" that the project of religiousness A meets with: the resistances of personal life to the implementation of high ethical ideals. In that case, emotions would certainly follow on passionate commitment to the project, and they would be analogous[8] to the emotions of frustration that Climacus discusses under the heading of "existential pathos" (CUP, 1:431-561).

Pathos

I have been proposing the word "emotion" as a key to understanding Climacus's moral and religious psychology. In some contexts of English, the word does not have a very worthy ring. It may be taken to refer to gratuitous and evanescent states of feeling, states which either tell us nothing about a person's deeper character, or tell us uncomplimentary things about it, states that are characteristically caused by the likes of too much beer or too little coffee. "Emotional" people, we may think, are ones whom minimal circumstantial vicissitudes can reduce to yelling, throwing things, sobbing, stage fright, self-pity, sweating, and blushing. They are susceptible to maudlin entertainments like 35¢ novels and B-grade movies, which "turn them on" or jerk the flusher of their eyeballs. If people are emotional it is because they are low on rationality and self-control.

If emotions were nothing but what this picture suggests, it is hard to understand why such explorers of the virtues as Plato and Aristotle, Augustine, Aquinas, David Hume, and Adam Smith gave them such a central place in their moral psychologies. It is hard to understand why the Gospels picture Jesus with such a rich emotional life including compassion, grief over sins, anger, joy, and sorrow.[9] It is hard to understand why the Apostle Paul's letters are peppered with references to and expressions of joy and

---

[8]Analogous, but certainly not identical. Since Climacus is discussing how to come to Christian faith, it is essential to his project that the telos (the eternal happiness) take the form of a personal relationship with God. The skeptic's telos, by contrast, is a kind of radical impersonal individuation. Consequently the highest pitch of existential pathos for the striving skeptic will be something like disappointment or self-directed anger, an emotion quite different from the sense of interpersonal guilt that is the highest pitch of existential pathos for the striving Christian.

[9]For a discussion of these emotions, see Benjamin B. Warfield, "The Emotional Life of Our Lord" in *The Person and Work of Christ*, ed. Samuel G. Craig (Philadelphia: Presbyterian and Reformed Publishing Co., 1950) 93-145.

hope, anger and gratitude, sorrow and compassion. And it is hard to understand why Kierkegaard's edifying works follow, in this respect, the footsteps of the New Testament and the classical moral psychologists. At any rate, I suggest that when Johannes Climacus speaks of existential pathos and dialectical pathos, he is following a long tradition of Christian and classical moral psychology, and our best English word for capturing what he is talking about is "emotion."

Like *Lidenskab*, *Pathos* does not have a single sense, but varies in sense by context. To love (probably in the sense of romantic attachment—*at elske*) is said to be pathos (CUP, 1:385); admiration of a hero, either of an esthetic or a religious sort, is said to be pathos (CUP, 1:388); even words and actions are said to be pathos: "In relation to possibility, words are the highest pathos; in relation to actuality, actions are the highest pathos" (CUP, 1:389-90). Thus we have the two senses that I have identified for *Lidenskab*, plus what I take to be an extension of one or both of these. To say that love is pathos is to say that it is an attachment (concern) on which a variety of emotions can be based; to say that admiration is pathos is to identify one emotion (based on a concern for great accomplishments); to say that action is pathos is to say that actions express emotions and their underlying concerns, and so serve as reliable indicators of their presence. *Pathos* and *Lidenskab* seem to differ, in the *Postscript*, in the weighting of their senses: Whereas *Lidenskab* as interest or concern seems to predominate, Pathos as emotion seems to predominate.

Climacus appears to confirm the idea that pathos is emotion and is based in passion as interest or concern when he says, "a person's passion [*Lidenskab*] culminates in the pathos-filled relation [*pathetiske Forhold*] to an eternal happiness" (CUP, 1:385). But he delimits pathos in a couple of ways. In the *Postscript* "Pathos" usually refers to "negative" or *unpleasant* emotions, and this is not surprising, given the stress on suffering, guilt, and offense in the last half of the *Postscript* (where most of the usage of *Pathos* occurs). He even seems to define pathos in terms of the negative and the tragic (as contrasted with the comic). "That the subjective existing thinker is just as positive as negative can also be expressed by saying that he has just as much of the comic as of pathos" (CUP, 1:87). Presumably the response to the comic does not count as pathos,[10] but this is not to say that Climacus never uses *Pathos* in reference to positive emotions. In fact, he indicates the contrary in the following passage.

> To *celebrate* a hero of faith is just as fully an esthetic task as to celebrate a war hero. If the religious is truly the religious, has passed through the ethical and has it in itself, then it cannot forget that religiously the pathos [*Pathos*] is not a matter of singing praises and celebrating or composing song books but of existing oneself. . . . esthetically the poet-production is the important thing, and the poet is the accidental.
> (CUP, 1:388; italics in the original)

Here it seems that the happy admiration of the hero of faith, whether it takes an esthetic or a religious form, counts as pathos. And, vocabulary aside, we can see that Climacus wants the class of existential, religious, subjective, and genuinely inward emotions to include positive ones, by his characterization of faith as a happy passion (*lykkelige Lidenskab*).

The distinction Climacus makes in the last quotation is important, and expresses his second delimitation of the concept. He repeatedly distinguishes existential or ethical pathos (what in a more classical vocabulary might be called emotions exemplifying virtue or indicating character) from esthetic pathos, which is somehow detached from the "existence" or character of the individual, and thus in a sense is not real pathos.

> In relation to an eternal happiness as the absolute good, pathos [*Pathos*] does not mean words but that this idea transforms the whole existence of the existing person. Esthetic pathos expresses itself in words and can in its truth signify that the individual abandons himself in order to lose himself in the idea, whereas existential pathos results from the transforming relation of the idea to the individual's existence. If the absolute τέλος [end, goal] does not absolutely transform the individual's existence by relating to it, then the individual does not relate himself with existential pathos [*existentielt-pathetisk*] but with esthetic pathos [*aesthetisk-pathetisk*]. . . .   (CUP, 1:387)

---

[10]In "Is Amusement an Emotion?" I have explored the question whether the mental state responding to comic representations should be counted as an emotion. *American Philosophical Quarterly* 25/3 (1988): 269-74.

The distinction between esthetic and existential pathos trades on at least four interconnected facts about emotions. First, a person's emotions—his hopes and fears, joys and sorrows, frustrations and satisfactions—can be among the deepest qualifiers and expressions of his "existence" (character, subjectivity, inwardness). But second, emotions can also be existentially shallow; they can veer, in varying degrees, toward being mere "feelings" that do not indicate much about the individual's heart. Third, the possibility of such shallowness is due to the human power of imagination. This is the power that makes distinctively human existence possible, but it is also the power of artifice that is most concertedly employed by the poet. Fourth, through the "magic" of word-craft and the power of his creative imagination, the poet can spin fantasies of feeling that are quite "moving" but which, from the point of view of the poet's actual human existence, are artificial and superficial.[11] This is not, of course, to say that poets are always emotionally superficial, but just to claim the possibility and danger of this; it is characteristic of one of the esthetes in *Either/Or* that he systematically dissociates from his emotions (see EO, 1:281-300).

These concocted or esthetic feelings are often deceptive or quasi-deceptive, inasmuch as their concocter is himself so charmed by the words and the fantastic feelings of emotion they generate that he takes the feelings to be expressions of his "heart," his char-acter, his deeper existence. Preachers, as wordsmiths who are pro-fessionally involved with religious concepts, are especially liable to take esthetic pathos for existential (ethical, religious) pathos, and induce their congregations to take the feelings generated by the preacher's eloquence as genuine religious pathos. It is also characteristic of the poet's attitude that he becomes diverted from the issues of his own existence which are expressed in his work, to the work itself as a product; instead of the work's being a school of his character, his own life becomes a fund of experience for the production of works of art. The danger of confusing esthetic and existential pathos is a chief motive of Climacus and Johannes de

---

[11]Ordinary human beings also commonly talk themselves into feeling emotions that do not run deep. I have explored this phenomenon in some detail in "Feeling One's Emotions and Knowing Oneself," *Philosophical Studies* 77 (1995): 319-38.

Silentio for stressing inwardness and even "hidden" inwardness, and warning against the snares of expression.

This danger is also Climacus's motive for saying that "In relation to possibility, words are the highest pathos; in relation to actuality, actions are the highest pathos" (CUP, 1:389-90). He does not, of course, literally mean to identify pathos with action. But action of an appropriate sort both *signals* existential hope, joy, gratitude, contrition, and so forth, and the passion for an eternal happiness from which these emotions spring, and *generates* the emotions and increases the passion.

> So when a man says, for example, that for the sake of his eternal happiness he has suffered hunger, cold, been in prison, in peril at sea, has been despised, persecuted, whipped, etc. [see 2 Corinthians 11:23-27], these simple words are testimony to ethical pathos inasmuch as they quite simply refer to what he, acting, has suffered.   (CUP, 1:390)

An almost sure sign that a person's pathos is esthetic is that it remains a matter of mere feeling, or feeling expressed only in words.

In chapter 4, division 2 of the *Postscript*, Climacus offers a somewhat systematic, developmental account of Christian pathos. His account posits three stages of "existential pathos" [*existentielle Pathos*] (CUP, 1:387) followed by a "new pathos" (CUP, 1:556) that is the specifically Christian kind of emotion, arising in response to the central character of the New Testament.

The initial stage of existential pathos (CUP, 1:387-431) occurs when a person becomes aware that an eternal happiness is the absolute telos of his life, and that by comparison all other ends are only relative, and thus ought to be subordinate. As always, this awareness counts as existential pathos only if the subject is willing to take *action* to give an eternal happiness the absolutely first place in his life, and to subordinate all other goals. Since Climacus is talking about the development of Christian emotion, we must suppose that an eternal happiness is at this stage at least dimly apprehended as a positive, obedient relationship with God, a state of mind and action in which God is respected as God and nothing else is respected as God. At this initial stage the stress is on pathos as concern (commitment), rather than as emotion, since the subject is intensely interested in leading a life of proper worship of God—so interested as to be willing to take action.

In the second and third stages, however, pathos as emotion predominates, built on the foundation of the interest in an eternal happiness, but in response to the difficulties of implementing the commitment. The second stage of existential pathos (CUP, 1:431-525) is marked by suffering [*Lidelse*] due to the fact that the commitment of the first stage is frustrated. The religious individual finds that the eternal happiness he is seeking is forever out of reach due to the weakness of his flesh and his ever-new back-sliding into giving relative ends the place in his life that only the absolute telos should occupy. The suffering at this stage takes the form of self-directed anger, anxiety about one's moral and spiritual status, impatience with self and life, disappointment and sorrow. In the third stage of existential pathos (CUP, 1:525-55), these negative emotions assume the aspect of a global, irremediable, and ever-increasing guilt. One is not only a failure at the project of relating oneself absolutely to the absolute telos and relatively to all relative ends; one is a failure at this by one's own doing and neglecting, and one has failed at it before the person of God. In this state of existential pathos one is ready, if one ever will be, to become friends with the God-man of the New Testament, who welcomes to himself those who labor and are heavy laden, and reconciles sinners to God while they are still helpless. But the difficulties are not yet over.

Dialectical Pathos

I turn now to that "dialectical" pathos which constitutes the virtue of distinctively Christian—that is, Christ-centered—faith. This is the virtue that Climacus calls "a happy passion" (PF, 54) and "the passion of faith" [*Troens Lidenskab*] (CUP, 1:563, 565). It is the religiousness characterized by "inward deepening... [which is] dialectical in second place" (556), wherein the individual relates himself or herself "to something outside himself in order to find the upbuilding" (561), something that is "paradoxically repelling and giv[es] rise to new pathos" (556). ·

Since the emotional dimensions of this religiousness are sketched rather abstractly in *Fragments* and *Postscript*, I propose to interpret it (and them) in light of a more concretely exegetical work, *Practice in Christianity*. Even *Practice* is somewhat abstract in its discussion of emotions, grouping a number of distinguishable emotional responses to Jesus under the general heading of "offense," and leaving inexplicit several of the positive emotions characteristic of faith. I shall attempt to aid the analysis a bit by asking what more particular emotions are at issue in the scriptural passages that Anti-Climacus expounds, and other related ones. As instances of aspect perception,[12] emotions pick up (or pick out, or at least attribute) particular aspects of the situations they are about, and this idea will help us to be more concrete as we seek to analyze the virtue of faith along with its counterpart state, offense.

Since *Practice* is written by a different persona than *Fragments* and *Postscript*, the interpretation must remain tentative and suggestive rather than strongly doctrinal; but there is not much to be said for being strongly doctrinal about Kierkegaard's writings anyway, since they are designed to discourage such reading. My interpretation of these writings as in line with classical thinking about emotions and virtues is offered in a similarly undogmatic, experimental spirit of suggestion, more interested in understanding the issues of moral and spiritual psychology than in arguing for a particular interpretation of Kierkegaard's writings.

Faith, in the present sense of the word, is always a relationship with Jesus of Nazareth. Since I am emphasizing the emotional aspects of virtues, I shall stress, as Kierkegaard and the New Testament writers do, the emotional dimensions of the believer's relationship to Jesus Christ. Thus when we speak of a "relationship," we will have in mind a pattern (disposition) of emotional response to that man; that is a very significant part of what the relationship *is*. Emotional response is a crucial index of ordinary friendship, enmity, or indifference—that is, "relationship." A friend is, in significant part, someone who rejoices when I am blessed, is saddened by my decline and fall, angered by those who undermine me and grateful to those who help me, who hopes for my well-

---

[12]For more discussion of emotions' perceptual character, see "Emotions as Access to Religious Truths," *Faith and Philosophy* 9 (1992): 83-94. For exegesis of Kierkegaard showing his sensitivity to emotions' perceptual character, see "Existence, Emotion, and Virtue: Classical Themes in Kierkegaard."

being and regrets having let me down. An enemy is one who holds me in contempt, or rejoices in my downfall or hopes for it, who is saddened when I do well, angry at those who help me and grateful to those who undermine me. Someone who is neither an enemy nor a friend is marked by emotional indifference in all these respects. Faith, as Anti-Climacus understands it in *Practice*, is like this: it is constituted, in significant part, by dispositions of emotional response respecting the man Jesus of Nazareth.

Characterizing faith as a "happy passion" suggests that the emotions that constitute it are "positive" in two senses of that ambiguous word. They are positive *about Jesus*, in that they evaluate him positively. He is seen, in these emotions, in his aspects of goodness, glory, helpfulness, worthiness, divinity. They are also, on balance, *affectively* positive, that is, pleasant. They will tend to be emotions like joy, gratitude, and hope—"happy" ones—though faith can also be exemplified in unpleasant emotions, notably contrition concerning one's own sins, and grief about the way in which Jesus is viewed and treated by unbelievers. By contrast, the emotions of offense are "negative" about Jesus, seeing him as impediment, intruder, false claimant, degrading to oneself, threatening rival, foolish, absurd. And they will be, on balance, unpleasant: anger, outrage, indignation, resentment, embarrassment, shame, dismay, repugnance, contempt, disappointment, fear.

Anti-Climacus is concerned throughout *Practice* with restoring a truthful perception of Christ. Just as Johannes Climacus wants to correct his contemporaries' impression of Christianity by making it "difficult to become a Christian, yet not more difficult than it is" (CUP, 1:557), it is part of the reintroduction of Christianity to Christendom to correct a false and "soft" (sentimentalized, "fantastic") picture of Christ, and replace it with the representation of a Christ who can evoke the range of emotional responses that Jesus is reported to have elicited from his contemporaries. Central to Kierkegaard's enterprise is the concept of Christ as the paradox, the shocking unity of God with this particular man Jesus of Nazareth. As Anti-Climacus points out, most of the negative emotion that Jesus aroused in his contemporaries could be traced to the extraordinary claim that his words and actions make (usually somewhat indirectly) about his identity. In the Invocation to *Practice*, Anti-Climacus prays,

> Would that we might see you as you are and were and will be
> until your second coming in glory, as the sign of offense and the
> object of faith, the lowly man, yet the Savior and Redeemer of the
> human race, who out of love came to earth to seek the lost, to
> suffer and die, and yet, alas, every step you took on earth, every
> time you called to the straying, every time you reached out your
> hand to do signs and wonders, and every time you defenselessly
> suffered the opposition of people without raising a hand—again
> and again in concern you had to repeat, "Blessed is the one who
> is not offended at me." Would that we might see you in this way
> and that we then might not be offended at you!   (PC, 9-10)

A virtue that is defined as a relationship of a certain sort with a
particular individual (an odd sort of virtue, in the context of the
history of the virtues) is attended with peculiar pitfalls, not the
least of which is to get the conception of the identity of that particular individual close enough to right to warrant the claim that
one is indeed related in the required way to *that* individual. Faith,
in the Christian tradition, is such a virtue. Kierkegaard and his
personæ are thus warranted in their concern to protect the possibility of offense—indeed a certain well-defined *kind* of offense—at
Jesus Christ as a condition for faith. For in protecting that possibility they are protecting the identity of Jesus Christ as the object of
faith.

Offense and faith are two ways (or families of ways) of
perceiving, with the "eyes of the heart" (Ephesians 1:18), certain
crucial features of Christ's person and activity: the reality of both
his lowly condition and his claim to be God and the contrast
between these; his assumption of our sin (need) and his claim to
be able to remedy our sin; his offer to give us rest by virtue of our
coming into a special relationship with him; his assumption of the
equality of all sinners.

These features of Christ can be seen in two ways: with joy,
gratitude, hope, contrition, trust; or with anger, dismay, repugnance, contempt, disappointment, resentment, fear, shame, embarrassment. A response of emotional indifference, such as seems
to characterize "christendom," is, by contrast, an indication of
failure or refusal to notice these crucial features of the historical
Jesus. But someone who cannot notice these features cannot come
into relationship with the man who is so fundamentally marked by

them, and thus cannot have the virtue that is constituted of that relationship. Of course it is possible that someone might be angry at Jesus without having *these* features in view, in which case he would not have experienced what Anti-Climacus calls *"essential offense."* One might also respond to Jesus with joy and gratitude, yet without "seeing" the features that would give rise to the emotions of essential offense. In that case the joy and gratitude would not exemplify the virtue of Christian faith. Neither person's subjectivity would be qualified by an encounter with the true Christ. Both offense and faith, then, are sets of ways of noticing real features of Jesus Christ, and noticing them with one's heart, noticing them "existentially." It is a goal of *Practice* to facilitate a "vision" of these features of the Christian story that gives rise to the possibilities of faith and offense.

All distinctively human emotions are dialectical in the basic sense of being shaped by thought: They are perceptions of their objects in one or more aspects which can be identified only via language and thought. But the emotions that rightly represent Jesus Christ are dialectical in a second, narrower sense (CUP, 1:557, 559): They are shaped by thoughts that "offend" against deeply ingrained, comfortable and righteous patterns and forms of human thought. The idea of a man who is God himself (not just an instance of the humanity that is in some sense naturally "divine" or made in the "image of God"), who, alone among human beings has the authority to forgive sins against God, a man who can call all of humanity to *himself* for salvation—this is an idea that strains the entire fabric of human moral thought. But it is this thought which enters into the structure of the emotions of offense, as well as the emotions of faith. It is this thought which shapes "dialectical pathos."

If Christ is who he claims to be, as Kierkegaard and his Climacus-personæ believe he is, then only the emotions of faith, and *not* those of offense, are true perceptions of him. The eyes of the heart that rejoices in Jesus Christ perceive him as the redeemer of the human race; the eyes of the heart that is grateful to Jesus Christ see him as the gracious giver of life to those who were dead in their trespasses and sins; the eyes of the heart that hopes in Christ see him as the surety of a glorious future. In the emotions of faith Christ is seen not only in his paradoxicality, but also in his goodness. This is what is missed in the emotions of offense, for they all have in common that Christ is seen as *bad* in one way or another. This is not only a misrepresentation of Christ as he is, but it is a failure to have the virtue that consists in loving and appreciating him. Offense and faith represent equally well the paradoxicality of the claims about Christ's identity that he makes through word and deed; but they are not equally accurate representations of Christ himself. The aspect perceptions which Kierkegaard calls offense clearly see one aspect, but not the other.

So much for some generalities. Let us turn to some particular instances of emotions of offense and faith in an effort to verify and illustrate these claims.

Some Particular Dialectical Emotions

Asked by emissaries from John the Baptist whether he is the one who is to come, Jesus refers to his miracles and preaching, and then says, "and blessed is he who takes no offense at me" (Matthew 11:6; see PC, 94). Given Jewish habits of mind and the claim implied by citing the passage from Isaiah, we may suppose that Jesus anticipates shocked outrage that he, in particular, should claim to be God's Messiah. Offense in this case is a distinctly Jewish indignation, based in the desire and expectation of the Messiah's glory, an indignation that this ordinary fellow should claim to be the Messiah. The relevant aspects that the offended Jew will hear in the report are culpable arrogance, the evil of demeaning Messiah, and the desert, on the part of Jesus, to be punished or got out of the way. From the perspective of Christian faith all of these perceived predicates of Jesus are misperceptions, but they get something right, namely the momentousness of Jesus' claim and the contrast of the humbleness of his person with current ideas about messiahship. The corresponding Christian perception is that of gladness that Messiah is here and that the news of this blessing is being shed abroad, and a new seeing of messiahship in the light of this man's humility. Thus Jesus is not a malefactor but a benefactor, not a degrader of Jewish expectations but, in his odd way, a glorifier of them; he is not culpable, but credit and praise are due him. This concern-based impression is the dialectical pathos indicative of faith, and it appreciates, as well as the offense does, that an unnaturally momentous, even "paradoxical," claim is being made.

Paul the Apostle notes that to the nations the crucified Lord often appears to be foolishness (μωρία; 1 Corinthians 1:23). This is the heathen counterpart of Jewish being offended (σκανδαλίζο-μαι). The emotion such heathen feel upon hearing the gospel is not indignation, but contempt. To them the announcement of a cruci-fied Lord just seems stupid or crazy; it seems to fall below the threshold of serious discourse. This may not seem like a very good example of dialectical pathos, and probably it isn't an ideal one. But still, it is a way of perceiving the departure from natural ways of thinking that is in fact being made in Paul's claim. Especially if the heathen does a lot of laughing and head shaking, this emotion is a way of acknowledging, with the heart, that a shocking thing is being said, and as such it is, in the view of Climacus and Anti-Climacus, a more perceptive response by light years than Christen-dom's yawning, emotionless repetition of Chalcedonian christolo-gy, processed by Hegelian demythologizing to keep it from exciting anybody.

In Matthew 26:31, 33 we read:

> Then Jesus said to them, "You will all be offended in me this night, for it is written, 'I will strike the shepherd and the sheep of the flock will be scattered'." . . . Peter declared to him, "Though they all are offended in you, I will never be offended."

Jesus speaks these words at the Mount of Olives, after the last supper. He is predicting the disciples' emotional response to his being taken into custody and treated as a lamb led to slaughter or a criminal to execution. The behavior associated with offense in this case is fleeing (the Revised Standard Version translates σκανδα-λισθήσεσθε ἐν ἐμοὶ with "fall away because of me"). The emo-tion in question is quite different from anger, outrage, indignation. Although fear is certainly present in the context, σκανδαλισ-θήσεσθε does not refer to fear (the disciples are not "afraid in Christ" or "afraid of Christ"). The emotion is instead something like disappointment with Christ, disgust with him, despair of him, loss of confidence in him. Offense here is a perception of Christ against a background of high expectations—indeed an ascription of divinity or at least Messiahship to him—that make the perception of his weakness and passivity, his abuse and suffering, an intolerable vexation, mortification, grief, disappointment. The counterpart faith response, which we see later in some of the disciples, is a confidence in Christ despite persecution, a trust that he abides with us in the worst of troubles, indeed that persecution is a sign of his blessing (Acts 5.41) and an opportunity to participate in his work (Colossians 1.24). In the joy referred to in these passages of scripture, the suffering is perceived in an aspect opposite to that of the garden: instead of looking like defeat, it looks like just the proper order of Christian work for this world. This joy is "dialectical" inasmuch as it is shaped by a pattern of thinking that departs, in a striking way, from ordinary thinking about good and bad, taking its point of departure from the Christian story of the incarnation of God.

"I am not ashamed (ἐπαισχύνομαι) of the gospel; it is the power of God for salvation to everyone who has faith, to the Jew first and also to the Greek" (Romans 1:16). Thus Paul identifies an emotion, sometimes experienced by Christians, that compromises the happy relationship with Jesus Christ. This emotion is the nagging vestige of existential heathenism in the Christian. In being ashamed of Jesus, the Christian sees him, as it were, through the contemptuous eyes of the Greeks or the angry eyes of the Jews, so that Jesus comes to look a little disreputable to the Christian himself. The Christian does not become an all-out unbeliever by this shame; it is in the logic of shame to construe as *belonging to oneself* whatever one is ashamed of. (The heathen and the unconverted Jew are not ashamed of Jesus, as they do not claim him as their own.) If, as is likely, the Christian's reason for being ashamed of Christ is the oddness or absurdity of the claim that this lowly man is God or that God has condescended to incarnate himself in this lowly man, then this shame is a case of dialectical pathos. Its faith counterpart is a certain "ignorance" (CD, 35) of the way unbelievers view Jesus, a full-hearted love for Jesus that doesn't "understand" why others are not equally enthusiastic about him. I use scare-quotes to indicate that I am speaking of a special, emotional kind of knowledge in which one is *unfavorably impressed* with the oddness or absurdity of the incarnation. The Christian does not really cease to know that Jesus comes across disreputable to unbelievers; but if his faith is completely healthy, then Jesus does not look at all disreputable to *him*. In perfect faith there is no place for being ashamed of Jesus, but only for rejoicing in him, hoping in him, being contrite before him and grateful to him. In mature faith the aspect perceptions constituting these emotions will involve or be qualified by the oddness or "absurdity," as Kierkegaard's personæ put it, of the incarnate Lord who is the object of the emotions. So the pathos is "dialectical in second place." But in this case, the impression of oddness or "absurdity" is *favorable* (to put it mildly): In the joy, hope, contrition, and gratitude that constitute the maturest and most aware Christian faith is an element of—what shall we call it? astonishment? awe?—that is expressed in the Apostle's statement that "God has revealed to us through the Spirit . . .

What no eye has seen, nor ear heard,
nor the heart of man conceived,
what God has prepared for those who love him.
                    —1 Corinthians 2:9 RSV, from Isaiah 64:4

5

Boom! The Earth Is Round!—
On the Impossibility of an Existential System

Julia Watkin

To illustrate the danger of attaching false security to objective truth, Johannes Climacus in Kierkegaard's *Concluding Unscientific Postscript* uses the amusing tale of an escaped lunatic's attempt to demonstrate his sanity. The lunatic hopes to convince people he is sane by the objective truth of what he says. He therefore (prompted by a ball he finds) keeps repeating to everyone an objectively true statement that occurs to him. "Boom!" he says, "The earth is round!" Not surprisingly, he fails to demonstrate his sanity, but, as Climacus points out, his failure does not concern the truth of the universally accepted fact that the earth is round. The problem lies in the inappropriate manner in which he associates that fact with his subjective situation. The lunatic's desire to state objective truth springs, however, from a sane realization that people seek the security of concrete facts that are independent of the human subject, facts that will eliminate the threat presented to human society by personal arbitrariness and craziness. Similarly, attempts by philosophers and scientists to work out "a system of existence," or a complete objective description of the world as it really is, can be viewed as aimed at avoiding the dangers presented by what Climacus describes as a purely "subjective definition of truth" (CUP, 1:194-95).[1]

In *Concluding Unscientific Postscript*, however, Climacus attacks not science and scholarship, which he sees as entirely legitimate in their proper sphere (see, e.g., CUP, 1:25), but pursuit of objective

---

[1] It looks as if Kierkegaard's view of objective truth involved correspondence and coherence, appropriate to the topic of discussion. Truth as "living for an idea" (JP, 5:5100) has, of course, to do with his view of subjective truth.

truth that treats all existence (including human subjectivity), in purely objective terms in the attempt to chart a complete objectively true system of existence. As he states it in his discussion of Lessing and striving for truth (CUP, 1:106-25), "a logical system can be given . . . but a system of existence cannot be given" (CUP, 1:109). In this paper I would like to take a close look at some of the arguments Climacus uses here in support of his claim that a system of existence cannot be given, in order to examine their applicability to current efforts in physics to arrive at a theory of everything. Particularly, I would like to consider the outlook of theoretical physicist, Stephen Hawking, and physical chemist, Peter Atkins, both of whom work with the idea of such a theory.[2]

Starting with Climacus in *Concluding Unscientific Postscript*, the first, introductory, objection he makes in his fourth section on Lessing concerning an existential system is that if one speaks of a system, one is speaking of something concluded. In other words, if a system is unfinished or incomplete it is not a system, only a bunch of hypotheses lacking the vital element of totality. Since existence in the sense of the entire contents of the universe is not finished, it is thus nonsense to speak of it as if it were a finished system, especially when, in the same breath, one admits that the conclusion is still lacking (CUP, 1:107, cf. 13).

Next (CUP, 1:109 a. a), Climacus allows that a logical system can be given or constructed and in its validation is objective in the way other forms of thinking (for example, the constructions of fantasy) are not, but he insists that nothing subject to existence in the sense of process must be included; one cannot import movement into logic.[3] His argument here is that logic is connected with

---

[2]I do not discuss the process theology/philosophy of Alfred North Whitehead, Charles Hartshorne, and Ian Barbour, because they intentionally go beyond the sciences yet do not aim to present a closed system of existence.

[3]Rem B. Edwards argues in his "Is an Existential System Possible?" (*International Journal for Philosophy of Religion* 17 [1985]: 201-208, esp. 201-202), that Kierkegaard-Climacus in developing the theme that a logical system is possible argues against its possibility. Edwards seems to think Climacus is talking about one kind of logicometaphysical Hegelian system. Yet Climacus is talking about two kinds of system: the grand Hegelian system of existence, and a logical system relating to existence which could well be complete and would not include movement. In other words, one can create propositional logical systems that relate to existence,

existence in so far as the items that figure in logic relate proposi-
tionally to existence or to existing objects ("all cats have claws"),
but that the fact of its lack of existential relation to existence is
what makes it hypothetical. I have yet to examine the paws of
four-dimensional felines, and if I deduce or conclude some facts
from foundation propositions about cats—build up a theory of
cats—I cannot and do not introduce the cats themselves into the
system. He argues that mathematics, too, have objectivity but they
have no relation whatever toward or from existence. That is, I use
the abstract symbols, can apply maths to concrete problems, but
while I can check logical propositions relating to cats by looking
at the actual animals, it would make no sense to go hunting for
square roots in the Grib forest (CUP, 1:109-11).

The other matter requiring attention is one's starting point, or
what Climacus calls "the dialectic of the beginning" (CUP, 1:111
b.). Here, he looks at the Hegelian existential system from the
standpoint of logic rather than existence. His specific objection is
to the notion of beginning from the beginning with a nothing that
is something, with the immediacy of "pure being." That is,
Climacus objects to the claim that a clean presuppositionless start
is made in relation to the bare idea of being—that things are.[4]

---

but not put all existence into a total logical *existential* system.

Jeffrey Turner and Devon R. Beidler, in "Kierkegaard's 'Johannes Climacus'
on Logical Systems and Existential Systems" (*Idealist Studies* [1991]: 21, 170-83),
state that by "a logical system" Climacus means "presumably one patterned after
Hegel's" (172). The authors argue that Kierkegaard scholars have been wrong to
see Climacus's critique as showing that there is an incompatibility between "the
System" and human existence. At a "deeper level" the reader is called upon to
"make sense of the claims that a logical system *is impossible* and an existential
system *is possible*" (170-71, cf. 172).

[4]E.g., Hegel, *Wissenschaft der Logik*. CUP, 2:211n.121:

As yet there is nothing and there is to become something. The beginning is
not pure nothing, but a nothing from which something is to proceed; therefore being, too, is already contained in the beginning. The beginning,
therefore, contains both, being and nothing, is the unity of being and nothing;
or is non-being which is at the same time being, and which is at the same
time non-being.

CUP, 2:211n.122:

But if no presupposition is to be made and the beginning itself is taken
immediately, then its only determination is that it is to be the beginning of

Climacus asks, "How does the system begin with the immediate, that is, does it begin with it immediately?" (CUP, 1:111-12). He points out that the system cannot begin immediately. If one assumes the System comes after its four-dimensional completed existence, the logical viewing or interpretation of it gets muddled up with the system in its actual existence. The observer assumes (impossibly) a backward-looking stance in relation to what has completely unfolded, and systematizes what is already a complete, unfolding system of existence. Nor can one treat the entirety of such a system as identical with the immediately-given material of the beginning phase. If one is speaking of the initial phase of the system this is not the same as speaking of the finished product. Climacus, however, denies that the System begins with immediacy in terms of its interpretation. As object of interpretation, the beginning of the existential system is achieved through reflection, and this is something else. The factor of reflection, of thought, decisively excludes the possibility of a system of existence, for where logic is concerned, it is nonsense to speak of absolute starting points, since, as we have seen, logic has to do with hypothesis: "A black cat is a black cat," but I propose the first term, the initial starting point, it does not present itself, even though there may be a black furry feline in the four-dimensional world just begging to be used as such a starting point. Similarly, not only does the entire layout of the System fail to present itself to the individual observer in an instantaneous intellectual totality, the initial foundation propositions do not give themselves either.

So one looks at existence and at its previous history and reflects on how the jigsaw puzzle fits together. But then, as Climacus

---

logic, of thought as such. All that is present is simply the resolve, which can also be regarded as arbitrary, that we propose to consider thought as such. Thus the beginning must be an *absolute*, or what is synonymous here, an *abstract* beginning; and so it *may not presuppose anything*, must not be mediated by anything nor have a ground; rather it is to be itself the ground of the entire science. Consequently, it must be purely and simply an immediacy, or rather merely *immediacy* itself. Just as it cannot possess any determination relatively to anything else, so too it cannot contain within itself any determination, any content; for any such would be a distinguishing and an interrelationship of distinct moments, and consequently a mediation. The beginning therefore is *pure being*.

points out, the next question is how I "bring to a halt the reflection set in motion in order to reach that beginning." Reflection (as Kierkegaard himself points out in a different context, in his Journals—JP, 3:3707), "has the notable quality of being infinite." That is, at least as long as a thinker is alive, and within all the usual limits of space and time, reflection goes on and on until it is broken off (CUP, 1:112-13).[5] There is no point at which reflection about existence is completed; it continues until the individual makes a "resolution" or chooses a cutoff point. Thus "the beginning can occur only when reflection is stopped," says Climacus, "and reflection can be stopped only by something else, and this something else is something altogether different from the logical, since it is a resolution," made by the existing person. A presuppositionless beginning of a reflection-stopping kind would have to be one breaking through the continuity of reflection and be on the lines of some miraculous package of information arriving from outside (CUP, 1:113). Since, however, the existing person does the breaking off in order to make a start, it is untrue to speak of an absolute beginning. Climacus points out that the Hegelians define the idea of "the immediate" as "the most abstract remainder after an exhaustive abstraction"—the stripping away of everything until one gets to the basic idea of the "thisness" of the universe without any presuppositions about it (CUP, 1:114). Climacus says he is pre-

---

[5]Climacus here jokes about Hegel's notion of the bad infinity (see Hegel, CUP, 2:213n.123):

. . . the infinite is not yet really free from limitation and finitude; the main point is to distinguish the genuine notion of infinity from spurious [schlecht] infinity, the infinity of reason from the infinite of the understanding; yet the latter is the *finitized* infinite, and it will be found that in the very act of keeping the infinite pure and aloof from the finite, the infinite is only made finite.

The infinite as thus posited over against the finite, in a relation wherein they are as qualitatively distinct others, is to be called the *spurious infinite*, the infinite of the understanding, for which it has the value of the highest, the absolute Truth. The understanding is satisfied that it has truly reconciled these two, but the truth is that it is entangled in unreconciled, unresolved, absolute contradiction; it can only be brought to consciousness of this fact by the contradictions into which it falls on every side when it ventures to apply and to explicate these its categories.

pared to accept this definition, but complains that it indirectly underlines the fact that there is no absolute beginning, for when *has* one abstracted from everything to get to the basic idea of the "thisness" of the universe? One can go on endlessly with the process of analysis. How does one begin from the beginning with nothing? If one could remove everything there would be nothing left, or if there were some basic bedrock left, it is hard to see how one would begin with nothing. How can one thus ignore the difference between thought and the existential world? Reflection does not stop of itself objectively (CUP, 1:115-16) as every absent-minded philosopher knows. It is the human subject who stops the reflection.

` Not content with these objections, Climacus also (CUP, 1:117g) takes a psychological magnifying glass to the state of mind of a Hegelian-style logical thinker—of the speculative idealists who want to insist on the identity of subject and object.[6] How does such a person die to the self—die to selfhood in terms of ceasing to act in existence—in order to arrive in such an intellectual universe, and how far does the imagination play a role?[7] How does one change oneself into speculative thought? That is, how does one, having identified oneself as a dot in the ongoing logicomental world-historical process one has thought up, really get inside the mental construction?

Here (CUP, 1:118 b.), Climacus goes on to the second part of his argument for which the first part has prepared the way: a logical (conceptual) system can be constructed, but it makes no sense to speak of a system of existence. Climacus reassures us, however, that he does not mean that there can be no system in existence or that the total workings of the universe do not fit together in a complete and completed totality—but this could only be for God, not for a finitely limited existing human spirit. As we saw, system implies concludedness, but "existence is the very

---

[6]See Niels Thulstrup: *Commentary on Kierkegaard's Concluding Unscientific Postscript* (Princeton: Princeton University Press, 1984) 229-30.

[7]Climacus later (CUP, 1:348) points out that all knowledge is a removal from existence, whereas in existence thinking, imagination, and feeling should be unified in an equality, i.e., one should not let any one of the three elements get out of balance (something Anti-Climacus deals with in *The Sickness unto Death*).

opposite." The striving individual has not completed his or her life-course let alone the universe in its entirety. Nor can one think system and existence together because as soon as one thinks of or about existence it is of something abstracted from existence.[8] In existence things are held apart, whereas what is systematic combines things in a totality of links and assumptions.

In connection with the attempt to chart a logically necessary system of existence, Climacus then returns to a previous attack (in *Philosophical Fragments*) on the Hegelian treatment of necessity in relation to the past. In the *Fragments* Climacus asserted that possibility and actuality are different in being and that the past can in no way become necessary through having occurred (PF, 72, 85-86), even though it is changeless in the sense that whatever has happened has happened and gives the illusion of completedness.[9] When the System thinker looks pastward, he or she is a viewer of all that has gone before and is not only placed in the odd situation of being unable to include his own future in that pastness, but also loses contact with ethics.

Loss of contact with ethics occurs firstly through the thinker's make-believe standpoint in which he or she takes some fantastical God's-eye position outside the universe, that is, outside existence. Since objective thinking, in that it concerns description of the world, has no relation to the individual thinker's personal life, daily life becomes an inconvenient appendage to the great work of System-building (CUP, 1:119, 122-23). Secondly, there is a loss of ethics in the Hegelian-style System because it contains ethics and morality in a necessary process. Yet in a necessary process there can be no freedom and hence no ethics, not even if one interprets

---

[8]Rem Edwards, in his article "Is an Existential System Possible?," 204, has difficulties with Climacus's objection, pointing out that if he thinks existence can be a system for God, he is thinking system and existence together. Yet Climacus is thinking only that existence could possibly be a system for God, as opposed to finite creatures within existence. While Edwards is correct to note that Kierkegaard has metaphysical assumptions about God and the universe, this does not seem to me to be quite the same problem.

[9]Specifically Kierkegaard as Climacus attacks the Hegelian assumption that "necessity is the unity of possibility and actuality." Against this Anti-Climacus comes to assert that "actuality is the unity of possibility and necessity." See here PF, 74; 299n.12; JP, 1:262; SUD, 36.

the universe pantheistically as a benevolent God-process (CUP, 1:119, 121-22).[10] The reality of personal existence thus disappears through being included in the System. As Climacus points out further on in the *Postscript*, both God and the individual are constrained in a "fantastical-objective life," God, because he is interpreted as a necessarily unfolding force, individuals, because they figure only as predetermined numbers in the ongoing stream (CUP, 1:156, 158-59).[11]

Nor is this all. Climacus also wants to know who is supposed to write or finish the system of existence. The options are a living human being or that it is a product of a fellowship of thinkers. But, asks Climacus, "in what final conclusion does this fellowship combine? How does it come to light?" (CUP, 1:120). Who is making the final construction, and how do individual thinkers relate to its making—especially if they disagree? Climacus's question is particularly pertinent here given that his own view of the universe (see, e.g. CUP, 1:159) clearly does not fit with the then dominant idealistic model he attacked.

In looking at the relevance of Climacus's objections to today's world, it needs to be noted that Kierkegaard, father of Climacus, was proficient in mathematics,[12] but he wrote prior to modern developments in mathematics and logic.[13] Climacus thus makes a

---

[10]The process of such a universe can be viewed, as it is by Kierkegaard's aesthete, in terms of a double understanding of "fate" as necessity and also as the incidental—as what "chances" one.

[11]While Hegel believes he has left a place for freedom in his System, Kierkegaard understands the Hegelian necessary process in fact to be of a hard deterministic nature. It should perhaps be noted here that my discussion of ethics and determinism in this paper is limited to the consideration of existential systems of this kind and is not directed towards the wider debate surrounding the compatibility of moral truth and universal physical determinism.

[12]He was a successful student at *Borgerdydskolen*. Per Krarup, *Søren Kierkegaard og Borgerdydskolen* (Copenhagen: Gyldendal, 1977) 25, 32, 34, tells us that Kierkegaard would have had only three hours mathematics a week (geometry and arithmetic). Kierkegaard seems to have had been taught to a high standard by G. F. Ursin, astronomer and later professor in mathematics at the Academy of Art. Cf. also here, Holger Lund: *Borgerdydsskolen i Kjøbenhavn 1787–1887* (Copenhagen: Wroblewski, 1887) 217-19; LD, 16-17.

[13]While one cannot here go into details concerning Kierkegaard's understanding of logic and mathematics, it must be remembered that Aristotle's view of logic

clear distinction between mathematical and logical systems (CUP 1:110-111) concerning their application to the world.[14] Where mathematics are concerned, however, he seems to anticipate the twentieth century divorce between mathematical axioms and physical reality when he states that mathematical systems have "no relation whatever toward or from existence but . . . only objectivity."[15] A logical system relates as hypothesis to the real world: it *is* linked to the real world in that it posits an actual state of affairs in the world, but the negative element is that it is only a hypothesis. As we saw earlier, since it may be erroneous in its objective application, it also does not apply to the actual world as firm fact. Despite Kierkegaard-Climacus's Euclidean and pre-Boolean situation,[16] the basic distinction Climacus is fairly making is between systems that are abstract from the world and constructions that relate hypothetically concretely to the world. It is the latter that Climacus sees as abused in the attempt to create a system of existence. Noting both that the situation of logic and mathematics has changed since Kierkegaard's time, but that their relation to the actual world is still in dispute,[17] we can now go back to the escaped lunatic and suggest that current efforts in physics to arrive at a theory of everything may well be an example of inappropriate association of objective truth with subjective situation, another version of a system of existence.

(that the general principles of logic are directly applicable to the external world) was dominant well into the 19th century. Boolean mathematical logic was unknown until 1847. Note here, Arnold B. Come, *Trendelenburg's Influence on Kierkegaard's Modal Categories* (Montreal: Inter Editions, 1991) 3-4, 16, and generally.

[14]Unlike Bertrand Russell, Climacus does not see mathematics as a development from logic. See Ray Monk: *Bertrand Russell: The Spirit of Solitude*, (London: Jonathan Cape, 1996) 142-44.

[15]On the divorce between axioms and actuality, see John D. Barrow, *Pi in the Sky: Counting, Thinking, and Being* (Oxford: Clarendon Press; New York: Oxford University Press, 1992) 13, cf. 11-13. It can also be noted that Kierkegaard sees mathematics as having an absolute certainty with no disproof possible (JP, 2:2296).

[16]On the divorce between logic and actuality in the twentieth century, see Barrow, *Pi in the Sky*, 15, cf. 16.

[17]See, Godfrey Vesey and Paul Foulkes, *Collins Dictionary of Philosophy* (London and Glasgow: Collins, 1990) 174-76.

Einstein was in advance of his time when he attempted to develop a unified field theory that would explain gravity and electromagnetism in one mathematical package. The 1980s and 1990s have seen a proliferation of attempts in physics to develop a theory that will unite the four forces of nature in one. In view of the difficulty of including gravity in the package, attention has been focussed on the Big Bang as the most fruitful testing ground for such a theory of everything.[18] We are presented with the picture of a universe that initially had no size and developed into the vast sea of galaxies known to modern science.[19] Compressed at the start are gravity, electromagnetism and the strong and weak nuclear forces that go their separate ways as the history of the universe unfolds. While two possible scenarios are predicted for the universe (infinite expansion or the big crunch),[20] progression and development are essential features of the situation, and completion is an essential feature of such a theory. Ideally, a set of equations will eventually account for the behaviour of matter under all circumstances.

As Paul Davies has pointed out in *The Mind of God*, if in arriving at such a total unification the theory becomes so constrained by mathematical requirements that it becomes unique, then "there could be only one unified system of physics, with its various laws fixed by logical necessity." If this were to be the case, then science could cease to be an empirical matter and become a branch of deductive logic, with the laws of nature "acquiring the status of mathematical theorems, and the properties of the world deducible by the application of reason alone."[21] It can be added

---

[18]See Michael White and John Gribbin, *Einstein A Life in Science* (London: Simon & Schuster, 1993) 248-58.

[19]Stephen Hawking, *A Brief History of Time: From the Big Bang to Black Holes* (London/Toronto/New York: Bantam Press, 1988) 74, cf. 11-12, 8-9, 117.

[20]Hawking, *A Brief History of Time*, 115, 173; John Boslough, *Stephen Hawking's Universe* (London: Fontana/Collins, 1984) 94-95.

[21]Paul Davies, *The Mind of God* (London: Simon & Schuster, 1992) 165-66. In *Theories of Everything* (Oxford: Oxford University Press, 1991) 11, John Barrow sees the modern quest for such a theory as the expression of the belief that the universe is "algorithmically compressible" and that there is "an abbreviated representation of the logic behind the Universe's properties that can be written down in finite form by human beings." The content of a Theory of Everything,

that there are those for whom the project of uncovering such a theory is related to God in that to know the theory will lead to the discussion of "why we and the universe exist," the answer to which would mean that we would know "the mind of God," even though the theory seems at the same time to make the idea of God redundant.[22]

In his book *A Brief History of Time*, Stephen Hawking is clearly interested in why there is a universe, and he discusses basic ideas about its origin and fate. As Anthony Flew has also pointed out,[23] Hawking dabbles with the idea of God, even though he retreats from it, and his later model of the universe (finite with no boundary) does not at all require either the idea of a beginning or of a God. With the later model he tells us there is no need to "appeal to God or some new law to set the boundary conditions for space-time,"[24] and when he asks why the universe goes to the bother of existing he also considers the possibility that the unified theory might be "so compelling that it brings about its own existence."[25] In an interview in 1992, Hawking explained that while he still thinks the universe had a beginning in real time, in the mathematics of imaginary time he finds the universe to be self-contained, so that as with the expression "the mind of God," the word "God" amounts to "the answer to [the] question" of why the universe bothers to exist, which in Hawking's case is an ultimate unified theory underpinning a consistent finalized model that would describe "everything in the universe."[26]

---

if found, "will be a piece of logically consistent mathematics." *Pi in the Sky*, 2.

[22]Hawking, *A Brief History of Time*, 175. In Hawking's case, he ends with "a universe with no edge in space, no beginning or end in time and nothing for a creator to do." See Hawking, introduction by Carl Sagan, x; also 175, 116, 136, 141. Peter Atkins appears to substitute science for God. See Peter Atkins, *Creation Revisited* (London: Penguin Books, 1994) 7, 111, 125; cf. Russell Stannard in *Doing Away with God?* (London: Marshall Pickering/HarperCollins, 1993) 139-40, cf. 63.

[23]Anthony Flew, "Stephen Hawking and the Mind of God," *Cogito* 10/1 (1996): 55-60.

[24]Hawking, *A Brief History of Time*, 136, cf. 46-47, 116, 122-27, 138, 140-41, 166, 173-75, cf. *Black Holes and Baby Universes and Other Essays* (London/New York: Bantam Books, 1993) 172-73.

[25]Hawking, *A Brief History of Time*, 174; cf. *Black Holes and Baby Universes*, 99.

[26]Hawking, *Black Holes and Baby Universes*, 172-73, 47, cf. 41-47.

In *Creation Revisited*,[27] Peter Atkins also favors the search for a unifying superlaw that is going to show that the physical world is necessarily as it is. The chain of causes and explanations goes back to a beginning. "In the end," states Atkins, "we shall possess a mathematical theory of the universe that matches it in every test: the fit of reality to the template will be exact and we shall have a theory of everything."[28] While Hawking speaks of the possibility of a superlaw compelling enough to bring about its own existence, Atkins, invoking the mathematics of chemistry and physics, provides us with a detailed explanation of the origin of the causal chain. Like Hawking, Atkins readily points out that: "No one is yet in a position to be definite about the final solution of the problem of cosmogony (the generation of the universe);" he also warns the reader that his argument will "increasingly resort to speculation."[29] Despite this, however, Atkins expresses total confidence in the human mind's ability to work out the "System." He sees the universe as having a deep logical, mathematical structure, the physical world having "the same logical structure as mathematics."[30] While there are causes and reasons, there are no reasons based on purposes, since purpose develops out of the necessary play of energy, atoms and evolution. It is an "interlocked mechanism," a "network of connections."[31] This network has its origins in chance. Atkins takes us back in time "beyond the moment of creation," to when there was no space and time, and describes in some detail how the universe came to bootstrap itself into existence in the Big Bang through time bringing points into being and points bringing time into being. Using the concept of "struc-

---

[27]Peter Atkins, *Creation Revisited*. Atkins's book is an updated version of his 1981 book *The Creation* (Oxford/San Francisco: Freeman, 1981).

[28]Atkins, *Creation Revisited*, 107, cf. 25; cf. comments on Atkins in Davies, *The Mind of God*, 164; Willem B. Drees, *Beyond The Big Bang* (La Salle IL: Open Court, 1990) 99.

[29]Atkins, *Creation Revisited*, 6; cf. Hawking, *A Brief History of Time*, 136-37.

[30]Atkins, *Creation Revisited*, 109, cf. 113, vii, 3, 7, 111. On 109 Atkins suggests that "the physical world has the same logical structure as mathematics. . . . mathematics works as a description of physical reality [because they] share the same logical structure."

[31]Atkins, *Creation Revisited*, 37, 39, 41.

tureless dust,"[32] Atkins concludes that the "universe can emerge out of nothing, without intervention. By chance."[33] Unlike Hawking, Atkins has no use at all for the idea of God.[34] The "natures of things determine their destinies," he says, and ultimately there is "only chaos, not purpose."[35]

In 1980, Stephen Hawking cautiously predicted the successful completion of a theory of everything by the end of the century.[36] While not all advocates of such a theory are as optimistic, and while most would not see themselves as presenting a "System," existence is clearly viewed as a system by some. For Hawking, such a theory does show that everything that happens in the universe is determined, even though he admits that the problems surrounding particle equations prevent us from ever being able to predict human behaviour.[37] Thus, although Hawking and those like him do not attempt to describe an entire ongoing System in terms of total content, they attempt to include total content in their description of the System of the universe, in that the entire content of the universe is seen as controlled by the laws governing its unfolding. While Hawking, Atkins and others admit, as we have seen, that the theory is still incomplete and hypothetical, they (undisturbed by this) tend to talk as if it is finished bar the shouting. They also assume that if a total theory combining the four forces had been written down, totality of explanation would have been arrived at, whereas this is far from the case.

We saw that Climacus did not object to the construction of a logical system, a conceptual system or major hypothesis built on initial assumptions. It can thus be argued that he need have nothing against the construction of a system or major theory, built on the foundation of laws arrived at inductively and with the help of mathematics. Nor should there be anything wrong with testing

---

[32] Atkins, *Creation Revisited*, 9, 129-43, 149.

[33] Atkins, *Creation Revisited*, 143.

[34] Atkins, *Creation Revisited*, vii, 17, 111, 125, 145.

[35] Atkins, *Creation Revisited*, 41, cf. 67, 155, 157.

[36] Stephen Hawking, *Black Holes and Baby Universes*, chap. 7: "Is the End in Sight for Theoretical Physics?" (1980 Lucasian professorship lecture reprinted in 1993). Cf. Peter Atkins, *Creation Revisited*, 107.

[37] Hawking, *Black Holes and Baby Universes*, 127-29, 83.

out the theory by looking at the situation in existence. The problem arises, however, with the turning of such a logical system into a system of existence. As Professor of Physics Russell Stannard has pointed out,[38] when scientists speak of the "Theory of Everything" "they are expressing the hope that one day they might be able to reduce physics," and only physics, "to a single law." What happens, though, is that popularizers of science, and some scientists, forget the hypothetical nature of science and also talk as if the theory covers all existence.[39] When scientists such as Hawking and Atkins assume that everything in the universe must be necessarily so, and not contingent, on Climacus's view they have gone beyond using a system constructed logically on the basis of principles derived from induction and mathematics, to the creation of an existential system. They take for granted certain assumptions about the theory, not least those having to do with the starting point.

Clearly the above-mentioned scientists and popularizers of science are not intending to begin from the beginning and with nothing, but they seem to fail to realize that their starting point is not presuppositionless. The beginning of such an existential system is achieved through mathematical reflection about scientific data and the work of modern scientists, but how does the existential system begin immediately with the immediately given data of the universe? Advocates of the existential system appear to begin with the assumption that only what can be measured is real, thus both Stephen Hawking and Peter Atkins, talk about the entire universe and yet both exclude the non-measurable bits. Hawking tells us that events before the Big Bang can have no consequences and that we should cut out all features of the theory of the universe that cannot be observed.[40] Atkins declares the "Why?" questions of the

---

[38]Stannard, *Doing Away with God*, 72-81.

[39]Stannard, *Doing Away with God*, 72-73; cf. Bryan Appleyard, *Understanding the Present* (London: Pan Picador, 1992) 1-3; cf. Hawking, *Black Holes and Baby Universes*, 127-29. Appleyard also accuses Carl Sagan and Jacob Bronowski of the fallacy of the omnipotence of science.

[40]He presupposes that philosophy and religion could have nothing concrete to say about his efforts to solve the "Why" of the universe and rejects some fields of research as a waste of time. He also attempts to eliminate the Big Bang

universe to be meaningless yet assumes science can explain everything.[41] Common to such all-embracing views of the universe are the assumptions that science is "ultimately capable of answering every question,"[42] that mathematics and the laws of physics constitute the sole bedrock of the universe and that there are only four forces holding the universe together.

If one looks at the question of the existential beginning of the system, one encounters either a tendency to strive to achieve a starting-point that definitively excludes what cannot be measured, as with Hawking's later development of the model of a finite universe with no boundary,[43] or one encounters, as with Atkins, an extremely detailed description of the state of affairs before time and the universe began. In Atkins's case he does attempt to "begin from the beginning and with nothing,"[44] describing exactly—almost as if he had been himself present before the start—how the Big Bang creation from nothing led by chance to the necessary universe. In both cases, the reflection concerning origins is stopped at what must be inadequate places if the theory of everything is really to be a system of existence. It is here that Climacus's comments about reflection have their application.

Although Atkins speaks of the limitlessness of reflection, it is in terms of the human brain as "an instrument of limitless power"[45] and not in relation to thought of the need to stop reflec-

---

singularity by creating a mathematical model of a self-contained universe. Hawking, *A Brief History of Time*, 55, 46, cf. 125, 136; Boslough, *Stephen Hawking's Universe* 49, 104-105, 18-19.

[41]Stannard, *Doing Away with God?* 139-40.

[42]Appleyard, *Understanding the Present*, 259; cf. 1-2.

[43]Hawking, *A Brief History of Time*, 136.

[44]Atkins, *Creation Revisited*, 149:

In the beginning there was nothing. Absolute void, not merely empty space. There was no space; nor was there time, for this was before time. The universe was without form and void. By chance there was a fluctuation, and a set of points, emerging from nothing and taking their existence from the pattern they formed, defined a time. The chance formation of a pattern resulted in the emergence of time from coalesced opposites, its emergence from nothing. From absolute nothing, absolutely without intervention, there came into being rudimentary existence.

[45]Atkins, *Creation Revisited*, vii.

tion through a resolution. Neither Atkins nor Hawking experience Climacus's realization that reflection concerning everything must so exceed the capability of the human mind to finish with it, that the thinker is forced to set limits to the scope of inquiry. When Hawking turns over to computers the problem of thinking through the theory of everything, he has scarcely started, let alone finished, the preliminary investigation of whether computers are the most suitable tools for uncovering such a theory. Atkins, on the other hand, confidently projects into the future the infallibility of the human mind to understand and define everything,[46] but needs to think through the implications of the present limitations of the mind, which limitations he is forced to acknowledge.[47]

A further problem concerns the possible identification of thought and being in the modern system of existence. Climacus objects to the problems presented by such an identification in the Hegelian model, but it is not irrelevant to consider the question when looking at the application of mathematics to existence in the modern "System." Here, we can note that Hawking seems to move from use of the mathematics of imaginary time as a useful way of solving the singularity problem to an extension of the actual universe into "another kind of time, imaginary time, at right angles to real time, in which the universe has no beginning or end . . . [which would] mean that the way the universe began would be determined by the laws of physics."[48] Atkins speaks of the possibility that "the logical structures of mathematics and the universe emerged simultaneously and are identical." He also seems to favour what he calls "strong deep structuralism" in which "mathematics and physical reality do not merely share the same logical structure . . . [they are] actually the same."[49]

---

[46]Hawking, *Black Holes and Baby Universes*, 68; Stannard, *Doing Away with God?* 140; Atkins, *Creation Revisited*, 111, cf. 115.

[47]Atkins, *Creation Revisited*, viii, 6, 111, 157, 121.

[48]Hawking, *Black Holes and Baby Universes*, 172, cf. 46, 81-83, 92-96, 121-22; *A Brief History of Time*, 134, 139, 143-44, and 185: imaginary time: "Time measured using imaginary numbers."

[49]Atkins, *Creation Revisited*, 115, 109, cf. 99, 101, 103, 111, 119. Atkins seems to take a platonic view of mathematics and that all humans can work them out.

Scientists, not least physicists, agree on the importance of mathematics in their disciplines, but it must be pointed out that Climacus would scarcely be happy with the identification of mathematics with the universe, the hypothesis Atkins seems to favour, in which "physical reality is mathematics and mathematics is physical reality,"[50] an identification that also seems to infect Hawking's later description of the mathematics of imaginary time, despite his instrumentalist approach. While disagreement continues as to whether mathematics is a human instrument or a Plato-style universe,[51] an identification of mathematics with the universe seems to be a way of identifying concepts and existence that fails to consider adequately the significance of the breakdown of the laws of physics at the point of the creation singularity and that mathematical postulates are selected presuppositions from among many different possibilities in mathematics. The limitations put forward in Goedel's theory of incompleteness may also have implications where total existential systems are concerned.[52] One can add to this that physicists seem to use beauty and not number as the final test in choosing a mathematical theory.[53] Finally one can emphasize the fact that mathematics simply have no reality for many people, and that in the discussion of the nature of mind, this fact too quickly has been treated as deficiency rather than difference.

Thus a modern Climacus may well ask whether some mathematical systemizers are not confusing the fact that nature, includ-

---

[50]Atkins, *Creation Revisited*, 109, cf. 99-125.

[51]Stannard, *Doing Away With God?* speaks of mathematics as "the language of physics"; Hawking, *Black Holes and Baby Universes*, 44, declares himself to be an instrumentalist; Davies, *The Mind of God*, discusses the two views of mathematics, 140-60.

[52]On Goedel and the possible implications for physics see Barrow, *Theories of Everything*, 37-38, 146, 181, 209-10; Barrow, *Pi in the Sky*, 18-19, 119-40, 284; cf. Davies, *The Mind of God*, 167. Stannard, *Doing Away with God?* 69, points out that there are an infinite number of possible geometries, each underpinned by a different set of postulates, and the physicist has to investigate experimentally which is the appropriate one for describing the state of affairs in the world. With a theory of everything one could not look at its underlying postulates because we belong to the universe, are described within the mathematical structure, and the original choice of postulates cannot be justified from within a mathematical structure.

[53]Davies, *The Mind of God*, 175-77, cf. 220.

ing human processes, can be described in terms of mathematics with the idea of their identity. Also, as Paul Davies points out,[54] even if one does emphasize the mathematics of the laws of physics, it does not answer the question of origins. To speak of "chance," as Atkins does, already points, through its reference to statistical permutations, to some other fact or factors existing beyond and behind the universe. Maybe even the fact that both Hawking and Atkins seem unable to avoid talking about God might be an indicator that they sense that a completed theory of everything itself does not itself provide the explanation for its existence.

We saw that Climacus also looked at the relation of the systematic thinker to the system. Here, we can note that since we are situated within the universe we cannot justify the choice of the underlying postulates of a theory of the universe, and attempts to describe a "pre-Big Bang" scenario[55] seem to involve a lively use of the imagination. In the case of Atkins he assumes a God's-eye view of the universe in order to describe it, while Hawking excludes everything human from it except the fate of the atoms of our bodies.[56] In viewing the model of his universe Hawking seems to place himself inside only as a bundle of lively particles among the many other bundles of lively particles.

Where ethics are concerned in the systematic universe, both Hawking and Atkins ought to have a problem on their hands regarding their individual lives. For Hawking, ethics ought to be an uncomfortable illusion, since he has driven himself into the position of having to act not by freedom but by necessity, while Atkins is in the slightly odder situation of having been determined by chance to act by necessity.[57] One might suggest here, that to the

---

[54]Davies, *The Mind of God*, 203-204, cf. 219-20, points out that natural selection cannot be the answer to why we have the particular set of laws of physics governing the universe we do.

[55]Hawking, *A Brief History of Time*, 46, discusses the possibility of events before the big bang but sees them as inaccessible. Atkins, *Creation Revisited*, 129, says: "Now we go back in time beyond the moment of creation, to when there was no time, and to where there was no space."

[56]Atkins, *Creation Revisited*, 129-57; Boslough, *Stephen Hawking's Universe*, 96.

[57]Hawking, "Is Everything Determined?" 127-39, in *Black Holes and Baby Universes*, argues that everything is determined, but that, because one cannot know what has been determined, one has to "adopt the effective theory that one

extent that Hawking and Atkins accept the objective truth of their theories, both in fact inappropriately associate objective truth with their subjective situation as long as they continue to live their personal lives by the light of what must be to them the myth of human freedom.[58]

To conclude, while Climacus's arguments were applied to a different worldview, it can be seen that that worldview shares several features in common with some of the modern attempts to make a system of existence. Although he was a citizen of Copenhagen just before the advent of modern logic and mathematics, I would like to suggest that his comments are insightful also in our time. He helps us to see that those who apply the theory of everything to all existence may be in an even sorrier situation than Climacus's lunatic, who, though crazy, was interested in maintaining the reality of his subjective freedom and did at least keep to an objective fact he could humanly handle.

---

has free will and that one is responsible for one's actions" (134). Atkins, *Creation Revisited*, seems to view creation as initiated by chance processes in which the behavior of things is then determined by their innate nature (e.g., 25, 39, 41, cf. 107). Cf. Davies, *The Mind of God*, 164.

[58]I consider this a fair criticism, given that Atkins and Hawking do not, at least in the works I mention in this paper, show how real freedom can be compatible with their understanding of the universe.

6

Deception in Service of the Truth:
Magister Kierkegaard and the Problem of Communication

Nerina Jansen

Kierkegaard thinks of communication as a mode of existence which is a vehicle for authentic self-expression. In modern society the changed position of the self in communication interferes, however, with the existential task of becoming what one essentially is. Kierkegaard's lifelong mission was to awaken his fellow human beings to an understanding of their own existential condition in order to help them improve the quality of their existence. Following from his viewpoint that the existential significance of a communication is determined, not by its content, but by the way it is conveyed (JP, 1:678), Kierkegaard's central question was: How does one communicate communication? This question is answered partly by his own carefully planned communication praxis and partly by his notes on the dialectic of ethical and ethical-religious communication (JP, 1:648-57), in conjunction with *Concluding Unscientific Postscript* and to a lesser extent sources such as *Philosophical Fragments*, *The Point of View for My Work as an Author*, and *Practice in Christianity*. In the discussion below the notes serve as starting point, while references to *Concluding Unscientific Postscript* and some of the other above-mentioned sources offer further elucidation of issues discussed.

Since *Concluding Unscientific Postscript* is normally regarded as the main source on the problem of ethical and ethical-religious communication, while the notes have hitherto received little attention, a few remarks about the *modus operandi* adopted in this paper are in order.

Kierkegaard was in fact concerned with the problem of communication from the beginning of his career as a writer. It is in *Concluding Unscientific Postscript*, however, originally intended as the conclusion to Kierkegaard's work, that Johannes Climacus offers us the clearest exposition of the topic as Kierkegaard envisaged it at that time. But soon the *Corsair* affair forced Kierkegaard to reconsider his role as a writer and, in particular, his views on the problem of ethical and ethical-religious communication. Against this background, the notes on the dialectic of communication, written during the year following the *Corsair* affair, constitute an important context for understanding his concern with the problem of ethical and ethical-religious expression. In fact, the notes provide a foundation for Kierkegaard's views on existential communication more generally.

The notes were apparently intended to clarify, elucidate, and elaborate on the principles and premises that had informed Kierkegaard's writing on the problem of communication up to the publication of *Concluding Unscientific Postscript*. Further elucidation of a couple of matters touched on in the notes is given in *The Point of View for my Work as an Author*, while the treatment of indirect communication in *Practice in Christianity* involves partly an application and partly a further development of some of Kierkegaard's basic ideas, more specifically in relation to the God-man as the sign of contradiction.

The notes neither diminish the importance of nor simply duplicate the viewpoints on communication expressed in *Concluding Unscientific Postscript*. Following from Kierkegaard's own existential struggle in defining his role as communicator and in coming to terms with the question as to how one may communicate communication, the notes provide a framework for approaching the treatment of the problem of communication both prior and subsequent to *Concluding Unscientific Postscript*. By means of the notes Kierkegaard is in fact providing a key to an understanding of what he was trying to say about ethical and ethical-religious communication.

But if the notes are so important, why did Kierkegaard never complete and deliver the lectures he intended to base on the notes? The answer to this question is suggested by Kierkegaard's observation that lecturing simply involves *talking about* ethical-religious truth. The lecturer does not reduplicate such truth in his or her own life. Stated differently, the lecturer does not comply with the requirement that the communicator in communication exist in what he or she communicates to the recipient (JP, 1:656). Kierkegaard emphasizes of course that he is not, in a stricter sense, a lecturer. If he were to deliver the lectures he would rather adopt a middle course between the strictly academic lecture and genuine ethical and ethical-religious communication, by using direct communication to make recipients aware of indirect communication. (I discuss both direct and indirect forms of communication in this paper.) However, Kierkegaard later became convinced that lecturing on ethical and ethical-religious communication was not an appropriate way for communicating with his recipients. Since he was by this time probably clear in his own mind about the forms of communication and his role as communicator, he never completed the notes or delivered the intended lectures.

However, from the viewpoint of coming to terms with his considerations concerning ethical and ethical-religious communication the notes are absolutely necessary.

The discussion below first describes the problem of communication in modern society, while the greater part of the essay examines Kierkegaard's dialectic of ethical and ethical-religious communication. The final section briefly sketches a context for reviewing his current relevance to communication theory.

A Critique of Modernity

Although Kierkegaard was by no means insensitive to new possibilities for individual self-expression in his day, the deepest meaning of modernity for him was the disappearance of the personal I (JP, 1:656). Modernity eliminates the possibility of religious subjectivity and inwardness which are definitive of authentic existence. In *Concluding Unscientific Postscript* and *The Dialectic of Ethical and Ethical-Religious Communication* (JP, 1:648-57) his critique focuses on objectivity, manifested preeminently in speculative philosophy and (Lutheran) religious orthodoxy, while in sources such as *Two Ages* he attacks the public, created by the daily press, as the embodiment of mediocrity.

A good starting point for understanding the problem of communication in modernity is the distinction between subjective and objective truth. For Kierkegaard, ethical and religious truth is subjective because human existence becomes meaningful only through personal appropriation. The truth is in us in that the ethical capability, which each and every human being possesses and which demands realization at every moment (JP, 1:649, section 10), enables us to recognize and acknowledge the truth. Assuming that everyone knows the ethical (JP, 1:649, section 13), communication of this capability is the art of luring the ethical out of the recipient (JP, 1:649, section 5). The reflection of inwardness belongs only to a subject (CUP, 1:73), a subject who is infinitely interested in his or her own existence. Because "his interestedness in existing is his actuality" (CUP, 1:314), the only actuality there is for an existing person (CUP, 1:316), ethical and ethical-religious communication takes place in the medium of actuality (JP, 1:649, section 28).

Objective thinking, however, is a theoretical and detached kind of thinking; it is universal and indifferent to a particular individual person (CUP, 1:72-73). The communication of objective truth takes place in the fantasy medium or the medium of imagination and is only an approximation (JP, 1:649, section 28). This kind of communication focuses on what is communicated, that is, on an object (JP, 1:649, section 8; CUP, 1:129). For example, the focus is on what Christianity is, not on how the thinker relates himself or herself to Christianity. Only the result counts, namely that the recipient must receive the message (JP, 1:653, section 2) and the individuality of the recipients is not taken into account. What is required from the recipient is intellectual understanding, and all recipients are treated in the same way. Because in modern society the emphasis falls on this kind of communication, one finds fantastic abstractions everywhere instead of recognizable human beings (JP, 1:650, section 9). The public, which Kierkegaard attacks *inter alia* in *Two Ages*, is such an abstraction par excellence.

Kierkegaard certainly did not deny the need for scientific and philosophical truth in modern society. When he objects that everything has become objective he is referring to a confusion created by modernity, namely that the art of existence is now communicated as scientific knowledge, while art is only understood aesthetically as fine art. When the ethical is communicated as scholarship and science (JP, 1:649, section 5) the result is that what it means to exist and what inwardness is becomes totally forgotten (CUP, 1:249). By arguing that inwardness cannot be communicated directly (CUP, 1:260) and that the more direct the communication, the less the inwardness (CUP, 1:242), Johannes Climacus draws attention to the inadequacy of direct communication as the only or primary mode for conveying an existential message. The reason for his concern becomes apparent when one bears in mind that "direct communication is the communication of knowledge" (JP, 1:653, section 1) and that all communication of knowledge, that is, communication of the results of objective thinking, is direct (JP, 1:651). Direct communication involves a straightforward statement as to what a particular matter is all about, and the knowledge conveyed has the same meaning for all recipients.

Direct communication is a suitable mode for conveying knowledge hitherto unknown to the recipient. What is required from the communicator in direct communication is competence and an ability to transmit knowledge to the recipient, while the only requirement for the recipient is to be in a position to receive the knowledge. Direct communication is a necessary first step in ethical-religious communication where recipients need to become acquainted with the contents of the Christian message (JP, 1:653, section 29). But to think that one is a Christian simply because one knows some factual content about Christianity is to deceive oneself (CUP, 1:380). As Johannes Climacus points out, Christianity is not a doctrine; it is an existential communication which requires subjective involvement and personal appropriation of meaning (CUP, 1:379-80). "Recipient" is an active word (JP, 1:649, section 7). What is sought is not intellectual understanding but self-knowledge (JP, 1:649, section 8), the prerequisite for becoming what one essentially is. Ethical and ethical-religious communication is therefore the communication of capability, not of knowledge (JP, 1:651). And to communicate capability requires a different mode of communication. Kierkegaard's dialectic of ethical and ethical-religious communication explains what is involved.

Kierkegaard's Dialectic of Ethical and Ethical-religious Communication

The mode of communication preeminently suited to ethical and ethical-religious communication is the indirect mode: "All communication of capability is indirect communication" (JP, 1:651).[1] Since ethical and ethical-religious communication differ in some respects I shall discuss them separately.

Ethical Communication

In the communication of ethical capability the emphasis falls on the recipient (JP, 1:651). Indirect communication is basically maieutic, a viewpoint which clearly reflects the influence of Socrates (JP, 1:649, section 19). The communicator's role is to assist the recipient in the birth of self-knowledge (PF, 14). To weaken the recipient's defences and help him or her become receptive to the message, the communicator must do everything possible to divert attention from his or her own person. In fact the communicator must work against himself or herself (JP, 1:649, section 31) to prevent the recipient from feeling any obligation towards the communicator. The formula for the maieutic relationship is "to stand alone—by another's help" (JP, 1:650, section 15). The message is open-ended and no definite outcome is envisaged because the end result is, and can only be, determined by the recipient. To be able to offer the recipient assistance requires, however, that the communicator exist in what he or she communicates (JP, 1:649, section 5). This requirement follows from the fact that indirect communication takes place in the medium of actuality and that actuality is "the existential reduplication of what is said" (JP, 1:653, section 17).

The indirect mode aims in the first place at cleansing the recipient from self-deception. The art of indirect communication is the art of "taking away" (CUP, 1:275). The maieutic's help is hidden behind the form of the communication. According to Johannes Climacus a confusing contrasting form of communication, which makes the knowledge appear strange to the recipient, is particularly useful when something needs to be taken away. The "knower's" knowledge is taken away until he or she manages to assimilate knowledge by overcoming the resistance of the strange form of the communication (CUP, 1:274-76).

---

[1]Kierkegaard refers to aesthetic capability as well. The communication involved in this case is indirect, or essentially indirect, instruction in art which places equal emphasis on the communicator and the recipient (JP, 1:657).

Indirect communication may be described as the placing together of dialectical contrasts without offering any explanation that may influence the recipient's interpretation (JP, 1:679). Contrasting alternatives place the recipient before a riddle he or she has to solve and for which all alternative interpretations are equally possible. In the absence of guidance on the part of the communicator the recipient can only come to a decision by self-consciously appropriating the message.

Alternative interpretations follow from the fact that communication involves double reflection. The recipient thinks the universal but, as existing in his or her own thinking, he or she becomes more and more subjectively isolated. The form of the communication needs to be considered as well: the communication must artistically possess just as much reflection as the existing thinker, existing in his or her thinking, possesses (CUP, 1:73-74). The first reflection concerns the expression of the communicator's thought, while the second reflection concerns both the relation between the communication and the communicator and the communicator's own existential relation to the idea (CUP, 1:76). To ensure that the recipient becomes subjectively involved in appropriating the message, his or her attention must be diverted from the communicator as a person. Double reflection requires therefore that the communicator continuously put qualitative contrasts in unity and refrain from supporting the communication with reference to his or her own existence. In this way a dialectical knot is produced, and the recipient is forced to untie the knot by himself or herself.

Central to the maieutic art is the use of deception (JP, 1:649, section 22; JP, 1:653, section 24) to lure the recipient into discovering the truth about himself or herself. Deception signifies that the communicator "first and foremost does not seem to be an earnest man" (JP, 1:649, section 24; JP, 1:653, section 23). The communicator must not appear to be earnest because the object of the communication is that the recipient becomes earnest, not by mimicking the communicator, but by the appropriation of the communication.

This attack "from behind" means that one does not begin directly with the matter one wants to communicate, but one begins by accepting the recipient's illusion. For example, Kierkegaard did not start his career as a writer by saying that he was a Christian while his recipients were not. He talked about aesthetic existence to recipients who were living in the illusion that the aesthetic was Christianity (PV, 40-41).

The maieutic art is preeminently the art of the ironist who appears to be serious while he or she is in fact jesting. The ironist incessantly alters the deception, thereby showing how well suited he or she is for conveying an indirect communication: "one can never mimic an ironist" (JP, 1:649, section 24). The ambiguous form of the ironic communication not only invites more than one interpretation; it deceives the recipient about the real intention of the communicator and ultimately of the communication. By being "detached" from his or her own life the recipient is able to see his or her existence "objectively" as a whole and to become aware of the unsatisfactory condition thereof.[2]

Irony is particularly useful for addressing an individual person. Because irony is absolutely unsocial and tends essentially towards one person as its limit, it focuses on what is peculiar to a particular recipient (PV, 54-55).

Indirect communication was for Kierkegaard inseparably bound up with pseudonymity. In Johannes Climacus's *Philosophical Fragments* and *Concluding Unscientific Postscript* the method of indirect communication reaches its full development.[3] In Kierkegaard's opinion he rendered a service to his age by bringing his pseudonyms into the center of life's actuality in order to familiarize persons again with hearing a personal I. The pseudonyms are particularly useful for this purpose because they have a something which makes them more bearable for a world that is quite unaccustomed to hearing an I (JP, 1:656). Because none of these poetised personalities, each of which pursues a onesided course to its very extreme, can be associated with Kierkegaard's own personality (CUP, 1:626) they act for him as a means of distancing himself (CUP, 1:252). By introducing different pseudonyms Kierkegaard was able to offer his recipients a variety of existential positions, thereby assisting them not only in coming to terms with themselves, but in choosing a more authentic mode of existence.

---

[2]J. D. Mullen, *Kierkegaard's Philosophy. Self-deception and Cowardice in the Present Age* (New York: New American Library, 1981) 39.

[3]Johannes Hohlenberg, *Den Ensommes Vej. En Fremstilling af Søren Kierkegaards Vaerk* (Copenhagen: Aschehoug Dansk Forlag, 1968) 126.

The maieutic art consists not only of the negative aspect of cleansing, but also the positive aspect of upbringing. In relation to the ethical (and ethical-religious) the genuine communication is training or upbringing (JP, 1:650, section 12). The assumption is that the person who is going to be brought up is able to become what he or she essentially is. By doing as well as he or she can at every moment, the recipient continues to get to know better what he or she is able to do and can gradually become what he or she is. Upbringing cannot be achieved through a communication of knowledge because in this case the person only gets something to know. Nor can it be achieved through instruction because here the emphasis falls on helping others understand, and in the final analysis they only understand what the communicator understands (JP, 2:1753). In ethical communication, on the other hand, the relationship is reciprocal: the communicator is the occasion for the recipient to come to self-knowledge, and the recipient is the occasion for the communicator to understand himself or herself (PF, 24).

Ethical-religious Communication

While ethical communication is unconditionally indirect, Kierkegaard describes ethical-religious communication as direct/indirect (JP, 1:651). Unlike the ethical, which everyone knows as the universally human, the religious in the Christian sense is not known as such. Although the communication of religious capability is indirect, a direct communication of some knowledge is first required (JP, 1:650, section 13; JP, 1:653, section 29). After the initial communication of knowledge the same relationship as in the ethical obtains (JP, 1:650, section 13).

In ethical-religious communication the communicator is emphasized (JP, 1:651). In this kind of communication the communicator has authority with respect to the knowledge that is communicated (JP, 1:653, section 28). However, when one bears in mind that between human beings the maieutic (Socratic) relationship is the highest (PF, 55), it becomes clear that God is the only communicator in ethical-religious communication (JP, 1:649, section 9). The human communicator dares only influence indirectly because what must be expressed is that he or she is but an apprentice of God who is everyone's master teacher. Ethically, the task is that everyone comes to stand alone in the God relationship (JP, 1:649,

section 20) and always has the task of his or her own development
(JP, 1:649, section 17).

In ethical communication the communicator is as much a
learner as the recipient and the recipient owes the communicator
nothing. In ethical-religious communication, however, the truth is
that the pupil owes God, the only teacher, everything. Understanding this truth requires that the learner be transformed and this can
only be made possible by the god who provides the condition for
understanding the truth (PF, 30). If the truth then lies not in the
subject but in a revelation that must be proclaimed, it follows that
the communication of the essentially Christian cannot be accomplished by the maieutic form alone, but must finally end in
witnessing (JP, 2:1957).

Kierkegaard describes witnessing as direct communication (JP,
1:670). In ethical-religious communication the human communicator acts maieutically so that the recipient may be cleansed of self-
deception. In this way the recipient is prepared for the process of
transformation which takes place during his or her communication
with God. When God becomes too powerful for the maieutic
relation, the recipient is turned into a witness (JP, 2:1957). It would
seem that witnessing is direct communication in so far as the
witness expresses in his or her life what he or she has come to
believe (JP, 1:659). However, for the witness, God is the authority,
not other human beings. While the witness's "communication"
addresses itself to one's fellow human beings, the witness himself
or herself addresses God. The God relation is personal and private
and, from the viewpoint of other human beings, it only communicates indirectly. Hence Kierkegaard notes that witnessing is a form
of communication that strikes the truest mean between direct and
indirect communication (JP, 1:670). This viewpoint is consistent
with his description of ethical-religious communication as being
direct/indirect (JP, 1:651). It seems that Kierkegaard's own communication during the last part of his life was influenced by these
considerations concerning witnessing.

Conclusion

Since Kierkegaard's dialectical theory of communication developed from his own communication praxis, it must be assessed with

reference to this context. Kierkegaard's entire *oeuvre* was written to awaken his fellow human beings. The very crux of his communication method, deception in service of the truth, shows that his writings are basically maieutic. The structure of the *oeuvre* as such reflects a placing together of contrasts without any explanation of what they (may) mean. Although *The Point of View for my Work as an Author* offers an explanation for the duplicity of the *oeuvre*, it is left to the reader to interpret the existential significance of the duplicity. The very fact that the recipient's involvement is sought suggests, of course, that there can hardly be a single "correct" interpretation of Kierkegaard's text. Moreover, Kierkegaard's deliberate attempts to make penetration of his work difficult makes any literal interpretation suspect.

The so-called "second authorship" provides the reader with some "knowledge" in that Kierkegaard *inter alia* explains, in his own name, Christian concepts and categories. The difference between direct and indirect communication is the dialectical contrast in his concept of communication. However, instances of direct communication must always be seen in relation to the purpose of his writing, namely to help the recipient appropriate the meaning of the message. Even a "direct" communication requires more than pure intellectual understanding.

It is doubtful whether Kierkegaard's own "direct" communication constitutes a pure type in contrast to his "indirect" communication. He notes, for example, that his indirect communication was always supported by a *more direct* form running parallel to it and that the pseudonyms were accompanied by "direct communication *in the guise of* (my emphasis) the upbuilding or edifying discourses" (JP, 1:656). Instead of placing them in airtight compartments, it seems more fruitful to think of direct and indirect communication on a continuum ranging from more to less direct.

The pseudonyms are by no means the only points of view represented by Kierkegaard's *oeuvre*. Who is the communicator in the edifying discourses for instance? Kierkegaard made it clear on several occasions that his discourses should not be seen as sermons since he was not ordained and therefore had no authority. Yet in the edifying discourses he conveys some knowledge in his own name, that is, he complies with his own prescriptions for a communicator who has authority, while he is convinced that he is without authority! *The Point of View for my Work as an Author* lends further support to a suggestion that Kierkegaard, whether he uses direct or indirect communication, always presents himself to his readers as a point of view. Apart from the fact that he himself never published his report to history (and this despite the purpose of the work) he tells us in the Introduction that he cannot explain his work wholly because his God relationship and several matters concerning his person are private (PV, 9). The work is concluded by Kierkegaard's poet who offers the reader an interpretation behind Kierkegaard's back, that is, the "direct" account ends with Kierkegaard donning yet another mask! The title for this work, contributed by his brother Peter, is, of course, unfortunate: the report to history can hardly be the (only) point of view for Kierkegaard's work!

Although his influence is not necessarily openly acknowledged, Kierkegaard is by no means dated as far as current developments in communication theory are concerned. During the past few years audience theory, for instance, has accentuated the need to take account of the involvement and participation of the recipient in determining the outcome of communication encounters. Kierkegaard may also rightly be seen as an important forerunner to poststructuralism, an approach which currently attracts a growing number of communication scholars. The comments that follow illustrate some affinities between Kierkegaard's viewpoints and developments in poststructuralism and suggest that there may be different ways of reading Kierkegaard. The notion of points of view suggests, for example, an affinity with poststructuralist thinking concerning the subject. For poststructuralists the subject is constructed through language and is socially and linguistically fragmented and decentered. This view comes close to the notion of a self adopting different points of view for self-presentation in different communication contexts. Kierkegaard's pseudonyms in particular come to mind in this connection.

Kierkegaard was, of course, one of the first authors to "absent" himself from his own communication, that is, to make himself a point of view. This theme has been taken up by poststructuralists such as Derrida and Foucault. Kierkegaard's styles of writing, the techniques he used and his masterful use of irony are also of interest to poststructuralist authors. Poole, for instance, notes that

Kierkegaard used all the major tools of deconstructive theory long before Derrida started focusing attention on them.[4]

Kierkegaard would probably not have agreed with all current developments in poststructuralist communication theory. However, a consideration of his critique is beyond the scope of the present paper. In view of the radical transformation in modes of communication during the second half of the twentieth century, brought about by fundamental social and cultural changes, a consideration of Kierkegaard's position concerning some major themes in poststructuralist communication theory may be worth considering in future research. Consider, for example, the poststructuralist view that communication is, among other things, a contest between persons in different social and power relations within different contexts, or the view that language, which for poststructuralists is constitutive of reality, is the key to an understanding of all human and social phenomena, including communication encounters.

Some of Kierkegaard's themes are certainly relevant to new media and developments in information technology which have in recent years significantly changed the *way* messages are conveyed. Particularly in the field of interactive media, such as computers, these developments focus attention on the positions of communicator and recipient and have implications for participation and response, especially on the part of the recipient. In this kind of small scale communication participation is possible for everyone who is in a position to use the medium. Since no one is physically present during the communication both communicator and recipient are "points of view." But they are not anonymous; they participate by using names which may even be their own names. Recipients reply to messages, that is, they give feedback which is believed to be virtually impossible in mass communication. Although feedback may entail the transmission of factual content, it also allows for the possibility of subjective involvement on the part of the recipient. There is no fixed and authoritative communicator as in mass communication; feedback implies not only that an exchange of messages takes place, but that communicator and

---

[4]Roger Poole, *Kierkegaard: The Indirect Communication* (Charlottesville: University Press of Virginia, 1993) 7.

recipient alternate. There is both indirectness and ambiguity in this kind of communication situation. For example, who is the communicator? Computers can be programmed to interrogate recipients who are then challenged to reply. Is the medium in this case the communicator, or is the communicator the person who programmes the computer? In addition, indirectness and ambiguity allow for unexpected rather than predictable outcomes, thereby suggesting that this kind of communication situation may enable participants to experience the encounter in a subjectively meaningful way. Characteristics such as these suggest that interactive media may be explored with a view to involving recipients in communication and exchanging different kinds of messages within contexts very different from those Kierkegaard knew.

Nobody would doubt the effectiveness of computers in transmitting factual content which requires intellectual understanding. But, as Kierkegaard has shown, the same media may be used for different purposes. In view of the possibilities for subjective involvement, made possible by developments in interactive media, it is not farfetched to suggest that this inherent potential may be explored in ethical and ethical-religious communication as well.

Limitations of interactive media also point to the relevance of some of Kierkegaard's concerns within the changing media landscape of the late twentieth century. Consider, for instance, that privacy is not guaranteed (information of a personal nature may be circulated by big computer networks) and that the possibility of fraud is ever present. The responsibility/irresponsibility of communicators may in fact be even more important today than in Kierkegaard's time.

While at present Kierkegaard does not attract the attention of communication scholars either with reference to the purpose of his writing or his views on Christian existence, his contributions to an understanding of communication are undoubtedly relevant to current developments in communication theory, such as poststructuralism, and approaches that highlight the active role of the recipient in communication.

7

Exemplars, Inwardness, and Belief: Kierkegaard on Indirect Communication

Edward F. Mooney

In its inexhaustible artistry, such a form of communication corresponds to and renders the existing subject's own [inexhaustible] relation to the idea.

[I]n our age we do not so much have philosophers as we have spectators of the exploits of philosophy.
—Johannes Climacus, *Concluding Unscientific Postscript*[1]

Indirect communication is a central theme of *Concluding Unscientific Postscript* and of Kierkegaard's authorship generally. It is central to Kierkegaard's use of pseudonyms and to his adoption of artistic means to bring his audience to an ethical or religious way of life. Irony and humor, prominent tokens of indirect communication, are favorite devices in all his work, and in the *Postscript* they also define specific transitional stages in spiritual development. In addition, the *Postscript* as a whole is an instance of indirect communication, for we are told, in its final pages, that none of it is to be taken at face value. If this work itself is a communication, its point is thereby obscured. Why tempt and tease readers with these multiple involutions?

At issue is not an insular concept but an entire mode of relationship between writer and reader, between speaker and hearer, between exemplars of a spiritual life and whoever recognizes or acknowledges such exemplars. The idea of indirect communication

---

[1]First epigraph, CUP, 1:419. (In this case I quote the Lowrie and Swenson translation: *Concluding Unscientific Postscript*, trans. Walter Lowrie and David L. Swenson [Princeton: Princeton University Press, 1941] 375.) Second epigraph, CUP, 1:80.

is so pervasive, in use and in mention, that finding one's way with it is like finding one's way out of a maze—just to discover that one has entered a larger one. In Kierkegaard's view our religious, artistic, and moral practices are corrupted by social conventionalism and a crude commercialism. They lack any spiritual focus. Our propensities for self-deception conspire with these hollow practices to keep us bound in illusion. But telling all this to another, or coming to realize it oneself, is no easy business. Moralism, preaching or abstract philosophizing won't work. There are no *direct* instructions for escape from such loss of self and spirit.

I. The Kantian and Hegelian Background

Kant's *Critiques* fix judgments in specific spheres of validity and importance. Art is distinguished from ethics, religion is separated from politics, and natural science is divorced from the more value laden worlds of art, ethics, or religion. Rules are articulated to provide the legitimation proper to each of these arenas of discourse. Kierkegaard wrote in Kant's wake, giving dramatic color and detail to the contrasts between ethics, art, philosophy, and religion, and altering Kant's map along the way.[2] However Kierkegaard did not share Kant's aim to minimize academic and political conflict over fields of intellectual endeavor by assigning proper jurisdictions.[3] He was obsessed instead by the existential question this geography posed: Could a life that was *lived out* in conventionalist or merely aesthetic terms be at all satisfactory? And if not, how could someone move toward a more satisfactory life—say a life lived partially under aesthetic but also under ethical or religious categories?

If Kantians thought a direct appeal to reason and critique would suffice for progress, Hegelians assumed, so it seemed, that the transitions would happen on their own through the relentless

---

[2]For the Kant-Kierkegaard connection, see R. Z. Friedman, "Kierkegaard: Last Kantian or First Existentialist," *Religious Studies* 18/2 (June 1982) and Ronald M. Green, *The Hidden Debt: Kierkegaard and Kant* (Albany: State University of New York Press, 1992).

[3]See Immanuel Kant *The Conflict of the Faculties,* trans. Mary J. Gregor (New York: Arbis Books, 1979).

engine of History. One was already on the train, regardless of one's thoughts about the matter, and would get carried along to whatever collective destiny awaited the assembled passengers. Kierkegaard was happy with neither of these answers. Rational critique could unsettle easy assumptions, but it could not reach deep enough to effectively move one toward a more satisfactory life. Although Kierkegaard can be viewed as extending rational critique in a Kantian vein, he saw this capacity as primarily negative, in the sense of challenging illusions rather than restoring realities. Our capacities for rationalization of the status quo, and our fears of losing defenses that keep anxiety somewhat at bay are too great for reason to decisively disable or remove them. In any case, he thought it was extravagant to hope that reason alone has the capacity to rebuild what it can dismantle.[4] With regard to the Hegelian response, Kierkegaard had no use for collective solutions to individual spiritual crises. Working through the transition, say from the merely aesthetic to the ethical, was an individual affair. Another might prod or prompt a move toward a more satisfactory life, but this would involve free responsiveness, not rational or historical inevitabilities. If advance was risky and unpredictable, so was communication about or embodying it. The essentials for spiritual life are not waiting quietly in simple slogans or even in lengthy texts.

Having pseudonyms present various viewpoints on life, and embody various stances, encourages our free responsiveness. We are addressed by art-like works appealing to our interpretative sensibilities rather than being informed by essays or self-help manuals or preached to in ways that intimidate or coerce. To see how art or ethics or reflective Socratic philosophy might animate one's life, surely a narrative portrait would help. Why not artistically *display* the "dialectical lyric" of a Johannes de silentio as he mulls through his multiple versions of the Abraham story in

---

[4]For the role of idealism and romanticism in shaping Kant's thought, see Frederick Beiser, *The Fate of Reason: German Philosophy from Kant to Fichte* (Cambridge: Harvard University Press, 1987); Rudolph A. Makkreel, *Imagination and Interpretation in Kant: The Hermeneutical Import of The Critique of Judgment* (Chicago: University of Chicago Press, 1990); and Susan Neiman, *The Unity of Reason: Rereading Kant* (Oxford: Oxford University Press, 1994).

Fear and Trembling, or *sketch out* the "comic pathetic dialectic" of a Johannes Climacus in the *Postscript* matching wits with Socrates on the nature of truth? In the immediate way a work of art allows us such direct encounter, we would get closer to what it would be like to take Abraham or Socrates as exemplars, closer to what a life lived under their lights could be. The artistry of a Kierkegaard producing the artistry of a Johannes de silentio or a Johannes Climacus can show how a life lived only as aesthetic whim or observation will fall apart, and how a life lived with the artistry of ethics or the ethicoreligious might hold together better, and *matter*. Because communication of moral seriousness requires the artistry of displaying someone *living out* the import of an indirect communication, artistry does not get discarded but is required as one depicts the moral-religious psychology of movement from the inadequacies of the aesthetic sphere of existence to the richer lives of the ethical or ethicoreligious spheres.[5]

Religion, philosophy, or ethics are ways of life, a matter of truly believing *in* something or someone. Conveying what is decisive about a way of life means exemplifying and expressing that life—not simply communicating a straightforward creed or set of beliefs. Indirect communication challenges reigning illusions about what matters. More important, it shows or lights up an exemplary life.

II. Direct Communication

In the obvious cases, transmitting or communicating straightforward beliefs that something is so is nonproblematic. I tell you it's raining in California or that my uncle has been incredibly rude. Unless you doubt my character, detect irony in my voice, or suspect that I have some devious end in mind, you will believe that these things are so when I tell you. The transmission will be direct and uncomplicated by the need for interpretation or worries

---

[5]See Sylvia Walsh, *Living Poetically: Kierkegaard's Existential Aesthetics* (University Park: Penn State University Press, 1994); and Jeffrey S. Turner, "To tell a good tale: Kierkegaardian reflections on moral narrative and moral truth," *Man and World* 24 (1991): 181-98.

about unresolved ambiguities. Here are some features of such straightforward, direct communication.

First, the idea that I have in mind to communicate is definite and for the purposes at hand, sharply etched. No penumbra of ambiguity, vagueness, or mystery occludes the idea conveyed; its content is immediately transparent. Second, as a communicator I have a direct lock on the idea to be conveyed, a seamless grip that eliminates gaps between me and the having of the idea. My mental gears, as it were, directly engage the thought with no play or space left over for interpretation or reflection. My "inwardness," as Climacus would say, is not an issue, for there's only a single reflection, "it's raining," to communicate, and no second reflection *about* that idea. Third, *your* mental gears lock in the idea that I transmit with the same ease that I transmit it.

Note that direct communication is not restricted to factual or theoretical matters. Evaluative or exhortative communications can be direct, as well. When teller and hearer are properly attuned, "Sit down!" or "You really should see your dad" are communications as direct as "It's raining in California."

The contrast between a direct communication (a single reflection) and indirect communication (where there is a reflection *about* an initial reflection—a "double reflection") is context sensitive. Even "It's raining" can involve my inwardness and elicit your subjective response: I write this sentence as an object lesson for linguistic analysis, attempting to transmit the skills of philosophical analysis, or I use it as a sample sentence for non- English speakers. Thus a recipient's capacity for interpretation, for grasping the appropriate sense and excluding inappropriate but conceivable senses, is put to work. In a small way one's subjectivity, one's motivation, alertness, sensitivity to context, readiness to accept the new, is engaged. On the other hand, if I have solidified a code with you such that "It's raining in California" is a private signal that I am about to arrive for a visit, then a direct communication would have occurred between us (though for outsiders, matters would be different).[6] I would know exactly what I meant in telling

---

[6]See the motto for *Fear and Trembling* where Tarquinius Superbus strikes off the head of the poppies in front of a messenger; later the messenger will repeat

you it was raining; I would have no worry about your capacity to understand me; and you would understand *me* unequivocally.

Other things being equal, you *trust* me when I report on the weather in California, trust that "It's raining" is not a stand-in for "I'm in the bleakest mood" or "It's raining term papers." Specifying the host of contextual presuppositions making direct communication possible would be rewarding, but it is not the job Johannes Climacus sets himself. His interest in direct communication is limited. It marks one end of an axis, the end where we receive telephone numbers and weather reports. It concerns knowledge that, as Climacus has it, can be simply "reeled off" (CUP, 1:75). If *this* end is nailed down, he can turn to the other end of the axis, to communication that is *indirect*.

III. Engaging Subjectivity

The most dramatic instance of indirect communication is Kierkegaard's use of pseudonyms to engage the subjectivity of a reader. Learning that he is not speaking directly forces us into an inquisitive, apprehensive, or frustrated position. *Why* are we not addressed directly? This opens a space for responsive interpretations, an aperture for imaginative, open-ended reflection. The pseudonym disrupts the convenience, ease, and automation of direct communication. Rebounding thought against thought without simple closure throws us into freedom. I shuttle among options: Does Kierkegaard have something to hide? Is the book written in code?[7] Does it perhaps say the *opposite* of what Kierkegaard thinks? Is Johannes Climacus's last hour revocation in the *Postscript* of all he has written in that tome (and others) to be taken

---

the gesture to signal the son to take revenge on his enemies. But this is not the core instance of indirect communication for the message will be unambiguous to its proper recipient.

[7]Codes are intended to be unambiguous once one has the translation key; hence they are direct communications that bypass subjectivity. See n. 6, above. However, we sometimes talk of "decoding" a poem, that is working to get the gist of what on the surface is opaque. So in this sense one's initial reaction to a Kierkegaardian pseudonym might be that there was something like a key to work out, even if in the long run one discovered, properly, that to even suppose that there was a strict translation key would be to have started on the wrong foot.

seriously? Can pseudonyms "talk" across their differences or is each hermetically sealed from others? I can wonder if only one or rather all or most of these interpretative options have some truth.

The impasse created by the realization that one of several pseudonyms speak (and not Kierkegaard himself) need not be a destructive impasse. It can be a creative one. Like a good metaphor, it can spawn an abundance of thought, feeling and images.[8] Working through these alternatives can engage my subjectivity to a degree unmatched by my reception of a direct communication of fact or theory or doctrine. I *experience* my mind or soul at sea. I am already thrown into an exercise of interpretative freedom, not just told *about* it.

From the side of the creator of a pseudonym, the aperture of subjectivity is also open wide, for he must think not only of what the *pseudonym* is to say or do, but how that saying or doing will be received by another, and how the distinction between pseudonym and creator is holding up. If proper distance is not maintained, the reader will mistake Kierkegaard for an authority on some matter of fact or doctrine to be communicated directly and with all urgency. However if Kierkegaard's task is to awaken *our* subjectivity, he must partially veil or disguise his seriousness, for authorities can intimidate or overpower as well as inspire and command. And even were he to inspire without intimidation, in yielding to his charisma, our freedom is at risk. Climacus makes this point by bringing out the contrast between Socrates' outwardly unfavorable appearance and his inner beauty.

Through the repellent effect exerted by the contrast, which on a higher plane was also the role played by his irony, the learner would be compelled to understand that he had essentially to do with himself, and that the inwardness of the truth is not the comradely inwardness with which two bosom friends walk arm in arm, but the separation with which each for himself exists in the truth. (CUP, 1:222). As Socrates must hide to protect his student from too easy a seduction, so Kierkegaard must hide so that his

---

[8]See S. Gillian Parker, *An Aesthetic Theory for Metaphor* (New York: Peter Lang, 1997) esp. chap. 6. I thank Gillian and Phil Clayton for an early reading of this essay.

reader may come to "exist in the truth." To hide is to intensify doubly reflected inwardness and to hope that this retreat will activate another's inwardness rather than their outrage.

Each pseudonym speaks from a unique position, in intimate address to a specific other, engaging in open-ended dialogue that in the broadest sense is a moral exchange, an instance of mutual moral reflection.[9] None can—or does—claim final moral or religious authority to possess the truth. "The secret of communication specifically hinges on setting the other free" (CUP, 1:74). This partially explains why Climacus appends to the very end of the *Postscript* a revocation of all he has so far asserted in his massive tome (CUP, 1:617-23). Furthermore, the revocation-containing appendix is followed by yet another appendix, "a first and last explanation" signed by Kierkegaard himself, a set of unnumbered sheets marking a break with the Climacus text. In this "final explanation" Kierkegaard distances himself from the pseudonymous works so far completed, including the *Postscript*.[10] In its final pages we have two gestures that distance the writer's own authority from the printed word in order, as I see it, to promote a reader's freedom to interpret. "Wherever the subjective is of importance . . . , communication is a work of art; it is doubly reflected, and its first form is the subtlety that the subjective

---

[9]A Kierkegaardian "theory" of practical reason has interlocutors face each other from a standpoint of respect, each engaging, without manipulating or coercing, the other's subjectivity: see Stephen Mulhall, "The Senses of *Sources of the Self*," in *Can Religion be Explained Away?*, ed. D. Z. Phillips (London: Metheun, 1996) and my *Selves in Discord and Resolve: Kierkegaard's Moral-Religious Psychology, from Either/Or to Sickness Unto Death* (New York: Routledge, 1996).

[10]The distancing gestures of both Climacus and Kierkegaard are, of course, incomplete. The *Postscript* is not withdrawn from publication. It remains for sale in bookstores. And leaving both Climacus's appendix "revocation" and Kierkegaard's unpaginated "first and last explanation" within the covers of an unabashedly pseudonymous text makes this two-step distancing itself partially suspect, the acts of a writer (or writers) still in partial ironic disguise. Paradoxically, the distancings may function both to call attention (directly) to the fact that what precedes is indirect communication—and also be themselves instances of indirect communication. If so, they are not to be taken entirely straightforwardly, but as freedom-enhancing existence-communications open to interpretation on roughly the same level as the rest of the *Postscript*. That is, despite appearances, they are not necessarily external and finally authoritative keys to the preceding text.

individuals must be held devoutly apart from one another and must not coagulate in objectivity (CUP, 1:79)."[11]

Kierkegaard (or Climacus) wants to convey to the reader an aperture for responsible appropriation, and nothing less. But how can a writer know that freedom has been conveyed? Is this even a reasonable hope, in a spiritless Copenhagen swallowed by interests of commerce and respectability? If Kierkegaard's overriding aim is to enable another to *become* ethical or Socratic or Christian, then he has reason to fear his work has failed. But if he's only thrown a bone to a bored intelligentsia, he'd rather take the whole book back. Thus the ambiguous gesture: it's handed to us with a note inserted saying not to trust a word.

IV. Unobtrusive Transfer

In its clearest instances, direct communication does not put our inwardness on notice; content passes from mind to mind without ruffling the feathers of subjectivity. But Kierkegaard (and Climacus) want to *alter* or *awaken* subjectivity—to strike to the spiritual quick: thus the *need* of irony or pseudonyms to startle or subvert our slumber. Communication that awakens subjectivity exploits contrast or tension between outer and inner forms of pathos. Socrates' outward appearance contrasted wildly with the beauty of his soul. His speech could seem negative or evasive, yet he emanated wisdom.[12]

> Pathos . . . [may be] expressed; but pathos in a contrary form is an inwardness that remains with the maker of the communication in spite of being expressed, and cannot be directly appropriated by another except through that other's self-activity: the contrast of the form is the measure of inwardness. The more complete the contrast of the form, the greater the inwardness, and the less contrast, up to the point of direct communication, the less the inwardness.   (CUP, 1:217)

---

[11]Translation emended.

[12]We are reminded here of the complaint of Alcibiades at the close of Plato's *Symposium* (221d-222b): Socrates seems ridiculous on the surface, yet within he is like an unattainable god one cannot but fall hopelessly in love with.

A disproportion or tension between inner and outer form is also present in having a pseudonym who speaks at cross purposes with his creator, or in having the ironic import of a line at cross purposes with its surface import. The proposal is that the greater the disproportion, contrast, or tension between inner and outer, the deeper the inwardness, and the more the recipient is forced back on her (or his) own interpretative resources. But this may seem to be an extreme position. Perhaps subjectivity can be awakened without such extreme measures, without vehicles that provoke or jolt us to awareness by wildly tensed oppositions.

If I tell you that I have just become a grandfather, it's easy to imagine my commitments, my passions, close at hand. This simple transmission can evoke interpretations: you can begin to wonder what my being a grandfather *means* to me. As communicator, there will be space for soliloquies where memories, anticipations of exchanges with friends and family, can resound and flourish. Reporting my grand-fatherly status can occasion reflections on who I am, time to evoke the contours of my life, the flow of generational advance. There is space for subjectivity to resonate, to rebound in your inwardness and in mine. I may find myself overtaken by the wonder and fear crystallized in the advent of a child, the fragile abundance of its coming to pass, and of my passing, and of the passing of a world that both pulls me forward and leaves me behind. My moral religious identity becomes engaged; a portion seeks and finds expression. The engagement may be episodic or perhaps signal a deeper turning point. Identity may shift in lasting ways, signaled by, but not limited to, the episode of my telling.[13]

Thus we can elaborate, and soften, Climacus's account by widening the scope of indirect communication to include cases where it is unobtrusive, where tensions between outer expression and inner import are largely invisible. Subjectivity transfer is not limited to the sophisticated artistry of pseudonymous communication or the arena of heightened religiosity, or the complex commu-

---

[13]Our subjectivity has its middle and surface strata as well as its deepest core, and its engagement can occur along a continuum. Understanding another person, another culture, another religion can evoke our subjectivity short of evoking our identity-commitments or core.

nications that prod the esthete to an ethical mode of life. Unobtrusive turning of a soul can permeate the unremarkable (yet remarkable) daily round, much as Johannes de silentio's shopkeeper knight of faith slips by invisibly, utterly lacking the fanfare of Father Abraham ascending Mt. Moriah.

Inwardness, indefiniteness of meaning, lack of closure, and a space for interpretation occur as matters of degree: "the *more* complete the contrast of the form [of inner and outer expressed feeling], the *greater* the inwardness, and the *less* contrast, *up to the point* of direct communication, the less the inwardness" (CUP, 1:217, my emphasis). From this angle, direct and indirect communication are not two distinct categories such that any communication can be located unambiguously as falling in one category or the other. Rather, direct communication defines one pole on a continuum, the pole of maximally impersonal objectivity. Some communication may fall midway between direct and indirect. Locating the opposing pole, maximal indirection, is more difficult than locating maximal directness. At the vanishing point of pure indirection, freedom moves from bearer to receiver with no tag to identify a uniquely certified transfer vehicle. There are an indefinitely large number of vehicles, none essential to the outcome. I might receive freedom from the glint of another's eye, from a rhetorical address, from the absence of my friend, from an exhortation, or from nothing specific that I could name at all. In instances of indirection, we can know abstractly *what* occurs (a freedom transfer); and often *that* it occurs; but *how* it comes about, either in general or in the "mechanics" of a specific case, remains largely unsayable, a secret.[14]

Kierkegaard works us from the merely aesthetic and conventionalist world "back" to a religious or ethicoreligious life of more sustained and resonant subjectivity. This requires artistry.

> Actually to communicate such a conviction [of the importance of inwardness] would require art, . . . enough art to vary inexhaust-

---

[14]*How* the communication of freedom arrives from friends or exemplary figures is wondrous, a "repetition": we cannot credit this reception to our willpower or talent alone. See my "Repetition: Getting the World Back," *Cambridge Companion to Kierkegaard*, ed. Gordon Marino and Alastair Hannay (Cambridge: Cambridge University Press, 1997).

ibly, just as inwardness is inexhaustible, the doubly reflected form of the communication. The more art, the more inwardness.
(CUP, 1:77)

V. Belief and Commitment

If I tell you I believe in honesty, you may credit my telling as truthful, and receive a belief by a kind of direct impress or transfer. You will believe *that* I believe in something, that my subjectivity is engaged. But belief about me can leave *your* subjectivity untouched. Commitments are not transferred by simple telling. I can tell you that I believe in the power of poetry to soothe or ignite the soul, but whether you catch that commitment in my telling of it is surely not straightforward.

To transfer my commitments to poetry to you, I'd take you aside, speak some aloud to you, tell you about my favorites and how my favorites have changed. I'd ask you about your interests, if they ever bordered on the poetic: I'd try to kindle, or rekindle your interest, by whatever means. In time, I might wonder if some of my commitment had rubbed off on you: maybe I'd suspect it in the sparkle in your eye. But I'd be cautious, for perhaps the sparkle comes not because you've come to share my passion for poetry but because you love the attention I've been showering. Keeping alive the sparkle in my eye might be more important to you than keeping alive the line from Wordsworth. Similarly, I might believe in civic duty or friendship and tell you of these commitments. I might tell you stories from my life, or bring you to spots where there was public work to do or where people suffered loneliness. But to awaken your moral passion or commitment would not be merely to tell you of mine.

Telling you that something matters to me does not license you to take it as important *to you*. To back a belief about what matters by citing another's belief is in Climacus's terms to "coagulate our identity in objectivity" (CUP, 1:79). An artful moral teacher will avoid moralizing, intimidation, and imitation. She (or he) may try to evoke a belief, so that it gets acquired by another, but gets acquired only because it stands *worthy* of embrace—precisely *not* merely on the grounds that a teacher *said* it was important.

There is a categorical distinction between direct and indirect communication, and most communication is complex enough to require both categories for its full explication. My subjectivity, my aperture for reflection cannot be transferred either *en bloc* or piecemeal to you; it's an *opening* within which substance or content can be appropriated and expressed, not itself a transferable substance or content. Nevertheless, you may find your own aperture of freedom widening in resonance with mine. "The secret of communication specifically hinges on setting the other free" (CUP, 1:74). If some of my subjectivity "rubs off" on you through a simple event, say my telling you I'm a grandfather, then there is a core element that can be directly communicated, a "mere fact." But to a listener properly attuned, the telling also marks an opening for interpretation. What *seems* a moment of only direct communication hides a place for indirect communication. You might say: "Perhaps you're confronting your mortality in that new-born child." If these words resonate, a communication has elicited my subjectivity. A proffered interpretation more or less directly communicated enters the fabric of indirect communication. So the apparent directness or indirectness of an expression's outer form is less crucial than the inwardness of speaker and recipient.[15] The conveyance of freedom through indirect communication allows production of interpretations that can be shared, tried out on others, and on oneself, more or less directly.

VI. Exemplars and Artistry

If I teach "Thou shalt have no disciples" in such a way that disciples gather around, or if I teach "The unexamined life is not worth living" as a random truth for mindless duplication on exams, then I have failed to communicate an appropriate concern. The outcome, as Climacus would say, is comic. I will not have exemplified the relevant truth in the telling. To fail in this regard is to have failed to convey decisive subjectivity, a capacity for *living* in a certain way. "The thinker must present the human ideal

---

[15]Direct communication *may* evoke another's subjectivity. An offhand apparently casual and indifferent aside may have soul-shattering effects: we are not in a position to predict, cause, or prevent decisive changes in another's subjectivity.

. . . as an ethical requirement, as a challenge to the recipient to exist in it" (CUP, 1:358).

Climacus wants the artistry of his Socrates to speak for itself, not be taken as a mask or disposable contrivance through which he, Climacus, or even Kierkegaard, speaks. Inwardness lets an author retreat to the wings, allowing artistically rendered exemplars to step forward. Exemplars show how to live in truthfulness to "the human ideal . . . as an ethical requirement."

The ethicoreligious individual is an *exemplar* of truth more than a truth *teller* because what she stands for is not something that can be simply told. Exemplifying or showing truth is distinct from stating truth. If an ethical or religious individual wishes to convey his truth, he must avoid the appearance and the reality of reducing it to a telling or a statement, even an *indirect* telling or stating, for indirect communication can completely *bypass* telling or stating. As Climacus has it, an exemplar is *forced* to bypass telling.

We can briefly reconstruct several of Climacus's arguments.[16] (1) The religious individual is constantly becoming, so what he says at moment x cannot convey the essence of his being at moment x+1. Yet if the truth to be exemplified concerns his life as it becomes, it must track the unfolding of his being; it cannot, and should not, be frozen at some arbitrary moment. (2) Telling the truth presupposes that we are (reasonably) certain of the truth told. But when I wish to convey inwardness, this is to transfer an aperture within which thought can occur, not to transfer a thought about which I am reasonably certain. (3) Direct communication typically aims for agreement. I tell you x in order to add to your stock of beliefs, and if I am successful, the x that I tell you will correspond exactly with or be duplicated by the x you come to believe through my telling. But if I am to convey what is exemplary about my religiosity, then you will be exemplary in terms of your *own* individuality, not by agreeing with my opinions or copying the expression of *my* individuality. (4) If you grasp my being exemplary, you will be changed. Abraham or Socrates are exemplary. Learning from them will turn my soul, turn my life.

---

[16]See James Kellenberger's helpful discussion, "Indirect Communication," *The International Journal for Philosophy of Religion* 16 (1984).

There is no telling how I absorb the lessons that they convey. As Socrates puts it, "I only wish that wisdom were the kind of thing that flowed from the vessel that was full to the one that was empty."[17] Repeating on cue "The unexamined life is not worth living" will not do for demonstration that Socrates has conveyed something essential to me any more than growing a beard in his likeness would accomplish this feat. Repeating the injunction "Always obey God!" or avowing my willingness to sacrifice what is most dear or climbing Mt. Moriah will not do for demonstration that Abraham has conveyed something essential.

Exemplars teach by setting a pattern that permits *successors*. But whether a student will succeed in establishing that she is *in fact* a successor is not something we can predict. Even retrospectively, it may be unclear whether someone is an heir, inherits the lessons the exemplar lived to teach. How a person today (or yesterday) follows the footsteps of Abraham or Socrates remains an "objective uncertainty," however passionately we may pursue the possibility of following their steps. We pursue exemplars for the possibilities they open. The first and negative phase is stripping something away: we realize we need clues, that we are not equal to every eventuality, that our questions outstrip our answers. Complacency is shattered. The second and positive phase is acquiring new insight, taking new steps, however tentatively, attempting to continue a succession the exemplar founds. Indirect communication knocks out the props and makes space for new ways of being, for transforming the relationships the recipient has to herself, to her world, her companions, her God, her traditions, her history.

An exemplar's life administers freedom and independence through indirect communication. Carrying on in the light of an exemplar is different from carrying on a doctrine, say of natural rights or of original sin, or carrying on a practice, say a ceremony of birth, marriage, or death. A handbook, catechism, or creed can remind us what must be carried on in ceremony or doctrine; we show we've objectively grasped their form by simple repetition. But to carry on in an exemplar's light is to move without a manual of directions or set of patterns to repeat. Accepting exemplars is

---

[17]*Symposium*, 175d.

commitment to them, trust in their light, and hope that one will have the vision and fortitude to see and follow the path they light up. But the path they light will be our *own*.

> No one is so resigned as God; for he communicates in creating, so as by creating to *give* independence over against himself. The highest degree of resignation that a human being can have is to acknowledge the given independence in every man, and after the measure of his ability do all that can in truth be done to help someone preserve it.   (CUP, 1:260)

The independence necessary between persons and the divine is maintained by the artistry of the divine, who on pain of taking freedom withdraws from creation. Just so, the independence—and dependence—necessary between person and person is maintained by their mutually reciprocating artistry and respect.

VII. Exemplars and Portraits

In double reflection, the first thought can be told; and a thought about the thought can also be told. However the intermingling or interpenetration of first and second reflections cannot be told. The relation between thoughts in doubly reflected inwardness is a synthesizing relation that is constitutive of self, or of a strand of self.[18] It is ongoing and thus eludes simple telling partially because a particular self in motion over time is a complex too rich to be exhaustively told. But there is a stronger, logical and not merely contingent basis for the gap between the inwardness of a self and a descriptive portrait of it.

The best portrait (conveyed by extensive and sensitive telling) will not leave the canvas or printed page to become a living self. Producing the reality that is a better self is distinct from producing an isolated portrait or snapshot of a self. What we learn in the light of an exemplar is not captured by doctrine or ceremony or telling, nor yet in narrative portraiture. Such lessons as become articulate are embodied concretely, "speak" through the ongoing existence of an exemplary life. "The [lived] concretion is the relation of the existence categories [thought, passion, imagination,

---

[18]See my *Selves in Discord and Resolve*, esp. chap. 8, for the self-relational web that constitutes a Kierkegaardian self in process.

relation to another, suffering, action] to one another" (CUP, 1:357).[19] These "existence categories" mark dimensions of reflection and action rebounding in embodied inwardness. In a proper synthesis, they jell, achieve dynamic equilibrium or integrity. One's existence crystallizes as a concrete particular.

Climacus writes that we should give *artistic style* to our lives (CUP, 1:357).[20] But sketched and reproduced as our existence, this artistry is clearly *not* a simple continuation of narrowly aesthetic self-portraiture. I can preen or sketch myself without moral striving. Exemplars will have little interest in commemorative or congratulatory self-portraits made to elicit the admiration of others. Portraits that are fanciful, narcissistic, or attached to merely interesting local detail, presentations that generally gloss over the seriousness of existence, are unreliable as ministering or prompting devices (CUP, 1: 358). The aim of ethicoreligious writing is to activate another's subjectivity, to effect a freedom transfer. Drawing one's soul in words or drawing it out in existence must be responsive to what is seriously required of persons—not the eccentric but the "universal" requirements that underlie virtuous, noble, or faithful lives. Thus one can come to exemplify in a text or a life what it could mean for a reader or listener to become true to whomever *they* may be or become. It is the artistry of an exemplar's *life*, its "existence communication," that is crucial.[21]

Climacus wants the universal—what for Hegel would be easily communicated—to be communicated by an existence communication to the particular person. But an "existence communication" is exactly what evades language-as-the-universal.[22] So the universal-

---

[19]See Walsh, *Living Poetically*, 208.

[20]Does this mean we should "sketch our own self-portraits in existence, reproducing in ourselves the human ideals toward which we strive"? Sylvia Walsh puts it this way in *Living Poetically*, 209. But we must distinguish, as Walsh herself does (240-41), merely fanciful self-commentary or self-portraiture from the demands of weaving a concrete life in actual existence.

[21]For the contrast between an "existence-communication" of "the universal" and "merely esthetic" portraiture, see CUP 1:358.

[22]Hence *Fear and Trembling*'s knight of faith, who cannot avail himself of the Hegelian universal-as-language, is consigned to silence. See my discussion in *Knights of Faith and Resignation: Reading Kierkegaard's Fear and Trembling* (Albany: State University of New York Press, 1991) 127-30. And as I have remarked, Plato's

to-be-communicated to the receptive reader is both something simple, say, "the virtuous, noble, or faithful life" and something that can't be said, can only be lived out. The problem of communication can be framed thus as a conundrum about conveying "the universal" to particular persons without the mediation of language-as-the-universal. Indirection then becomes the solution to this conundrum. But the failure of narrative portraiture to achieve the aim of turning round a life can be seen more clearly from another angle. Switching perspectives, the failure can be seen as a matter of disregarding a categorical distinction. An apple most true to its own kind will never be an orange; it *must* fail in this regard. A portrait most true to its kind (most true to what a good portrait must be) will never be a self; it *necessarily* fails to be a self. If the aim of Kierkegaard's and Climacus' writing is to effect a change in selves, then good writing, direct and indirect, can minister or pave the way, but it cannot deliver the goods—that is, write out a better self.

VIII. Indirect Communication: A Summary

The religious individual must avoid direct communication. For one thing, people become defensive when preached at; for another, they should not be responding to the power or charisma of a preacher. But we can approach the impossibility of direct communication from another angle. The life task of an ethicoreligious individual is to communicate an ethicoreligious identity, to express it in word and deed and life. Such an expression cannot be directly communicated for the simple reason that direct communication is communication that by definition leaves out the communicator's subjectivity. Attempting to communicate a decisive moral-religious core *directly*—that is, in disregard of that core—is attempting a logical impossibility; but worse, it is a moral and religious fault.

Climacus wonders how an artist is present (or absent) in his work. Indirect communication can conceal an author's existence to let an art work speak for itself, as when a pseudonym speaks for

---

Socrates finds himself, in a sense, silenced, or at least impeded, in his communications: "I only wish that wisdom were the kind of thing that flowed from the vessel that was full to the one that was empty." *Symposium*, 175d.

himself. The art work calls for interpretation, and so calls on the freedom of the recipient to interpret: it does not wear (all) its meaning on its sleeve. A direct communication is determinant, largely to be rejected or accepted outright, not wondered over or worked on interpretatively. But art works are not alone in speaking to us indirectly in a way eliciting and requiring our freedom of interpretative response. Persons, too, especially exemplary persons, can elicit our interpretative response. They communicate through creating works of art, products to circulate in book shops and museums. But they also elicit our interpretative response through the artistry of their activities and being, by what they say, but also by what they don't say, or by the way they walk or by the way they laugh, or by the way they regard or disregard their children or their friends. Thus an exemplary life speaks, but through the medium of existence, not of art. And what it speaks is more than uttered words.

An author may distance herself in order to let her art work speak, but she may also become an exemplary person whose *life* speaks with artistry. A life itself can be whole (or fissured), open to interpretation (or resisting interpretation) in such a way that author and life-authored coalesce, become inseparable. Socrates does not write, but he is author of his life in a way that makes his artistry indistinguishable from that life; he stands artfully before us eliciting and requiring our response: "The subjective thinker's form [. . .] is his style. . . . His form must first and last be related to existence, and in this regard he must have at his disposal the poetic, the ethical, the dialectical, the religious" (CUP, 1:357). Exemplars solicit our freedom and display virtue. What makes them indirect and not merely direct communicators is their "acting in asserting," the fact that any asserting is woven into a companion context of action and response, these acts and assertings (and questionings and proddings) woven into a wider and extended narrative fabric that is the exemplary life.[23] "The subjective thinker

---

[23]"Acting in asserting" is a phrase Kierkegaard uses in his "Job Discourse," discussed in my *Selves in Discord and Resolve*, chap. 3. Contemporary "speech-act theory" is here anticipated, although Kierkegaard's stress is on a saying's embeddedness in the "act" of an entire *life* rather than its role in a relatively isolated event such as my promise to return a book.

is not a scientist-scholar; he is an artist. To exist is an art. The subjective thinker is aesthetic enough for his life to have aesthetic content, ethical enough to regulate it, dialectical enough in thinking to master it" (CUP, 1:351).

Double reflection allows for a gap between saying and sayer to be exploited by an artist to conceal and reveal; it also allows for a life where that gap has been closed, where saying and sayer are one and exemplary, and, as Kierkegaard will write, the saying is duplicated in the life—or, since a life is ongoing and a saying may be episodic, we have a continuous, numinous and concrete *reduplication* of saying and sayer in the exemplary life.[24]

---

[24]See the role of "reduplication" in Kierkegaard's *Eighteen Upbuilding Discourses*, trans. Howard V. Hong and Edna H. Hong (Princeton: Princeton University Press, 1990) 169, 484-85.

8

Beyond a Joke: Kierkegaard's Concluding Unscientific Postscript *as a Comic Book*

Hugh S. Pyper

I am not a religious person but simply and solely a humorist.
—CUP, 1:501

Concluding Unscientific Postscript is a joke. That in a nutshell is the thesis I wish to put forward here. It presents itself as a joke and it is only by taking its character as such entirely seriously that we can deal in earnest with its message. It is no secret that irony, humor and the comic are featured throughout the book as matters of discussion and have important theoretical status as transitional modes between the stages of existence. The tone of the writing itself is by turns playful, satirical, ironic and mock serious. It is not these features which I propose to deal with directly here, however. Rather, I wish to call attention to the overall structure and presentation of the work. It is at this level, not in the components of its argument and rhetoric, that we shall see that the work is a joke, and, furthermore, that it could be nothing else if it was to be adequate to the task it sets out to perform.

Such a claim is not original. The point is well made by Andrew Burgess in his exhaustive investigation of the category of the comic in Kierkegaard's authorship.[1] He summarizes the findings of his computer-assisted analysis by pointing out the pervasiveness of the theme of the comic throughout most of the authorship, but finds it in particular at those points where the structure of the author-ship is discussed. He sees the whole authorship as essentially

---

[1]Andrew J. Burgess, "A Word-Experiment on the Category of the Comic" in *International Kierkegaard Commentary: The Corsair Affair*, ed. Robert L. Perkins (Macon GA: Mercer University Press, 1990) 85-121.

comic, regarding that category as the most useful of those which Kierkegaard addresses precisely because it is concerned with communication. What is found funny depends on the culture, the values and even the maturity of the listener. This orientation to the listener is what makes the category of the comic so useful to Kierkegaard.

Burgess goes on to relate this specifically to the *Concluding Unscientific Postscript*: "Even such a massive philosophical piece is written from the standpoint of the subject—specifically, the subject who is wondering about the problem of becoming Christian. It comes as no surprise, then, that an everyday conception of the comic fits the pattern of the *Postscript* without modification when it is used to describe what the *Postscript* is doing. . . . at the right time, *Postscript* may be a colossal joke."[2] It is this claim which is the purpose of this paper to develop.

To plead such a case calls for doughty advocates. In the brief compass of this discussion, two will furnish us with the bulk of our support. Firstly we shall turn to Gérard Genette, who in his book *Seuils*[3] has undertaken a witty and comprehensive analysis of what he terms the "paratext." This he defines as "that by which the text makes itself a book, and offers itself as such to its readers, and more generally to the public."[4] The term covers title, dedication, editorial matter, prefaces, footnotes, epigraphs—all the attendant matter of the text. It can, of course, itself be part of the fiction it accompanies. Sir Walter Scott's elaborate devices of fictional editors and correspondents to whom the text is addressed form an instance of this. Yet the point is that, fictional or not, these devices serve to entice, to orientate or indeed to disorient the reader.

It is in these supplements that we may find what a Freudian might term "the return of the repressed" where things are said that are excluded from the main text and yet have to be stated, matters the author may be uneasy about which cannot quite be hidden. As with a conjuror's feint, the device of the preface, the appendix, the footnote, may be used to distract the audience's

---

[2]Burgess, "Word Experiment," 118, 119.
[3]Gérard Genette, *Seuils* (Paris: Éditions du Seuil, 1987).
[4]Genette, *Seuils*, 7.

attention from the real sleight of hand of his or her discourse. As we marvel at the illusion the text produces, the mundane mechanism at work may be hidden in the margins of our perception.

Kierkegaard's work shows more than an awareness of this principle. Indeed, at the end of the *Postscript* we find it spelled out that if a man loudly proclaims his opinion, the ironist will find, not in what is "written in large letters" but in a subordinate clause, or a "hinting little predicate" (CUP, 1:615), the evidence that the good man is not of this opinion.

This hint itself confirms *Concluding Unscientific Postscript* as a prime site for the investigation of the paratextual. It is self-confessedly a supplementary text. It presents itself as a "Postscript," as an addendum, to the *Philosophical Fragments*. This presentation, already clear in the title, is developed further in the attendant texts to the book. It has a cluster of these, like the moons round a planet: a preface, an introduction, and a two-part appendix, consisting of "An Understanding with the Reader" and "A First and Last Explanation." This "concluding unscientific postscript" itself concludes with not one but two postscripts and we will see later how inconclusive these are.

The title of a book is for Genette the first and all-important means of attracting the reader. Kierkegaard's title *Afsluttende uvidenskabelig Efterskrift* is what Genette terms a *rhematic* rather than a *thematic* title.[5] By this is meant that it is related to the form rather than the content of the book, informing the reader what it is and how it says it rather than what its contents are. Once again, the validity of focusing on the structure of the book is confirmed. As an enticement to the casual reader, however, this title verges on the self-defeating. What interest it does raise is perhaps in its very quaintness, raising the possibility of self-parody.[6]

---

[5]Genette, *Seuils*, 82.

[6]In the "Editor's Preface" to the 1941 translation of the *Postscript*, Walter Lowrie recounts David Swenson's tale that "attracted by the quaint name of a book *Concluding Unscientific Postscript to the "Philosophical Fragments"* he took the book home and "read it all that night and all the next day, with the profoundest emotion." *Concluding Unscientific Postscript*, trans. David F. Swenson and Walter Lowrie (Princeton: Princeton University Press, 1941) xi.

Furthermore, all the terms of this title are susceptible to various translations. *Afsluttende* carries the same ambiguity as the English "Concluding"—it can refer to that which brings something to an end in formal terms but also to the drawing of conclusions, the provision of a solution to a problem. *Uvidenskabelig* is not simply "unscientific" but covers a much wider range which in the context might bear the translations "unsystematic" or "unscholarly." The verb *efterskrive* in Danish carries not just the etymologically straightforward connotation of "after-writing" (*postscriptum*) but the derived meaning of "forgery" or "counterfeit." "Final unscholarly forgery" may be a forced translation, but it emphasizes the point that none of the terms present the contents in a positive light.

Of course these three words do not comprise the whole title. The full title explains that this is the postscript to the *Philosophical Fragments*. Immediately the casual reader is put off by the hint that she or he had better read that work first. Quite apart from that implication, this brings us to a series of questions over the consequences of describing any work as a "Postscript."

Genette discusses postscripts under the title of *postfaces*.[7] He characterizes them as the point at which an author may say to his reader "Now you know as much as I do; let's chat." He points out that they lack two vital functions of a preface. Coming after the work, they cannot serve "to gain or to guide the reader," as Genette puts it, to tell him or her why and how to read the text. The postface can only hope to have either a curative or a corrective function. A whole work set up as a "postscript" then seems to hold out relatively little prospect of enlightenment to its readers as it can only serve to regulate their reading of another prior work.

If Genette's generalizations hold out no great hopes for such a work, the internal account of the genesis of this specific postscript is, if anything, less encouraging. In the introduction, it is explained that the *Postscript* is the fruit of a casual promise of a sequel to *Philosophical Fragments*, although indeed a promise which the

---

[7]Genette, *Seuils*, 219.

writer had already matter in hand to fulfil.[8] As such, the sequel is a work which, so Climacus argues, "every young graduate in theology" (CUP, 1:10) will be capable of writing. When Climacus praises *Philosophical Fragments* for not following the "feminine practice of saying the most important thing in a postscript" (CUP, 1:11), he again by implication seems to reduce the importance of the *Postscript*. Even the length of the book seems to be an arbitrary and therefore not particularly significant matter. In one sense, the book could be of minimal length as it does not develop the thought. In another it could be an endless supplement as it is presented as the accumulation of historical detail around the issue. The whole book, then, could be seen as a potentially infinite accumulation of learned footnotes, where the real issue is ultimately not enhanced but submerged in the mass of material, where the footnotes, so to speak, occupy the place of the text and relegate the question to be addressed to the margins.

How much harder, we might ask, could an author try to put a reader off reading his book? The answer turns out to be: "quite a lot." The introduction then moves into a warning against the power of the introduction. We are presented with the examples of the orator, who bedazzles his hearer with the power of his eloquence without ever dealing with the issue, the systematician, who promises that all will become clear at the end, but who also confesses the end has not yet been reached, and the scholar who confuses a striving toward perfection with a striving toward the issue (CUP, 1:12). An introduction which warns against introductions is an archetypally self-consuming text. Finally, however, Johannes Climacus presents the issue to be dealt with in the *Postscript*: the question as to how he, Johannes Climacus, is to share in the happiness that Christianity presents.

> I, Johannes Climacus, born and bred in this city and now thirty years old, an ordinary human being like most folk, assume that a highest good, called an eternal happiness, awaits me just as it awaits a housemaid and a professor. I have heard that Christiani-

---

[8]The promise occurs in this remark near the end of *Philosophical Fragments*: "[I]n the next section of this pamphlet, if I ever do write it, I intend to call the matter by its proper name and clothe the issue in its historical costume" (PF, 109).

ty is one's prerequisite for this good. I now ask how I may enter
into relation to this doctrine.   (CUP, 1:15-16)

To present the question in this way is not immodesty, he claims,
but "merely a kind of lunacy" (CUP, 1:17). Presumably, then, the
ensuing book is the product of an act of lunacy. Again, this is not
obviously a selling point. Here at last, however, we have some
prospect of interest. We are offered a question and thereby enticed
with the implicit promise of an answer. The quest for this answer
may sustain us through the bulk of the book's argument.

What then are the reader's feelings when finally the first
postscript to the *Postscript*, "An Understanding with the Reader,"
is reached (CUP, 1:617)? In this "Understanding" Climacus admits,
before the accusation can be made, that this whole book has been
superfluous. Moreover, he asks that no one bother to appeal to it,
because it contains a notice of its revocation: "What I write
contains the notice that everything is to be understood in such a
way as it is revoked" (CUP, 1:619).

This remark might justify the fact that so far our discussion has
hardly touched upon the main text of the *Postscript*. Johannes
Climacus has pulled the rug from under the reader's feet and has
told us not to bother citing the text. What kind of a trick is this?
The reader who has diligently waded through the text, and few
readers will not find it quite hard going at times, is entitled to feel
a little cheated. Where is the answer to the question that Climacus
posed which induced us to devote our attention to reading this
text?

One reader who clearly reflects this sense of being deceived by
the *Postscript* is Derrida. He cites the paratextual apparatus of
Concluding Unscientific Postscript in a long footnote to his characteristically vertiginous essay on the paratextual which itself forms a
self-consuming preface to the collection *Dissemination*.[9] With the
Postscript very much in the wings, he writes of the claim inherent
in a postface to provide the truth of the preceding discourse. He
then turns to the status of a pretended postscript: "The *simulacrum*
of a postface would therefore consist of feigning the final revela-

---

[9]Jacques Derrida, *Dissemination*, trans. Barbara Johnson (London: Athlone
Press, 1981) 1-51.

tion of the meaning or functioning of a given stretch of language."[10] But there is a further twist when such a simulacrum is playacted. "While pretending to turn around and look backward, one is also in fact starting again, adding an extra text, complicating the scene, opening up within the labyrinth a supplementary digression, which is also a false mirror that pushes the labyrinth's infinity back forever in mimed, that is endless, speculation."[11] If this is so, then such a feigned "concluding postscript" is an oxymoron. Far from concluding the discourse, it opens up an endless speculation.

Whatever its general validity, this reads as a fairly straightforward account of what seems to be going on in *Concluding Unscientific Postscript*. The *Postscript* purports to tie the themes of the *Philosophical Fragments* to the historical and then all responsibility is disclaimed. The "First and Last Understanding," at least at first sight, serves to reveal not the meaning but the meaninglessness of the foregoing text.

We might well feel inclined to echo the words of Lewis Carroll's Alice at this point. Excited by the prospect of a riddle when the Mad Hatter asks her, "Why is a raven like a writing desk?" Alice is exasperated when eventually the Hatter and the March Hare confess blithely that they haven't the slightest idea of the answer: "Alice sighed wearily. 'I do think you might do something better with the time,' she said, 'than waste it in asking riddles that have no answers'."[12]

Indeed, but it is precisely at this point that another line of attack on this problem may prove fruitful. Just this problem of why anyone would waste time on such a pursuit is taken up by Sigmund Freud, the second of our champions. In a footnote added in 1912 to his *Jokes and their Relation to the Unconscious*, he tells the story of a man at dinner who dips his hands in mayonnaise, runs them through his hair and then, seeming to notice his mistake, re-

---

[10]Derrida, *Dissemination*, 27n.27.

[11]Derrida, *Dissemination*, 28n.27.

[12]Lewis Carroll, *Alice's Adventures in Wonderland* and *Through the Looking Glass* (Harmondsworth: Puffin, 1962) 96.

marks to his neighbor, "I'm sorry, I thought it was spinach."[13] Why would anyone make such an absurd and meaningless remark?

Rather startlingly, a remarkably similar story is to be found in an inordinately long footnote in *Concluding Unscientific Postscript* (CUP, 1:514-19). Climacus gives a series of random examples to demonstrate his contention that the comic is present wherever there is contradiction and where one justifiably avoids the pain of the contradiction because it is inessential. Amongst these examples is the rather odd incident of an absentminded man who reaches his hand into a spinach casserole and then, realizing his mistake, excuses himself by saying, "Oh, I thought it was caviar" (CUP, 1:516).

How intriguing, given what we have been saying about the importance of the marginal, that both these writers have hit upon a very similar joke and that both have thought fit to place it in a footnote, in Freud's case in a footnote to a footnote. What grist to the mill of a deconstructive critic for whom, as Christopher Norris writes:

> [I]t is often in the margins or obscure minor passages of a text—in the footnotes, perhaps, or a casual parenthesis—that its strains and contradictions stand most clearly revealed. . . . The very fact that they bear a problematic relation to the rest of an author's work—or beyond that to the ruling assumptions of philosophic discourse—may have caused them to be tucked away out of sight in a footnote or simply passed over by commentators in search of more enduring truths. It is precisely by seizing on such uncanonical texts, passages or details that deconstruction seeks to resist the homogenizing pressure of received ideas.[14]

What then do the two make of this story? In Freud's account, this exchange counts as "idiocy masquerading as a joke."[15] Climacus, in a wonderfully Kierkegaardian phrase, regards it as absentmindedness "raised to the second power" (CUP, 1:516n). Their contrasted reactions make the point that the same comic narrative affects different hearers rather differently. Freud reads it

---

[13]Sigmund Freud, *Jokes and their Relation to the Unconscious*, Pelican Freud Library 6, trans. James Strachey (Harmondsworth: Penguin, 1976) 190n.1.

[14]Christopher Norris, *Derrida* (London: Fontana 1987) 134.

[15]Freud, *Jokes*, 190n.1.

as a deliberate, and indeed somewhat malevolent, attempt to discomfit the hearer, whereas Climacus sees it as a rather endearingly compounded form of distraction.

The matter of the reception of such tales will occupy us further, but for the present let us remain with the problem of the motivation of the teller. Freud gives what could well stand as two separate accounts of the pleasure afforded to the teller. Firstly, this mechanism allows the pleasure of spouting nonsense to be liberated. Secondly, the teller gains pleasure from misleading and annoying his listener, who can salvage some satisfaction from resolving to tell the story in his turn. Here we find the fundamental principles of Freud's analysis of the function of jokes. The pleasure of jokes consists in the lifting of inhibitions, either inhibitions which enforce the "proper" use of language or inhibitions about the subjects which can be spoken of. Freud tends to focus on puns and other plays on words where he sees a principle of economy at work. At a purely verbal level, by making one lexical item perform several semantic functions, the joke economizes on effort, and the excess energy is liberated in the form of laughter. At the level of meaning, the joke may allow an "economy of affect." In other words, serious and troubling matters are spoken of in a way which deflects attention from their emotional import, again liberating emotional energy in the form of laughter. Puzzling over the verbal conundrum to find the "thought content" of the joke deflects attention from the emotional content.

Samuel Weber,[16] however, homes in on this particular story which Freud appends as a footnote to a footnote with deconstructive zeal. Why does Freud feel he has to supplement his text with this absurd story? Weber's answer is that in such nonsense jokes there is *no* thought content. The joke works, if it does, by refusing the attempt to sort out a sensible meaning from the verbal play. Freud, Weber argues, was driven to add this supplementary footnote because this strange form of joke, a joke which is playing with the conventions of joking, threatened to undermine the elaborate account of humor that Freud propounded.

---

[16]Samuel Weber, *The Legend of Freud* (Minneapolis: University of Minnesota Press, 1982) 113-14.

Weber uses the term "shaggy dog story" to describe this form of humor. He seems to be focusing on the refusal of the traditional shaggy dog story to offer the kind of neat condensation of language in a "punch line" that is the promise of the standard joke. This is only part of the story, however. The art of the shaggy dog story is not simply that it is a meta-joke, a joke on the conventions of joking, but also that it parodies narrative conventions.

Freud makes much, as we have seen, of the importance of condensation and economy in the joke work: brevity is the soul of wit. The shaggy dog story, on the other hand, makes a virtue of its ability to spin out the thread of the listener's attention to the greatest length possible with the least expenditure of material. It is narrative at its most ductile. If we follow the line of Peter Brooks in his *Reading for the Plot*,[17] the listener's engagement in any narrative depends both on the promise of closure and on the deferral of that closure. Narrative happens in the space between the promise and the fulfillment. But this is true not only of narrative but of any sustained utterance.

In such terms, *Concluding Unscientific Postscript* can be seen as a prime example of a shaggy dog story, indeed a St Bernard amongst such stories. It does not have a conventional plot, perhaps, but it is set up as providing the answer to the question Climacus has posed himself. Even the simple promise to answer a question sets up a tension of expectation and fulfillment, in itself sufficiently engaging to underpin countless quiz shows on television, all the more so when the reward of the question answered is coupled to the offer of a cruise to the Bahamas. The joke, or what is set up as a joke, operates in the same way, offering not only the promise of closure, but the additional reward of laughter, of the pleasure of the effects that Freud enumerates in his consideration of humor. A comic narrative can then be spun out perilously far because the reward at the end is not simply the answer to a question but also the catharsis of laughter.

---

[17]Peter Brooks, *Reading for the Plot: Design and Intention in Narrative* (Cambridge MA: Harvard University Press, 1992). See esp. chap. 4, "Freud's Masterplot: A Model for Narrative."

The shaggy dog story gains its effect from its ability to hold the listener's attention with the promise of such a reward which at the end it withholds, leaving the listener with a banal denouement. The genre, however, would not survive long if the only reward was for the teller to pull a fast one on the listener and for the listener perhaps to join ruefully in the laughter as he realizes that he has been fooled. The listener may well be aware that this is the game and be intrigued by watching the teller's skill in spinning out the story, by a sense of complicity in the overturning of a convention and even by the skill in which false clues are laid which lead to the bathetic climax. The stories need be neither the rather malicious assault on the listener that Freud seems to envisage, nor simply a product of absentmindedness, as in Kierkegaard's reading.

It seems to me that *Concluding Unscientific Postscript* is quite consciously set up as a philosophical/theological shaggy dog story, something that promises a conclusion which it then withdraws but which offers another sort of reward to its readers—the incidental rewards of watching the master strategist at work, the rewards of humor, but also a supplementary pleasure, something that takes it beyond a joke.

As such, however, is it not simply a hypersubtle and highly artificial device, remote from any serious engagement with philosophical issues and a mere irresponsible game with language? I believe that the opposite is the case. Both Freud and Kierkegaard offer support to the view that in fact a text such as the *Postscript* offers a clear view of how the comic is not a parasitic form of language and discourse but a window into the intrinsic limitations and possibilities of what language can do. The comic, Climacus argues, is all-pervasive. "On the whole," he writes, "the comic is everywhere" (CUP, 1:462)—although we should not miss the hint of contradiction and the comic in the juxtaposition of "on the whole" and "everywhere." Nevertheless, such a statement surely argues for caution in designating the comic as in any sense parasitic on language.

This insight is borne out by Freud's account of the aetiology of the comic.[18] He argues that the first function of speech is pleasure. The child gains physical satisfaction from trying out his or her developing speech organs and from the aural stimulation of chiming sounds and the effort of mimicry. The notion of responsible speech, of answering or posing a question which could be answered, one form of speech production which seems to entail another, is a derived state. The comic for Freud gains its place in adult discourse because it allows for the temporary lifting of the inhibitions which adult responsibility places upon us. In this sense, the "serious" use of language is derived from the playful.

The change that comes about in the development from childhood is also discussed in the unfinished work *Johannes Climacus*. There is consciousness in the child, but doubt is outside it, Kierkegaard reports Climacus as arguing. This means that for the child, who is immediacy, everything is true, but at the same moment everything is untrue. Immediacy cancels the question of truth. As soon as the question of truth arises, so does untruth. Indeed, so Climacus argues, it is untruth that makes it possible for consciousness to be brought into relation with something else. For Climacus, the agency by which this is brought about is language. This is spelled out rather cryptically at the beginning of the second part of *Johannes Climacus*, where Johannes is confronted with the question as to whether mediacy or immediacy comes first. Which is parasitic on the other? This he dismisses as a nonquestion, as by the time that consciousness is in place to ask the question, the two are mutually coimplicated. "Immediacy is reality, language is ideality, consciousness is contradiction. The moment I make a statement about reality, contradiction is present, for what I say is ideality" (JC, 168). If contradiction is present, then so is the potential for the comic as Climacus defines the comic as an apprehension of contradiction.

The heart of language is contradiction—saying against. We speak not to mimic a static world but to bring about change in a world in flux. What we say always "speaks against" a situation, always counters another and encounters another. Both comedy and

---

[18]Freud, *Jokes*, 174-75.

tragedy arise from this opposition of language and world. How many of the great tragedies turn upon a vow, a promise, an oracle or prophecy which lures the hero into an inexorable and crushing collision between word and world. The tragic hero despairs of the way out of this contradiction and dies. The comic, however, holds to the way out—the clever parry of the quip, the verbal feint, the disguise adopted and then shed. The union of the tragic and the comic is in this fundamental characteristic of language, in the fundamental structure of communication. Neither the comic nor the tragic is a parasitic or derived function of language. Rather it is the neat formulations of the systematists and the polite platitudes of social discourse which are the parasites on language which leach it of its passion.

So both Freud and Kierkegaard can be adduced as witnesses to the fundamental role of the comic in language. That being said, Freud's principal concern in his book on jokes is to account for the fact that jokes have to be *told*. Given the function of the comic in language and the apprehension of the comic in contradiction, we have yet to account for the need to tell a joke to another party in order to make that person laugh. What lies behind this apparent compulsion to communicate? Ordinarily, those who tell jokes do not laugh at their own witticism and so this need to repeat the joke is not a simple need for the teller to experience again the pleasure of the catharsis the joke offers. What kind of transaction, then, is involved here? In terms of the *Concluding Unscientific Postscript*, what leads to the writing of the work? Why does this joke need to be told?

The title of the chapter where Freud's discussion is to be found itself bears out this aspect of the question: "The Motives of Jokes—Jokes as a social process."[19] Freud insists on the transactional nature of humor. The joke in the end depends on the hearer, what Freud calls the "third person." The "second person," which need not be a person, is the subject of the joke. As his analysis progresses, Freud gives increasing weight to this audience. In the end, it is the listener who makes or breaks the joke. A joke, he says, is a "double-dealing rascal which serves two masters at

---

[19]Freud, *Jokes*, 191-211.

once."[20] Everything in jokes that is aimed at gaining pleasure is calculated with an eye to the third person, to the audience, as though there were internal and insurmountable obstacles in the way of that pleasure in the first person. He concludes that we are compelled to tell a joke to another person precisely *because* we are unable to laugh at it ourselves.[21] It is the hearer's laughter which liberates the teller.

It is not ultimately in the control of the teller of the joke whether the listener will laugh. Jokes, indeed, provide a fascinating case of the negotiation of authority in language. Laughter is to an extent involuntary, and a good comedian can reduce us to a state of "helpless laughter." However, the same comedian may well "die" in front of a different audience which sees no reason to laugh or may be offended rather than amused by his or her material. So, paradoxically, the comedian makes the audience laugh but cannot *make* them laugh. She or he is more than the simple occasion for laughter—she or he has an intention of causing laughter and a repertoire of techniques to draw on,—but the teller cannot guarantee success.

We have already quoted Burgess on the importance of the joke as the epitome of communication for Kierkegaard. A quotation from *Stages on Life's Way* makes this point succinctly. "To believe the ideality on the word of another is like laughing at a joke not because one has understood it but because someone else has said it was funny. In that case, the joke can really be omitted for the person who laughs on the basis of belief and respect; he is able to laugh with equal *Emphasis* [significance]" (SLW, 438-39). Here Kierkegaard uses the example of jest as the clearest instance of the role of the subjective in the receipt of communication. It also neatly reveals the essential fallacy of Climacus' strategy in the *Postscript* and therefore the necessity of its revocation. Why do we read the *Postscript* if it is not in some sense to believe on the word of another? The joke has to be made so that the effect of omitting it can be made clear. The truly comic is not the contradiction between Climacus' aims and the impossibility of their achievement,

---

[20]Freud, *Jokes*, 208.
[21]Freud, *Jokes*, 209.

but between the infinite and the finite, between the ideal and the actual.

The fact that the work which promises to answer Climacus' question turns out to have been a joke is not simply the result of an elaborate evasion of Climacus' question. The question posed by Climacus is such that it could only lead to an absurd answer and a revocation. Superficially, it may seem plausible, even important, but it is an impossible formulation. Climacus defends his question on the grounds that, unlike the dry objectivity of the systematicians who only ask what Christianity is, his concern is with the central issue of the subjectivity of Christianity. If that is his aim, then his question rests on assumptions as absurd as the explanation that accounts for dipping one's hand in spinach by explaining that one thought it was caviar. He wants to know how he can gain the goods of Christianity without gaining the goods, or, in other words, how he can receive the benefits of the transformation wrought by Christianity without being himself transformed. Johannes Climacus is to undergo the transformation of Christianity but somewhere, the old Johannes must persist in order to be able to act as reporter and commentator on the process.

There is no way in which the question how to gain the goods of Christianity can be posed as such an item of discussion. It is not possible on Climacus' own account to inspect the life of the religious as it consists in hiddenness. One might as well ask why a raven is like a writing desk. Unless one knows the answer, there is little point in posing the riddle. As *Philosophical Fragments* points out, the answer is a matter of infinite interest, not simply a piece of knowledge to catalogue alongside others. There is no way in which the question as posed could be intelligibly answered. That is the basic point which the elaborate devices of the *Postscript* are designed to bring home to the reader, who, if he or she is intrigued by the title of the book, may well be the kind of interested but detached, humorous individual who takes the absurdity of Climacus' question seriously. As we have seen, the title itself together with the other paratextual features make the book attractive to those who share delight in the subversive power of language, in the clever manipulation of literary conventions, in a sense of irony. A particular readership has been winnowed out, a readership which is in sympathy with Johannes Climacus and who may well fall into the same kind of absurdity to which he is prone.

This absurdity, however cannot be communicated directly. The obstacle to plain speech here is not simply an inhibition, an imposition of the ego on the unconscious as Freud would have it, but the category of the absurd. Humor and the comic are the results of the realization of the contradiction, the incommensurability, between the finite and the infinite, the human and the divine, made concrete in the figure of the God-man. Where Freud accounts for humor and the role of the jest in terms of an interplay between different aspects of the individual human mind mediated through communication, Kierkegaard's thinking starts from the possibility of communication and an account of human being which sees it as characterized by its relation to the eternal and the infinite.

Burgess points out, however, that the danger in designating the authorship as comic is that it all too easily lays one open to the very trap that Kierkegaard was so concerned to point out and which the *Corsair* epitomized: a too easy definition of the comic. Kierkegaard's papers reveal that the *Concluding Unscientific Postscript* was intended originally literally to conclude the authorship (JP, 5:5873). In this work, he had gone as far as he could to lead the reader to the brink of the religious, trusting to the reader's apprehension of the true comic which embraces both jest and earnestness.

Arguably, it was the realization of the error of this presupposition which prompted him to continue his writing in a new way, discarding the devices of pseudonymity and indirection. It was immediately after the publication of *Concluding Unscientific Postscript* that he became embroiled with the satirical magazine, the *Corsair*. In response to the ridicule that he was subjected to as a result of this affair, with heavy irony Kierkegaard records his former opinion that the most difficult task is "to deal with the comic in fear and trembling." As such, it follows that only a few are truly capable of the comic. Now he is told that things are the other way round. Everyone else in Denmark is capable of the comic and he stands out by his renunciation of any reputation for the comic (COR, 179). "As a matter of fact, everybody in Copenhagen but me understands the comic," he concludes sourly (COR, 188).

The key to the comic is contradiction, but this is also the condition for the tragic. The difference, according to Climacus, is that the comic vision always has its eye on the way out. "The tragic is suffering contradiction and the comic is painless contradiction" (CUP, 1:514). It knows there is an escape from the contradiction whereas the tragic vision does not and therefore despairs over the way out. The illegitimate comic, however, consists in holding to an illusory way out, either a fantastic resolution of the contradiction, or a failure to appreciate the nature of the contradiction. The trouble with a comic book is that it may encourage people in an illegitimate apprehension of the comic.

In the end, the reader always has a way out of a book—he or she can simply stop reading it. In this sense, it is possible to read *Concluding Unscientific Postscript* as purely a comic book that provides its own way out in its reiterated insistence that it is not even worth reading. We might even share Freud's verdict of such a production and see it as "idiocy masquerading as a joke." We can shut the book—and go home. A book can only ever be an occasion, a transaction. *Concluding Unscientific Postscript* is not unique in this. It shares this characteristic in common with all books. To pretend otherwise would involve a contradiction between what the book claimed and what it could do, in itself enough to qualify it as a joke. What it does evince is a particular self-conscious reduplication of the joke which can recall us from our absentmindedness.

Yet it may be that the book itself becomes the occasion that brings us face to face with the contradiction at the heart of our very notion of our selves. In that sense, it may prompt us to go beyond the joke. The religious is something beyond both the comic and the tragic. Abraham, for instance acts in the hope of a resolution of the dilemma of losing his son or obeying God in the knowledge that there is humanly speaking, no way out. That sense cannot be communicated, but only lived. As soon as religiousness manifests itself, it becomes legitimate material for the comic. Climacus indicates that on the level of the apparent, the humorous is the highest state in that it sees clearly the contraction between the inner and the outer, but the truly religious category is defended "by the comic against the comic" (CUP, 1:522). Religiousness escapes the comic by incorporating it and so as a higher principle is defended against it. Because religiousness is hidden, it cannot come into contradiction with anything and therefore is immune from the comic.

The nearness of the existing humorist and the religious is to be seen in their common awareness that suffering is not an accident of existence but something that stands in essential relation to existing. The humorist is aware of this, but makes the "deceptive turn" by revoking everything in jest. "He touches the secret of existence in the pain but then he goes home again" (CUP, 1:447). "The ironist levels everything on the basis of abstract humanity; the humorist on the basis of the abstract relation with God, inasmuch as he does not enter into the relationship with God. It is precisely there that he parries with a jest" (CUP, 1:448n).

The humorist is quoted as refusing to attempt to answer the riddle of existence as, in the end, the one who proposed it will answer it anyway. Climacus uses the simile of the riddle printed in a daily paper with the answer printed the next day, accompanied by the name of an old maid who had guessed the riddle. But as the answer is printed, the humorist argues, she only anticipates common knowledge by one day (CUP, 1: 451). Of course, the fallacy in this is to assume that the important thing is to add the answer to the riddle to one's stock of knowledge. The important thing, surely, is not what the answer is, but arriving at the answer, even if that answer is no answer. Kierkegaard offers the reader the opportunity to enact that experience.

The ideal reader to whom Climacus addresses himself in the "Understanding" will understand that "to write a book and to revoke it is not the same as refraining from writing it" (CUP, 1:621). To elaborate a theory of humor, as the *Postscript* does, is one thing, but it is another to see the joke. When the book is revoked, the theory of humor still stands, for those who have the leisure to be interested in such things, and a very illuminating theory it is. But as an answer to Climacus's question, it only goes to show that the question could not be asked, and so, therefore, the whole enterprise has to be erased. Yet, as in mathematics, arriving at an absurd answer which needs to be rubbed out may not solve the immediate question, but may well be an important moment in learning to see how the problem is to be tackled. It may also be an important lesson in persistence and serious engagement.

The humorist, says Climacus, knows the depth of suffering—and then goes home. The religious consciousness, however, has no home to go to. There is still a barrier between the humorist's consciousness of the contradiction and his or her sense of that consciousness. For the religious, that contradiction is constitutive of the consciousness that is aware of it.

Thus there is no place for the religious to evade the contradiction which the humorist knows but does not yet live. There is no way to evade being posed the riddle which only God can answer. The humorist may close the book and walk away. The religious reader is left living the unanswered riddle.

9

The Reality of the World
in Kierkegaard's Postscript[1]

M. G. Piety

The objective of this paper is to debunk the long-standing myth that the metaphysics of Kierkegaard's *Concluding Unscientific Post-script* is fundamentally antirealist, or "acosmic." One of the most respected statements of this view is Louis Mackey's article, "The Loss of the World in Kierkegaard's Ethics,"[2] so I shall use it as the point of departure for the present essay.

Mackey begins his article by acknowledging that Kierkegaard's metaphysics are basically realist.[3] He argues, however, that this realism is implicitly contradicted by two remarks in the *Postscript* that are central to the argument of this book: "(1) The ethical reality of the subject is the only reality. (2) All realities other than his own, the subject encounters only in the mode of possibility, by thinking them."[4]

The difficulty, argues Mackey, is that the claim that one encounters the reality of others only in terms of possibility appears to imply that other people cannot affect one directly. More particularly, it appears to imply that the presence of other people cannot directly require that one relate to them ethically. One may

---

[1]This paper has benefitted greatly from criticisms and revisions suggested by Paul A. Bauer, Hubert L. Dreyfus, George Pattison, and Robert L. Perkins.

[2]Louis Mackey, "The Loss of the World in Kierkegaard's Ethics," *Review of Metaphysics* 15/4 (June 1962): 602-20. Repr. first in *Kierkegaard: A Collection of Critical Essays*, ed. Josiah Thompson (Garden City NJ: Doubleday & Co./Anchor Paperback, 1972) 266-88; and then in Louis Mackey, *Points of View* (Tallahassee: Florida State University Press, 1986). Subsequent references to this article will be to *Points of View*.

[3]Cf. Mackey, *Points of View*, 145.

[4]Ibid., 143.

choose to behave ethically toward the people with whom one comes into contact, but the operative word here appears to be "choose." That is, it appears the claim that one is related to the reality of others only in terms of possibility implies one is absolutely free to choose to relate to them ethically or not as one pleases. It thus appears that ethical commitment, on Climacus's view, is generated from the individual's freedom alone rather than from the response of the individual to the reality of the needs of others or of the ethical demand itself.[5] That is, it appears that the reality of the world drops out of the ethics of the *Postscript*.

It is clear, however, that Johannes Climacus, the pseudonymous author of the *Postscript*, did not intend his remarks to be interpreted in this way. "[T]o make the subjective individual's ethical actuality the only actuality," he observes, "could seem to be acosmism. That it will so appear to a busy thinker who must explain everything, a hasty pate who traverses the whole world, demonstrates only that he has a very poor idea of what the ethical means for the subjective individual" (CUP, 1:341).

I will argue that the purported acosmism of the *Postscript* has its roots in the confusion of epistemological with ontological issues as well as in the mistaken supposition that Climacus subscribes to the existentialist view that human freedom is absolute. The metaphysics of the *Postscript*, I will argue, is inherently realist and it is this realism which provides the foundation for the views on ethics that are expressed in this work.

1. Reality and Actuality

What must be addressed first is whether the remarks in the *Postscript* which provide the foundation for the charge that this work is fundamentally acosmic will, in fact, support such an interpretation. The first difficulty concerns the fact that Climacus never claims that the only reality there is for an existing individual is his own ethical reality. What he claims is that "[t]he only *actuality* [*Virkelighed*] there is for an existing person is his own ethical actuality" (CUP, 1:316).[6]

---

[5]Cf. ibid., 152.
[6]Emphasis added.

"Reality" (*Realitet*) and "actuality" (*Virkelighed*) have been assumed by English-speaking Kierkegaard scholars in the past to be synonymous in Kierkegaard's authorship.[7] This is undoubtedly a result of the fact that the Danish "*Virkelighed*" was often translated as "reality" rather than actuality in the first English translations of Kierkegaard.[8] It is, however, now nearly universally agreed that these expressions are *not* synonymous.[9] "Reality," Gregor Malantschuk argues, refers, according to Kierkegaard, to the "presence [*tilstedeværelse*]" of a thing "without any further determination of how it came to be there,"[10] whereas, "actuality" is always the result of a process of actualization.[11] Ideas, according to Kierkegaard, have reality as such and so does every *created* thing, but only the latter have actuality as well.[12] That is, only the latter have "come into existence" (PF, 74).

This distinction between reality and actuality can be seen in Climacus's remark in the *Postscript* that "[e]xistence is always the particular; the abstract," he argues, "does not *exist* [*existerer ikke*]" To conclude from this, he continues however, "that the abstract does not have reality [*Realitet*] is a misunderstanding" (CUP, 1:330).

The reality of the world is never questioned by Climacus. One cannot help but believe in the reality of the world on his view.[13]

---

[7]Cf., e.g., Mackey, *Points of View*, 146n.4.

[8]Cf. ibid., and *Postscript*, Swenson-Lowrie translation, 292.

[9]Cf., e.g., Robert Widenman, "Kierkegaard's Terminology and English," *Kierkegaardiana* 7 (1968): 116-18; Gregor Malantschuk, *Nøglebegreber i Søren Kierkegaards tænkning*, ed. Grethe Kjær and Paul Müller (Copenhagen: C. A. Reitzel, 1993) 210-12, and Anton Hügli, *Die Erkenntnis der Subjektivität und die Objektivität des Erkennens bei Søren Kierkegaard*, Basler Beiträge zur Philosophie und Ihrer Geschichte (Basel: Editio Academica, 1973) 103.

[10]Malantschuk, *Nøglebegreber i Søren Kierkegaards tænkning*, 210. Unless otherwise noted, all translations are my own.

[11]Ibid., 210. Cf. PF, 73-75 (i.e., the section entitled "Coming Into Existence").

[12]Cf., e.g., JP 2:1587 (The translation of this entry is highly problematic. Considerations of space do not permit a detailed explication of it here. It will thus suffice to direct the reader to the original text.); CUP, 1:330; Mackey, *Points of View*, 146n.; Malantschuk, *Nøglebegreber i Søren Kierkegaards tænkning*, 210-12; and Widenman, "Kierkegaard's Terminology and English," 116.

[13]Cf. C. Stephen Evans on how genuine skepticism is impossible according to Climacus: "Kierkegaard and Plantinga on Belief in God: Subjectivity as the

The reality of other people is thus self-evident according to Climacus. Assurance, he asserts, that the people with whom one comes into contact are really there is equivalent to one's sense impressions of these individuals.[14] It is "nonsense" he argues, for example, to demand of someone with whom one comes into contact that he or she prove he or she is "really there [*er til*]" (CUP, 1:39).[15] A person's actuality is not equivalent, however, to his mere presence. It is not something that can be sensed. "Actuality," according to Climacus, "is interiority infinitely interested in existing" (CUP, 1:325).

Just as the reality of the world is simply assumed by Climacus, so is the reality of ethics simply assumed.[16] The actuality of human beings, as it is presented in the *Postscript*, is inherently ethical.[17] It is a result of the efforts of the individual to bring his existence into conformity with his understanding of how he ought to exist.

Ground of Properly Basic Religious Beliefs," *Faith and Philosophy* 5 (1988): 30. This is clearly Kierkegaard's own position (cf., e.g., WL, 230, and Martin Slotty, "Die Erkenntnislehre S. A. Kierkegaards," diss., Friedrich-Alexanders-Universität, Erlangen, 1915, 20). The impossibility of universal doubt is, in fact, one of the themes of *Johannes Climacus* (JC, 113-72).

[14]Compare this with Kierkegaard's claim that it is possible to "sensibly convince oneself" of the presence of another person and that person, Kierkegaard continues, "can quite sensibly convince one that he is really there [*er til*]" (OAR, 108). The Danish text of this passage appears in *Nutidens Religieuse Forvirring. Bogen om Adler*, ed. Julia Watkin (Copenhagen: C. A. Reitzel, 1984) 142.

[15]Cf. PC, 204, and Slotty, *Die Erkenntnislehre*, 22. The Hong's translate *er til* as "exists." Existence is, however, a technical term for Kierkegaard that is often used by him in a manner synonymous with "actuality" (i.e., *Virkelighed*; cf., e.g., PC, 129). The expression *er til* is etymologically related to *Tilværelsen* (cf. Christian Molbech, *Dansk Ordbog, Anden forøgede og forbedrede Udgave* [Copenhagen: Gyldendal, 1859], *Anden Deel*, s.v. *Tilværelse*) and should thus be understood to refer to reality rather than actuality.

I want to make clear here that I am not arguing that it is Kierkegaard's position that we "know" other people are real. Whether our belief in the reality of other people amounts to knowledge is irrelevant to the argument of the present essay.

[16]Cf. Alastair Hannay's assertion that "Kierkegaard's psychology flatly acknowledges the reality of ethics and attempts no scientific explanation of it" (Alastair Hannay, *Kierkegaard* [London/New York: Routledge, 1982] 160).

[17]Cf. CUP, 1:328. It is important to acknowledge, of course, that every created thing, on Climacus's view, has actuality and that *only* human actuality is inherently ethical.

"[A]ctuality," explains Climacus, "is not the external action but an interiority in which the individual annuls possibility and identifies himself with what is thought in order to exist in it" (CUP, 1:339). That is, it is the result of the individual's annulling the possibility of the correspondence between what he thinks he ought to do and what he does, by the establishment of the actuality of such correspondence.[18] A person's actuality is thus equivalent, on Climacus's view, to his ethical development. That is, "[E]xisting ethically," he argues, "*is* actuality" (CUP, 1:319).[19]

The difficulty with distinguishing the technical senses that the expressions "reality" and "actuality" have in the *Postscript* is that it is not clear that they are always used by Climacus in these senses. It is thus possible that when he argues that "[t]he only actuality there is for an existing person is his own ethical actuality" (CUP, 1:316) and that he is related to every other actuality only in terms of possibility, what he means by "*Virkelighed*" is what he normally means by "*Realitet*." In order to determine whether this is the case, we will have to go to the section of the *Postscript* from which this reference has been taken.

"Existing ethically," argues Climacus, "is actuality, but instead of that the age has become so predominantly an observer that not only is everyone that but observing has finally become falsified as if it were actuality" (CUP, 1:319).[20] The concern of the passage in question is explicitly epistemological, as is apparent from the following reference. "All knowledge about actuality is possibility. The only actuality concerning which an existing person has more than knowledge . . . is his own actuality" (CUP, 1:316). That is, the concern of the passage in question is not whether one will choose to behave ethically toward people with whom one comes into contact, but whether "the ethical" is something that can be observed in the "world" or in human history as the Danish theologian and former tutor of Kierkegaard, Hans Lassen Martensen, argued it could.[21] This is, in fact, a recurrent theme of the *Postscript* which,

---

[18]Actuality, according to Climacus, annihilates possibility; "not merely the possibility that is excluded but even the possibility that is accepted" (PF, 74).

[19]Emphasis added.

[20]Cf. CA, 22.

[21]Cf. CUP, 1:320.

it has been argued, is actually a polemic directed against Martensen's "peculiar epistemology [*egenartet Erkendelseslære*]."[22]

Climacus never asserts that other people are possibilities in the sense that one may or may not choose to be obligated to relate to them ethically. It is not the reality of other people that becomes possibility from the perspective of the subjective, existing individual, it is their moral character. It is not, however, this character in itself (i.e., ontologically), but only to the extent that it is an object of knowledge (i.e., epistemologically). That is, one's judgments of the moral character, or ethical development, of other people are possibilities in the sense that they may or may not correspond to reality.

The reality of the world is never questioned in the *Postscript*. Climacus develops no formal defense of realism because such a defense would be superfluous. We cannot help but believe in the reality of the world on his view. It is the reality of other people, rather than their actuality, toward which we are ethically obligated according to Climacus. That is, we are not obligated to behave ethically only toward people who are themselves ethically developed, or engaged in a process of such development. Christianity asserts that our ethical obligation is toward our "neighbor [*Næsten*]" (WL, 44-60), and our neighbor, explains Kierkegaard, is the person "we see" (WL, 159-174).

This may sound like far too theological a metaphysics to impose on the *Postscript*, a work by a pseudonym who denies he is a Christian. It is important in this context to appreciate, however, that religion and Christianity are not synonymous on Climacus's view and that Climacus is clearly religious in the more general sense.[23] Even more important, however, is the fact that there is reason to believe he is religious in the specifically Christian sense.

I have argued elsewhere that Climacus deliberately undermined the purported objectivity of the *Philosophical Fragments*, that to accept what he said in the "Interlude" section of this work was to express an implicit bias in favor of a Christian rather than a

---

[22]Arild Christensen, "*Efterskriftens Opgør med Martensen*," *Kierkegaardiana* 4 (1962): 48.

[23]That is, he never questions whether there is, in fact, a God.

Socratic interpretation of existence.[24] Kierkegaard writes in his journal that Climacus compresses the content of Christianity "to its least possible minimum simply in order to give all the more powerful momentum toward becoming a Christian" (JP, 6:6574).[25] One may legitimately wonder, however, why an author who was not a Christian would try to lead his reader in the direction of a Christian interpretation of existence. Christianity or, more specifically, what it means to become a Christian is the subject of both the *Fragments* and the *Postscript*. But why would someone who was not a Christian go to such lengths to describe what was really involved in becoming a Christian?

If we look closely at Climacus's purported denials that he is a Christian, what we find is not that he denies that the Christian interpretation of existence is the true interpretation, but that he is reluctant to identify himself as a Christian lest he be criticized for falling short of the ideality of Christian existence.[26] By denying that he is a Christian he can thus direct attention away from an examination of the extent to which his life is an expression of Christian truth and toward the issue of what it means in general to become a Christian.

---

[24]M. Piety, "A Little Light Music: The Subversion of Objectivity in the *Fragments*," in *International Kierkegaard Commentary: Philosophical Fragments* and *Johannes Climacus*, ed. Robert L. Perkins (Macon GA: Mercer University Press, 1994) 47-62.

[25]The Hongs' translation actually reads, "In the pseudonymous writings the content of Christianity has been compressed . . . , " etc. The Danish phrase that the Hongs have translated as "In the pseudonymous writings" is, however, *Hos pseudonymen* which translates literally as "as the pseudonym has it/according to the pseudonym" (cf. Jens Axelsen, *Dansk-Engelsk Ordbog* [Copenhagen: Gyldendal, 1984] s.v. *hos*). The heading under which the reference appears is "On Professor Nielsen's Relation to My Pseudonym Johannes Climacus." It is thus clear that the reference here is not to the pseudonymous writings as a whole, but to Climacus's writings in particular.

[26]Cf., e.g., CUP, 1:466 and 1:617-23. It is interesting to note in this context that Kierkegaard never denies Climacus is a Christian, but only emphasizes that Climacus himself denies this (cf., e.g., JP, 6:6431; 6:6433; 6:6439; Pap. X[1] A 636 and Pap. X[5] B 20 [there is no English translation of these passages]; JP, 6:6349; 6:6597; and 6:6598). Even more important in this context, however, is the fact that Kierkegaard asserts in *The Point of View for My Work as an Author* that Climacus does not describe himself *directly* as a Christian (PV, 145-146n.) which would seem to imply that he *is* in fact describing himself indirectly as a Christian.

Kierkegaard appears to have believed, however, that this rhetorical strategy on Climacus's part would be relatively transparent to his readers; thus he refers in a letter to Rasmus Nielsen, a professor of philosophy at the University of Copenhagen, to Climacus's "humorous" denial that he is a Christian.[27] That is, Climacus's denial is "humorous" because it is otherwise obvious that he is a Christian and that he is denying it only to direct attention away from himself and toward the issue with which he is concerned as an author.[28]

The fact, however, that it appears Climacus is what one might call a closet Christian does not necessarily make him immune to the criticism that his thought is acosmic. That is, the fact that there is an ethical-religious distinction, on his view, between an individual's reality and his actuality does not in itself demonstrate that his thought is essentially realist. One could argue that even if Climacus's claim that one is related to the actuality of others only in terms of possibility were correctly understood to refer not to the reality of these people, but to their moral character as a possible object of knowledge, the extrapolation from possibility in the epistemological sense to possibility in the ethical sense would still be compelling to the extent that human freedom is portrayed in the *Postscript* as absolute, or equivalent to *liberum arbitrium*.

If moral commitment, according to Climacus is, in fact, something that one can either choose to have or not to have as one pleases—i.e., if there is nothing which influences one in either direction, then it would appear that even from an ethical perspective, the reality of other people is translated, according to Climacus, into possibility. That is, if one could legitimately be said not to appreciate that there were any such thing as ethical obligation except in a hypothetical sense, then the metaphysics of the *Postscript* would be fundamentally acosmic.

---

[27]LD, 298-99. I am indebted to Paul A. Bauer for bringing this remark to my attention.

[28]Humor, I believe, plays a far more important role in Kierkegaard's thought than has traditionally been appreciated by scholars (cf., e.g., C. Stephen Evans, "Kierkegaard's View of Humor: Must Christians Always be Solemn?" *Faith and Philosophy* 4 [1987]: 176-86).

2. Liberum arbitrium

There are surprisingly few references to freedom in the *Post-script* and what references there are can only properly be understood when placed in the context of what is generally appreciated about Kierkegaard's views on freedom as these views are expressed other places. In general, it appears that Kierkegaard rejects the notion that human freedom can be equated with *liberum arbitrium*.[29] Genuine *"liberum arbitrium,"* he argues in his journals "is really never found" (JP, 2:1240). Vigilius Haufniensis, the pseudonymous author of *The Concept of Anxiety*, calls such freedom "a thought-unthing [*Tanke-Uting*]" (CA, 49),[30] and argues that "[t]o maintain that freedom begins as *liberum arbitrium* (which is found nowhere, cf. Leibniz) that can choose good just as well as evil inevitably makes every explanation impossible" (CA, 112).[31]

Several prominent Kierkegaard scholars have argued that human freedom is limited on Kierkegaard's view.[32] The interpretation of Kierkegaard as a proponent of the view that this freedom is absolute continues, however, to be popular, both among Kierkegaard scholars and among philosophers in general. It is widely believed, for example, that the foundation of subjective commitment, according to Kierkegaard, is an absolutely free choice.

This can be seen, in particular, in the interpretation Alasdair MacIntyre has given of Kierkegaard's views on the nature of ethical commitment. That is, MacIntyre argues that the foundation of

---

[29]Cf. Poul Lübcke, *"Selvets ontologi hos Kierkegaard," Kierkegaardiana* 13 (1984): 58.

[30]Thomte actually translates *Tanke-Uting* as "nuisance for thought." It is not clear, however, whether *Tanke-Uting* refers to the inability of thought to comprehend *liberum arbitrium*, or whether it is meant to imply that such freedom is, in effect, a figment of the imagination, or something which has no existence outside of thought. I have chosen the literal translation of *Tanke-Uting* (i.e., thought-unthing) because it preserves this ambiguity.

[31]Cf. EO II, 173-74.

[32]Cf., e.g., Birgit Bertung, *Kierkegaard, Kristendom og Konsekvens* (Copenhagen: C. A. Reitzel, 1994) 60, 77, and 83; Hügli, *Die Erkenntnis der Subjektivität und die Objektivität des Erkennens bei Søren Kierkegaard*, 224; and Gregor Malantschuk, *"Studier i Frihedens Bevægelse hos Søren Kierkegaard," Frihed og Eksistens* (Copenhagen: C. A. Reitzel, 1980) 235-49.

ethics, according to Kierkegaard, is nothing other than the individual's free choice to accept an ethical *Weltanschauung* as definitive.[33] That is, ethical prescriptions are valid, on this interpretation, only to the extent that they are accepted as valid by a given individual. The difficulty is that the view that ethical prescriptions derive their force purely from an individual's choice to view them as forceful inevitably makes every explanation of why anyone would ever make such a choice impossible. That is, it appears, as MacIntyre points out, that "no rational justification can be given" for this choice.[34] One cannot, for example, choose to accept ethical prescriptions as valid on the grounds that this is the right thing to do because this would betray that one had already accepted them as such.

The question is thus whether Kierkegaard in fact subscribes to such a view of the foundation of ethics and, in particular, whether this view can be found in the *Postscript*.[35] I asserted above that Climacus never questions the reality of ethics. It is clear, however, that he does not believe everyone is immediately in possession of an ethical world view in the sense that everyone consciously subscribes to this view. He is, in fact, particularly interested in how it is that one comes consciously to hold such a view.

One of the characteristics of an ethical world-view, according to Climacus, is that it sees suffering as essential to human existence. This is not, he acknowledges however, a view of existence to which one is immediately inclined to subscribe. "[T]he life-view of immediacy," he asserts, "is good fortune" (CUP, 1:433). That is, the view of life that is immediately appealing considers that life is basically pleasant and that suffering is thus a result of misfortune. "Misfortune," Climacus observes, however, is for the immediate individual

> like a narrow pass on the way of immediacy. Now he is in it, but essentially his life-view must continually imagine that it will in turn end because it is something alien. If it does not end, he

---

[33]Alasdair MacIntyre, *After Virtue* (Notre Dame IN: University of Notre Dame Press, 1984) 38.

[34]MacIntyre, *After Virtue*, 40.

[35]Cf. C. Stephen Evans's argument against "voluntaristic" readings of Climacus's works in "Kierkegaard and Plantinga," 29-30.

despairs, whereby immediacy ends, and the transition to another understanding of misfortune is made possible, that is, to comprehending suffering, an understanding that does not merely comprehend this or that misfortune but essentially comprehends suffering. (CUP, 1:434)

Only an ethical, or ethical-religious, interpretation of existence comprehends suffering on Climacus's view. One does not actually choose such an interpretation of existence, according to Climacus, however, one merely chooses not to deceive oneself concerning the significance of one's subjective experience.[36]

"The ethical," argues Climacus in the *Postscript*, is both "easy to understand" (CUP, 1:472).[37] and "infinitely valid *in itself*" (CUP, 1:142).[38] Not only is ethical knowledge unproblematic on Climacus's view, "[t]he ethical," he argues, "is the only certainty, to concentrate upon this the only knowledge that does not change into a hypothesis at the last moment, to be in it the only secure knowledge" (CUP, 1:152).

We saw in the preceding section that Climacus is concerned in the *Postscript* to discredit the view that the ethical is something that can be observed in the world or in human history. "In order to study the ethical," he argues, "every human being is assigned to himself" (CUP, 1:141). That is, "each individual," on his view, "actually and essentially comprehends the ethical only in himself, because it is his co-knowledge with God. In other words, although in a certain sense the ethical is infinitely abstract, in another sense it is infinitely concrete, indeed, the most concrete of all" (CUP, 1:155).

The ethical is "concrete" in that knowledge of it, on Climacus's view, is simply part of the way a person is constructed. This is not to say, again, that everyone consciously subscribes to an ethical

---

[36]This is a considerable refinement of the views I expressed in "Kierkegaard on Rationality" (*Faith and Philosophy* 10 [1993]: 365-79; repr. in *Philosophy of Religion: An Anthology of Contemporary Views*, ed. Melville Y. Stewart [Boston: Jones and Bartlett, 1996]). This refinement is, in part, a product of comments and criticisms I received from Hubert L. Dreyfus and Stuart E. Dreyfus.

[37]Emphasis added. Cf. Kierkegaard's claim in his journals that "the thing which a person [*et Menneske*] actually ought to do is always easy to understand . . . infinitely easy to understand" (JP, 3:2874).

[38]Cf. Hannay, *Kierkegaard*, 160, and Slotty, *Erkenntnislehre*, 40.

life-view, but that experience would inexorably lead anyone to this view who did not systematically deceive himself concerning its significance. Ethical knowledge is, in this way, built into the essence of the individual. It is for this reason Climacus refers to ethical knowing as "essential knowing" (CUP, 1:198). It is also for this reason that Christianity, on his view, "is not a matter of knowing" (CUP, 1:215).[39]

When Climacus argues that ethical knowledge is "the only knowledge that does not change itself into a hypothesis at the last moment," he is making a clear distinction between the individual's appreciation of what he actually ought to do and what it would be the case he ought to do *if* he decided to adopt an ethical *Weltanschauung*. The latter represents what one could refer to as a hypothetical imperative. A hypothetical imperative represents how one ought to behave *if* one wished to be ethical. When Climacus argues, however, that ethical knowledge is "the only knowledge that does not change itself into a hypothesis in the last moment," the imperative in question is categorical. To be aware of what Climacus refers to as "the absolute ethical distinction between good and evil" (CUP, 1:134) is to be aware that one is obligated to instantiate the good,[40] independently of whether one wishes to be so obligated. "The ethical," according to Climacus, is "the absolute" (CUP, 1:142).

Climacus is not concerned in the *Postscript* to get his reader to accept ethical prescriptions as valid. He assumes the reader has already done this. Neither is he concerned to enlighten his reader as to the precise substance of these prescriptions. He assumes the reader already knows this. What he is most interested in appears to be what one could call the dialectic of self-deception or what he refers to as the phenomenon of the "subtle conscience" (CUP, 1:604) that endeavors to explain away a responsibility while

---

[39]Kierkegaard argues that Christianity is not essentially concerned with knowledge, but with the transformation of the individual's will. That is, the problem is not that the individual does not know what he ought to do, but that he does not want, or will to do what he knows he ought (cf. JP, 4:4953, 6:6966, 2:1202; WL, 96; EUD, 215; and SUD, 94-95).

[40]Cf. Kierkegaard's claim that "[t]he most limited poor creature cannot truthfully deny being able to understand this requirement" (FSE, 35).

remaining unaware that this is what it is doing.[41] The "subtle conscience" knows very well what it ought to do, it just doesn't *want* to do it.[42] It is for this reason Climacus speaks throughout the *Postscript* about the importance of "willing" the ethical.[43]

One does not, according to Climacus, choose to accept ethical or ethical-religious prescriptions as valid, one chooses not to deceive oneself concerning either the substance of these prescriptions as such or the issue of whether one has succeeded in living according to them. That is, when Climacus speaks about the importance of willing the ethical he is making an appeal to the reader's conscience, which according to Kierkegaard, is a "witness who is always and everywhere present" (SV XII, 285). The reader is indirectly asked to acknowledge that she has not lived, and is not living as she should. It is for Climacus only in the sense that a person chooses not to deceive herself in this way, that she is truly free. That is, freedom on Climacus view, is not equivalent to *liberum arbitrium*, but is associated rather with the ethical,[44] or with willing the good.[45] "[T]he person," he explains, "who rubs the

---

[41]Cf. CUP, 1:604.

[42]"Every person," argues Kierkegaard, "always understands the truth a good deal farther out than he expresses it existentially. Why does he not go farther out then? Ah there's the rub! I feel too weak (ethically too weak) to go as far out as my knowledge extends [*som jeg erkender*]" (JP, 2:2301). The difficulty is that although Kierkegaard argues that "[i]n this way everyone becomes guilty before God and must make this admission" (JP, 2:2301), people do not want to make this admission. Rather than admit that they have failed to behave as they knew they ought to have behaved, they try to conceal from themselves their inherent ethical, or ethical-religious knowledge (Cf. SV X, 174; JFY, 158-59; FSE, 117-18, and JP, 1:523) in an effort to deceive themselves into believing there is nothing wrong with their behavior. "[T]his," argues Anti-Climacus, "is how perhaps a great many people [*en stor Mængde Mennesker*] live, they work gradually at eclipsing their ethical and ethical-religious knowledge which would lead them out into decisions and conclusions that their lower nature does not much care for" (SUD, 94). Cf. JP, 3:3705.

[43]Cf., e.g., CUP, 1:135-37 and 1:343.

[44]Cf. CUP, 1:135.

[45]Cf. CUP, 1:136. Climacus also refers to guilt as an expression of freedom in the negative sense (i.e., as an expression of the failure to actualize one's freedom to do the good. Cf. CUP, 1:534).

wonderful lamp of freedom becomes a servant—the spirit [of the lamp] is the Lord" (CUP, 1:139).[46]

3. The Religious Dimension of Ethics in the Postscript

It should now be clear that the ethics of the *Postscript* is not founded on acosmism. There is never any question in the *Postscript* of whether other people are in fact real. Not only are other people real, on Climacus's view, their mere presence makes an immediate appeal to our conscience, which he asserts is our "co-knowledge" with God.[47]

But if there is no question concerning the reality of other people in the *Postscript*, what about the reality of God? Climacus's remark that "God is negatively present in . . . subjectivity" (CUP, 1:53) seems to imply that we can only assume God is the ultimate source of our ethical knowledge. God, it appears, is no more than a postulate.

It is important, in this context, to appreciate, however, that the claim that "God is negatively present in subjectivity," is intended to refer to the potential for a concrete God relationship that resides in human subjectivity, it is not meant to reduce all God relationships to such negative presence.[48] God is negatively (i.e., potentially) present, according to Climacus, in the existence of a person who does not yet believe, but he is clearly positively (i.e., actually) present in the existence of the person who does believe. Belief, according to Climacus is, in fact, the means by which one comes to know God. That is, one becomes acquainted with God, on

---

[46]Cf. Kierkegaard's claim in *Works of Love* that "[d]uty . . . makes a person dependent and at the same moment eternally independent. 'Only law can give freedom.' Alas we very often think that freedom exists and that it is law that binds freedom. Yet it is just the opposite; without law, freedom does not exist at all, and it is law that gives freedom" (WL, 38). Cf. also JP, 2:1241, 3:3281; EO II, 174; and Lübcke, *Selvets ontologi*, 58.

[47]Cf. CUP, 1:141.

[48]Cf. Cornelio Fabro's observation that Kierkegaard scholars have "too often reduced the meaning of Kierkegaard's work to its negative moment," in "Faith and Reason in Kierkegaard's Dialectic," *A Kierkegaard Critique*, ed. Howard A. Johnson and Niels Thulstrup (New York: Harper & Brothers, 1962) 158.

Climacus's view, through belief in Christ.[49] When Climacus argues that our ethical knowledge is knowledge we share with God, the God he is referring to here is thus not merely an empty postulate, but the real source of this knowledge.

It may seem at times to the reader of the *Postscript* that Climacus wants to reduce divine reality to absurdity and paradox. Climacus argues, however, that "[w]hen I believe, then assuredly neither faith nor the content of faith is absurd" (JP, 6:6598).[50] This claim may appear, at first, to be at odds with his claim in the *Postscript* that if an individual "understands that it [i.e., Christianity] is not the absurd, then he is *eo ipso* no longer a believing Christian" (CUP, 1:558). The argument of the *Postscript*, however, is twofold. Climacus argues first, that "*viewed objectively*, it [Christianity] is the absurd" (CUP, 1:210) and second, that this is *not* the proper perspective from which to view Christianity.[51]

"Christianity," argues Climacus,

> wants to give the single individual an eternal happiness, a good that is not distributed in bulk but only to one, and to one at a time. Even though Christianity assumes that subjectivity, as the possibility of appropriation, is the possibility of receiving this good, it nevertheless does not assume that as a matter of course the subjectivity is all set, as a matter of course has even an actual idea of the significance of this good. This development or remaking of the subjectivity, its infinite concentration in itself under a conception of the individual's highest good, an eternal happiness, is the developed possibility of the subjectivity's first possibility.

---

[49]Cf. PF, 68-69. "[T]o know [*kjende*] God" in the sense of to be acquainted with him, argues Kierkegaard, "is crucial and without this knowledge a human being would become nothing at all" (EUD, 326). Kierkegaard's authorship is rich with references to acquaintance knowledge of God (cf., e.g., EUD, 321, 326; and JP, 1:1351) or of Christ (cf., e.g., PC, 172).

[50]Cf. C. Stephen Evans, *Kierkegaard's "Fragments" and "Postscript": The Religious Philosophy of Johannes Climacus* (Atlantic Highlands NJ: Humanities Press, 1983) 239-40; and Sylvia Walsh, "Echoes of Absurdity: The Offended Consciousness and the Absolute Paradox in Kierkegaard's *Philosophical Fragments*," *International Kierkegaard Commentary: Philosophical Fragments*, 33-62.

[51]This point is made so often throughout the *Postscript* that it would be impractical to provide a list of references here. CUP, 1:130 is, however, a particularly straightforward reference and may thus be helpful for the reader who has not yet appreciated that this is a central theme of the *Postscript*.

> Christianity, therefore, protests against all objectivity; it wants the
> subject to be infinitely concerned about himself. (CUP, 1:130)

"Like," argues Climacus, "is understood only by like" (CUP,
1:52). This means that since Christianity, on his view, is essentially
something subjective, it can only properly be understood from a
subjective perspective. "With reference," he explains, "to a kind of
observation in which it is of importance that the observer be in a
definite state [e.g., a subjective state], it holds true that when he is
not in that state he does not know anything whatever" (CUP, 1:52).
That is, since Christianity is essentially something subjective, one
must be passionately or subjectively engaged with it in order to
understand it. "Christianity," argues Climacus, "cannot be observed objectively" (CUP, 1:57).

Christianity, on Climacus's view, is "absurd" when viewed
merely objectively. That is, its absurdity cannot be rationalized
away as Martensen, for example, attempts to do in his *Christian
Dogmatics*.[52] What Climacus objects to is not that faith can give the
believer insight into the nature or substance of Christian truth, but
that it can give the believer insight into the purported objective
necessity, or inherent rationality of this truth.

4. The Reality of the World in Kierkegaard's "Postscript"

The development of an individual, according to Climacus, is
associated, as we saw in part two, the appropriation of ethical-
religious truth in the sense that the individual brings his or her
existence into conformity with the ideal of how one ought to exist
that is provided by God through his or her conscience. Freedom,
as we saw in part one, is equivalent to the decision to establish
such conformity. Hermann Deuser explains, however, that "the
chance of freedom—to be able to decide to do the good . . . —exists only if the self, in the act of deciding, stands in relation to
something else. That is, the chance exists only if the self does not
produce itself and have merely itself as a goal."[53]

---

[52]H. Martensen, *Christian Dogmatics*, trans. William Urwick (Edinburgh: T.&T.
Clark, 1866).

[53]Hermann Deuser, "*Kierkegaards Verteidigung der Kontingenz: »Daβ etwas
Inkommensurables in einem Menschenleben ist,«*" *Kierkegaardiana* 15 (1991): 113 (my

The reality of the world is never questioned in the *Postscript*. The concern of this work is epistemological rather than ontological. Belief in the reality of the external world is more fundamental, on Climacus's view, than is skepticism concerning this reality. Climacus is thus not in the least interested in the skeptical question of whether there is an external world or a moral law. He is interested rather in the nature of ethical knowledge and the ethical consequences that this has.

Because our conscience, according to Climacus, is the source of our ethical knowledge, this knowledge is essentially reflexive. That is, it tells us how we ought to relate to those around us as well as whether we have been successful in this regard. It cannot, however, give us any definitive information about the ethical significance of the behavior of others. I can extrapolate from my own experience and speculate about what my conscience might tell me if I were in a situation similar to that of another person, but since I cannot actually "make myself into the other person" (CUP, 1:321), I can never be certain that I have properly understood his situation. Our judgments concerning the ethical significance of the behavior of others are thus merely possibilities in the sense that they may or may not correspond to reality.

But if ethical knowledge is essentially reflexive, then it is inherently unethical to judge the behavior of others. It is a confusion of the essence of the ethical to suppose, as speculative philosophy does, that it can be observed in the world.

Speculative philosophy, the target of much of the polemic of the *Postscript*, has, on Climacus's view, lost sight of the essence of the ethical as a direct result of its striving for objectivity. The essence of the ethical is subjective in the sense that it resides in each individual's conscience. Yet speculative philosophy abstracts from individuals as such. It is, in fact, the activity of speculative philosophy of abstracting from the world, from particular individuals and the concrete relations between them that, for Climacus, makes it comic.[54] That is, speculative philosophy, on his view, has "forgotten in a kind of world-historical absentmindedness what it

---

translation); and SUD, 13-14.

[54]Cf., e.g., CUP, 1:190, 1:357, 1:533.

means to be a human being, not what it means to be human in general . . . , but what it means that *we*, you *and* I *and* he, are human beings, each one of us individually" (CUP, 1:120).[55] It is, one could argue, the antirealism of speculative philosophy that is the target of much of the polemic of the *Postscript*. That is, the problem with speculative philosophy, on Climacus's view, is precisely that it has confused the concrete world with the abstraction of the "world historical."[56]

The reality of the world is the foundation upon which the ethics of the *Postscript* rests. If the world, according to Climacus, had no reality (*realitet*) in itself, it would be impossible, on his view, for the individual to achieve actuality (*virkelighed*). That is, the actuality of human beings is synonymous in the *Postscript* with their ethical development. Our ethical, or ethical-religious, obligations are not, however, things we can fulfill in isolation from the rest of the human community. Climacus in fact ridicules the suggestion that we should, in order to develop ethically-religiously, isolate ourselves from "the confusion of the world" (CUP, 1:415 and 1:459). It is, on his view, precisely in "life's multiplicity" (CUP, 1:415), or in our relations to the individuals with whom our activities bring us into contact, that our actuality as human beings is painstakingly won.

---

[55]Emphasis added. The Hongs' translation actually reads "each one on his own." This is not incorrect. It seems to me, however, to lend credence to the acosmic interpretation of Kierkegaard. The Danish phrase translated by the Hongs as "on his own" is *hver for sig* which may also be translated simply as "each" (cf. Axelsen, s.v. *hver*, and Molbech, *Første Deel*, s.v. *hver*).

[56]Cf. J. Heywood Thomas's claim that "Kierkegaard's self-appointed task in philosophy was to provide a corrective for what he regarded as the System's obsessive concern or preoccupation with the world-historical," "Kierkegaard's View of Time," *Journal of the British Society for Phenomenology* 4 (1973): 33.

10

Kierkegaard and Approximation Knowledge

Thomas C. Anderson

There seems to be general agreement that one of Kierkegaard's primary goals in writing the *Postscript* was to show the tremendous limitations and fallibility of a human being's cognitive powers. In fact, many commentators claim that Kierkegaard is epistemologically a skeptic, and they cite especially the *Postscript* to support their position (even though its author is the pseudonymous Johannes Climacus). For example, Mackey asserts that the very intent of the *Postscript* is to show that every belief and every truth claim about reality have no cognitive warrant.[1] Popkin also believes that skepticism is the final result of Kierkegaard's epistemology; he writes, "When we search for true knowledge we end up in complete skepticism."[2] Many others similarly claim that Kierkegaard holds that it is in principle impossible, at least without God's help, for humans to know if any particular explanation or interpretation of reality is true. Price succinctly sums up this interpretation. He asks, "What then can I know?" and replies, "Nothing, says Kierkegaard, nothing with any degree of real certainty; nothing about God, nothing about the world as it really is."[3]

---

[1]L. Mackey, *Kierkegaard, a Kind of Poet* (Philadelphia: University of Pennsylvania Press, 1971) 179-80; 189-92.

[2]R. Popkin, "Kierkegaard and Skepticism," in *Kierkegaard, A Collection of Critical Essays*, ed. J. Thompson (Garden City NY: Doubleday, 1972) 368.

[3]G. Price, *The Narrow Pass* (London: Hutchinson, 1963) 113. Others who advance this interpretation are K. Nordentoft, *Kierkegaard's Psychology*, trans. B. Kirmmse (Pittsburgh: Duquesne University Press, 1978) 334-39; J. Gill, "Kant, Kierkegaard, and Religious Knowledge," in *Essays on Kierkegaard* (Minneapolis: Burgess Pub. Co., 1969) 66-67; A. Hannay, *Kierkegaard: The Arguments of the Philosophers* (London: Routledge & Kegan Paul, 1982) 153.

On the other hand, most of the above authors do recognize that Kierkegaard admits the possibility of, and stresses the need for, self-knowledge. Yet, not all realize the full ramification this admission has on his alleged skepticism. Furthermore, while granting that Kierkegaard believes that truths about one's self are obtainable, some limit such truths just to one's own individual reality[4]—a position that I will critique later. Of course, almost every interpreter agrees that Kierkegaard believes that an individual person aided by God's grace and revelation can attain a number of truths about reality, whether or not such truths can be fully comprehended.

Various reasons have been offered in support of labeling Kierkegaard a skeptic. In this paper, however, I will address only one of them, namely, Climacus's repeated assertions in the *Postscript* that all empirical knowledge of reality is only "approximation." Some interpret this to mean that such knowledge can, at best, approach but never achieve truth about empirical reality.[5] It will become clear in the course of this paper that I do not agree with that interpretation.

In what follows, I will first set forth the views of Johannes Climacus on this issue and, then, seek to determine the extent to which Kierkegaard accepts Climacus's position. I will use the following criteria to determine which *Postscript* positions are in fact Kierkegaard's own.

1. Any position stated both by Climacus and by Kierkegaard in works published under his own name will be considered to be Kierkegaard's.

2. Any position presented in those works published under the pseudonym Anti-Climacus (*Sickness Unto Death* and *Practice in Christianity*) will be considered Kierkegaard's. This is because this later pseudonym was used not because Kierkegaard disagreed with, or dissociated himself from, the content of these

---

[4]Price, *The Narrow Pass*, 113-21; Nordentoft, *Kierkegaard's Psychology*, 339-40; Hannay, *Kierkegaard*, 152-53; A. Shmueli, *Kierkegaard and Consciousness*, trans. N. Handelman (Princeton: Princeton University Press, 1971) 43-45.

[5]For a discussion of other reasons why Kierkegaard is considered to be a skeptic, see my article "The Extent of Kierkegaard's Skepticism," *Man and World* 27 (1994): 271-89.

works, but because he did not want to imply that he was living Christianity at the level of perfection presented in them.[6]

3. Finally, passages in his *Journals* where Kierkegaard clearly states his acceptance of a position of a pseudonymous author will be considered his own, as, of course, will entries which correspond to positions taken in the above mentioned works.

Section I
Empirical Knowledge as Approximation

Climacus's Position

In the *Postscript*, Climacus offers a number of reasons for his apparent skepticism about empirical knowledge, or, more precisely, for designating such knowledge as "approximation." Let us investigate his comments carefully to see just what he means by the use of that term.

1. In the first place all empirical beings, including human knowers, are in the process of becoming. This means, Climacus writes, that "truth itself is in the process of becoming and is [only] by way of anticipation the agreement between thinking and being" (CUP, 1:190, translation modified). The point apparently is that truth, meaning the (fixed?) conformity or correspondence of thought and being is unattainable because of the continual change of both knower and known. Climacus refers to such truth as a *desideratum*, a goal which would be achieved only if becoming reached its end and ceased. The best we can obtain, he says, is "approximation" to this goal.

2. A second reason Climacus offers for calling empirical knowledge "approximation" is a typical anti-foundationalist one. He points out that the "beginning [of empirical knowledge] cannot be established absolutely" by thought itself but is in a sense arbitrary. One reason it is arbitrary is because it is the knower who *decides* the "limits" of his or her investigation of any empirical data. Thus, for example, since all the members of a certain group cannot be studied, generalizations about the entire group rest on

---

[6]JP 6:6433, 6446, 6461. See also the translators' introduction to SUD, xx-xxii.

the selection of a limited sample. Such generalizations are, therefore, inevitably approximations (CUP, 1:149-50). Furthermore, any existing human being's knowledge takes place from one of many limited perspectives or points of view. No individual can attain an unlimited, absolute, God's eye view of reality. Now neither the selection of a particular perspective nor the selection of the data to be investigated are themselves guaranteed by a presuppositionless, indubitable, intellectually intuitive, self-evident foundation. The selections rest ultimately on will, that is, on free choice. I take it this is what Climacus means when he says "every beginning [of empirical knowledge]...does not occur by virtue of immanental thinking but is made by virtue of a resolution, essentially by virtue of faith" (CUP, 1:189).

3. A third reason why Climacus designates empirical knowledge as only approximation is because its object, empirical being, is contingent. The *Philosophical Fragments* explains this in more detail than does *Postscript*. Accepting Leibniz's distinction between necessary truths of reason and contingent truths of fact, Climacus places all empirical knowledge in the latter category, arguing that such knowledge always lacks certitude or necessity, precisely because the beings it seeks to know lack necessity.[7]

In summary, since empirical reality is in constant change, since all empirical knowledge is perspectival and begins in choice, since empirical beings are thoroughly contingent, human knowledge of empirical reality is only approximation. Climacus himself states that conclusion, "objectively there is no truth for existing beings, but only approximations . . . " (CUP, 1:218, 224).

Yet in spite of such assertions, I am not convinced that Climacus, the detached humorist, personally agrees with all the positions he presents nor do I believe that the views that he sets forth are as thoroughly skeptical as many make them out to be. I say this for a number of reasons. In the first place, a thorough-going skepticism about the truth of all knowledge of empirical reality would be incompatible with other positions Climacus clearly holds. Moreover, such a skepticism has internal difficulties that Climacus is well aware of. Finally, and this has been over-

---

[7]See the Interlude in PF, 72-88, and pp. 23, 30, and 81.

looked by many, when Climacus labels empirical knowledge an approximation, he very often does not mean that such knowledge cannot achieve truth, but only that it cannot achieve intellectual *certitude* or *necessity*. Let me elaborate.

For one thing, the claim that true knowledge of empirical reality is unobtainable involves internal difficulties common to all forms of skepticism, and Climacus is well aware of this. He recognizes, for example, that there is a "basic certainty" (CUP 1:335ftn) contained within all skepticism. Specifically, to argue that, because both the knower and the object of knowledge are changing, no true empirical knowledge is possible, presupposes that we do in fact possess true knowledge of empirical beings, at least in general, namely, that they are concrete, particular things that change. Speaking of change, if one defines empirical truth, and Climacus does, as the conformity or agreement of thought with being, then, unless one considers reality to be a radical Heraclition flux, and Climacus clearly does not, the mere fact that things change, and are contingent, does not preclude true knowledge of them *in their relatively stable features*. Climacus surely understands this for he expresses his agreement with Aristotle on this point (CUP, 1:312-13). He does, after all, give the empirical statement "the earth is round" as an example of an objective truth (CUP, 1:194-95)—and one could think of countless other statements about empirical reality which he would accept as true (e.g., Copenhagen is in Denmark). In fact, as we shall see in the next section, he claims to have a great deal of true knowledge about one kind of changing, contingent being, the human self.

Furthermore, if Climacus actually believes that empirical knowledge cannot attain truth, this would render unintelligible his statements that such knowledge consists of approximations. If empirical reality is unable to be truly known, it would be impossible to know whether any attempted explanation of it was close to the truth or not, nor would one have any objective basis for choosing among differing explanations. Yet Climacus never suggests that he believes that every interpretation of reality is equally arbitrary or has an equal claim to truth. Need I point out that he obviously considers his own explanation of the general character of empirical reality, and of the human self, to be, if not absolutely true, more true than those offered by idealism, romanticism, rationalism, paganism, or Christendom. This has to mean that he is not totally skeptical about the human ability to grasp some truths about empirical beings.

In fact, much of the skepticism about empirical knowledge which is found in the *Postscript* rests upon a very rationalistic and/or idealistic understanding of the nature of truth.[8] This becomes clear when one notes that the term approximation is often used, not to mean approximation to truth, but approximation to certitude about an eternal, finished, absolute system of knowledge. In this light, let us look at each of the three reasons set forth above which he gives for challenging the truth of empirical knowledge.

1. In spite of the fact that in the *Postscript* he defines empirical truth as the conformity of thought and being, a definition which, as I indicated, does not of itself preclude true knowledge of changing beings, immediately after giving that definition Climacus proceeds to limit such truth or conformity to the realm of the totally eternal and unchanging. Speaking like an idealist who identifies truth only with the completed, and, therefore, unchanging, system, he states that in the empirical realm truth is a goal which can only be approximated or anticipated because "the empirical object is not finished" and the knower is coming to be (CUP, 1:189-90). In other words, empirical knowledge is called approximation in comparison to an *eternal finished* (idealist) system. Note, however, this does not mean that such knowledge cannot be in conformity with presently existing empirical beings, and, therefore, true in that sense.

2. Climacus's statements about the arbitrary character of the beginnings of empirical knowledge also have a rationalistic/idealistic ring to them. On the one hand, some statements seem to assume, with idealism, that truth lies only in the whole, in an absolute and total grasp of reality. Otherwise, the mere fact that human knowledge is always from finite perspectives would not of itself mean that it is an approximation. All that necessarily follows from the perspectival character of human knowledge is that no individual

---

[8]Thus, I agree with Robert Perkins that it is Hegelian idealism and not empirical realism that Kierkegaard is against in CUP. See his "Kierkegaard's Epistemological Preferences," *International Journal for Philosophy of Religion* 4 (1973): 198-200, 214.

can reach an absolute, unlimited, point of view from which to grasp the truth about the whole of reality. The fact that human knowledge is perspectival does not of itself mean that an individual cannot grasp any truth about reality, nor that his or her grasp of reality is illusory or inaccurate, nor that he or she colors or structures or creates the features of that which he or she knows. Climacus himself draws none of these conclusions from the perspectival character of human knowledge. On the contrary he states that "all knowledge and all apprehension has nothing to give from itself" to the object known (PF, 80, translation modified). Moreover, the fact that knowledge is perspectival does not of itself preclude the possibility of one perspective allowing a more complete or deeper grasp of the real than another, a position Climacus certainly holds about his own views. To repeat, only if truth is identified with a nonlimited (hence nonperspectival) absolute realm of knowledge can human knowledge be considered to be just an approximation because it involves a limited point of view.

I might add that the fact that empirical knowledge does not begin with presuppositionless, indubitable, intuitively self-evident principles also does not render it unable to truly grasp reality—unless one assumes with classical rationalism that only necessary truths, those whose opposite is impossible, can furnish a proper foundation for knowledge. True knowledge is simply that which corresponds to reality, as Climacus himself recognizes; no more, no less.

3. Finally, to call empirical knowledge an approximation because generalizations about empirical data are in principle falsifiable by new data does not mean that empirical knowledge cannot be true but only that it cannot be absolutely certain or necessary. Of course, the more data that supports an inductive generalization, the more it approaches or approximates certitude. But not all empirical knowledge involves induction from incomplete data, and even generalizations that do may in fact be true, that is, be in conformity with reality, even though they are in principle falsifiable. To repeat, Climacus's use of the term approximation here means, not approximation to truth (whatever that could mean), but approximation to *certitude*. Similarly, for Climacus to designate all empirical knowledge as approximate because its object is contingent or nonnecessary, is to say, as he does, that empirical knowl-

edge is not certain in the sense of logically necessary. The opposite of any statement about empirical reality is logically possible. This is not, however, to say that empirical knowledge cannot be true, that is, be in agreement with reality. Thus, when Climacus states that all historical knowledge, and in fact all knowledge of contingent beings, is only "approximation knowledge," he is claiming that the best it can do is approach, but never become, *certain* knowledge, *necessary* knowledge, that whose opposite is impossible. He is not saying, however, that such knowledge can never be in conformity with reality.[9]

Thus, we see that the skepticism about empirical knowledge set forth by Climacus, specifically his claim that all such knowledge is only approximation, is not nearly as radical as some believe. It rests on a highly rationalistic/idealistic conception of true knowledge, one which identifies true with necessary, logically certain, absolute, eternal, complete.[10] Given such a conception, to say that knowledge of empirical reality is approximate simply means it is never necessary, logically certain, absolute, eternal, or complete. Whether Kierkegaard actually intends to portray Climacus as one who himself accepts this grand idealistic conception of truth, or whether, as I suspect, he uses his pseudonym to show his rationalistic/idealistic contemporaries that their conception of truth renders it unattainable for existing subjects, is not clear to me. In any case, the fact remains that if the author of the *Postscript* simply sticks with the classical definition of truth as the correspondence of thought with reality, a definition he himself offers, there is no need for him to deny that humans can achieve true knowledge of empirical beings. Indeed, Climacus does assert that knowledge, even certain knowledge, is possible of at least one empirical being, namely, one's self. That assertion buttresses my interpretation of

---

[9]In my opinion the Interlude of PF makes it clear that knowledge of contingencies is uncertain, but not necessarily untrue. Likewise see CUP, 1:23-24, 30, 81, 152-53.

[10]Perkins, "Kierkegaard's Epistemological Preferences," makes a helpful distinction between the Hegelian idealism which Kierkegaard (or Climacus) opposes and a Socratic humanistic idealism which he accepts. For the source of truth in the latter see nn. 21-24 below.

his statements about empirical knowledge as approximation and I will pursue this point in section II.

Let us turn now to Kierkegaard and attempt to determine what he himself holds about the truth claims of empirical knowledge.

Kierkegaard's Position

In works published under his own name or that of Anti-Climacus, Kierkegaard's main concerns are religious. Only infrequently does he utter statements directly pertaining to epistemology, and even then the context is not philosophical but theological. Although they often discuss the relation between faith and knowledge, these works, unlike Climacus', set forth no general theory of knowledge. Thus, it is not possible to determine whether every single conclusion or argument presented by Climacus is accepted by Kierkegaard; all we can do is attempt to discover whether the basic position or positions of the *Postscript* about empirical knowledge are Kierkegaard's own.

I find little or no indication that Kierkegaard himself is skeptical about the human ability to attain true knowledge of empirical reality. For one thing, he certainly expresses his disagreement with the rationalistic/idealistic definitions of truth (as necessary, logically certain, absolute, eternal, complete) which was the foil of Climacus's remarks about empirical knowledge as approximation. Furthermore, in his religious writings, when he does speak of human knowledge of empirical reality, such as history or natural science, Kierkegaard does not say that such knowledge cannot attain truth; in fact, he is sometimes willing to grant that it can.[11] The question that concerns him is, rather, even if history or natural science possesses true knowledge, is this truth important or relevant to an understanding of spirit and to the subjective task of becoming Christian? He usually concludes that it is not, and it may even be "dangerous" for it may "distract" one

---

[11]At PC, 27, for example, Kierkegaard speaks of history "proving" particular truths. Also, in CD he states that objective thought can be "true and profound" (CD, 207).

from his or her ethical task, the task of being spirit.[12] In one passage he puts it this way:

> The main objection, the whole objection, to the natural sciences can be expressed formally, simply, and unconditionally in this way: It is incredible that a human being who has infinitely reflected about himself as spirit could then think of choosing the natural sciences (with empirical material) as the task for his striving.   (JP, 3:2820)

Indeed, natural science "becomes especially dangerous and corruptive when it wants to enter into the realm of the spirit" (JP 3:2809), for it can only deal with the physical. It is also worth mentioning that Climacus's favorite word, approximation, almost never occurs in works Kierkegaard wrote under his own name or the pseudonym Anti-Climacus, and when it does it is almost exclusively used in an ethicoreligious, not an epistemological, context.[13] There are a few *Journal* entries, and they probably express Kierkegaard's own view, which refer to the fallibility of human knowledge of empirical reality since inductive generalizations are "merely statistical" (JP 1:1072) and "an approximation process" (JP 3:2809). However, as I argued above, the most one could infer from such statements is that empirical knowledge is not certain or necessary; they do not assert that such knowledge cannot be true.

It is the case that Kierkegaard, like Climacus, stresses the perspectival character of human knowledge. In an early *Upbuilding Discourse*, for example, he writes, "what one sees depends on how one sees ...how the observer himself is constituted is indeed decisive" (EUD, 59). In later works, he repeatedly contrasts the radically different interpretations the so-called natural man and the Christian have of things like guilt, suffering, love, natural inclinations, even of Christianity itself. He emphasizes that ultimately

---

[12]PC, 31; EUD, 134-35. For Kierkegaard's comments on natural science see JP, 3:2809-24.

[13]Except for JFY, 208-209, the word approximation does not even appear in the various indexes compiled by Hong and Lowrie to works Kierkegaard published under his own name or as Anti-Climacus. In *Journal* entries such as 2:2809, 2813, and 4:4267, where he refers to natural science as approximation, the term seems to mean that such science can attain no real knowledge about spirit or the ethical and religious. Hence it is "qualitatively irrelevant" (JP 3:2809).

each individual must freely choose (with God's grace) to accept or not accept the Christian perspective. In the same vein, *Works of Love* states that "every event, every word, every act, in short, everything can be explained in many ways," and adds that variations in explanation are possible because of free choice (WL, 291). For example, one can choose to love another and then his or her explanation of the other's behavior will be significantly different from that offered from the viewpoint of a nonlover. Such statements by Kierkegaard indicate that Climacus's view is his, namely, human knowledge does not ultimately rest on indubitable, intellectually intuited, self-evident principles, but on freely chosen starting points, based on light-hearted or serious intent. Accordingly, Kierkegaard's own position appears to be: "That by which a beginning [of "science and scholarship"] is made is a resolution" (JP, 2:2292).

Still, as I explained above, there is no contradiction in holding that human knowledge is perspectival and rooted in freely chosen starting points, and at the same time claiming that it can be in conformity with reality, that is, true. I will not repeat my arguments but simply remark that Kierkegaard himself expresses little doubt about the truth of *his* explanations of reality nor about their superiority, and the superiority of *his* perspective, over rival ones.

Thus, as far as empirical knowledge is concerned, I am extremely reluctant to attribute the alleged skepticism of the *Postscript*, that humans cannot attain truth about empirical reality, to Kierkegaard himself. As I indicated above, I have serious doubts that it should even be attributed to Climacus once one understands that his statements about empirical knowledge as approximation are directed against rationalistic/idealistic conceptions of truth. Of course, one cannot prove the negative, but at least I can argue that in the absence of any clear evidence in his own writings that he believes that empirical knowledge is unable to attain truth, it seems gratuitous to saddle Kierkegaard with such a skepticism, especially if one considers the implicit realism behind all his thought.

Let me conclude this section on this point, for it seems clear that Kierkegaard and Climacus do both implicitly accept the basic views of classical realism. Granted, realism as an epistemological theory is never explicitly defended in detail by either of them, yet is it not obvious in every one of his works that Kierkegaard and all his pseudonymous authors acknowledge the existence of particular beings independent of the knower, and believe that these beings can be known to some degree?[14] One can also point to Kierkegaard's and Climacus's repudiation of Hegelian Idealism or pure thought precisely because it identifies reality with that which is only in the realm of thought. Kierkegaard's and Climacus's complaint that such identification leaves out actual reality, namely, concrete individual temporal beings, is further confirmation of their realism. Moreover, in the *Postscript* itself, while admitting that Kant's skepticism about the ability of thought to know reality cannot be overcome by thought itself, since that very power is called into question, the author nevertheless categorically rejects such skepticism. What one must do with it, he says, is just "break" with it, and dismiss as a "temptation" any question about the reality of a thing-in-itself eluding thought. Such questions, he states, arise only when thought becomes too self-reflexive and selfishly seeks to think itself (its own content), thereby refusing to do its job of thinking *other things*.[15]

Since I cannot imagine that anyone would seriously deny that Kierkegaard and his pseudonymous author implicitly, at least, adopt this basic position of epistemological realism, I will dwell on this no further but turn instead to the most clear case where Climacus and Kierkegaard do allow true and certain knowledge of one kind of empirical reality, namely, knowledge of the human self. As we shall see, the extent of such knowledge is much wider than is realized by many who label Kierkegaard and Climacus skeptics.

---

[14]In other words, I agree with Mackey that the basic assumptions of classical realism are in the background of Kierkegaard's writings as "beliefs-which-it-is-not-necessary-to-call-into-question," 270, of "The Loss of the World in Kierkegaard's Ethics," in *Kierkegaard*, ed. Thompson. If I understand him correctly, Robert Perkins also considers Kierkegaard to hold an empirical, realist metaphysics and epistemology, in "Always Himself: A Survey of Recent Kierkegaard Literature," *Southern Journal of Philosophy* (Winter 1974): 543. In *Passionate Reason* (Bloomington: Indiana University Press, 1992) 138, C. S. Evans says Kierkegaard is a realist like Plato and Aristotle.

[15]CUP, 1:328, 335.

Section II
Knowledge of the Self

Climacus's Position

One of the major themes of part two, section II of the *Postscript* is that every individual should be a subjective thinker not a detached objective one. That means, Climacus says, that "in all his thinking [the individual] has to include the thought that he himself is an existing person" (CUP, 1:351). The subjective thinker should continually strive to understand himself; indeed, such self-knowledge is the only certain knowledge an individual can attain. In his exposition, Climacus, in fact, sets forth quite a large number of items that each individual can and should come to know about the self.[16] (1) A person can understand that the greatest ethical task he or she has is to become a self or subject in the fullest sense; (2) A person can come to see that this demands passionate interest in one's self and repeated free decisions to (3) appropriate or live what he or she knows from self-reflection he or she should be, and this involves (4) knowing and unifying into a concrete harmony his or her human faculties of imagination, feeling, passion, and thought.[17] More generally, a person can understand that becoming a self means (5) "to become a whole human being" (CUP, 1:346), that is, to express in his or her individual existence "the essentially human" (CUP 1:356). The latter statements presuppose, of course, that one knows, or can know, what is essentially human. This point is extremely important for it shows that Climacus believes that subjective reflection gives one not just an understanding of his or her unique individual self but also knowledge of the general nature or essence of the human self. This should not surprise us since the statements about the human self which Climacus makes throughout the *Postscript* are set forth not just as descriptions of one individual self, Johannes Climacus, but as true and applicable to every human self as such.

---

[16]See the whole discussion in CUP, 1, part II, sec. II, chap. I, "Becoming Subjective."

[17]CUP, 1, part II, sec. II, chap. III, @4.

However, some who consider him a skeptic about the powers of human understanding claim that Climacus believes that true knowledge of the self can be gained only through Divine Revelation.[18] It is true that Climacus states that from the Christian point of view non-Christians are wrong in thinking that they have within themselves the power to grasp the truth about themselves, for the non-Christian does not realize how radically human beings are gripped by sin and how sin renders them unable to understand themselves. Since the remedy for sin can only be supplied by God, only God can furnish the condition which enables us to grasp truth.[19] Now Climacus does say all this, yet he also presents Socrates, the personification of philosophy, as able to know many things about the self.[20] He also states that many such truths are grasped in religion A, the religion of immanence, which is the religion which "has only universal human nature as its presupposition" (CUP, 1:559) and "can be present in paganism" (CUP, 1:557). True knowledge about the self is explicitly said to be attained by the self's reflection on itself, a kind of Platonic "recollection" (PF, 87),[21] and it is sharply distinguished from the revealed truths of Christianity (for example, original sin, forgiveness, Christ, the God-man, etc.) which "did not arise in any human heart" (PF, 109). It seems evident, then, that Climacus believes that a great deal of knowledge about the self can be attained by a human being.

Let me explicitly draw out the implications of all this on my earlier interpretation of Climacus's alleged skepticism about empirical knowledge, specifically his designation of it as approximation. As we saw above, a close reading of the texts showed that Climacus so labels it for three reasons: (1) all empirical objects change; (2) all such knowledge is perspectival and rests on choice not on intuitively self-evident principles; and (3) empirical beings

---

[18]See the authors cited in nn. 3 and 4 above.

[19]PF, 13, 51, 62-65.

[20]CUP, 1:204-206; PF, 11-13, 20, 31, 87.

[21]For Climacus's discussion of religion A and its source of knowledge see CUP, 1:204-13, 555-61. See also the texts cited in the previous footnote. On this point I agree with L. Pojman, *The Logic of Subjectivity* (University AL: University of Alabama Press, 1984) chap. 3, and C. S. Evans, *Kierkegaard's Fragments and Postscript* (Atlantic Highlands NJ: Humanities Press, 1983) chap. 8.

are contingent. But to say this is to say that such knowledge is never necessary, logically certain, absolute, eternal or complete; that is, it is not true in a rationalistic/idealistic sense. It is not to say that empirical knowledge cannot be true, meaning be in conformity with reality. The fact that Climacus holds that humans can have true knowledge of the self verifies this. After all, the self changes continually and is contingent. Knowledge of it is not based on necessary self-evident first principles and it is surely perspectival (e.g., a self can be grasped from an aesthetic or an ethical or a religious perspective). Since Climacus asserts that knowledge of the self can be certain, that must mean that designating empirical knowledge as approximation is not to be taken as skeptical about the possibility of true knowledge of (at least one) empirical reality. What, then, about Kierkegaard?

Kierkegaard's Position

Anyone acquainted with Kierkegaard's religious writings knows that throughout them he stresses the need for each individual to achieve an understanding of him or herself if he or she is to become a true Christian. Like Climacus, he repeatedly contrasts impersonal objective knowledge with knowledge that concentrates on the self and insists on the need for the latter. In *Judge For Yourself*, for example, he distinguishes between a type of knowledge or understanding that simply knows, and one that understands one's self inwardly and in the direction of concrete action.[22] Also, like Climacus, Kierkegaard believes that reflection on one's self yields not just an understanding of one's unique individual self, but an understanding of the essential nature of the self. This is evident if one notes that in his religious writings Kierkegaard is not simply engaged in his personal autobiography when he stresses the need for self-reflection and self-understanding. He continually makes general statements about the nature of the self and its path (the stages) to faith, statements obviously meant to apply to *all* selves.

Furthermore, again like Climacus, Kierkegaard holds that some knowledge of the self is attainable by human understanding; it need not come only through Divine Revelation. *The Sickness unto*

---

[22]JFY, 35-45. Also see CD, 154-55, 207-208, and PC, 48-49, 205-206, 233-34.

Death makes this clear for in it, as he sets forth the human progression in self-knowledge, he indicates that some (partial) knowledge of the self is possible this side of Christian revelation. For example, he describes individuals who, though not believers, are somewhat "conscious of being despair and therefore conscious ... of having a self in which there is something eternal" (SUD, 47). Now to say that one is aware of having a self with something eternal is to say that he or she is aware, to a some degree, of the nature of that self. Furthermore, Kierkegaard describes and ranks various types of despair in terms of their increased insight into the nature of the self as spirit, and many of these forms of despair are explicitly said to be present in non-Christians.[23] Thus, at the end of his descriptions he states that these "gradation[s] in the consciousness of the self," are "within the category of the human self, or the self whose criterion is man" (SUD, 79).

Accordingly, whether or not they agree on every detail, it is clear that Kierkegaard holds Climacus's position that we can, in spite of our radical sinfulness, arrive at a number of truths about the nature of the self by our own powers. A number of *Journal* entries make it plausible to assume that, like Climacus, he believes that knowledge of the self's nature is available by recollection, that is, by reflection on the mind's inner content. In one he states that Plato's view that "all knowledge is recollection" is "beautiful," "profound," and "sound," and that "All philosophizing is a self-reflection of what already is given in consciousness" (JP, 2:2274).[24] Of course, Kierkegaard believes that ultimately only the Christian message brings the *fullness* of truth, as well as the power to accept it. Yet this hardly means that what the non-Christian knows about the self is completely false or unimportant. It seems necessary, then, to draw the same conclusion that we did in Climacus's case. Kierkegaard is not thoroughly skeptical about the possibility of human knowledge of empirical beings, at least not when it comes to knowledge of the human self.[25] We can be even stronger. Not

---

[23]SUD, 29-31, 47-74.

[24]Also see, JP, 1:649; 3:3085 and 3606.

[25]The possibility of human knowledge of empirical beings other than the self has special difficulties of its own which I have treated at length in "The extent of Kierkegaard's skepticism."

only is such knowledge possible, it is absolutely necessary for an individual to attain some understanding of his or her self, especially of his/her freedom and limitations, his/her obligation to be a self, his/her need for the eternal, his/her weakness and guilt, prior to any revelation. For only if one gains such knowledge will they ever become receptive to God's revelation of their sins and Christ's atonement and forgiveness.

However, to insist on the necessity of such knowledge of the self raises problems of its own if one takes seriously the *Postscript's* strong statements about the inverse relation between objective truth (including, presumably, objective truths about the nature of the self) and subjective truth (i.e., the subjective appropriation of truths). But that is an issue for another paper.

11

Having Lessing on One's Side

Alastair Hannay

Why does Kierkegaard have his pseudonym give prime space in the *Postscript* to a long-dead *littérateur*? Surely not to seek respectable sponsorship for unfashionable ideas; that would be contrary to the work's manifest message that authority has no place in matters of faith. Indeed in the very first sentence of the main chapter, Climacus himself assures us he is not invoking Lessing to have someone to "appeal" to (CUP, 1:72).[1] Nor is it just a matter of giving credit to sources; the two chapters dedicated to Lessing form far too elaborate an expression of gratitude for that. There are other possibilities: Kierkegaard may have seen in Lessing's scant comments on the leap a conveniently sketchy and therefore congenial basis upon which to define his own conception. Further, as an able apprentice of Lessing's ironic style, he might hope that favorable comparison would allow some of the great man's literary prestige to rub off on his own efforts. Not least, an advertised alliance with such a cultural eminence could show those who refused to recognize Kierkegaard's genius locally that his talent could well make its mark in less parochial surroundings.

None of these trivial explanations, whatever partial truths they hide, hits the mark. The real explanation is of a far more subtle and strategic character and is to be found in the text. Ostensibly Climacus presents his tribute to Lessing as an independent thinker's call for outside help. A poor lodger, he looks down wonderingly from the heights of his garret and sees all that is being done to expand the building and improve the facade, but cannot help worrying about the foundations. Commentators often

---

[1]Except for some brief phrases, the translations of *Concluding Unscientific Postscript* are all modified.

identify the building with Hegel's System, but it is perhaps better identified nearer to home with the cultural Hegelianism of J. L. Heiberg. Heiberg was a professed Hegelian but as it happens, in light of his eclectic reputation as poet, dramatist, and critic, also Copenhagen's best qualified candidate for the position of local Lessing. The real Lessing, of course, was not a Hegelian. So much the better. Nor indeed, though professing himself a Spinozist, had Lessing articulated any consistent or systematic philosophical position. Indeed, so eclectic had been the real Lessing's contribution to late eighteenth-century German culture, and so piecemeal his expressed views on philosophical matters, that all attempts to place him in the philosophical landscape would be in vain. In a comment, whose style also gives excellent support to one of our subsidiary explanations, Climacus says:

> Lessing, of course, has long since been left behind, a vanishing little way station on the systematic railway of world history. To rely on him is to damn oneself, to confirm every contemporary in the objective judgment that you cannot keep up with the times, now that one travels by train—and the whole art is to jump into the first and best carriage and leave it to world history.
>
> (CUP, 1:67-68)

For Climacus the advantage of Lessing is that he is a writer whose work the expanding Hegelian edifice has been unable, or not even thought fit, to accommodate. Deference to the *Fragments'* motto "Better well-hanged than ill-wed" would of course always lead Kierkegaard to avoid having his work interpreted and judged by the System. But in his polemic against the System it would serve his purpose well if he could find an ally that the System itself had been unable to assimilate. Better well-hanged than ill-wed, but better still to be well wed than not wed at all.

Climacus's irony tells us there would clearly be no harm in a marriage with someone so *passé* as Lessing. But such a high-profile wedding needs some more solid tie than the mere ability to survive the System. What might that be? The answer could be a common (but of course in Lessing's case posthumous) interest in presenting exclusion from the System as due to a common point of view from which the System itself can be successfully debunked. This is in essence the gist of my discussion. The argument consists in a scale of increasingly defeasible but never implausible claims:

first a very easily defended thesis to the effect that Kierkegaard presents Lessing in the guise of a subjective thinker; second, the claim that this provides the affiliation he needs to place his own authorship on the immediate and recent cultural landscape, not least in relation to a notion much current in the late eighteenth century, that of the leap of faith; third, the not implausible contention that, of the main actors on the cultural scene from that period, an alliance with Lessing alone afforded the negative identification Kierkegaard needed; and finally, the significant but here unargued suggestion that the alliance constitutes not just another philosophical position but a point of view from which rational inquiry's own limits come into view.

We must note how carefully prepared is Climacus's portrait of Lessing. First everything upon which Lessing's fame rests is stripped off: we are told to disregard the scholar, the legendary librarian, the poet, the turner of phrases, the aesthetician, sage, etc. (CUP, 1:64-65). These are the externals which have been duly flagged on the map of eighteenth-century German culture, but fortunately too scattered to be collected under a single rubric suited to the System. Once out of the way, they can be replaced by a plausible portrait of a subjective thinker. Accordingly, in the second and longer of the two chapters on Lessing, Climacus first of all attributes to Lessing two theses which are clearly his own rather than positions textually attributable to the historical Lessing himself. One of these clarifies the difference between objective and subjective thinking and introduces the notion of double reflection as characteristic of the subjective thinker. The other ties comedy and pathos to the same subjective thought, presenting the idea that what sounds like a joke can nevertheless be meant and grasped as deep earnest. In this way, by as it were being made a relative of Socrates, Lessing becomes an even better match. The plan clearly is to present Lessing as someone whose ironical remarks can be interpreted as expressions of subjectively reflected thought. Through the mediation, so to speak, of Socrates, these theses crucial to Climacus's exposition are linked to Lessing's name and used as boundary markers to define the hermeneutic horizon within which to interpret the theses "actually" attributable to Lessing.

Chief of these latter is Lessing's use of Leibniz's distinction between contingent truths and truths of reason to state that eternal truths of reason cannot be inferred from accidental truths of history. This thesis forms the background to the problem raised by the *Fragments*: how to base an eternal happiness on something historical. Then in the *Postscript* to the *Fragments*, our topic here, Leibniz's distinction defines the parameters of what Climacus following Lessing calls the leap, and which, whatever it turns out to mean, is central to Climacus's notion of faith. Since faith is in turn the principal topic of the *Postscript*, we can see how under Climacus's astute direction Lessing has been brought out of world-historical obscurity and placed polemically in center stage.

If history records only externals then of course the Lessing brought to life in these two chapters is not the historical Lessing. But that does not prevent it being the actual Lessing. Of course, equally, it may be nowhere near the actual Lessing—we simply cannot tell. However, that is what the position to be outlined would lead you to expect. Whether or not the portrayal is ficti-tious, there is a sense worth noting in which any portrait of a sub-jective thinker cannot help but be a fiction. The picture Climacus presents is nevertheless on all accounts far from incredible, especially in light of the fourth thesis in which Lessing confesses to being a searcher rather than a finder. Lessing says that, offered the choice by God, he would prefer the lifelong pursuit of truth to truth itself,[2] which underpins Climacus's admiring observation that Lessing has no "result." To his contemporaries Lessing appeared to personify the Enlightenment. But it would be nearer the truth to say that Lessing was the Enlightenment on the move. His thought was that of an inquirer who never adopted or attempted to develop a clearly defined position; his positions changed and evolved as he engaged with the movements of the time, upon which his comments exerted a great influence in turn—in his drama, his work on aesthetics, and above all in his criticism. So much was Lessing on the move, indeed, that it is often hard to say where his thinking counts as the current state of the Enlightenment

---

[2]"Eine Duplik" (1778), *G. E. Lessing's gesammelte Werke* (hereafter GW) Neue rechtmässige Ausgabe (Leipzig: G. J. Göschen'sche Verlagshandlung, 1857) 9:98.

art or forms the makings of fundamental criticism. Yet, throughout the changes, Lessing's attitude appears consistently to have reflected the kind of trust in human self-sufficiency, in the long run, that forms the deep basis of all Enlightenment thought. Lessing saw mankind as he saw himself, as in constant development, not self-consciously on course towards absolute self-consciousness, as the System would later have it, but precisely with the kind of opportunistic contextuality which allowed Lessing's writings to escape the System's clutches. Though not all of Lessing's actual views would appeal to Kierkegaard,[3] there is something in Lessing's attitude to Christianity which would certainly attract him; always sympathetic to Christian ideals, Lessing remained neutral towards the ways in which these ideals were expressed in current forms of Christian belief and practice.

Thus the kinship Climacus seeks with Lessing, in the ironic spirit of Lessing himself, lies at the level of subjective thinking, that is, the thinking of someone in continual development and never resting on a "result." How deep a kinship he seeks we cannot tell, but we might test the plausibility range here by boldly hypothesizing on Climacus's, or at least Kierkegaard's, behalf that Lessing's grasp of subjective thinking was good enough for him to have been able to write the *Postscript* himself. What better way of having Lessing on your side than by allowing that he could have written your book? Especially when you have elevated Lessing to the stature of a Socrates. Historically, of course, he could not have done that; world history was still awaiting Hegel's arrival, and Climacus himself remarks that Lessing never had to contend with the principle of mediation (CUP, 1:106).

---

[3]What could Kierkegaard make of a thinker who at one time or another held (i) that individuals can get a head start at birth by bringing their spiritual gains with them from a previous existence (and generation), (ii) that freedom was *not* such a good idea because it induced anxiety (*Philosophische Aufsätze*, 1776)—Lessing thanked his God that he was "under necessity, that the best must be"—and who ended up believing (iii) that the resort to religion was in any case a sign of human immaturity (*Die Erziehung des Menschengeschlechts* [1780], GW, 9:399-425). But in mitigation and in the context of the fourth thesis attributable to Lessing, it would be perfectly in order to doubt that Lessing considered any of these to be "results."

Nevertheless, kinship at the level of subjective thought is still not enough to provide a basis for Kierkegaard's alliance with Lessing. If subjective thought were enough he might have settled straightaway for Socrates. What we need is to be found in the indications provided by scattered remarks to the effect that Lessing had a better grasp than his contemporaries of the notion of a leap of faith and, connected with this, as Kierkegaard writes in a journal from 1848, a considerably clearer notion of the true problem concerning the relation between Christianity and philosophy than "the common herd of modern philosophers." This problem is specified in the threefold theme of the *Fragments*: how to reach a historical point of departure for an eternal consciousness, how such a point of departure can be of more than historical interest, and how to build a personal happiness on a piece of historical knowledge? Kierkegaard adds: "Lessing uses the word *Sprung* [leap] as if its being an expression or a thought didn't matter. I take it as a thought . . . " (JP 3:2342, 2370, trans. altered).[4]

Exactly what distinction Kierkegaard had in mind here is not clear, especially since Climacus will later tell us that the leap is not a thought but a decision. Maybe he means that the word expresses a thought about a decision; at any rate, as we shall see, Climacus does tend to think that, when he talks about a leap, Lessing plays with words and images rather than with concepts. To try to grasp what it is that Lessing has understood better than the common herd of modern philosophers, let us by way of a contrast Climacus himself intends look at the two representative thinkers mentioned in the chapters on Lessing: Hamann and Jacobi. It is significant that both are well known for their contributions to what is called the spirit of the counter-Enlightenment. Accordingly, one question we shall have to face is why Kierkegaard the alleged irrationalist should cast in his lot with Lessing, the great Enlightener himself, rather than with these two renegades and potential existentialists.

Answering that question requires uncovering some of the anatomy of the period during which the currently somewhat glibly named Enlightenment Project had lost much of its impetus and had begun to be undermined. What was undermining it was the

---

[4]For Lessing's use of the word *Sprung* see GW, 9:84-85.

apparent inability of the program of free inquiry and criticism to achieve its anticipated political goals. As in any time when culture divides, parties form, and thinkers jockey for position on one side or the other, it was also a time of creeds.[5] The Enlightenment's own official creed had been reason but in the movements constituting the counter-Enlightenment it was exactly faith in reason that had begun to crumble, due as much as anything to the transparency reason had been able to bring upon itself, above all in the critical philosophy of Kant. Kant remained a rationalist, but in some quarters faith in reason gave way to—in a manner of speaking to be made a little clearer below—faith in faith. In others even the grounds for faith in faith appeared to crumble as the conspicuous successes of natural scientific reasoning appeared to destroy the very humanist assumptions upon which the original Enlightenment goals were based.

The thinkers we are considering remained unaffected by this deeper crisis. This meant that their break with the Enlightenment was a correspondingly ambiguous affair. Often the Enlightenment is in retrospect spoken of as if it were based on a narrow conception of human rationality, reason in a "thin" sense. It is not just more accurate but also more revealing to regard the Enlightenment as a movement of thought based on a basic trust in the human being's capacity to secure its own basis for the traditional supports of human life (morality, religion, and the state); Enlightenment was to replace a capricious tradition and unsupported appeals to revelation, scriptural authority and the like. But then any nascent doubt in the ability of human powers of systematic reasoning itself to perform this role need not in the first instance lead to an abandonment of the high aims of Enlightenment itself. One may suppose rather that the first natural reaction within the Enlightenment horizon will be to appeal to some other human capacity, or perhaps review the account currently given of what human capacity amounts to. Such a review may lead in the end to revision even of such a key notion as that of reason itself, as happened in

---

[5]For an informative account of this aspect of the period and of the background to the present paper's topic in general, see Frederick C. Beiser, *The Fate of Reason: German Philosophy from Kant to Fichte* (Cambridge MA and London: Harvard University Press, 1987).

the cases of both Kant and Hegel. That is to say, one need not abandon the project of reconstituting human values and practices on a human basis simply because human reason as currently conceived proves inadequate to the task.

An example of this was the new liberalism which appeared late in the eighteenth century in such figures as Schiller, Humboldt, and Forster, though also Lessing and Jacobi were involved. Here we find the shrinkage of reason compensated by an attribution to individuals of a *native* ability to take care of their own welfare, religion, and morality. The new liberalism urged characteristically that states should protect human rights but not actively intervene in promoting stability and welfare. That would be to inhibit an innate human capacity to promote them, and thus in the end to destroy it. Seen in this light, even the extreme form of liberalism—anarchism—is simply a projection of Enlightenment thought. It assumes a human talent to produce organization at the level of the individual from below. A romantic dream no doubt, but still within the terms of the project.

The same, however, can be said of Romanticism itself and the *Sturm und Drang*. Here too we have an extension of Enlightenment faith, even if the typical interpretation of Romanticism sees it, as did Hamann himself, as a polemic against the Enlightenment. Hamann, an early hero of Kierkegaard's, proposed the life of artistic feeling and expression, or indeed of lived experience in general, as the proper source of the truths humanity needed and to which reason had been inappropriately applied. One can indeed say, of course, that Hamann saw in lived experience the locus or source of truths that would lead to a radical revision of the humanizing project of the Enlightenment, so that in effect through Hamann that project acquired a nature and dimension it had all along lacked, and that therefore this is indeed a polemic against the Enlightenment. But by looking at the Enlightenment in terms of its goals rather than its chosen method, we may see both the liberal and the romantic developments as attempts to save the project itself. Both developments involve typically "immanent" points of view, pushing reason aside to give room to a power of appreciation and apprehension which has been unnecessarily ignored and suppressed. That this is not the normal way of looking at the Enlightenment project, least of all that of those like

Hamann who began to criticize it, is due mainly to the project's being identified with those philosophers who despite these criticisms continued to believe that the crucial human truths could be established by reason, as they conceived that capacity, alone.

Hamann called his new sense of life and artistic feeling "faith." But there is no invocation here to look or leap *beyond* reason. Hamann, for whom the rational horizon merely defines the limits of a shallow, debilitating intellectuality, proposes instead a *return* to experience not a leap beyond it. As has often been pointed out, there is a strong "existentialist" strain in Hamann to which Kierkegaard early responded.[6] Not only does the appeal to lived experience as the place to which to address significant human questions, as well as the place from which to ask them, have its clear counterpart in the writings of Climacus, but what Hamann himself wrote based on his own lived experience provides an important source for just those psychological concepts Kierkegaard was to exploit in his own "experimental" writings, e.g. anxiety or dread.[7] Kierkegaard is also clearly influenced by the way Hamann reappropriated the Enlightenment's hero, Socrates, to turn the tables on the Enlightenment by focusing on Socratic ignorance.[8]

Hamann's thought, however, lacks dialectic. Although for Hamann "faith is not the work of reason, and therefore cannot succumb to its attacks," there is no thought of faith being antagonistic to reason. And even if faith "happens as little for reasons as do tasting and sensing,"[9] it still happens in much the same way as do these latter. Hamannian faith is an immediate trust in one's sense of things. And although Kierkegaard acknowledges Hamann's understanding of how the common understanding of religion errs, he does not see Hamann occupying the point of view

---

[6]See the Journal entries from 1836 to 1837 (among them JP, 2:1539-43).

[7]See, e.g., CA, 162n., and JP, 1:96.

[8]See *Papirer* V B 55,14: "The greatest humorist (Hamann) has said concerning the greatest ironist (Socrates), that what made Socrates great was that he distinguished between what he knew and what he did not know." Cf. JP 2:1554 and J. G. Hamann, *Sokratische Denkwürdigkeiten*, ed. Sven-Aage Jørgensen (Stuttgart: Reclam, 1968).

[9]J. G. Hamann, *Sämtliche Werke, Historisch-kritische Ausgabe*, ed. J. Nadler (Vienna: Herder, 1949–1957) 2:74.

of religion developed by Climacus in the *Postscript*. And, whether due to inadequacy of perspective or to his own failure to do the perspective justice, Hamann's criticism did not in fact survive in a way that would make him a suitable ally for Climacus.

What about Jacobi? In spite of his zealous criticism of current exponents of Enlightenment thought, Jacobi still held on to the "humane" goals of the Enlightenment. Since he was also satisfied that he had identified the limits of reason, for him the choice was obvious. If you cannot prove the existence of God and the immortality of the soul in the way that, for instance, Mendelssohn thought one could,[10] you must accept these vital truths on faith. For Jacobi, reason's cognizance of its own limits leads the rationalist to atheism but in his uncritical refusal to countenance that conclusion he, too, is a proper heir of the Enlightenment and his faith merely a change of horses in midstream—from faith in reason to faith in faith itself. Anticipating one side in the recent debate between Popper and his critics as to whether rationalism is inherently irrational because itself the result of a basic choice which therefore cannot itself be rational, Jacobi saw faith as a basic human attitude to which even the rationalist must resort to choose reason.[11] This and a continued belief in revelation, and also his "leap of faith," earned for Jacobi an anti-Enlightenment and irrationalist label. But exactly as with Hamann's so-called irrationalism, Jacobi's was merely a concern to keep reason within its own bounds—bounds that do not define the limits of human understanding in a large sense but, when defined, give room to another mode of human understanding.

Later on in the *Postscript*, in the conclusion of his chapter on subjective truth, Climacus acknowledges the contributions of both Hamann and Jacobi. But he finds neither of them suitable for his project. Typical of the tone of high irony preserved throughout the two chapters on Lessing, Climacus's manifest and ironic reason for not allying himself with either of these thinkers is the inherent or

---

[10]Moses Mendelssohn, *Morgenstunden oder Vorelesungen über das Daseyn Gottes* (Berlin, 1785; rev. ed. 1876). See Beiser, *The Fate of Reason*, 72, 78, 94.

[11]F. H. Jacobi, *Werke*, ed. F. Köppen (Leipzig: Fleischer, 1819–1820) IV/1:210-11, 223.

simply *de facto* inability of their work to resist Hegelian compart-mentalization.

> I won't hide the fact that I admire Hamann, though freely admitting the pliancy of his thought lacks proportion, and his extraordinary vitality lacks self-control for working in any coherent way. But his aphorisms have the originality of genius, and the pithiness of the form is entirely suited to the casual throwing off of a thought. Life and soul, and to the last drop of his blood, he is captured in a single phrase: a highly gifted genius's passionate protest against an existential system. But the System is hospitable, poor Hamann! you have been reduced by Michelet to a §. Whether some stone marks your grave I do not know; whether it is now trodden under I do not know; but this I do know, that with the devil's might and main you have been pressed into the §-uniform and pushed into the ranks.
>
> (CUP, 1:250)

For someone protesting vigorously against enrollment in a system, being pushed into the ranks is a fate no better than to have been brought into a bad marriage with the system itself. Indeed it is worse; as the metaphor implies, it means being forced to fight on all the same, but on the wrong side. Certainly, Hamann's single-minded and passionate protest against a rational metaphysics of life was a blow in the right direction; and it was a shame, if true, that he had been rendered impotent by being acknowledged by the System. But Kierkegaard's real criticism of Hamann is that the appeal to lived experience is still the expression of an aesthetic point of view. This is made clearer by noting that, in Hamann's case, reason and faith are not actually in conflict with each other, they simply have different roles, lived experience now being given the due of which the Enlightenment's "thin" reason had unfairly deprived it. Hamann's understanding of the roles of faith and reason is not unlike that commonly ascribed to Wittgenstein, a language game view in which reason and faith each has its independent part in the complex structure of our language-based practices; so that it would be wrong to apply the standards of one language game to the practices of the other. But if reason is not in conflict with faith, then faith neither is nor requires a leap beyond reason, one merely switches from one game to the other, simply making sure not to confuse the standards appropriate to each.

Jacobi too is dismissed for surviving merely as a section in the System's Encyclopedia.

> Poor Jacobi! Whether anyone visits your grave I do not know, but I know that the §-plough overturns all your eloquence, all your inwardness, while a few scant words are registered as what you amount to in the System. There it is said of him that he represents feeling with enthusiasm. . . .

As Climacus says, "a reference like that makes game of both feeling and enthusiasm, whose secret is precisely that they cannot be reported secondhand . . . " (CUP, 1:257).

But "now to Lessing" (CUP, 1:95). If Jacobi's weakness was to have said too much, clearly Lessing's merit is to have said very little and, with respect to what he did say, to have "remained a riddle." His strength, as Climacus says, is that "it was quite impossible to have Lessing killed and world-historically butchered and tinned in a §" (CUP, 1:107). That could be said to be the ironical explanation, to be read as evasive humor by those able to grasp only secondhand explanations. The serious point, to be picked up firsthand by subjective thinkers, has to do with the leap and what it means to have faith. It is here that Climacus turns the "riddle" of Lessing to his own, and he would assume Lessing's, advantage.

The third thesis, an actual thesis of Lessing's in this case, is that "accidental truths of history can never serve as proof for eternal truths of reason, and the transition by which one would base an eternal truth upon historical testimony is a leap" (CUP, 1:93).[12] According to Climacus, what Lessing "constantly" opposes is the "direct transition from the historically reliable to the eternal decision" (CUP, 1:96), or any attempt to "quantify oneself into a qualitative decision" (CUP, 1:95). Lessing uses the distinction between historical contingency and necessary truths of reason to mark the illegitimacy of any attempt to convert the purely historical facts on which Christianity is based into the eternal Facts con-

---

[12]G. E. Lessing, "Über den Beweis des Geistes und der Kraft," *Theologische Streitschriften*, GW, 9:82. The short piece (only eight pages) also includes the occurrence of the familiar Aristotelian expression "metabasis eis allo genos" (qualitative change) referred to by Climacus (CUP, 1:98).

stitutive of Christian faith. As historical contingencies they cannot amount to the eternal truths embodied in Christian belief. As Lessing says, "The letter is not the spirit, and the Bible is not religion, so that objections against the letter, or against the Bible, are not ipso facto objections against religion."[13] Climacus reminds us that Lessing describes the unbridgeable gap between letter and spirit as a "ditch" that is "repugnant" and "wide,"[14] and also that Lessing says he has tried, "often and earnestly" but without success, to leap over it (CUP, 1:98).

There are several puzzling aspects to Lessing's remarks. Apart from the fact that, as Climacus immediately points out, they involve serious conceptual confusions, there is doubt even as to the direction in which Lessing would have us believe he has attempted the leap. As Climacus formulates the problem of the *Fragments*, you might expect the problem to be that of the transition from the historical to the eternal. But as the quotation above indicates, Lessing seems already to be standing on the other side, the side of reason for which historical evidence is at least in principle neither here nor there. What in that case could have motivated his attempt to leap in the direction of the historical and contingent? Perhaps the wish to span the gap between the point where his reason had brought him to a stop and those Facts (of Christianity) for which, according to Leibniz's distinction, no historical research is relevant. But then it is even unclear whether Lessing is serious in claiming that the ditch played a part in his own intellectual life at all. In another context he accepts that truths attested to only historically might well be those we are after in any case. He is on record as denying the theistic belief in an independent creation,[15] and happy

---

[13]G. E. Lessing, *Axiomata*, GW, 9:210, 211. Cf. Beiser, *The Fate of Reason*, 58. Lessing's remarks here are part of his dispute with H. M. Goeze (see *Anti-Goeze*, GW, 9:241-322), an orthodox Lutheran pastor in Hamburg, who had reacted against Lessing's publication (with commentary) of an attack on positive religion by H. S. Reimarus (*Apologie oder Schützschrift für die vernunftige Veregrer Gottes*). Lessing had received the manuscript, withheld by its author during his lifetime because he feared the effect of its publication, from Reimarus's daughter, Elise (cf. CUP, 1:103, where Kierkegaard refers to her as Emilie).

[14]G. E. Lessing, "Über den Beweis des Geistes und der Kraft," GW, 9:85.

[15]Short notes, "Über die Wirklichkeit der Dinge ausser Gott," 1763, published in 1795 in his brother Karl G. Lessing's *Lessing's Leben* (Leipzig, 1887).

with the idea that there is nothing outside the divine mind even if the world contains contingencies (in which case God does too). The problem is then that if Lessing had no personal concern with the distinction, why should he call the ditch "repugnant"?

Although Climacus fails to comment on this, focusing instead on the metaphor of width, it is still worth asking why Lessing should use the term "repugnant." But we are reduced here to guesswork. Perhaps Lessing was saying that since no one could claim to bridge the gap rationally the very attempt would be repugnant because intellectually disreputable. But then he also admits to having made such repugnant attempts himself. Or is Lessing, as just suggested, simply describing his own frustration at not being able to reach the truths in question? The puzzle remains; although we will come upon another possible interpretation, the real explanation may simply be Lessing's talent for the dramatic expression. Climacus himself suggests it may be just a "stylistic turn of phrase" on Lessing's part (CUP, 1:98).

As for width, Climacus points to two glaring mistakes in Lessing's account. First, the "leap" is a decision ("the category of decision," says Climacus), which means that you either do it or don't do it, there is nothing that can be called trying or failing to do it. The idea of "having been quite close to doing something" has in itself something of the comical about it, but "to have been very close to making the leap is nothing whatever" (CUP, 1:99). Second, if there can be no trying to leap, then "earnest" cannot pertain to the attempt, and Climacus's next comment is that the notions of trying and earnest can only apply here in the attempt "with the utmost earnest to make the ditch wide," indeed "infinitely wide," so that it becomes "equally difficult for someone who cannot jump at all, whether the ditch is wide or narrow" (CUP, 1:99). Here the attempt is in the intellect; whatever it is positively to make the leap of faith, it cannot be done unless one grasps the absolute nature of the distinction between the contingent and the eternal.[16]

---

[16]Climacus also notes that, in referring to accidental historical truths, Lessing might be allowing there could also be historical truths that were not accidental, but assumes that "accidental" is intended as a "genus predicate" (CUP, 1:98).

It is worth considering here what we ordinarily mean by leaping over a distance. Ordinarily, surely, such a leap is an attempt to treat the distance as if it were nothing, an attempt which, if successful, reduces to taking the gap, as one would say, "in one's stride." Taking a gap in our stride, whatever training may have been involved in making our stride sufficiently long, is in effect to make nothing of the distance which, before we trained, may well have seemed beyond us. But none of this resembles what Kierkegaard suggests we should be doing. What Kierkegaard calls the "leap" is not a leap from one foothold to another; the trick is rather, as Johannes *de silentio* says, "to transform the leap in life to a gait, to express the sublime in the pedestrian absolutely" (FT, 41, trans. altered). In short, it is the leaper who changes, not the location. Outwardly the leaper just keeps going, and if there is anything corresponding to a space or a void, it is the thought that, for all the leaper *knows*, the ground over which he continues to walk might not be what in his faith he believes it to be—not the space of his own and of God's possibilities but what Kant once referred to as the "black abyss" of a world without providence.[17] From this it is tempting to conclude that Kierkegaard's notion of faith is badly represented by the notion of a leap, even that it is not a notion with which Kierkegaard would have liked to be as closely associated as he has become in the encyclopedias of latter-day "§-ploughers." We might even conjecture that the reason why Climacus resorts to the notion of a leap in the *Postscript* is mainly to provide Lessing with an opportunity to make a mockery of the whole notion, at least as conceived in the "leap"-literature of the time. In any case, we should be wary of treating the notion too figuratively.

One thing at least is clear. Climacus presents Lessing's words about the leap as essentially comical. Their comical nature is presented as the visible aspect of that Socratic combination of comedy and pathos which characterizes the existing thinker. Climacus goes so far as to concede that Lessing himself has in fact employed his

---

[17]Immanuel Kant, "Gedanken bei dem frühzeitigen Ableben des Herrn Friedrich von Funk," *Werke, Akademie Text Ausgabe*, ed. W. Dilthey et al. (Berlin: de Gruyter, 1979) 2:37-44. See Beiser, *The Fate of Reason*, 333n.49.

earnest in the appropriate manner, that is, to make the ditch wide
rather than "try" to leap over it—wide enough to give room for
this combination of pathos and comedy. He describes Lessing's
whole account as that of a "wag" (*Skjelm*) (CUP, 1:99), as indeed
it would have to be if Lessing's earnest is that of a subjective
thinker. In conclusion Climacus subtly brings Lessing's humor to
bear on Hegel by introducing a "more popular" way of poking fun
at the leap: "you shut your eyes, you seize yourself by the scruff
of the neck *à la* Münchhausen, and then—then you stand on the
other side, on the other side of sound common sense, in the
promised land of the System" (CUP, 1:99).

The presentation is a subtle mix of irony and polemical
strategy, but the argument underlying it is no less subtle. Climacus
admits that Lessing has "very little to say" about the leap and
therefore there is little to be said about "Lessing's relation to the
leap." Nor is it "altogether dialectically clear what Lessing has
wanted to make of it" (CUP, 1:105). Yet on the way he has been
careful to bestow on Lessing just those features which would
indeed lead one to expect him to say very little. His words have
acquired a Socratic "complexion" (CUP, 1:102), and in addition to
"poetic imagination" he has the "skeptical ataraxy and religious
sensibility needed to become aware of the category of the religious" (CUP, 1:65). Lessing's evasive facetiousness can, in short, be
read as Socratic jest, just as the brevity of his comments can be
taken to demonstrate his constant ability "cleverly to exempt
himself, his dialectical insight, and inside that his subjectivity, from
every busy delivery service to the bearer" (CUP, 1:68)—all of
which, again, is consistent with the thesis that Lessing is a
subjective thinker. Climacus's argument in a nutshell is this:
Lessing says little about the leap, but the little he does say is
consistent with a genuine understanding of the leap, which will
then explain why he says so little.

The clearest picture we are given of Lessing as someone able
to avoid answering in ways which would betray his grasp of what
the question asked is in Climacus's rendition of part of the famous
conversation between Jacobi and Lessing, a report of which Jacobi

published after Lessing's death.[18] Here, says Climacus, we have Lessing's "last word" on the leap. This last word follows Lessing's famous confession to Jacobi that he is a Spinozist. The original goes as follows (LS, 69):

Lessing: So we won't be parting company over your *credo*?
Jacobi: We don't want that by any means. But it isn't in Spinoza that my *credo* lies.
Lessing: I would hope it doesn't lie in *any* book.
Jacobi: Not just that. I believe in an intelligent and personal cause of the world.
Lessing: Ah, so much the better! Now I must be about to hear something quite new.
Jacobi: Don't get too excited on that account. My way out is with a *salto mortale*; but you aren't one to take much pleasure in standing on your head?
Lessing: Don't say that, just as long as I don't have to follow suit. And you're going to end up on your feet anyway, aren't you? So, if there's no mystery, I want to see what's in it.

Then following a fairly lengthy discussion of fatalism, the conversation resumes as follows:

Jacobi: As I see it, the researcher's first task is to reveal and to disclose existence (*Dasein zu enthüllen*). . . . Explanation is only a means, a way to this goal: it is the first goal but never the last. The last goal is what cannot be explained: the irresolvable, immediate, and simple. . . .   (LS, 78)

To this Hamannian proposal Lessing ironically responds:

Lessing: Good, very good, I too can use all that; but I can't do it in the same way. On the whole, your *salto mortale* does not displease me; and I can see how a man with a head of that kind will want to stand on his head to get somewhere. Take me with you if it works.
            (LS, 79, quoted by Kierkegaard in German, CUP, 1:102)
Jacobi: Just step on the elastic spot which catapulted me out and it will go of its own accord.
            (LS, 80, quoted by Kierkegaard in German, CUP, 1:102)

---

[18]F. H. Jacobi, "Über die Lehre des Spinoza in Briefen an den Herrn Moses Mendelssohn" (LS), in *Jacobis Spinoza Büchlein*, ed. Fritz Mauthner (München: Georg Müller Verlag, 1912) 63-80.

Lessing: That already requires a leap that I can no longer ask of
my old legs and heavy head.
        (LS, 80, quoted by Kierkegaard in German, CUP, 1:102)

By publishing his account of this conversation in 1785 Jacobi
hoped to bring the Enlightenment's faith in reason into disrepute.
If Spinozism is where reason takes you, so much the worse for
reason. Climacus's account does justice to this part of Jacobi's
intention by taking Lessing's ironic reply to be a recommendation
to lighter heads and younger legs to accept the invitation which
Lessing declines. But in Climacus's hands the remark that "anyone
with young legs and a light head can very well leap" (CUP, 1:103)
is aimed ironically at Jacobi himself. For Jacobi has not understood
the full dimensions of the leap. He has failed to see that the leap
is an "isolating act" and so cannot be taught or conveyed, or done
in company. The Lessing to whom the "possible" thesis on the
dialectic of inwardness and communication has already been
attributed sees the folly in Jacobi's asking him to leap with him,
and in declining, Lessing makes it sound as though the leap
spanned a ditch so that once again it is its width that is too much
for his heavy head and old legs. Really, however, it was Jacobi
who made the absurd suggestion that there can be a "transition"
to a decision (CUP, 1:102), hence the possibility of a run-up and
failure to gather sufficient impetus. Lessing is simply humoring
Jacobi, "realiz[ing] very well that the leap, or the crux, is qualitatively dialectical and allows no approximating transition."
Lessing's answer is therefore "a jest" (CUP, 1:103). Climacus
concludes his account of the Jacobi-Lessing exchange by summariz-
ing the psychological difference between the two: "Lessing rests in
himself, feels no need of fellowship; so he parries ironically and
slips away from Jacobi on his old legs" (CUP, 1:103).

Of course the fact may have been that Lessing slipped away on
his old legs simply to avoid further badgering by the persistent
Jacobi. However, Jacobi exploits Lessing's last word for his own
ends. And Climacus does the same. He wants to point out that
faith for Jacobi is a cheap surrender of his human gift of understanding. No doubt it is also an uncritical faith, a faith in "truths"
already identified and aimed at under the aegis of reason, and
with the slack now seen to be left by an ineffectual reason conveniently made up by faith. But faith, as Kierkegaard's pseud-

onyms present it, requires you to open yourself to practical uncertainties and to the realization that Enlightenment goals can only be secured by a relationship to God—in other words through a radical break with Enlightenment. Furthermore, if your interest in continuing beyond the bounds of human possibility is in any genuine sense religious, the leap you envision will disqualify you if you fail to evince a grasp of the fact that religious belief engages the whole person and not just the intellect. In short, Jacobi's anti-Enlightenment stance is confined to the criticism of reason. What Jacobi egregiously lacked, in Climacus's language, is that "passionate dialectical abhorrence [Avsky] for a leap" which makes the ditch "so infinitely wide" (CUP, 1:99).

But that abhorrence is just what, in Climacus's portrayal, we are prodded into thinking Lessing did possess—which now provides us with that other possible explanation of why the ditch appeared so "repugnant." Here it is not because leaping from finite to infinite, or vice versa, is intellectually disreputable; nor is the repugnancy the frustration typically felt by a rationalist who would have so liked his reason to convey him across. It is the abhorrence one feels at the brink when one acquires enough negative dialectic to realize what is risked when the gap between finite and infinite is itself infinite.

Whatever Lessing meant by the phrase, it is undeniable that the commitment to reason and the acceptance of Spinozistic conclusions—and for Jacobi it was these which were repugnant—brings Lessing within reach of the existential dialectic expounded in the two chapters we have been exploring. The moral then, surely, is that precisely because it involves a clear break with the Enlightenment, this latter is a better background against which to grasp Kierkegaard's thought than the various moves made to save it in the so-called counter-Enlightenment. The crux is that Climacus's leap is reserved for those whose commitment to reason is strong enough for them to feel the full force of Johannes *de silentio*'s "shudder of thought" (*Tankens Gysen*) (FT, 9, trans. altered).

According to Beiser's rewarding account, Jacobi's publishing the record of the conversation was calculated to bring the weight of Lessing's reputation behind the counter-Enlightenment, making it clear, as he puts it, that it was Lessing and not Mendelssohn

who was the "true Socrates of his time."[19] The Enlightenment
Socrates was the tireless seeker of truth. But, as we noted, the
tireless search was proving fruitless. Beiser describes Jacobi as
preparing the hemlock that would solve the tragic Socratic
dilemma confronting mainstream Enlightenment thinkers once it
became obvious that the program was not achieving its expected
goals. Lessing was to be portrayed as someone willing to see the
vanity of philosophy—a determinist who saw that rational
speculation, consistently carried out, leads in the end to atheism
and to fatalism. The solution was to leap out of philosophy.
Hamann, as we saw, and as Kierkegaard noted, had gone even
further and turned Socrates, the persistent confessor of ignorance,
into a counter-Enlightenment symbol. Climacus's chapters on
Lessing are in the same tradition. Like Jacobi, Climacus sees
Lessing as a Socrates whose jest betrays a sense of the objective
uncertainty of all that is important (cf. CUP, 1:210). Like Socrates,
Lessing with his wit and evasiveness can be someone who
"conceives infinity in the form of ignorance" which must then be
expressed in the form of irony, in speech which to the uninitiated
must sound like that of a "madman" (CUP, 1:83).

But what does Climacus make of Lessing's Spinozism? In referring to it he neither approves nor indeed comments. He does, however, say on the strength of a remark of Lessing's reported by
Jacobi (LS, 80) that it is "no wonder" that Lessing was declared a
pantheist (CUP, 1:104). But there need be nothing wrong with pantheism from Kierkegaard's point of view, so long as it does not
take a form that prevents it developing into true Christianity. In
the *Postscript*, however, pantheism is clearly associated in a bad
sense with Hegel, who offers no future in that direction. The publication of Jacobi's *Briefe* led in fact to the famous Pantheism Controversy which, as Beiser says, "threw the *Aufklärung* back on the defensive," in the end "completely [changing] the intellectual map of
eighteenth-century German."[20] The way in which Spinoza was received was part and parcel of that change, and by Kierkegaard's
time Spinoza belonged to the likes of Herder and Goethe. Spino-

---

[19]Beiser, *The Fate of Reason*, 77.
[20]Ibid., 44.

za's pantheism had come to be associated, in a way that Jacobi had not calculated, with Hamannian "lived life" under one or another aspect. Spinoza's texts were now treated as a mould into which to pour whatever existential ballast one needed to flesh out their "geometry." Kierkegaard would hardly be attracted to that Spinoza, and we gather from the distribution of entries on Spinoza in the journals that, although he had read the *Tractatus* as a student, it was not until 1846 that he looked seriously at the *Ethics*. But there is nothing in principle that would have prevented him appreciating Lessing's Spinozism, at least as Jacobi understood it—as the best that reason can do.

One might still question Climacus's consistency, in the very chapter which crucially denies the possibility of an existential system, in praising someone who he acknowledges is a confessed Spinozist. Of course, one could say that Spinoza's system is not existential, and so it does not make the mistake of Hegel whose System did have such pretensions. But a failure even to raise existential issues can hardly be a virtue in a work whose clear aim is to move those issues to center stage. Again, however, in terms of the dialectic which Climacus is concerned to elucidate in the *Postscript*, and if we grant Lessing his own reading of Spinoza, the portrayal of Lessing as a rationalist, and committed to staying within the bounds of reason, is essential to the portrayal of Lessing as the thinker who understands what is meant and what is not meant by the "leap." Only someone who knows that he stands at the brink can grasp what is involved in going beyond.

Finally, there is that question again of how Kierkegaard can "attach himself" to Lessing on the subject of the leap in a work whose clearest message is that in this matter appeals to authority have no place. We noted at the beginning that Climacus says he is not invoking Lessing as an authority. Yet in a subtle twist of counterfactual reasoning he contrives to have it both ways. Lessing is appealed to as someone who would agree that, if he could be appealed to, then the project that calls for his support would not be the right one. There can be no acknowledgement, but at least you know that if there was, then someone has certainly got it wrong. Attachment on that point should be beyond reproach.

You see, that's how hard it is to approach Lessing in religious matters. If I were to present the individual ideas, ascribing them to him directly and in parrot fashion, if I were to enfold him politely, obligingly in my admiring embrace, as the one to whom I owed all, then he might smilingly disengage himself and leave me in the lurch, an object of ridicule. If I were to keep his name quiet, come out bawling joyously over this matchless discovery of mine, which no one before me had made, then that *polumetis Odysseus* [wily Odysseus], if I imagined him there, would no doubt put his hand on my shoulder and, with an ambivalently admiring look on his face, say: "You are right in this, if only I'd known." And then I, if no one else, would understand that he had the better of me.   (CUP, 1:71)

In the same way that true knights of faith can never be teachers, only witnesses (FT, 80), truly religious writers can never cite each other as authorities (see ibid.). For Kierkegaard there is something in the nature of the relation of religious discourse to religious experience that makes it clear to one who understands that discourse (and therefore its relation to experience) that *if* another writer were to embrace him as a colleague, the right thing to do would be to look at one's watch and plead another appointment. A religious thinker seeing someone do that might suspect he had found an ally.

12

Retracing the Circular Ruins of Hegel's Encyclopedia

William McDonald

Preliminary Expectoration

Let us construct a thought experiment [*Experiment*].[1] Let us suppose Kierkegaard's "authorship," from *Either/Or* to *Concluding Unscientific Postscript*, is a polemical reduplication of Hegel's system of speculative philosophy, which is represented most comprehensively by his *Encyclopedia of the Philosophical Sciences in Outline*. An extensive comparison of these works would be logistically unworkable within the scope of this essay, so I propose the following modification to the thought experiment. Since the *Phenomenology of Spirit* precedes Hegel's *Encyclopedia* and anticipates the essentials of the whole system,[2] it might be read as a preface to the *Encyclopedia*. Climacus's *Concluding Unscientific Postscript*, on

---

[1]Howard and Edna Hong translate *Experiment* as "imaginary construction." They educe good reasons for not always simply translating it as "experiment." See the extensive discussion of this in the translators' "Historical Introduction" to R, xxi-xxxii. Nevertheless, "imaginary construction" is often rather cumbersome. Throughout this paper I will use "thought experiment" or some variant of "imaginary construction" as the context requires. The other important qualification of the use of the term in Kierkegaard's work is that it usually refers to the construction of a different narrative voice within the text, for experimental purposes. For further discussion of the notion, together with references to the use of the term elsewhere in Kierkegaard, see R, 357-62.

[2]Cf. Rudolf Haym: "[I]t is not saying too much when I claim that anyone understands Hegel's philosophy if he completely masters the meaning of this preface"; Hermann Glockner: "[T]he most important of all Hegel texts . . . whoever has understood the preface to the *Phenomenology* has understood Hegel." Both are quoted in *Hegel Texts and Commentary: Hegel's Preface to His System*, trans. and ed. Walter Kaufmann (Notre Dame IN: University of Notre Dame Press, 1977) 1.

the other hand, retrospectively recuperates Kierkegaard's "author-ship," repeating much of it in review. Since I will be arguing that the rhetorical structures of the *Encyclopedia* and the "authorship" stand in an inverse relation to one another, I propose to compare the "Preface" to Hegel's *Phenomenology of Spirit* (as preface to the "system") with Johannes Climacus's *Concluding Unscientific Post-script* (as postscript to the "authorship"). In the "Preface" to the *Phenomenology of Spirit* Hegel announces the impossibility of writing a preface to a philosophical system. In the "Appendix" to *Postscript* Climacus revokes everything he has said. The question of prefaces (and postfaces) is central to the rhetorical structure of both works. A comparison of Hegel's "Preface" and Climacus's *Postscript* will give us, in condensed form, an insight into the archi-tectonics of both Hegel's *Encyclopedia* and Kierkegaard's "author-ship," and a chance to observe differences in their philosophical rhetoric as modes of communication and pedagogy.

Experimenting Foreword

The use of an imaginary construction, as Johannes Climacus has argued, allows a crucial difference to be discerned by the reader. This is the contrast between narrative points of view, which allows the reader to see a difference within the pseudonym's account. Often this contrast consists in an ironic distance between the pseudonymous narrator and his imaginary construction. The narrative thereby loses its monologic authority and the reader is left in doubt. The prime effect intended by this split narrative is to establish "a chasmic abyss between reader and author and [to fix] the separation of inwardness between them, so that a direct understanding is made impossible" (CUP, 1:263).

This ironic distance within a split narrative is one of the defining hallmarks of modernist literature.[3] Another hallmark is the totalizing structure of the grand narrative, wherein all differ-ence is teleologically subsumed without remainder. In Hegel's work these two modernist features coalesce: (i) While he does not use imaginary constructions to create ironic distance between

---

[3]Cf. Jean-François Lyotard, *The Postmodern Condition*, trans. Geoff Bennington and Brian Massumi (Manchester: Manchester University Press, 1984) 33-34.

coexisting narrative voices, he does differentiate points of view within his work. The narrative point of view of *The Phenomenology of Spirit*, for example, evolves in the course of the book in the manner of a *Bildungsroman*, so that successive sections of the book are only intelligible to a reader who has followed the dialectical evolution of the narrative in the preceding stages; and (ii) Hegel's systematic recuperation of all of history, of everything encyclopedically, is paradigmatic of the grand narrative. In Hegel's modernism these two features are reconciled by difference being accommodated within the unifying structure of the grand narrative. The narrative consists in the retrospective account of how differences have contributed to the formation of the absolute point of view which now accounts for them.

In Kierkegaard's pseudonymous "authorship," on the other hand, the ironic distance applies not only within each narrative structure but to the whole. Not only is each of the pseudonymous works partitioned in ways which break up the narrative unity, often by the creation of "imaginary constructions" of characters by the pseudonymous authors, but the whole "authorship" stands in the same relation to Kierkegaard as the imaginary constructions stand to the pseudonymous authors. Kierkegaard is the "author of the authors," just as they are authors of characters who are authors (CUP, 1:625-27). From the point of view of the humorist Climacus, the "authorship" redoubles the totality of the Hegelian system, but in such a way that what is most important remains outside, viz., the individual *existing* in faith before the absolute paradox (CUP, 1:271-72). Narrative contrast is used to disrupt retrospective mediation of difference, to maintain a decided distinction between inner and outer. This includes the maintenance of a distinction between narrators and characters inside the books, and the existing individual reader outside the books. The mock "grand narrative," to be found particularly in *Postscript*, functions to exceed the seamless totality of retrospection by rhetorical repetition. It is largely in virtue of this antisystematic excess and the hyperbolic proliferation of narrative voices and textual segments, together with his unremitting irony, that Kierkegaard is seen as a proto-postmodernist.[4] Yet his work also retains strong modernist elements, including the pursuit of a unifying "life-view" (*Livs-Anskuelse*) and attempts at retrospective totalization of his work.[5]

Inverse Relations

Both the "authorship" and the *Encyclopedia* ostensibly aim at an absolute *telos*. The *Encyclopedia* aims to lead the reader from relative ignorance (or at an ideal extreme from pure immediacy or even from nothing at all) to absolute knowledge. The "authorship" aims to lead the reader away from the immediacy of sensuous desire and the snares of reflective knowledge to the edge of Christian faith, which is a precondition for the absolute *telos* of eternal salvation.

Both works develop dialectically. That is, their movement occurs by virtue of responding to perceived conflicts between contrasting positions. The response in turn leads to further conflict, which evokes another response. Hegel seeks to resolve the conflicts

---

[4]See, e.g., Christopher Norris, *The Deconstructive Turn: Essays in the Rhetoric of Philosophy* (London/New York: Methuen, 1984); John Vignaux Smyth, *A Question of Eros: Irony in Sterne, Kierkegaard and Barthes* (Tallahassee: Florida State University Press, 1986); Pat Bigelow, *Kierkegaard and the Problem of Writing* (Tallahassee: Florida State University Press, 1987); Sylviane Agacinski, *Aparté: Conceptions and Deaths of Søren Kierkegaard*, trans. Kevin Newmark (Tallahassee: Florida State University Press, 1988); Mark C. Taylor, *Altarity* (Chicago: University of Chicago Press, 1987). For critiques of postmodern interpretations of Kierkegaard, see, e.g., Sylvia Walsh, "Kierkegaard and Postmodernism," *International Journal for Philosophy of Religion* 29/2 (1991): 113-22; Ronald L. Hall, *Word and Spirit: A Kierkegaardian Critique of the Modern Age* (Bloomington: Indiana State University Press, 1993). For further consideration of Kierkegaard's relations to modernism and postmodernism, see n. 20 below.

[5]The attempt at a retrospective self-interpretation in PV undermines much of what the "authorship" aspired to achieve. It is a mastering moment of reappropriation *within the realm of thought* of the duplicity and martyrdom implicit in the "authorship," and thereby loses the existing individual Søren Kierkegaard. See Agacinski, *Aparté: Conceptions and Deaths of Søren Kierkegaard*, 120-26. On the notion of "life-view" and the related notion of "life-development," as deployed in *From the Papers of One Still Living*, see Sylvia Walsh, *Living Poetically: Kierkegaard's Existential Aesthetics* (University Park: Pennsylvania State University Press, 1994) 30-41.

within a comprehensive and consistent system of knowledge; the "authorship" seeks to maintain contrasts (between existential types, between knowledge and faith, between inner and outer, between human and divine), but to find religious atonement by means of faith despite the ineluctable contradictions inherent in Christian paradox. The inversion in this respect is really in terms of the means of achieving resolution or atonement: by means of systematic knowledge or religious faith. For while Climacus caricatures Hegel as though he ultimately aims to reduce all difference to identity within absolute knowledge, Hegel himself explicitly rejects such monotonous reduction:

> To pit this one piece of information, that in the absolute all is one, against all the distinctions of knowledge, both attained knowledge and the search and demand for knowledge—or to pass off one's absolute as the night in which all cows are black—that is the naivete of the emptiness of knowledge.[6]

The shape of each dialectic is the converse of the other. While Hegel's dialectic is apparently circular,[7] it is in fact spiral. It returns to its starting point only to view it from a metaperspective, which itself was formed in the journey away from the starting point. In our beginning is our end, but now transfigured by a heightened perspective. The "authorship" is apparently spiral, but in fact circular. It seems to move from the aesthetic, through the ethical to the religious, returning to the beginning from a higher perspective. But in fact it is always caught within the immanent sphere of writing, which occupies a realm of possibility only. Writing, and thought, can never transcend the limits of pure possibility (at least according to Climacus). Climacus, who as humorist seems to occupy the highest narrative point of view within the dialectic of the "authorship," which arguably begins with irony, says:

> Humor, when it uses Christian categories, is a false rendition of the Christian truth, since humor is not essentially different from

---

[6]*Hegel's Preface to His System*, 26.

[7]Cf. Tom Rockmore, *Hegel's Circular Epistemology* (Bloomington: Indiana University Press, 1986). Cf. also: "The true is its own becoming, the circle that presupposes its end as its aim and thus has it for its beginning—that which is actual only through its execution and end." *Hegel's Preface to His System*, 30.

irony, but is essentially different from Christianity, and is essentially not different from Christianity otherwise than irony is. It is only apparently different from irony by apparently having appropriated all the essentially Christian, yet without having appropriated it in a *decisive* way (but the essentially Christian consists precisely in decision and decisiveness), whereas what is essential for irony, recollection's withdrawal from temporality into the eternal, is in turn essential for humor. . . . Humor, when it uses Christian categories (sin, forgiveness of sin, atonement, God in time, etc.), is not Christianity but a pagan speculative thought that has come to *know* all the essentially Christian.   (CUP, 1:271-72)

So, despite its tortuous peregrinations, the "authorship" gets no further, with respect to its absolute goal, than its beginnings in irony. Or at most it achieves with respect to the modern age what Socratic irony achieved for the classical age, viz., an internal critique of received opinion (*doxa*) which clears the ground for new beginnings. In short, whereas Hegel's dialectic is positive, progressive and ascending, the dialectic of the "authorship" is a negative dialectic, a mere propaedeutic to a negative theology (which may or may not be an effective propaedeutic to a positive Christian faith).

Both Climacus and Hegel give only a promise, or a philosophical sketch, of the dialectical journey to their respective goals. Both also criticize systems of knowledge which only make promises.[8]

Preface to the System

The paradox of prefaces arises in philosophical works which are structured like a *Bildungsroman*, namely, a work whose narrative voice evolves in the course of the work itself, so that the endpoint can only be understood by a consciousness which has itself followed the same evolutionary, or dialectical, trajectory. A preface stands at the beginning of the book, but typically presents anticipations of the results of the book. But readers of a *Bildungsroman* will be in no position to understand the results or conclusions of the book until their consciousness has been led by the narrative through its dialectical trajectory. So the reader will be in no position to understand the preface prior to reading the book. Typically

---

[8]Cf. *Hegel's Preface to His System*, 24; CUP, 1:9-10.

the author writes the preface after the book has been written, so it should more accurately be called an anticipatory postface.[9]

The paradox of prefaces is highlighted by asking the question: Is the preface inside the book or outside the book? If it is inside the book, then it is part of the book and loses its status as preface. If it is outside the book, then it seems it can have no organic connection with the book and so becomes a redundant appendage. This becomes extremely important when we inquire into the structure of Hegel's *Encyclopedia*. Hegel divides the books which comprise this compound work into particular philosophical sciences, and universal philosophical science. The former have specific empirical content, while the latter is pure logical thought. The paradox of prefaces only applies, according to Hegel, to the attempt to preface works of universal philosophical science. Because particular philosophical sciences have contingently empirical elements they cannot present themselves in the pure logical form of the concept as it unfolds itself. They need to be introduced to the learner, not because of the learner's incapacity to assimilate the thought, but because of the learner's specific ignorance of the material. But with universal philosophical science, where the subject matter ideally presents itself in immediate transparency, no introduction of specific knowledge is necessary. In universal philosophical science, if there is a difficulty for the learner it is due to incapacity rather than empirical ignorance.

There can be no preface to universal philosophical science because any anticipation of the result will be empty. The result can only be understood properly by working through the full logical presentation in the body of the text, without prior mediation. The preface would therefore be superfluous. If the preface were a necessary part of the presentation of the concept, it would no longer be preparatory or prefatory; it would be incorporated into the body of the text proper as an integral part of the complete logical presentation.

---

[9] Cf. Jacques Derrida, "Outwork, prefacing" in *Dissemination*, trans. Barbara Johnson (Chicago: University of Chicago Press, 1981) 20. Derrida discusses the Hegelian paradox of prefaces, but with little reference to Kierkegaard's work, which anticipates Derrida's by well over a century.

Hegel's *Encyclopedia* comprises various types of philosophical science: phenomenology of spirit, philosophy of nature, and logic. It is an exercise in the coordination of all areas of philosophical knowledge (at least in outline). The word "encyclopedia" comes from the Greek *enkyklios* ("circular" or "in circulation," i.e., "customary") and *paideia* ("education"). Its etymological sense, then, is "either 'circular, viz., all-embracing' or 'customary education,' and more particularly a survey either of all the arts and sciences or of a particular field in systematic and alphabetical order."[10] All the areas of knowledge in Hegel's *Encyclopedia* are capable of having mediating prefaces except logic. Yet it is necessary for consciousness to be prepared for the recognition of logical presentation. Therefore the other philosophical sciences offer programs of knowledge and training in philosophical consciousness so that the individual reaches the state of culture necessary to recognize pure logic. This prompts Johannes Climacus to remark:

> It would then become a question of the importance of the Hegelian phenomenology for the system, whether it is an introduction, whether it remains outside, and if it is an introduction, whether it is in turn incorporated into the system. (CUP, 1:117)

That is, are these preparatory texts part of the necessary presentation of universal philosophical science, or do they lie radically outside it? If they are radically outside, how can they serve as preparatory?

Hegel's solution to this problem is to conceive of the preface as a self-consuming artifact.[11] Because of the gap between consciousness at the cutting edge of science and the less developed consciousness of most other people (or the analogous gap between the author, who has completed the voyage of dialectical development through the text, and the reader who has not), it is necessary to rehearse the less developed consciousness in the preliminary stages. Once learners have been rehearsed sufficiently in various particular analogues to the universal philosophical science, their consciousness is deemed receptive to recognition of the concept.

---

[10]Michael Inwood, *A Hegel Dictionary* (Oxford: Blackwell, 1992) 86.

[11]Cf. Stanley Fish, *Self-Consuming Artifacts: The Experience of Seventeenth-Century Literature* (Berkeley: University of California Press, 1972).

But because the particular philosophical sciences are not exactly analogues of the universal science of philosophy, they must be discarded at the point where logic begins. It is not that the particular philosophical sciences are false or misleading, but because of their particularity and historicity they are bound to be presented in formalistic, empirical, and ceremonial guises that are anachronistic from the point of view of pure logic. They all make concessions to the incompletely developed consciousness of the reader, by means of a feigned regression to the reader's stage of consciousness. By the time readers reach a sufficient level of development, however, consciousness becomes radically self-reflexive. Then readers can be led to see that the very forms (of the particular philosophical sciences) which brought them to their current state of consciousness are anachronistic and tendentious, and must be discarded before going further. Therefore Hegel wrote in the preface to the *Phenomenology* that a preface to a work of universal philosophical science is impossible.[12] This statement simultaneously condemns the *Phenomenology* to lie outside universal philosophical science, and retracts phenomenology as a preface to the works of logic at the core of the *Encyclopedia*. Phenomenology resembles the ladder of Wittgenstein's *Tractatus*, which has to be "thrown away" once it has been used to get to a position where the ladder itself can be seen to be an impediment to further progress.[13]

But there is something suspect about this Hegelian account. The problem is that the progression from training in the particular philosophical sciences to autonomous recognition of pure logic is posited not as a progression but as a leap. Now the question arises whether this leap is the same in kind as those made in the dialectical syntheses in the particular philosophical sciences, or whether it is radically different. The dialectical syntheses in the particular philosophical sciences are taken to be determined by the historical evolution of consciousness as a matter of necessity. Is the leap from training in the particular philosophical sciences to recognition of pure logic also a matter of the exigences of the historical

---

[12]*Hegel's Preface to His System*, 6.

[13]Ludwig Wittgenstein, *Tractatus Logico-Philosophicus*, trans. D. F. Pears and B. F. McGuinness (London and Henley: Routledge & Kegan Paul, 1961) 74.

evolution of consciousness? If it is, then the particular philosophical sciences are continuous with universal philosophical science, insofar as they are necessary preliminary stages in the apprehension of universal philosophical science. But then the particular philosophical sciences are part of universal philosophical science, or inside it. If the leap is different in kind from that made in dialectical synthesis, then logic will be isolated within the encyclopedic system as an alien body. It will be unteachably isolated in its own inside, like the Kierkegaardian demonic inclosing reserve (*Indesluttethed*). If it is isolated in this way then the Hegelian teachings of the particular philosophical sciences will not just be incomplete and anachronistic, but false—insofar as they teach that reason coming to know itself to be all reality is the result of a necessary historical dialectical process. But they are not presented as false. They are presented as particular forms of *knowledge* within the encyclopedic compass of absolute knowledge.

It seems Hegel's *Encyclopedia* is committed to rehabilitating the self-consuming prefatory works of particular philosophical sciences to the inside of absolute knowledge. It is not their contents but their forms that are anachronistic and tendentious. At the same time as they become part of the inside, the particular philosophical sciences alienate universal science from its inside, because they do not allow universal science to fulfill its requirement of being autonomously self-presenting. As Climacus puts it, "Hegelian philosophy culminates in the proposition that the outside (*Udvortes*) is the inside (*Indvortes*) and the inside the outside" (CUP, 1:296; translation modified). The universal philosophy will include everyone and everything, so that ultimately it can have no outside. Its outside is a feigned moment, for pedagogical purposes, though this feigning is also a necessary stage in the self-presentation of the concept. If the system has no outside, neither does it have an inside. It is all reality, though in order to distinguish itself from nature this panidealism will have to make use of provisional distinctions. When reason ultimately comes to realize that it is all reality, it will realize that its provisional distinctions were only provisional, for the sake of attaining a particular form of consciousness, and will revoke them.

Hegel assumes, in the first instance, that the reading public consists of those who have not yet reached the pinnacle of culture

(*Bildung*) represented in the results of the book of logic. This public, because it lacks culture, still dwells in a form of consciousness belonging to an age when formalism reigned. Therefore it requires as a matter of ceremony that the book be introduced by a preface. But because the preface does not correspond to the scientific consciousness, the public that requires it must be led into the light of science. Therefore Hegel constructs prefaces that deconstruct themselves, that fall away like empty husks, once scientific consciousness is reached. Hegel begins with indirect communication, using simulations of the forms required by the uncultured, in order to exercise the public in the particular philosophical sciences. This exercise will give the reading public the necessary training in dialectical thought and self-reflexivity to allow it to recognize the necessity of the deconstruction of the very means of the exercise. Then the reading public will be receptive to direct communication. Once this final perspective is attained the reading public will be able retrospectively to reinterpret the indirection of the communication in the particular philosophical sciences as the most direct communication possible for the uncultured. Lack of culture is reinterpreted as a necessary stage on the path to culture and thus as a part of culture. Indirection is reinterpreted as a necessary device to attain direct communication and thus as a part of direct communication.

Preface to Transgression

It is this whole difficult paradoxical relation between the inside and the outside of absolute, or ultimately redemptive knowledge that Kierkegaard plays with in his pseudonymous "authorship." He prefaces this "authorship" with invisible antithesis in *The Concept of Irony*[14] and ends with humorous reconciliation in *Concluding Unscientific Postscript*. Climacus concludes the latter itself with "An Appendix: An Understanding with the Reader," though this "conclusion" is succeeded by "A First and Last Explanation" by S. Kier-

---

[14]On the invisible difference of irony in his dissertation, see Agacinski, *Aparté: Conceptions and Deaths of Søren Kierkegaard*, 33-78. For some considerations against the claim that Kierkegaard is ironical toward Hegel's proclaimed mastery of irony, see Sylvia Walsh, *Living Poetically*, 13-14.

kegaard. This pseudonymous "authorship" is succeeded by several more pseudonymous works, which are included as part of the "authorship" in a later retrospective self-interpretation which Kierkegaard withheld from publication (PV, 10). Climacus refers to himself as a humorist, and in the appendix to *Postscript* claims to revoke everything said in it. He adds that to say something and then to revoke it is not the same as never having said it at all (CUP, 1:621).[15] In effect this is a declaration that the "authorship" is a self-consuming preface. The pseudonym Johannes Climacus (John the Climber) parodies the notion of a *scala paradisi*—a ladder by means of which one can climb up to heaven (or redemption or the absolute). It is possible to construct enormously long and complicated ladders, such as Hegel's *Encyclopedia* or Kierkegaard's intricately baroque reduplication of it. Hegel's *Encyclopedia* is one of the most hubristic assaults on heaven since the tower of Babel. Kierkegaard's parodic reduplication of it, and Climacus's humorous revocation of it, reduce it to babble. At the end of the ladder the only options are to climb down again, or to make a leap of faith. Climacus gets to the end of the ladder, laughs, tells us how to make the leap, but in telling us also tells us that reading about it won't help. He remains within the immanence of humor, and thereby stays on the ladder.

In reconstructing the "authorship's" retracing of Hegel's *Encyclopedia* we also need to be aware that there is a dialectical evolution of perspectives within the "authorship" with respect to the polemic against Hegel's system. If we retrace this evolution to the pre-authorship works, we can see a dialectic that begins with immediate *mimesis*, changes to a virulent strategy for textual production, then moves from irony, through satire and parody, to humor.[16]

Kierkegaard's early attempts at writing were largely mimetic. They were modelled on established forms. Some of his writing was almost a verbatim transcript of other people's work, such as his lecture notes from Martensen's course on the history of philoso-

---

[15]Note that the reader whom Climacus addresses when talking about revocation is only an "imagined reader" (*indbildt Læser*), i.e., an imaginary construction.

[16]Cf. P, 9-11.

phy.[17] But since one of the forms on which he modelled his writing was that of romantic individualism, he came to develop an individual aesthetic style. Nevertheless, this was still not madly eccentric. At the outset of his career as a writer Kierkegaard sought acceptance by his contemporaries, in particular from the Heiberg circle. His early published work bears the imprint of that aim. While it is still mimetic, part of the Heibergian style he used was acerbic criticism. This he directed at Hans Christian Andersen in *From the Papers of One Still Living*.

This critical *mimesis* was used as a mask in order to enter the Heiberg circle. It is similar to the strategy adopted by a virus to enter a cell. A virus consists of genetic material encapsulated in a protective shield of protein. The cell it penetrates has receptor molecules on its surface for the reception of the molecule's own hormones, which are vital to the cell's functioning. The virus enters the cell by virtue of the shape of its protein shield, which exactly replicates the shape that fits one of the cell's receptor molecules. The virus can only reproduce itself when its genes are free. Therefore, once it is inside the cell it sheds its protein shield. But nor can the virus produce its own protein, so it takes over the cell's own protein production mechanism. By this means it is able to manufacture protein shields for its clones, which can then enter other cells, use their protein manufacturing mechanisms, and disseminate further clones.

The virus has no master plan, no intentionality, in using this means of reproduction and dissemination. It acts in pure immediacy, according to its nature. Kierkegaard sought an identity as a writer. The Heiberg cell provided excellent opportunities for literary production and dissemination. The protein shield in this case was the Heibergian combination of romantic aestheticism and Hegelian speculative philosophy. But Kierkegaard's ultimately virulent nature was recognized by the Heibergian "T-cells" and he was rejected (or never fully accepted).

It was really from this point that the virus began to mutate. Kierkegaard immersed himself in his dissertation on irony, thereby learning the subtlest arts of dissimulation. In particular irony

---

[17]*Papirer* II C 25 (in XII 280-331).

taught him how rhetorical repetition could be an invisible means of critique. Understanding irony was also what launched Kierkegaard's dialectic of indirect communication, whereby writing became not a matter of conveying finished truths to the ignorant, but of acting as midwife at the birth of the reader's subjectivity.

In writing *Irony* Kierkegaard gained a deep understanding of a means of repeating something while keeping it at a distance. He had originally intended to write his thesis on Roman satire,[18] so he was obviously attracted to devices which use a combination of *mimesis* and critique. "Johannes Climacus, or *de omnibus dubitandum est*" features the first sustained appearance of Johannes Climacus, the philosophical climber. His preoccupation in that work was with beginning (philosophy). The writing of *De omnibus* immediately precedes the publication of *Either/Or. Fragments* is the second work in which Climacus appears, this time as author. It concerns the interlude (*Mellemspil*), between the contemporary of Christ and the follower at second hand (JC, 72). Climacus's final work, *Postscript*, works with the problematic of conclusions, or how to finish off the system. In this way writings which feature Climacus frame the "authorship" with a triadic philosophical structure. Hegel's *Encyclopedia*, too, is divided into three main sections: "The Science of Logic," "The Philosophy of Nature," and "The Philosophy of Spirit."

Whereas Hegel assumes that the reading public initially consists of the uncultured, Kierkegaard, at the outset of the "authorship," assumes it consists of the cultured, specifically those formed in the image of Hegelian speculative philosophy. Kierkegaard sees the problem of the age to be precisely too much "culture"—in the abstract speculations of Germanic reflection. Kierkegaard's task is to begin his "authorship" with a work in a form recognizable to the type of consciousness of his reading public, and gradually to move toward the form desired. Because the reading public is assumed to be steeped in the culture of Hegelianism and German romanticism, the "authorship" begins with a work of sophisticated aesthetic reflection, the first part of which gives a portrait of the romantic ironist (EO, 1).

---

[18]*Papirer* II A 166 (September 1837).

Parallel with the prefatory works of Hegel's particular philosophical sciences, the prefatory works of the Kierkegaardian "authorship" gradually introduce movements of thought, categories, terms, and problematics analogous to those that form the content of the ultimate goal, which in Kierkegaard's case is the presentation of Christian faith. Also parallel with Hegel's prefatory works, Kierkegaard's prefatory works deconstruct themselves at the point where the reader has been sufficiently trained in dialectics and self-reflexivity to see that these are only prefatory works and must be left behind.

But because Kierkegaard's "authorship" begins with the assumption that the reading public is already cultured, the aim of the "authorship" is not to provide it with even more culture. The aim is not to *give* the reader anything, but to *take something away* (CUP, 1:275). That which the "authorship" will take away is the whole speculative, complacent, bourgeois confidence in world historical dialectic, and in the capacity of science to explain the whole of reality (without remainder).

The pseudonymous "authorship" begins on the level of culture of the reading public in the "age of reflection," and works up to its climax in Climacus's *Concluding Unscientific Postscript*. The *Postscript* deconstructs itself, and the whole of the preceding "authorship," by the ultimate proclamation that it is all to be *revoked*. The whole "authorship" (at least on Climacus's interpretation) is designed to fall away like an empty husk, because ultimately, according to the religious philosophy it presents, there is nothing merely human one can do to achieve eternal salvation—one has to rely on divine grace.

In presenting itself as postscript/postface to the "authorship," *Postscript* makes a feigned movement.[19] It is only the simulacrum of a postscript, a simulacrum of the moment of mastery where, with cultured retrospective awareness, one can look back over the path travelled in order to cast it away as a redundant ladder, as an

---

[19]Cf. Derrida, "According to the logic of sublation, the postface provides the truth both of the preface (always stated after the fact) and of the entire discourse (produced out of absolute knowledge). The *simulacrum* of a postface would therefore consist of feigning the final revelation of the meaning or functioning of a given stretch of language." *Dissemination*, 27.

instrument required by historical circumstance, but whose function has been fulfilled. It is only a simulacrum because, under the incognito of humor, Climacus's joke is that the whole analogy of ladders and dialectical stages is part of the cultured consciousness to be jettisoned. There is no analogy to the real inside (paradoxical faith decisively appropriated by the existing individual), so one cannot approach it by mediation and approximation. All analogies are only analogies "under erasure." Kierkegaard's task is to wean the cultured away from the complacent illusion that they can enter the highest form of religious consciousness in easy stages, by the *ein, zwei, drei, Kokolorum* method (CUP, 1:117). His task is the Socratic one of inducing *aporia*, of making the task more difficult. This he does by isolating each reader in subjectivity and passion by means of the whole prefatory "authorship" with its double reflection, split narratives, paradoxes, contradictions and self-deconstructive mechanisms.[20]

A First and Last Question

If the parallels between the "authorship" and Hegel's *Encyclopedia* are more than an imaginary construction by a zealous commen-

---

[20]Hegel's paradox of preface/book is a variant of what Foucault calls "the analytic of finitude," which the latter sees as definitive of modernity. The analytic of finitude is the attempt in the wake of the breakdown of "classical age" representation and analytical taxonomy, to find the *basis* for absolute truth in an analysis of the modes of human finitude. The paradigmatic attempt to do this is found in Kant's transcendental deductions. See Michel Foucault, *The Order of Things: An Archaeology of the Human Sciences* (New York: Vintage, 1994) 312-35. On analogy with this, Hegel's universal philosophical science (or "the book") is the transcendental condition for absolute knowledge to be reached by intensive training in the "prefatory," immanent, finite, particular philosophical sciences. Kierkegaard's deconstructive strategies of resistance to Hegel's modernist "analytic of finitude" (or movement from approximation knowledge to absolute knowledge) align him with postmodernism, though not in the way envisaged by Foucault. Foucault saw the modernist paradigm based on the finite human subject as giving way to an antihumanist concern with structures, especially linguistic and institutional structures which position subjects in relations of power. Kierkegaard held onto the humanist subject, though his relational understanding of the self stands in some tension with humanism. On the "death of the subject" see Foucault, *The Order of Things* 386-87.

tator, it seems they were either intentional, coincidental or guided by providence (*Styrelse*). But I think the real explanation is something different from all of these. While it is difficult to demonstrate that the whole "authorship" was sketched out in advance, it is possible to show that Kierkegaard was preoccupied with the structure of the Hegelian system and that he was also concerned to structure his own "authorship" as a totality. As a result, while he worked on the substance of each of his publications, he was able both prospectively and retrospectively to take into consideration the developing shape of the overall "authorship."

As far as intentions go, we have the retrospectively announced intention of Climacus to "find out where the misunderstanding between speculative thought and Christianity lies" (CUP, 1:241). Two months earlier he had decided to be an author (CUP, 1:234). This decision occurred approximately four years before writing *Postscript* (CUP, 1:185). This would date the decision to 1842, when "Johannes Climacus, or *de omnibus dubitandum est*" was begun. Before he manages to publish anything, Climacus finds that his project has been preempted by the pseudonymous works, at each step of his plan (CUP, 1:251). Climacus's works provide a philosophical frame to the "authorship," at least if we include the unpublished *De omnibus* as a "preliminary expectoration" to the "authorship" and recall that Kierkegaard was tempted to give up writing after *Postscript*.[21] Perhaps we also have an adumbration of the idea even earlier, in a journal entry which compares Hegel to the original Johannes Climacus: "Hegel is a Johannes Climacus, who does not storm the heavens by setting mountain upon mountain—but enters them by means of his syllogisms."[22]

---

[21]*Papirer* VII A 4 (February 7, 1846): "My idea is now to become ordained as a priest. I have now for several months asked God to help further, since it has now long been clear to me that I ought no longer be an author. . . . "

[22]*Papirer* II A 335 (January 20, 1839). F. J. Billeskov Jansen has argued that from as early as 1839 Kierkegaard was critical of Hegel's dialectic for itself exemplifying what Hegel called "the bad infinity." This criticism took a literary form that revolves around doubling and narrative splitting. See F. J. Billeskov Jansen, "Kierkegaard—Narrator," in *Kierkegaard—Poet of Existence*, ed. Birgit Bertung (Copenhagen: C. A. Reitzel, 1989) 21-22.

We also have the retrospective self-interpretation in *Point of View*. This argues strongly that the "authorship" should be read as a totality. Kierkegaard gives due acknowledgement to providence in the writing of the "authorship," and in so doing disavows a conscious intention to have planned the whole "authorship" from the outset himself (PV, 72). Yet he also acknowledges that the "authorship" is structured rigorously as a whole:

> No, I must say truly that I cannot understand the whole, just because to the merest insignificant detail I understand the whole, but what I cannot understand is that now I can understand it and yet cannot by any means say that at the instant of commencing it I understood it so precisely. . . . (PV, 72)

Whatever the intentions of either Kierkegaard, Climacus, or providence, we can discern a structure in the "authorship" that seems to coincide in too much detail with that of Hegel's *Encyclopedia* to be mere coincidence. In the middle of Kierkegaard's ludicrously baroque redoubling of the structure of Hegel's *Encyclopedia* is a small work called *Prefaces*. This work is not a book: it consists of nothing but prefaces (which are not the prefaces to any books), and a postscript. The pseudonym Nicolaus Notabene has been forbidden by his wife to be an author. By the sophistical definition of an author as someone who writes books, Notabene can indulge his passion for writing with a good conscience by writing nothing but prefaces and postscripts. The strategic positioning of this work provides the key to how seriously Kierkegaard modelled the rhetorical structure of his pseudonymous "authorship" on the Hegelian problem of writing a preface to absolute knowledge.[23]

---

[23]*Prefaces* occurs approximately midway through the "authorship," depending on what is counted as belonging to the "authorship." Prior to the publication of *Prefaces*, beginning with *Either/Or*, Kierkegaard published nine "books." *Prefaces* was published on the same day as *The Concept of Anxiety*. After *Prefaces*, up to and including *Postscript*, Kierkegaard published seven works. These include the reissue in collected form of the remaindered *Upbuilding Discourses* from 1843 and 1844, and two articles in *Fædrelandet* by Frater Taciturnus. After *Prefaces* and up to, but not including *Point of View*, he published twelve works. See the chronology in JP 5:ix-xi.

In general the "authorship" avoids getting to *die Sache selbst* (the subject matter itself) by not consisting of "books." The "authors" are not real authors, but imaginary constructions of Kierkegaard. They write prefatory works, indirect experiments in particular existential points of view, postscripts, reviews, but never direct communications about faith. Writing as humoristic redoubling is not authorship; it contains no authority. Nor does it essentially get beyond irony,[24] but merely exposes the pretentions of speculative philosophy to the mocking laughter of a "higher madness" (CUP, 1:448; translation modified). By constantly redoubling itself in imaginary constructions, the whole "authorship" separates the reader from the authority of the author, thereby acting as midwife for the birth of the reader. Only then can the reader begin on the subject matter of faith in the decisive category of existence:

> once again to read through solo, if possible in a more inward way, the original text of individual human existence-relationships, the old familiar text handed down from the fathers.
>
> (CUP, 1: 360)[25]

---

[24]Humor is in a sense a "higher stage" with respect to Christianity than irony is, since it comprehends all the essential categories of Christianity, including the paradox of the incarnation, guilt and sin. But it comprehends these categories only in the modality of thought, i.e., possibility, and does not appropriate them existentially. As a result, humor falls short of faith in essentially the same manner as irony does. Cf. CUP, 1:271-72.

[25]This reading of Hegel and Kierkegaard gives a new slant to what Derrida refers to as "religions of the book." See Jacques Derrida, *The Gift of Death*, trans. David Wills (Chicago: University of Chicago Press, 1995) 80. Kierkegaard's authorship amounts only to a "religion of the preface."

13

"A Highest Good . . . An Eternal Happiness": The Human Telos in Kierkegaard's Concluding Unscientific Postscript

John D. Glenn, Jr.

Both works published under the name of Johannes Climacus are concerned with eternal happiness—or, at least, with the conditions for coming to possess it. The title page of the *Philosophical Fragments* poses the question "Can an eternal happiness be built on historical knowledge?" (PF, 1), and Climacus[1] proceeds to explore the presuppositions and implications of either a negative or a positive answer to his question.

He takes the Socratic doctrine of recollection to represent the negative position; it holds that human beings are *eternally* (rather than by virtue of anything historical) in possession of "the condition" for attaining eternal truth and happiness. An affirmative answer, Climacus suggests, only makes sense in certain quite remarkable circumstances—first, that human beings are self–deprived (in a state for which he proposes the term *sin* [PF, 15]) of that condition, and, second, that "the god," out of love, enters into human existence to restore it.

Climacus does not, in the *Fragments*, question whether eternal happiness is real, or what it might be like; in fact, between the initial posing of his question and his concluding remarks, the term "eternal happiness" appears at only two points in the *Fragments* (PF, 12, 58). For the most part, his reflections are carried out in a spirit of ironic detachment, and only at the end of the *Fragments*

---

[1] I will comply here with Kierkegaard's insistence that he not be identified with any of the pseudonymous authors—that he was rather "the author of the author or the authors" (CUP, 1:627).

(PF, 109) does he acknowledge—what every reader has of course realized—that the position to which his reflections have primarily been devoted is that of Christianity.

In the *Postscript*, however, despite its many continuities with the work to which it is the "postscript," things stand very differently. Here, rather than focusing primarily on the "objective" conditions for eternal happiness—that is, the appearance of "the God in time" offering this happiness to individual human beings—Climacus deals with the subjective conditions for the *reception* of this gift. And from the very beginning, eternal happiness—which he refers to as "highest good" and "highest *telos*"—and Christianity which claims to provide it, are regarded as matters of utmost personal concern:

> I, Johannes Climacus, . . . an ordinary human being like most folk, assume that a highest good, called an eternal happiness, awaits me just as it awaits a housemaid and a professor. I have heard that Christianity is one's prerequisite for this good. I now ask how I may enter into relation to this doctrine.
>
> (CUP, 1:15-16)

Such concern for one's own eternal happiness—and *not* any sort of personal arbitrariness or irrationality—is the highest expression of "subjectivity" in the distinctive sense in which Climacus uses the term.[2]

In the *Postscript*, moreover, Climacus speaks of eternal happiness in a way that virtually invites the question of how it is to be described, or defined. Yet he declines any attempt to describe it, or to define it in any direct manner. Even so, in setting out his conception of the proper *relation to* this "highest good" Climacus provides at least indirect indications of what sort of reality he takes it to be.

In this essay, I will outline the chief elements of Climacus's account of the right relation to an eternal happiness, and consider what understanding of the meaning of eternal happiness this account suggests. I will also consider how Climacus's account relates to Aristotle's and Kant's conceptions of the "highest good,"

---

[2]For a distinction between different senses, or sorts, of subjectivity, see CUP, 1:130-31.

and will argue that there are, in particular, important similarities to aspects of Kant's conception—but also notable differences. Finally, I will briefly indicate how Climacus's reflections are rooted in the New Testament—and note, in conclusion, what in this light seems to be a remarkable *lacuna* in his account.

Climacus's use of the terms "highest good" and "highest *telos*" in reference to eternal happiness suggests that relevant comparisons can be made to certain of his philosophical predecessors. The most obvious of these is Aristotle, who in the first book of the *Nicomachean Ethics* poses the question of a human being's highest good and highest end, and proceeds to identify this as "happiness." This is, at least, the usual translation of the Greek *eudaemonia*, although it is clear that as Aristotle uses the term it carries more the sense of an (objectively-determinable) well-being which, while inclusive of pleasure, is not to be identified with any feeling-state *per se*.

As to the perennial question of the relation between happiness and virtue, Aristotle links the two by arguing that happiness consists primarily of a life of virtuous activity—this being the life which is most fulfilling of our human (rational) nature. He eventually identifies the life of intellectual activity—specifically, of contemplation—as the most humanly fulfilling life, and the highest happiness possible for a human being;[3] he even calls such a life "divine," yet without claiming that such happiness can be, for a human being, eternal.[4]

In modern philosophy, probably the most distinctive use of the term "highest good" is that of Kant. Climacus does not directly refer to the Kantian doctrine,[5] but a brief comparison between it and the Aristotelian conception may provide a useful background for approaching Climacus.

---

[3]See *Nicomachean Ethics*, 1177a-78b. All quotations of Aristotle are taken from *The Basic Works of Aristotle*, ed. Richard McKeon (New York: Random House, 1941).

[4]In the *Metaphysics*, he says that the god's activity of eternal thought "is a life such as the best which we enjoy, and enjoy for but a short time" (1072b).

[5]For an excellent exploration of Kant's influence on Kierkegaard, see Ronald M. Green, *Kierkegaard and Kant: The Hidden Debt* (Albany: State University of New York Press, 1992).

The most crucial point here is that Kant conceives of the highest good as a *synthesis* of two *distinct* elements—moral virtue and happiness. On this point, his conception poses a sharp alternative to Aristotle's notion of the homogeneity of the highest good.[6] According to Kant, virtue is the *supreme* good,[7] the good which is to be chosen unconditionally, whereas happiness should be subordinated to it. Together, in this relation of condition to conditioned, they comprise the *highest* good. We are obligated, according to Kant, to seek a world in which virtue is rewarded by (proportionate) happiness; we have, moreover, the right to hope for our own happiness, to the extent that we strive to make ourselves worthy of it.

This conception is the basis of Kant's arguments for the "practical postulates" of immortality and the existence of God. The former is necessary if it is to be possible for an individual to attain perfect virtue—that "complete fitness of intentions to the moral law [which] is holiness."[8] The latter is required if obedience to one's duty to work for a world in which happiness is proportionate to moral worth is not to be undermined by the difficulty of regarding such a state of affairs as even possible. We can only conceive of its possibility, according to Kant, under the condition of the existence of "a being which is the cause (and consequently the author) of nature through understanding and will, i.e., God."[9]

At least at first sight, Climacus's understanding of eternal happiness as highest good may appear closer to Aristotle's doctrine than to Kant's. It is a homogeneous, not a synthetic conception of the highest good—and his substantive term for this good is (at least in translation) "happiness." One might even wonder whether Climacus's adoption of his own eternal happiness

---

[6]By "homogeneity of the highest good" I mean the notion that every appropriate human end—including virtue—is good only insofar as it is part of or contributes to a *single* ultimate end, happiness. Aristotle does vacillate somewhat on the matter, saying at one point (*Nicomachean Ethics*, 1097b) that we do choose many things other than happiness—such as "honor, pleasure, reason, and every virtue"—for themselves, "but . . . also for the sake of happiness."

[7]Kant, *Critique of Practical Reason*, trans. Lewis White Beck (Indianapolis: Library of Liberal Arts, 1956) 115.

[8]Kant, *Practical Reason*, 126.

[9]Kant, *Practical Reason*, 130.

as "highest good" indicates that he has fallen into a form of eudaemonism, which from a Kantian perspective would be no less immoral merely because it places the aimed-for happiness in another world.[10]

Matters are, however, considerably more complex than this. Although Climacus's use of the terms "highest good" and "highest *telos*" suggests an affinity with Aristotle, he is at points highly critical of the Aristotelian position. First, in regard to its valorization of intellectual activity, Climacus argues that, since the human being is a "synthesis of the temporal and the eternal," the *intensification* of existence, which he proceeds to describe as taking the form of ethical striving, is more appropriate than any "speculative happiness" resulting from a thinker's attempt to escape time, to be "exclusively eternal" (CUP, 1:56). However, Climacus's *ultimate* target here is not so much Aristotle as his own Hegelian contemporaries, with their emphasis on contemplation of world history; thus his jibes at those who believe that objective observation of world history "is the *ethical* answer to the question of what I am to do ethically" (CUP, 1:133).

That Climacus's understanding of the highest good is even further from that of Aristotle is also, and perhaps more surprisingly, given his identification of that good as a form of "happiness," indicated by his occasional, yet always critical remarks regarding eudaemonism.[11] This suggests that, in respect to the highest good, Climacus may be closer to Kant than to Aristotle. And this is amply supported by many things he says, beginning with the main thesis which emerges from his reflections on what he calls "the objective issue of the truth of Christianity" (CUP, 1:19-57). Here he argues that neither historical nor philosophical inquiry can arrive at an objective decision regarding the truth of Christianity. But this is not due merely to the impossibility of attaining objective

---

[10]C. Stephen Evans points out this difficulty, and attempts to defend Climacus from such an interpretation, in *Kierkegaard's "Fragments" and "Postscript"* (Atlantic Highlands NJ: Humanities Press International, 1983) 141-47. I am in basic agreement with Evans's approach.

[11]See especially a footnote at CUP, 1:426. Climacus regards eudaemonism as a kind of hedonism—which is perhaps not entirely fair as an interpretation of Aristotle.

certainty regarding Christianity's historical claims, or to the fact that, in basing access to eternal truth on historical fact, Christianity places itself essentially outside the sphere of philosophical speculation. It consists above all in the fact that the "objective"—by which he means, personally indifferent—approach to Christianity is inconsistent with the *infinite passion* for which Christianity calls (CUP, 1:50-57).

From this emerges one of Climacus's most crucial claims: namely, that the possibility of an individual's acquiring eternal happiness is *essentially* contingent on his or her subjective interest in it. Although not claiming to have "comprehended" Christianity, Climacus says, "I have at least understood . . . that it wants to make the single individual eternally happy and that precisely within this single individual it presupposes this infinite interest in his own happiness as *conditio sine qua non* . . . " (CUP, 1:16). And he develops this thought even more provocatively:

> It is not impossible that the individual who is infinitely interested in his own eternal happiness can some day become eternally happy; on the other hand, it is certainly impossible that the person who has lost a sense for it (and such a sense can scarcely be anything but an *infinite* concern) can become eternally happy.
> (CUP, 1:16)

This assertion has a degree of intuitive plausibility. On reflection, however, it is perhaps not at all obvious. Even granting that it might well be in some sense *inappropriate* for a person who had never been concerned with his or her eternal happiness to receive it, is this *impossible*? Is Climacus claiming that such a person would not be *happy* . . . if he or she were *eternally* happy?

At least part of the answer to this question seems to be that the term here translated "happiness"—*Salighed*—is not to be regarded as precisely analogous with "happiness" in the everyday sense, even if the latter were unqualified and of infinite duration. Abrahim H. Khan has argued this persuasively in a very thorough and helpful study of this term in the wider Kierkegaardian corpus.[12] "Bliss" and "blessedness," he notes, are possibly superior

---

[12]Abrahim H. Khan, *Salighed as Happiness?: Kierkegaard on the Concept Salighed* (Waterloo, Ontario: Wilfrid Laurier University Press, 1985). The book also contains

translations of *Salighed*, but he also points out that *Salighed* has sometimes been employed in Danish translation of the Bible where "salvation" appears in the English, and suggests that the best course may be to leave it untranslated.[13]

Whatever the best translation of the *term* (and I will continue here to follow the Hongs' translation) the *logic* of Climacus's claims indicate that he conceives of "eternal happiness" *not* as a satisfaction, even a complete satisfaction, of the self or subject's *given* desires, but as a state of spiritual fulfillment requiring the deepening of oneself and the transformation of one's desires. That is, it is *not* to be identified with "happiness" in the ordinary sense—the conditioned component in Kant's conception of the highest good—but is much closer to what Kant called the *supreme* good—virtue or, more precisely, holiness of will.

In emphasizing that "infinite interest" in one's own eternal happiness is necessary for coming to possess it, Climacus at times even seems close to *identifying* infinite interest and eternal happiness. This is particularly the case in a passage where he describes how "objective" inquiry regarding the truth of Christianity can undercut the appropriate subjective interest:

> The subject's personal, infinite, impassioned interestedness (which is the possibility of faith and then faith, the form of eternal happiness and then eternal happiness) fades away more and more because the decision is postponed . . . as a direct result of the results of the learned research scholar. . . . One has become too objective to have an eternal happiness, because this happiness inheres precisely in the infinite, personal, impassioned interestedness. . . ."   (CUP, 1:27)

In saying that "infinite . . . interestedness" is "the form of eternal happiness and then eternal happiness," or that this happiness "inheres" in such interest, is Climacus identifying infinite interest in eternal happiness *as* eternal happiness? Such at least *apparent* circularity is a recurrent feature of Climacus's reflections;[14] another, closely-related example is passages in the *Postscript* where

---

a useful bibliography.

[13]See Khan, *Salighed as Happiness?*, 90-91, 110-11.

[14]And of Kierkegaard's writings in general, as, e.g., in the description of the self as "a relation that relates itself to itself" (SUD, 13).

Climacus seems to construe subjectivity as concern for one's own subjectivity.[15]

The simplest explanation for all this is, I think, that Climacus is convinced of the importance of second-order desires for both the constitution and the fulfillment of the self. But it would be erroneous (entirely apart from the logical difficulties involved) to say that he takes eternal happiness to be *identical* with infinite interest in (one's own) eternal happiness, rather than a crucial component or requirement of it.[16] The phrase "form of" in the quoted passage should probably be read along somewhat Kantian lines. Kant speaks of space as the "form of all appearances of outer sense," in that it is the a priori subjective condition for the reception of the manifold of external sensibility.[17] "Infinite interestedness" would, analogously, be the "form of" eternal happiness in the sense of being its anticipation, and a subjective condition for its reception.

At this, and other points, a reader of Climacus might be tempted to think that taking an "infinite interest" in one's eternal happiness is an attempt to earn or merit it. But Climacus denies this notion, which he attributes particularly to the Middle Ages (CUP, 1:404-405). His own understanding of the right relation to one's eternal happiness is that it is *not* a matter of meriting, or even *trying* to merit it.[18] It is rather, as I understand him, that of trying to *live as* one to whom the possibility of eternal happiness has been offered—and for whom it is thus inappropriate to absolutize some lesser "good." He describes the proper relation to eternal happiness, as "highest good," in a formula which is profound in its simplicity, yet daunting in its practical implications: One's task,

---

[15]E.g., see CUP, 1:129-31. A similar example is the claim that subjective interest in the truth in some sense *is* the truth (CUP, 1:199-205).

[16]A relatively simple analogy here might be the claim that a good parent is one who *wants* to be a good parent. Wanting to be a good parent is not sufficient, but does seem to be necessary, for being one.

[17]Kant, *Critique of Pure Reason*, trans. Norman Kemp Smith (London: MacMillan, 1963) A26/B42.

[18]His understanding of guilt and sin in human existence would make it impossible for him to say that any of us can merit eternal happiness.

he says, is "simultaneously to relate oneself absolutely to one's absolute *telos* and relatively to relative ends" (CUP, 1:387).

Such an attitude does *not* require, as some in the Middle Ages thought, that lesser ends be *renounced*—only that they be *relativized*. Yet Climacus—never one to make our task too easy[19] —adds that, although such renunciation is not *essentially* required for the proper relation to eternal happiness, *approaching* the stance described in his formula does call for it as a preliminary spiritual exercise—"practicing the absolute relation through renunciation" (CUP, 1:431). Thus, in the end, he agrees neither with monasticism *nor* with those of his contemporaries who disdained the monastery yet seemed to be wholly caught up in pursuing worldly goals.[20]

It is in connection with the formula of relating oneself "absolutely to one's absolute *telos* and relatively to relative ends" that Climacus introduces a basic theme of his reflections: *suffering*. His point is *not*—although he is certainly aware—that finite existence inevitably involves suffering. Rather, it is that, insofar as each of us is strongly inclined to absolutize some merely relative end, making eternal happiness one's absolute *telos* requires a "dying to immediacy" (CUP, 1: 460-63). The *essential* religious suffering, as Climacus conceives it, is *chosen*; it is that involved in continually resisting, and attempting to transform, one's tendency to subordinate the "highest *telos*" to some finite and relative end.[21]

This is by no means the only way in which Climacus takes suffering to be inherent in the religious life. An individual who is concerned to have the right relation to his or her own eternal happiness will be further enmeshed in suffering by consciousness of *guilt*—the awareness that his or her existence regarded as a whole is lacking in respect to maintaining such a relation. And,

---

[19]See his account of how he became an author (CUP, 1:185-88).

[20]Climacus's counterpolemic against contemporary rejection of "the monastery" is a recurring theme of the *Postscript*; if Climacus ever overstates a point—does anyone doubt this?—it is important to remember that he was struggling against what he regarded as an attitude of extreme spiritual complacency.

[21]It is remarkable that Climacus takes the essential religious suffering to be one "of which there is on the whole very little mention in the New Testament" (CUP, 1:453). It seems that here, and I think elsewhere, Climacus's account of what he calls "Religiousness A" leads him to slight certain distinctive features of Christian existence; see below, 260-61.

within the sphere of "Religiousness B"—Christianity in a strict sense—consciousness of *sin* produces further suffering. All in all, in the latter sections of the *Postscript* Climacus succeeds in fleshing out in manifold ways his claim that, although "there is no suffering in the eternal happiness, . . . when an existing person relates himself to it, the relation is quite properly expressed by suffering" (CUP, 1:452).

Climacus's assertion that eternal happiness can neither be described nor, in any direct sense, defined, is another crucial feature of his reflections. As to the first part of this claim, he insists that it is not only *impossible* for an existing individual to describe eternal happiness, it would also be *inappropriate*; to do so would be to construe eternal happiness as an aesthetic, rather than an ethical or religious reality. He imagines a "serious man" who asks, "Is it not possible to find out for certain, clearly and briefly, what an eternal happiness is? Can't you describe it to me 'while I shave,' just as one describes the loveliness of a woman, the royal purple, or distant regions?" (CUP, 1:392) And he responds, with an emphatic refusal:

> It is good that I cannot do it, . . . because . . . I might succeed—in once again subsuming eternal happiness under esthetic categories so that the maximum of pathos would become the marvelousness of description, even though it is a task that esthetically is enough to despair over—esthetically to have to make something out of an abstraction such as an eternal happiness.   (CUP, 1:392-93)

This response to the quite intelligible desire (from the standpoint of any spiritually imperfect human being) for a description of eternal happiness is yet another indication that Climacus conceives it as very different from "happiness" in any ordinary sense, the latter being quite appropriately subsumed under aesthetic categories.

Climacus sharpens his point further. Not only should one not seek any description of *what* eternal happiness is; one should not seek any certainty *that* it exists. Again, he imagines "a serious man" asking, "But is it certain and definite that there is such a good, is it certain and definite that there is an eternal happiness in store?—because in that sense I surely would aspire to it; otherwise, I would be lunatic to risk everything for it" (CUP, 1:422). In response, Climacus suggests that there *should* be no objective assurance of such a thing.[22] For that would transform into a good trade, or a good bet, a commitment that should be spiritually "infinitizing." Reliance on the assurances of philosophers or clergy regarding the reality of eternal happiness, Climacus says, would hinder an individual, prompting him "to want to make an intellectual transaction, a profitable stock-exchange speculation, instead of a daring venture, . . . a simulated pass at the absolute, although he remains completely within the relative . . . " (CUP, 1:423).

Climacus's reasoning here is close to that of Kant, who argues that conviction of the existence of God, of rewards for virtue and punishment for vice, can, and properly should, only *follow* moral commitment, not be its basis. If the reality of God were evident to human knowledge, Kant says, "most actions conforming to the law would be done from fear, few would be done from hope, none from duty. The moral worth of actions, on which alone the worth of the person and even of the world depends . . . , would not exist at all."[23]

I have suggested that Climacus's understanding of eternal happiness is analogous to Kant's conception of virtue, or holiness of will. But that claim must be strongly qualified. Kant believes that a formula for the latter can be given—namely, the categorical imperative. But although Climacus provides a formula for the right *relation to* our "highest good," he neither conveys, nor seems to accept, any comparable statement defining that highest good itself.[24]

---

[22]At another point, Climacus says that "the person who wills does not want to know" anything about eternal happiness "*except that it exists*" (CUP, 1:394; emphasis added). This apparent inconsistency does not, however, mean that he abandons the basic claim that the passionate, "infinitizing" attitude appropriate in relation to this *telos* is most compatible with considerable objective uncertainty regarding it.

[23]Kant, *Practical Reason*, 152-53. See Green, *Kierkegaard and Kant*, for a much fuller account of such parallels between Kierkegaard's writings and Kant's.

[24]One basic difference between Climacus and Kant would seem to rest on the difference between an ethics based on the idea of rational autonomy and a "theonomous" ethics. Most of Kierkegaard's pseudonymous writings are to some extent concerned with this matter, but I am unable to discuss it at any length here.

This aspect of Climacus's thought emerges especially when he says that "nothing else can be said of eternal happiness than that it is the good that is attained by absolutely venturing everything" (CUP, 1:427). It is, it seems, as if we were told—with no objective warrant of the truth of the matter—that there is a good surpassing every other good, to which every other good must be subordinated (and, if necessary, sacrificed), yet were not told *what* that good is. Even referring to it as "eternal happiness," given the differences which he suggests between it and "happiness" in any usual sense, and our general inability to conceive it concretely, may convey very little more.

What this inability to describe or positively define eternal happiness, taken together with the thesis that the proper relation to it requires the relativization of every other end, would seem to call for is—although Climacus does not use this term—an existential *via negativa* as the appropriate form of the relation. That is, what we are called to *enact* in our passional and choosing existence, in relation to our "highest good," is that it is *not* this, *not* that—that it is *other* than any specifiable finite goal. Yet we are to do this without regarding finite goals as worthless, and without the despair which would follow if we were to believe that there is no "highest good," no final fulfillment, no ultimate meaning to existence.

Translated into the language of temporality, such a "not this, not that" becomes a "not now, not yet." The individual who attempts to maintain the proper relation to an eternal happiness is not to regard any temporal state as one in which he or she can remain at rest, or—as probably all human beings are tempted to do—to hope for such a state, for a "paradise on earth," or even for repose in some state of spiritual realization. On this point, Climacus is emphatic:

> The absolute *telos* is present only when the individual relates himself absolutely to it, and they cannot, as an eternal happiness relating itself to an existing person, possibly have each other or tranquilly belong to each other in existence, that is, in temporality. . . .   (CUP, 1:397)

In sum, eternal happiness is to be related to as something which is (to borrow a word-pair, if not a concept, from Professor Derrida) *different*, in that it is *other than* any finite goal, and *deferred*, in that it is to be regarded as always essentially *future*, not something that can be realized at any point in time. The stance of the individual who maintains an appropriate relationship to an eternal happiness as highest *telos* involves a certain spiritual lightfootedness,[25] a certain distance—which is nevertheless quite different from both ironic detachment and monastic renunciation—with respect to every finite end. He, or she, will not at any time cease striving, nor be brought to despair by any disappointment.

Yet, even if this is a proper account of what Climacus is suggesting, it must be added that he proceeds to call it into question. Having asserted that eternal happiness cannot be possessed in time, he notes, late in the *Postscript*, that Christianity claims otherwise! Part of the paradox of Christianity, he says, is that it posits that eternal happiness can be attained "*in time through a relation to something else in time*" (CUP, 1:570).

In both the *Fragments* and the *Postscript*, Climacus has stressed the "paradox" that, according to Christianity, the possibility of the human being's *attaining* eternal happiness is qualified by the eternal God's appearance in history, and a temporal decision to accept or reject Him. Here he seems to go one step further, suggesting that not only the possibility of *acquiring* eternal happiness, but eternal happiness *itself* is temporally qualified due to the distinctive Christian conception of "the God in time."[26]

What does this mean? Climacus provides no real explanation. On what basis does he assert it? This latter question raises a more general one, which perhaps should be addressed first: Given Climacus's demurrals regarding the possibility of describing or defining eternal happiness, what authority does he have for what *he* says about it, even for these demurrals themselves? He would

---

[25]Cf. Johannes de Silentio's image of the dancer at FT, 41.

[26]One *might* wonder whether Climacus is hinting at a immanentized conception of eternal happiness as somehow possessed *wholly* "in time." But only if one takes him to be committed to some sort of total "demythologization" of religious concepts would this be plausible—and I see no reason that he should be interpreted in this fashion. For a pointed response to the suggestion that Kierkegaard did not believe in an afterlife, see Gordon D. Marino, "Salvation: A Reply to Harrison Hall's Reading of Kierkegaard," *Inquiry*, 28:441-49.

seem to be one of the least likely of thinkers to claim the benefit of any private *gnosis*.

Here the answer seems to be that, in general, what Climacus says about eternal happiness is said on the basis of the New Testament,[27] although he makes few explicit references to specific scriptural passages. Granted that Climacus does not claim to be a Christian, he is throughout the *Postscript* concerned with the proper relation to Christianity, which is quite consistent with his concepts being drawn basically from the well of the New Testament.

It is true that the term "eternal happiness" does not appear in the New Testament. But what Climacus says about eternal happiness seems to be based on what is said there in somewhat different terms—"the Kingdom of God," "the Kingdom of Heaven," "salvation," "eternal life" or "everlasting life," and the term "blessed," as this is employed in the Beatitudes. The latter, along with some of Jesus' "parables of the Kingdom," seem to have especially shaped Climacus's assertions about "subjectivity" and "infinite interest" as necessary for the reception of eternal happiness. The Beatitudes suggest that the "kingdom of heaven" belongs particularly to those who are aware of their need for it ("the poor in spirit"), and fulfillment to those who "hunger and thirst after righteousness" (Matthew 5:3, 6). In Matthew 13, the kingdom of heaven is likened, first, to a treasure hidden in a field, and then, in the parable of the "pearl of great price," *not* (as one might expect) to the pearl, but rather to the man who sells all that he has in order to buy it. Here, it seems, in simpler terms, is Climacus's thesis that "the subject's personal, infinite, impassioned interestedness" can be regarded as "the *form of* eternal happiness" (CUP, 1:29; my emphasis).[28]

This provides a basis for answering the more specific question raised earlier, concerning Climacus's unexplained suggestion that "Religiousness B" or Christianity posits eternal happiness as attainable *"in time through a relation to something else in time"* (CUP, 1:570). For in the Johannine writings, and particularly the Fourth

---

[27]For discussion of the New Testament sources of Kierkegaard's general understanding of *Salighed*, see Khan, *Salighed as Happiness?*, 88-90.

[28]I am grateful to the Rev. William C. Morris for, among many other things, the understanding of the Beatitudes and Jesus' parables expressed in his sermons.

Gospel, everlasting life is spoken of as something which can be possessed even *now*—if only in an imperfect and anticipatory manner. St. John, moreover, seems to regard it as present above all in the life of Christian *love*. "We know that we have passed from death into life," he says, "because we love the brethren" (1 John 3: 14).

This suggests one final reflection, though: When the *Postscript* is read in relation to the New Testament, one remarkable fact emerges. It is that, although Climacus is in many respects a very concrete thinker, his conception of Christian existence is in some ways quite *abstract*. He has very little to say about much of the concrete *content* of the Christian life, and in particular about something quite central to that life—love of one's neighbor.

Kierkegaard was very much concerned with this dimension of Christian life. One might even say that, in *Works of Love*, where love of God, the right kind of love of oneself, and love of one's neighbor are treated as intimately related,[29] he suggests that such love in a sense unites what Kant conceives as the two distinct elements of the highest good. Love, Kierkegaard says, following St. Paul, "is the fulfilling of the law" (WL, 91)—if we love, we fulfill the requirements of duty.[30] And when Kierkegaard asks, in terms that are strongly reminiscent of Climacus—"What . . . is the *highest good* and the greatest *blessedness*?"—his answer is "Certainly it is truly *to love*, and next, truly *to be loved*" (WL, 239; my emphases).[31]

Kierkegaard was certainly aware that love of one's neighbor involves its own risk and suffering—the sort of suffering which would seem to be the essentially Christian suffering.[32] But in *Works*

---

[29]"To love yourself in the right way and to love the neighbor correspond perfectly to one another; fundamentally they are one and the same thing" (WL, 22). "*To love God is to love oneself truly; to help another person to love God is to love another person* . . . " (WL, 107).

[30]Here I must again refrain from dealing with the very real issues concerning the respective merits of an ethics of rational autonomy and a "theonomous" ethics.

[31]"Blessedness" and "highest good" here are *Salighed* and *høieste Gode*, respectively—"happiness" (in "eternal happiness") and "highest good" also in the English translation of the *Postscript*.

[32]See above for Climacus's conception of the essentially religious suffering.

of Love he tries to show how commitment to love of one's neighbor provides meaning, fulfillment, and hope—even when such love is not requited. He would seem to be in accord with the New Testament, and Christian tradition, in suggesting that such love offers at least an anticipation of the full reality of what Climacus calls eternal happiness.

Of all this, however, Climacus says nothing. Perhaps he thought he had said enough—for his purposes. And perhaps a *via negativa* is essential preparation for a *via affirmativa*.

14

Resignation, Suffering, and Guilt
in Kierkegaard's Concluding Unscientific Postscript to "Philosophical Fragments"

David R. Law

Resignation, suffering, and guilt are discussed in the three subsections of part A (CUP, 1:387-555) of Climacus's discussion of "The Issue in *Fragments*." They thus belong to the immanent dialectic of Religiousness A. In examining these three concepts, then, we shall gain an insight into the way the human being acquires and sustains a relationship to an eternal happiness. In doing so, we shall simultaneously gain an insight into Religiousness B, for Religiousness A is the "terminus a quo" (CUP, 1:558) for Religiousness B and "must first be present in the individual before there can be any consideration of becoming aware of the dialectical *B*" (CUP, 1:556, cf. 557).

Before we can embark upon an analysis of these concepts, however, there are some preliminary problems that must first be addressed. These concern the principles upon which the immanent dialectic of resignation, suffering, and guilt is based.

(a) Eternal Happiness

What is an eternal happiness? For Climacus this is an illegitimate question. If an eternal happiness could be defined or described, then it would *ipso facto* be *finite* and consequently could not be an *eternal* happiness. Climacus pours scorn on those who demand a definition of eternal happiness and who would be willing to relate themselves to it only when a definition has been provided (CUP, 1:392, 395). The important point to grasp is that eternal happiness is concerned with the *existence* of the individual human being: "For an existing person, an eternal happiness relates itself essentially to existing, to the ideality of actuality . . . " (CUP, 1:387-88).

Climacus links the concept of eternal happiness to that of the absolute or highest telos: "eternal happiness . . . is the absolute τέλος (CUP, 1:397). This too is impossible to define.

> And this highest τέλος is not a something, because then it relatively corresponds to something else and is finite. But it is a contradiction absolutely to will something finite, since the finite must indeed come to an end, and consequently there must come a time when it can no longer be willed. But to will something absolutely is to will the infinite, and to will an eternal happiness is to will absolutely, because it must be capable of being willed at every moment.   (CUP, 1:394)

The absolute telos, then, is infinite, for it requires the individual to will it infinitely. This means that everything else, all finite ends, must be subordinated to the absolute telos, for if this is not the case, then the absolute telos simply ceases to be the absolute telos. In Climacus's words: "If it does not *absolutely* transform his existence for him, then he is not relating himself to an eternal happiness; if there is something he is not willing to give up for its sake, then he is not relating himself to an eternal happiness" (CUP, 1:393). Summing up, an eternal happiness is the absolute and highest telos, which has to be willed absolutely.

The next stage of Climacus's argument is to link the concept of the absolute telos to that of God. There are several passages where Climacus seems to employ "eternal happiness" synonymously with "God" (e.g., CUP, 1:43, 446). In relating himself to the absolute telos, then, the resigned individual is simultaneously relating himself to God: "The absolutely differentiating one relates himself to his absolute τέλος, but *eo ipso* also to God" (CUP, 1:413).

Summing up, an eternal happiness is the absolute telos which is God. The issue Climacus wishes to address is how the human being can establish a relationship to this absolute telos and thereby acquire an eternal happiness.

(b) The Composite Self

A second principle that underlies the concepts of resignation, suffering, and guilt is Climacus's understanding of human existence as a synthesis of the infinite and the finite: "Existence is composed of the infinite and the finite; the existing person is infinite and finite" (CUP, 1:391). The task facing the individual is that of bringing these into the correct relationship, which means subordinating the finite elements of the self to the infinite. Only in this way can a relationship with an eternal happiness come about. As Climacus puts it, "Now, if to him an eternal happiness is his highest good, this means that in his acting the finite elements are once and for all reduced to what must be surrendered in relation to the eternal happiness" (CUP, 1:391; cf. 420). As we shall see, resignation, suffering, and guilt constitute the individual's attempts to carry out such a subordination of the finite to the infinite and thereby bring about a relation to an eternal happiness.

(c) Pathos

This is the term Climacus employs to express the relation of the individual to an eternal happiness. Pathos entails the individual's transformation of his or her existence in such a way that the individual's existence comes to express a relation to an eternal happiness. In Climacus's words: "In relation to an eternal happiness as the absolute good, pathos does not mean words but that this idea transforms the whole existence of the existing person" (CUP, 1:387). That is, the issue Climacus addresses in the *Postscript*, and this is where the significance of pathos lies, is the individual's transformation of his or her existence in such a way that the absolute telos that is eternal happiness comes to be embodied in this existence. The individual must be "transformed into the actuality of the idea" (CUP, 1:387), or, as Climacus also puts it: "The pathos that corresponds to and is adequate to an eternal happiness is the transformation by which the existing person in existing changes everything in his existence in relation to that highest good" (CUP, 1:389; cf. 409).

Resignation

The task of the individual, then, is to sustain a relation to the absolute telos that is an eternal happiness or God. This requires that the human being develop into the position where such a relationship becomes possible. The first movement in this process is "resignation."

Resignation is the means by which the individual establishes whether he or she is related to an eternal happiness. Resignation achieves this by carrying out an "inspection" of the individual's immediacy:

> The individual himself can then easily examine how he relates himself to an eternal happiness or whether he relates himself to it. He needs only to allow resignation to inspect his entire immediacy with all its desires etc. If he finds a single fixed point, an obduracy, he is not relating himself to an eternal happiness. . . . If, however, the inspecting resignation discovers no irregularity, this shows that the individual at the time of inspection is relating himself to an eternal happiness.   (CUP, 1:394-95)

That is, resignation undertakes to ensure that the individual is oriented towards the absolute telos (CUP, 1:402). Resignation is able to achieve this by virtue of the fact that it makes an *absolute distinction* or, as Climacus also puts it, an *absolute differentiation*, between relative ends and the absolute telos: "The absolute distinction is equipped to clear the way just as a policeman does in a procession; it clears away the crush, the mob of relative ends, in order that the absolutely differentiating one can relate himself to the absolute" (CUP, 1:413).

The distinction resignation makes between the absolute telos and relative ends should not be understood as a deprecation of the finite, however (CUP, 1:413). Absolute orientation towards the absolute telos does not mean that the individual divorces him or herself from the finite; this is simply impossible, for the human being exists in the sphere of the finite and is, as we have seen, a synthesis of the infinite and the finite. Nor can the absolute telos be *expressed* or *actualized* in relative ends, for this would reduce the absolute telos to the level of those relative ends. The individual's task is rather to continue in the finite but to have the source of his or her being and action in the absolute telos. Climacus writes:

> It is not true, either, that the absolute τέλος becomes concrete in the relative ends, because resignation's absolute distinction will at every moment safeguard the absolute τέλος against all fraternizing. It is true that the individual oriented toward the absolute τέλος is in the relative ends, but he is not in them in such a way that the absolute τέλος is exhausted in them.
> (CUP, 1:400)

Resignation, then, is the means by which the individual orients the self absolutely toward the absolute telos and by which the absolute telos is distinguished from relative ends.

Thus far resignation has been concerned with orienting the human being toward the absolute telos. This function on the part of resignation is without doubt important, but it does not in itself bring about a relation to the absolute telos. Climacus is aware of this and thus introduces the concept of renunciation in order to supplement and fill out the concept of resignation: "The first true expression of relating oneself to the absolute τέλος is to renounce everything" (CUP, 1:404). Renunciation is necessary because the individual cannot simply and straightforwardly relate him or herself to the absolute telos, for "the actual individual is, after all, in immediacy and to that extent is actually in the relative ends absolutely" (CUP, 1:431). Thus "the individual begins, not, please note, by simultaneously relating himself absolutely to the absolute τέλος and relatively to the relative ends, because by being in immediacy he is exactly reversed, but he begins by practicing the absolute relation through renunciation" (CUP, 1:431). The first step in the individual's absolute orientation towards the absolute telos, then, is the renunciation of finite ends. Only then does a relation to the absolute telos become possible.

The renunciation required by resignation does not mean, however, that the human being should attempt to flee finite existence by, for example, entering a monastery. On the contrary, the person is called upon to relate to the absolute telos and express this relationship in his or her own existence while nevertheless remaining within the sphere of the finite. The point is that the individual's life is no longer determined by the finite but by the relation to the absolute telos: "In immediacy, the individual is firmly rooted in the finite; when resignation is convinced that the individual has the absolute orientation toward the absolute τέλος, everything is changed, the roots are cut. He lives in the finite, but he does not have his life in it" (CUP, 1:410). This holding on to the absolute in the midst of the finite is a "strenuous double movement" (cf. CUP, 1:409), for "it is difficult simultaneously to relate oneself absolutely to the absolute τέλος and then at the same moment to participate like other human beings in one thing and another" (CUP, 1:407, cf.

422). This strenuousness is increased still further by the fact that the resigned individual can never rest easy—there is no "reward" for the act of resignation (CUP, 1:397, cf. 405)—but must constantly hold fast to and repeat this resignation: "the task is to gain proficiency in repeating the impassioned choice and, existing, to express it in existence" (CUP, 1:410; cf. 406, 409).

How, then, is this "resigned" mode of existence expressed in *concrete* terms? What does the life of the resigned individual look like? Resignation should not, Climacus emphasizes, result in the monastic life. Monasticism is to be commended, for "the monastic movement is a passionate decision, as is appropriate with respect to the absolute τέλος" (CUP, 1:402) and is thus "far preferable in its nobility to the wretched brokerage wisdom of mediation" (CUP, 1:402). The weakness of monasticism is that it seeks to give an *external* expression of what is an inward, existential reality (CUP, 1:405, 408, 413). This is in contrast to the resigned individual, who, although he or she too, like the monk, "is a stranger in the world of finitude, . . . does not define his difference from *worldliness* by foreign dress (this is a contradiction, since with that he defines himself in a worldly way)" (CUP, 1:410). Indeed, as far as outward appearance is concerned, the resigned individual looks like everyone else, including those who have not made the movement of resignation: "His life, like the life of another, has the diverse predicates of a human existence, but he is within them like the person who walks in a stranger's borrowed clothes . . . ; he is incognito, but his incognito consists in looking just like everyone else" (CUP, 1:410). Thus the resigned individual may be found in a diversity of different professions and occupations. Such a person may be a councilor of justice or even a king (CUP, 1:409-10). What is decisive is that through resignation the individual no longer invests his or her whole existence in such activities, but even when engaged in them, is absolutely oriented towards the absolute telos. Thus although the resigned human being remains in the finite and carries out the tasks and duties that arise from his or her particular position in the realm of the finite, such a person has removed "the vital power of the finite in the moment of resignation" (CUP, 1:411). This, Climacus emphasizes, "does not necessarily mean that the existing person becomes indifferent to the finite" (CUP, 1:413), but rather that "the maximum of the task is to be able simultaneously to relate oneself absolutely to the absolute τέλος and relatively to the relative ends, or at all times to have the absolute τέλος with oneself" (CUP, 1:414).

Resignation, then, is a complex concept. Its most basic meaning is acceptance of the incommensurability of the finite and the infinite. This acceptance involves more than a mere intellectual awareness of incommensurability, however, for it requires the individual to act upon this incommensurability and structure his or her life accordingly. Thus resignation also has the meaning of renouncing the finite and the temporal. Thereby the individual achieves a form of existence in which a relationship to the absolute telos that is God and the acquisition of an eternal happiness become possible.

Suffering

The relation to the absolute telos brought about by resignation is, however, only the *initial* expression of existential pathos. It correctly expresses the insight that "existential pathos is action or the transformation of existence" (CUP, 1:431) and that "the appointed task is simultaneously to relate oneself absolutely to the absolute τέλος and relatively to relative ends" (CUP, 1:431), but has not yet won through to a full understanding of the difficulty this task involves. Climacus describes this difficulty in the following terms: "But this task must now be understood more specifically in its concrete difficulty, lest the existential pathos be revoked within aesthetic pathos, as if it were existential pathos to *say* this once and for all, or once a month, with the unchanged passion of immediacy" (CUP, 1:431). That is, the problem with resignation is that it does not stress clearly enough that the absolute relation to the absolute telos must be sustained through time in all the concrete experiences of human existence. The danger is that the individual may give merely notional assent to resignation, accepting intellectually the necessity of relating absolutely to the absolute telos, while failing to express this existentially in his or her life. What is needed, then, is a deeper comprehension of the existential task involved in the absolute relation to the absolute telos. This deeper comprehension is provided when resignation is supplemented by what Climacus calls "the *essential* expression of existential pathos" (CUP, 1:431), namely *suffering*:

"Just as resignation saw to it that the individual had the absolute orientation toward the absolute τέλος, the continuance of suffering is the guarantee that the individual is in position and keeps himself in position" (CUP, 1:443).

Suffering as a Universal Human Condition

Scattered through his analysis of suffering are several passages which seem to indicate that Climacus conceives of suffering as a universal human condition and that the task facing the human being is to find some creative way of dealing with this. This is indicated by the fact that if the concept of suffering in the *Postscript* were reserved exclusively for the suffering that results from dying to immediacy, then we would not expect the aesthetic individual to suffer, since he or she is not engaged in dying away from the world. Climacus, however, informs us that the aesthetic individual *does* suffer. This suffering takes the form of the experience of *misfortune*.

The aesthetic individual, Climacus tells us, is nondialectical: "the nondialectical individual changes the world but remains himself unchanged, because the aesthetic individual never has the dialectical within himself but outside himself, or the individual is changed in the external but inwardly remains himself unchanged" (CUP, 1:433; cf. 461, 537, 572). That is, for the aesthetic individual there is no incommensurability between the infinite and the finite: "He is the happy unity of the finite and the infinite" (CUP, 1:453). The aesthetic individual is simply what and who he or she is and exists in a (usually) happy relationship with the external world, upon which he or she is dependent for pleasure. Climacus describes the aesthetic lifeview in the following terms: "*Immediacy is good fortune*, because in immediacy there is no contradiction; the immediate person, viewed essentially, is fortunate, and *the lifeview of immediacy is good fortune*" (CUP, 1:433). Should something intervene to interrupt the individual's happy relationship with the external world and hinder the fulfilment of his or her desires, then the individual understands this in terms of misfortune and becomes unhappy.

The aesthetic individual does not have an *essential* relationship to this suffering, however; that is, the aesthete does not understand it to impinge upon his or her very being, but considers it merely to be an external problem brought about by a temporary interruption of his or her good fortune. Such an individual is confident that, once the impediment has been removed, the suffering will cease and he or she will be able to return to the original state of happiness (CUP, 1:434, 449). This means that the aesthete does not understand suffering, for such a person does not conceive of it as essential to human existence but as merely accidental (CUP, 1:447, 451). Indeed, if no misfortune were ever to befall the aesthetic individual, he or she would remain unaware of the existence of suffering (CUP, 1:433). Even when misfortune comes, Climacus writes, "he *feels* the misfortune, but he does not *comprehend* the suffering" (CUP, 1:433; cf. 443).

In the whole of Climacus's discussion of the aesthetic attitude to suffering there is *no question of this suffering being due to the individual's dying to immediacy.* On the contrary, the individual is firmly rooted in immediacy and feels no urge to part company with it. If suffering does not originate in dying to immediacy, then where does it have its source? The answer is that it must be a universal feature of human existence.

This concept of suffering as a universal human condition can also be found in Climacus's description of the humorist. The humorist, Climacus tells us, "has an essential conception of *the suffering in which he is*" (CUP, 1:447; emphasis added) and his "profundity is that he comprehends suffering together with existing and that therefore *all human beings suffer as long as they exist*" (CUP, 1:447-48; emphasis added). The humorist, in contrast to the aesthetic individual "comprehends the meaning of suffering as *inherent in existing*" (CUP, 1:449; emphasis added). These passages all make clear that for the humorist suffering is an intrinsic feature of all human existence. Indeed, it is the great profundity of the humorist over the aesthete that the humorist "comprehends suffering together with existing" (CUP, 447-48, 451). That is, the humorist does not relate him or herself to suffering externally, as was the case with the aesthetic individual, but understands it to be an essential expression of the human condition: to exist is to suffer. Once again, what is significant here, is that suffering is understood to be a universal characteristic of human existence and not merely something experienced by those engaged in dying to immediacy.

The humorist's attitude to suffering, although marking an advance on that of the aesthete, is nevertheless flawed, for although such a person recognizes the essential connection between existence and suffering, he or she is not *fully* aware of the meaning of suffering: "He comprehends the meaning of suffering in relation to existing, but he does not comprehend the meaning of suffering. He comprehends that it belongs together with existing, but he does not comprehend its meaning otherwise than that suffering belongs together with it" (CUP, 1:447). Consequently, "Humor comprehends suffering together with existence but revokes the essential meaning of suffering for the existing person" (CUP, 1:451; cf. 447). It is in this awareness of suffering and yet withdrawal from it that humor lies: "The humorist comprehends the profundity, but at the same time it occurs to him that it most likely is not worth the trouble to become involved in explaining it. This revocation is the jest" (CUP, 1:448; cf. 449).

The only adequate response to suffering is the religious response. Unlike the aesthetic individual the religious person understands suffering as an essential feature of human existence: "Just as the faith of immediacy is in fortune, so the faith of the religious is in this, that life lies precisely in suffering" (CUP, 1:436). Consequently, the task is not to attempt to avoid suffering, for this would mean failing to live authentically; the challenge is rather to face up to and accept the suffering that is the human lot: "from the religious point of view all human beings are suffering, and the point is to enter into the suffering (not by plunging into it but by discovering that one is in it) and not to escape the misfortune" (CUP, 1:436). This requires the religious individual to be conscious of suffering even when he or she is in what from the aesthetic perspective is good fortune: "Viewed religiously, the fortunate person, whom the whole world favors, is just as much a suffering person, if he is religious, as the person to whom misfortune comes from outside" (CUP, 1:436). Indeed, "the religious person continually has suffering with him, wants suffering in the same sense as the immediate person wants good fortune, and wants and has suffering even if the misfortune is not present externally, because it is not misfortune he wants, since then the relation would still be aesthetic and he would be essentially undialectical within himself" (CUP, 1:434-35; cf. 447). Thus, unlike the aesthetic individual, the religious person makes suffering the subject of his or her reflection, rather than seeking for ways of *avoiding* suffering: "Viewed religiously, the point . . . is to comprehend the suffering and remain in it in such a way that reflection is *on* the suffering and not *away from* the suffering" (CUP, 1:443; cf. 451).

Here too it is noticeable that Climacus speaks of suffering as a universal human condition, irrespective of whether the individual is engaged in the process of dying to immediacy or not. As we have seen, from the religious perspective all human beings are suffering and the task is to accept this and find some creative way of dealing with it.

Suffering as Dying to Immediacy

Suffering is not only a universal human condition, it can also arise from the human being's engagement in what Climacus calls "dying to immediacy." This type of suffering arises from the individual's attempt to transform his or her existence into a form capable of sustaining an absolute relation to the absolute telos. This requires that "the absoluteness of the religious [be] placed together with the specific, a combination that in existence is the very basis and meaning of suffering" (CUP, 1:483).

Wherein does this suffering lie? Why should bringing the absoluteness of the religious into relation with the specific result in suffering? Why does the individual suffer when he or she attempts to express the conception of God in his or her life? The reason is that God and the human being are absolutely different. Despite this absolute difference, it is nevertheless the individual's task to bring his or her existence into relationship with God. A genuine relationship between two parties, however, can only be established on the basis of equality. If a relationship is to come about between two *unequal* parties, as is the case between God and the human being, then one of the two parties must acknowledge this and adopt the appropriate status in relation to the other party. That is, what Climacus seems to mean by "equality" is that the status of both parties must be recognized if a genuine relationship is to come about. It is in this contradiction, namely in the fact that the individual is called upon to bring his or her existence into relationship with that which is incompatible with human existence, that suffering lies.

The cause of this suffering is that to sustain a relationship with God, the human being must undergo a process of self-transformation. The person must acquire a form capable of sustaining a relationship with the absolute telos that is God. This requires that the human being die to immediacy: "The effect that a person's conception of God or of his eternal happiness should have is that it transforms his entire existence in relation to it, a transformation that is a dying to immediacy" (CUP, 1:483). Climacus unpacks the nature of dying to immediacy by means of the concepts of "self-annihilation" and "becoming nothing before God." These two concepts make the same point from different perspectives. "Self-annihilation" makes clear what dying to immediacy entails, namely the breaking down and removal of the egocentricity of the human being. "Becoming nothing before God" describes the nature of the human being's God-relationship that comes about through dying to immediacy. Nothingness before God, which in concrete terms expresses itself as humility, is an expression of the absolute difference between God and the human being, and is therefore the only adequate expression of their relationship to each other (CUP, 1:492).

This process of dying to immediacy is not an easy process. Its goal is that the human being should ultimately "feel absolutely captive in the absolute conception of God"; not, however, on isolated occasions but constantly, "because the absolute conception of God is not to have the absolute conception *en passant* but is to have the absolute conception at every moment." When achieved, "this is the cessation of immediacy and the death warrant of annihilation" (CUP, 1:488).

This demand to have the absolute conception at every moment brings with it another level of suffering. This suffering comes about because "absoluteness is not directly the element of a finite existence" (CUP, 1:483). That is, in striving for an absolute relation with the absolute telos the human being is out of his or her element. The person is like a bird imprisoned in a cage, a fish out of water, or an invalid on his sickbed (CUP, 1:483-84). Yet the religious individual's plight is worse than this, because "the captivating conception is everywhere present and at every moment" (CUP, 1:484). This results in the utter annihilation of the human being and in the insight that he or she is utterly helpless.

> Even though the conception of God is the absolute help, it is also the one and only help that is absolutely able to show a person his own helplessness. The religious person lies in the finite as a helpless infant; he wants to hold on to the conception absolutely, and this is what annihilates him; he wills to do everything, and while he is willing it, the powerlessness begins, because for a finite being there is indeed a meanwhile. He wills to do everything; he wants to express this relation absolutely, but he cannot make the finite commensurate with it.   (CUP, 1:484)

What Climacus seems to be saying here is that at this stage of his development the suffering individual has made only the movement of infinity, as Johannes de Silentio puts it in *Fear and Trembling* (FT, 38, 40-46, 69, 100). That is, the individual has severed the connections with the finite in his or her relation to the absolute telos, but has yet to find a way back to the finite. Yet he or she must find a way back to the finite, for the finite is the realm in which every person lives. As Climacus puts it, in dying to immediacy the individual has attained to "the suffering of annihilation . . . when he in his nothingness has the absolute conception but no *reciprocity*" (CUP, 1:484; emphasis added). The individual has, to employ the language of Constantin Constantius, yet to experience *repetition*, the paradoxical event whereby the person regains all that he or she had lost in making the movement of infinity.

The individual, then, is ill, having divorced him or herself from the finite in the relation to the absolute. Consequently, the person lies stranded like a beached whale, for it is the finite and not the absolute that is the human being's natural element. The relation to the absolute, however, makes a person incapable of acting in the finite: "In the state of illness, the religious person is not capable of joining the God-conception together with an incidental finitude such as going out to the amusement park" (CUP, 1:486). This means that the individual is presented with a new difficulty. Having cut his or her roots in the finite, the person must return to the finite and bring the relationship with the absolute telos into relation with the finite ends and trivial activities of human existence. This is a difficult task because "the more unimportant something is, the more difficult it is to join the God-conception together with it" (CUP, 1:487). It is not in relationship to the great events of life that the concept of God must be introduced but in the most trivial and everyday of events. "It is right here," Climacus tells us, "that the relationship with God will be known" (CUP, 1:487). Thus having discovered his incapacity to relate to the finite by virtue of his relation to the absolute telos the individual is presented with a new difficulty, namely, "the difficulty is: with God to be capable of it" (CUP, 1:486).

How, then does the religious individual succeed in returning to the finite once he or she has died to immediacy? Climacus answers this question thus: "We left the religious person in the crisis of sickness; but this sickness is not unto death. We shall now let him be strengthened by the very same conception that destroyed him, by the conception of God" (CUP, 1:488). Just as it was dying to immediacy in relation to the absolute telos that brought about the religious individual's sickness, so too is it the conception of God that heals this sickness. How does this come about? Here we run up against a typical feature of Kierkegaard's authorship, namely that when we reach the crucial stage of the individual's God-relationship, he breaks off the discussion with the assertion that it is impossible for him to go further and that it is now up to each individual to make the final movement. Thus Climacus does not provide us with an analysis of how the conception of God cures the religious individual of his or her illness, but instead writes:

> Every human being is gloriously structured, but what destroys so many is, for example, this confounded talkativeness between man and man about what must be suffered but also be matured in silence, this confession before human beings instead of before God, this candid communication to this one and that one of what ought to be a secret and be before God in secret, this impatient hankering for makeshift consolation.   (CUP, 1:489)

That is, respect for the divine-human relationship prohibits open discussion of this relationship. This is a relationship that is sustained within the inwardness of the human being. If it is dragged out and made a topic of conversation, if the religious individual betrays his or her hidden inwardness in order to seek consolation for suffering from friends and companions, then the God-relationship disintegrates into blather. The true religious individual will not engage in such activity (CUP, 1:489-90).

Nevertheless, Climacus does give us some idea of how the individual is able to return to the finite. The individual achieves this and is able to visit the amusement park because it is an expression of his or her humility and *eo ipso* a relationship with God.

> And why does he enjoy himself? Because the humblest expression for the relationship with God is to acknowledge one's humanness, and it is human to enjoy oneself. If a woman can succeed in totally changing herself just to please her husband, why should the religious person in his relationship with God not succeed in enjoying himself if this is the humblest expression for the relationship with God?" (CUP, 1:493)

Beyond this we cannot go, for a person's suffering and the God-relationship it expresses are concealed in the hidden inwardness of the religious individual.

The Relationship between Suffering as a Universal Human Condition and Suffering as Dying to Immediacy

Climacus does not explain the relationship between suffering as a universal condition and suffering as dying to immediacy. Indeed, he seems to understand them as one and the same thing. If this is the case, then it indicates a lack of clarity in Kierkegaard's thought, for, as we have seen, two distinct types of suffering are present in the *Postscript*. Suffering as a universal human condition arises from existence itself; it is a given feature of human existence over which the human being has no control. Suffering as dying to immediacy, however, arises from the individual's attempt to relate absolutely to the absolute telos. It is not a given feature of human existence but is something that the individual freely takes upon him or herself in relationship to God. Is there any way of bringing these two types of suffering together into a coherent whole? Although this is a task Climacus himself does not undertake, it is possible that there is an underlying unity to the two forms of suffering. Such a unity can be posited if we understand suffering as a universal human condition to function as a prompt to the process of dying to immediacy. That is, the universal givenness of suffering can create, to employ Karl Jaspers' phrase, a "boundary situation" in which the individual is forced to reassess his or her life. All three types of human being—the aesthete, the humorist, and the religious person—are confronted by the reality of suffering in human existence and need to find some creative way of dealing with it. The aesthete's solution is to understand suffering as something external that will eventually pass, allowing a return to happiness. The humorist understands suffering to be a defining feature of human existence—to exist is to suffer—but does not penetrate to the *significance* of suffering for human existence. Like the humorist, the religious person understands the essential relation of suffering to existence, but whereas the humorist stops at this point, the religious individual imposes a *religious* framework upon his or her suffering by placing it in relation to God. That is, the suffering that is the universal human lot indicates the task facing the religious individual, namely that human existence should not retreat from or attempt to avoid suffering, but should understand it as the means by which the human being is detached from dependence upon the finite. This insight only becomes valid, however, when the individual expresses it in his or her own existence by freely accepting the suffering that arises from attempting to sustain an absolute relation to the absolute telos.

Guilt

It would appear, then, that the individual has at last arrived at the point where he or she can relate absolutely to the absolute telos. The individual has made the movement of resignation whereby he or she subordinates finite ends to the absolute telos, and has embarked upon the process of dying away to immediacy that makes a relationship to the absolute telos possible. It would seem, then, that the individual has fulfilled all the conditions for a relationship to the absolute telos. This, however, is not the case, for suffering leads not to an absolute relation to the absolute telos but to *guilt*.

What, then, is the nature of this guilt and how exactly does it come about? When attempting to answer these questions we run up against a similar problem to that encountered in our discussion of suffering, namely that Climacus seems to be working with a variety of different conceptions of guilt.

Guilt as a Universal Human Condition

That Climacus understands guilt to be a universal human condition is clearly indicated by his statement that guilt is a universal given and that it is this that makes individual instances of guilt possible: "In everyday affairs, total guilt, as a *universally given*, gradually becomes so taken for granted that it is forgotten. And yet it is this totality of guilt that ultimately makes it possible for someone to be guilty or not guilty in the particular" (CUP, 1:529; emphasis added). Further evidence that Climacus views guilt as a fundamental feature of human existence is provided by his repudiation of those who claim that the universality of guilt exonerates the human being from responsibility for his or her own personal guilt. Such individuals argue that "inasmuch as the guilt is explained by existing, the existing person seems to be made guiltless; it seems that he must be able to shove the guilt onto the one who placed him in existence or onto existence itself" (CUP, 1:528). If this argument were valid, then "the guilt-consciousness is only a new expression for suffering in existence" and guilt would not need to be treated as an independent category but as an appendix to the discussion of suffering (CUP, 1:528). Climacus rejects this, arguing that to absolve oneself of responsibility for guilt is an implicit confession that one is guilty, for a truly guiltless person would not address this question. For a guiltless person the question of who bears responsibility for guilt would simply not arise. In denying responsibility for guilt, then, the individual succeeds only in denouncing him or herself as guilty. This is the terrible, entrapping dialectic of guilt: "Its dialectic is so cunning that the person who totally exonerates himself simply denounces himself, and the person who partially exonerates himself denounces himself totally" (CUP, 1:529). Responsibility for guilt, then, lies with the individual and is a condition that affects all human beings, irrespective of whether they acknowledge it or not.

Guilt Arising from Dying to Immediacy

This form of guilt stems from the failure of suffering to bring about an absolute relation to the absolute telos. The problem is that the individual's dying to immediacy through suffering is not *total*. This is due to the fact that the time the person spends acquiring the conditions for sustaining a relation to the absolute telos is time in which he or she has not yet related him or herself to the absolute telos.

> Even at the moment the task is assigned, something is already wasted, because there is an "in the meantime" and the beginning is not promptly made. This is how it goes backward: the task is given to the individual in existence, and just as he wants to plunge in straightaway . . . , and wants to begin, another beginning is discovered to be necessary, the beginning of the enormous detour that is dying to immediacy. And just as the beginning is about to be made here, it is discovered that, since meanwhile time has been passing, a bad beginning has been made and that the beginning must be made by becoming guilty, and from that moment the total guilt, which is decisive, practices usury with the new guilt.   (CUP, 1:526)

The individual's inability to sustain an *absolute* or *total* relation to the absolute telos thrusts him or her into total guilt.

Guilt as the Juxtaposition of Finite Guilt and the Absolute Telos

Guilt should not, Climacus emphasizes, be understood as the result of particular, finite actions. Guilt that results from specific actions is childish or aesthetic guilt and is characterized by its intermittence or lack of continuance: "Aesthetically, the dialectic of guilt is this: the individual is without guilt, then guilt and guilt-lessness come along as alternating categories in life; at times the individual is guilty of this or that and at times is not guilty" (CUP, 1:537). Such guilt-consciousness is thus "comparative" in nature (CUP, 1:531). Its distinctive feature is that it has "its criterion outside itself" (CUP, 1:531).

What childish or aesthetic guilt lacks is a consciousness of the necessity of joining guilt together with the absolute telos: "Child-ishness and the comparative guilt-consciousness are distinguished by not having a comprehension of the requirement of existence: *to join together*" (CUP, 1:531). As a result guilt is merely fragmentary and episodic in nature. When specific instances of guilt are brought into relation with the absolute telos, however, guilt becomes a "totality-qualification" (CUP, 1:529) or a "totality-catego-ry" (CUP, 1:549). That is, the individual comes to understand guilt not merely as the sum of isolated, particular episodes within existence, but as a concept that applies to the whole of the person's life:

> The priority of the total guilt is no empirical qualification, is no *summa summarum*, because a totality-qualification is never produced numerically. The totality of guilt comes into existence for the individual by joining his guilt, be it just one, be it utterly trivial, together with the relation to an eternal happiness.
>
> (CUP, 1:529)

When it is brought into relation to the absolute telos that is an eternal happiness, then, guilt becomes a total determinant in the life of the existing individual.

The Relationship between the Three Forms of Guilt

How are these three apparently different forms of guilt related? Climacus does not himself spell out explicitly the solution to this problem. The most likely explanation, however, is as follows. In attempting to relate himself or herself to the absolute telos the human being discovers only that he or she is incapable of sustaining such a relationship. A single incident of guilt, when brought into relation to the absolute telos, is sufficient to plunge the individual into total guilt, because in this moment of failure to relate to the absolute telos the human being distances him or herself from the absolute telos. The distance created by this failure can never be made up, for the relation to the absolute telos is an absolute relation: "The slightest guilt, even if the individual henceforth were an angel, when joined together with the relation to an eternal happiness is sufficient, because the joining together yields the qualitative category" (CUP, 1:529). The insight the individual gains through his or her attempt to relate absolutely to the absolute telos, then, is that it is not possible to sustain such a relationship and that this incapacity on his or her part is guilt.

This does not mean, however, that the individual *causes* total guilt through joining together finite instances of guilt with the absolute telos, although Climacus's language can sometimes create this impression. This cannot be the case, for, as we have seen, guilt is "a universally given." It is not something first brought into existence by the individual's guilt. It must be noted that when Climacus speaks of guilt coming into existence through the joining together of finite guilt and the absolute telos, he qualifies this statement with the phrase "for the individual"; e.g. "The totality of guilt comes into existence *for the individual* by joining his guilt . . . together with the relation to an eternal happiness" (CUP, 1:529; emphasis added). That is, in bringing his or her finite guilt into relation to the absolute telos, the individual does not cause or create guilt but becomes *conscious* of the universal givenness of guilt in human existence. We could perhaps express the point Climacus is making by saying that in committing acts of guilt the individual is forced to posit the ontological priority of the total guilt which makes these acts of guilt possible.

With the guilt that comes about through dying to immediacy, the problem is considered from the perspective of the absolute telos. That is, what is required of the individual in order to sustain an absolute relation to the absolute telos? The answer is that all those elements of the self that impede such a relation—finite wishes, egocentricity, and so on—must be put to one side. The failure of the individual to sustain this constantly and the fact that there was a period prior to his or her decision to relate absolutely to the absolute telos when such a relation was not sustained means that the individual is thrust into guilt.

In the case of the guilt that arises from the juxtaposition of finite guilt with the absolute telos the problem is considered from the perspective of the instances of finite guilt committed by the individual. When the individual attempts to bring his or her life into relation with the absolute telos, it is discovered that these instances of guilt make impossible an absolute relation to the absolute telos. This casts a new light on the individual's guilt. It must now be understood as a total determinant of the person's existence, because each instance of guilt, even the most trivial, has shattered the possibility of an absolute relation to the absolute telos. The whole of the individual's existence is distanced from the absolute telos.

All these forms of guilt express the underlying truth that human existence as such is separated from an absolute relation to the absolute telos. Consequently, all human existence is guilty.

Guilt and the God-Relationship

In attempting to sustain a relationship to the absolute telos, then, the individual succeeds only in discovering his or her absolute guilt. This might give rise to the conclusion that an absolute relation to the absolute telos is impossible, for is not the end-result of resignation and dying to immediacy merely the discovery of the apparently insuperable distance that lies between the human being and the absolute telos? This, Climacus tells us, would be a mistaken conclusion.

> Indeed, one would think that this consciousness [of guilt] expresses that one is not relating oneself to it, decisively express- es that it is lost and the relation abandoned. The answer is not difficult. Because it is an existing person who is supposed to relate himself to it, but guilt is the most concrete expression of existence, the consciousness of guilt is the expression for the relation.   (CUP, 1:527-28)

That is, it is precisely through becoming conscious of guilt that the individual comes to sustain a relationship to the absolute telos. This relation seems to come about in two closely related ways.

Firstly, guilt-consciousness expresses the fact that the individu- al is not related to the absolute telos. It is precisely this disrelation- ship that constitutes the relationship between the human being and the absolute telos:[1]

> Thus the essential consciousness of guilt is the greatest possible immersion in existence, and it also expresses that an existing person relates himself to an eternal happiness . . . , expresses the relation by expressing the disrelationship.   (CUP, 1:531)

That is, in understanding him or herself as absolutely distanced from the absolute telos, the individual acquires an understanding of the human being's true position before God. The individual thereby comes into a relation with God because he or she has at last adopted the correct attitude of the creature to the Holy and Almighty Creator. This does not mean that the individual now comes *closer* to an eternal happiness. Climacus writes: "In the eter- nal recollecting of guilt-consciousness, the existing person relates

---

[1]I have followed Lowrie in translating *Mishold* as "disrelationship," rather than "misrelation," which is Hong and Hong's preferred transla- tion, because the latter implies a *distorted* relationship. This confuses the point Climacus is making, which is that it is through *distance* or *separation* that a relationship with the absolute telos becomes possible.

himself to an eternal happiness, but not in such a way that he now has come closer to it directly; on the contrary, he is now distanced from it as much as possible, but he still relates himself to it" (CUP, 1:535). The relationship between the human being and the absolute telos is expressed, then, through *distance*. This means that, underlying the distance or disrelationship between the human being and the absolute telos, there is a tenuous point of contact: "In the relation that is the basis of the disrelationship, in the intimated immanence that is the basis of the dialectic's separation, he is closely bound up with happiness, by the finest thread, as it were, by the help of a possibility that continually perishes . . . " (CUP, 1:535-36). In guilt, then, there still exists an *Anknüpfungspunkt* between the human and the divine. This is because through the eternal recollection of guilt the human being has arrived at an awareness of the eternal that underlies existence.

The second way in which a relationship is brought about between the individual and the absolute telos is through increased existential pathos: "Guilt-consciousness is the decisive expression for the existential pathos in relation to an eternal happiness" (CUP, 1:533). That is, the existential pathos by which the individual sweeps away those finite elements that stand in the way of a relationship to the absolute telos, has reached a higher and more intense expression than was the case with resignation and suffering. This is because the greater distance posited by guilt makes it far more difficult to relate to the absolute telos, which radically increases the existential pathos: "The dialectical that is present here, still within immanence, creates a resistance that intensifies the pathos" (CUP, 1:535)

This existential pathos is intensified still further by the fact that guilt-consciousness is not a momentary event or temporary action carried out by the individual but is a constant feature of his or her existence. That is, once the person has broken through to the insight that he or she is guilty, the human being cannot return to the previous mode of existence, which would be a relapse into an aesthetic or childish conception of guilt (CUP, 1:533), but *recollects* his or her guilt-consciousness: "Thus the decisive expression of guilt-consciousness is in turn the essential continuance of this consciousness or the eternal recollecting of guilt, because it is continually joined together with the relation to an eternal happiness" (CUP, 1:533). The individual must constantly relate him or herself through guilt-consciousness to an eternal happiness and express this relationship in every, even the most trivial, aspect of life. This is the art of existing.

> To relate oneself existentially with pathos to an eternal happiness is never a matter of occasionally making a huge effort but is constancy in the relation, the constancy with which it is joined together with everything. The whole existence-art consists in this, and in this, perhaps most of all, human beings fall short.
>
> (CUP, 1:535)

"Existential pathos," then, as Climacus puts it a few paragraphs later, "is not the pathos of the moment but the pathos of continuance" (CUP, 1:536). The result of this is that recollection of guilt becomes the highest expression of existential pathos: "Recollection's eternal storing up of guilt is the expression for existential pathos, the highest expression, even higher than the most inspired penance that wants to make up for the guilt" (CUP, 1:538). Through guilt-consciousness, then, the individual experiences a deepening of existential pathos.

This is the reason that guilt-consciousness is a *forward* movement, despite the fact that it places a greater distance between the individual and the absolute telos and makes the task of relating to an eternal happiness considerably more difficult. It is a forward movement because it constitutes an advance in the individual's self-understanding and existential pathos. As Climacus puts it, "This backward movement is nevertheless a forward movement inasmuch as immersing oneself in something means to go forward" (CUP, 1:527; cf. 534)

But in what way does this constitute an advance over suffering? Why is the existential pathos of guilt-consciousness deeper and more advanced than that of suffering? The decisive difference, Climacus informs us, is that "the negative expression is decidedly stronger: the relation is distinguished by the totality of guilt-consciousness" (CUP, 1:532-33). Guilt-consciousness is more advanced than suffering, because the relation it sustains to the absolute telos is even less direct and more inward than suffering. The relation of guilt-consciousness to the absolute telos is a stage more distant or, as Climacus puts it, "repellent" than suffering: "suffering is the direct reaction of a repelling relation; the guilt-consciousness is the repelling reaction of a repelling relation" (CUP, 1:533). The difference, then, seems to lie in the fact that guilt imposes a greater distance between the individual and the absolute telos than does suffering. Suffering is value-neutral; it is merely the means by which the individual molds him or herself into a form capable of sustaining a relationship to the absolute telos. Guilt, however, is not value-neutral. The individual is unable to sustain a relationship to the absolute telos, even by means of suffering, and bears the responsibility for this. Thus suffering is a direct relation because it presupposes and proceeds on the assumption that a relationship with the absolute telos is possible once certain impediments have been removed. Guilt-consciousness understands the impediments to be far more deep-seated. They cannot be removed, for the impediments constitute the very self of the individual. The highest insight is to acknowledge this, and in acknowledging it one advances into a self-understanding and acquires an existential pathos that is more advanced than that of suffering.

Conclusion

Resignation, suffering, and guilt constitute the individual's attempt to sustain a relationship to the absolute telos that is God and to acquire an eternal happiness by means of the subordination of the finite elements of the self to the infinite. They seem to be an abstract, philosophical unfolding of a principle that lies at the heart of the Christian Gospel: "He who loves father or mother more than me is not worthy of me; and he who loves son or daughter more than me is not worthy of me; and he who does not take his cross and follow me is not worthy of me. He who finds his life will lose it, and he who loses his life for my sake will find it" (Matt. 10.37-39; cf. 8.22; 16.25; Mark 8.35; Luke 9.24; John 12.25). That is, finite relations, including even close relations such as family, must be renounced if a relationship with Christ is to come about. Of course, in Climacus's analysis this is not expressed in relation to Christ, for this would take him out of religiousness A into religiousness B. Nevertheless, the principle that the finite elements of the self must be subordinated to the absolute telos through resignation, suffering, and guilt, seems to have firmly biblical roots. Before bringing our discussion to a conclusion, it is necessary to place our three concepts in their broader context.

Although the *Postscript's* treatment of resignation, suffering, and guilt stand in continuity with their treatment in the earlier works, there is one respect in which Climacus's analysis differs from that of the other pseudonyms. As Wilfried Greve rightly points out,[2] in the *Postscript* these three concepts are given an ontological grounding in the form of Climacus's analysis of the relationship between the infinite and the finite. For this reason the portrayal of the three concepts in the *Postscript* is far more abstract than is the case with the more concrete portrayals offered in the earlier pseudonymous works, where resignation, suffering, and guilt are explored in the context of the personal problems of poetic individuals.

Another interesting point that emerges from our discussion is that there seems to be a parallel between Climacus's examination of religiousness A and his earlier analysis of subjectivity and truth. Indeed, it seems that religiousness A and its three concepts of resignation, suffering, and guilt are the deeper unfolding of the principle that "subjectivity is the truth," especially when we recall that the truth with which Climacus is concerned is existential, and ultimately religious, truth. The discussion of how the individual sustains an relation to the truth is an alternative formulation of the later discussion of how the individual can establish an absolute relation to the absolute telos. The validity of this view is established by the fact that Climacus's development of the principles of religiousness A mirrors his development of the concept of subjectivity. Both principles are based on the presupposition that the human being possesses the capacity to sustain a relationship to the truth/absolute telos. Both end with the conclusion that this is not the case and that the foundations upon which they are constructed are flawed. "Subjectivity is truth" ends with the insight that "subjectivity is untruth" (CUP, 1:207), while religiousness A reaches its climax with the insight that the human being is totally guilty. That is, Climacus's analyses of truth and of religiousness A

---

[2]Wilfried Greve, *Kierkegaards maieutische Ethik* (Frankfurt am Main: Suhrkamp, 1990) 247.

both end with the insight that the human being is not able by means of his or her own powers to establish a relation to the truth/absolute telos. Climacus's introduction of the concepts of resignation, suffering, and guilt in the latter part of the *Postscript*, then, can be regarded as a deeper unfolding of the existential consequences contained in the principle "subjectivity is the truth."

Our analysis of resignation, suffering, and guilt also places us in a better position to understand the relationship between religiousness A and B. It should be stressed that these two forms of religiousness are not in competition with each other. Religiousness A is indispensable for religiousness B. The individual must have developed the intensity of inwardness of religiousness A through resignation, suffering, and guilt, if he or she is to enter Christian religiousness. This does not mean that there is a natural progression from religiousness A to religiousness B, or that we can bypass religiousness A and go straight to religiousness B, thereby avoiding resignation, suffering, and guilt. To do so would be to fall back into aesthetic Christianity (CUP, 1:558), which, as Hirsch succinctly puts it, is merely "paganism masquerading as Christianity."[3] The role of religiousness A and its three concepts of resignation, suffering, and guilt is to protect Christianity from such deterioration into aestheticism. Furthermore, the existential attributes accompanying our three concepts, namely consciousness of utter human incapacity before God and radically heightened pathos, are qualities which must also appear in religiousness B. The significance of religiousness A is thus that it clears the ground for Christian religiousness. It is for this reason that it is the indispensable "terminus a quo" for religiousness B.

That a human being's God-relationship is something that should be the very center of his or her life and must be expressed not just on great occasions but also in the most trivial activities and problems of everyday existence is surely a view with which no religious individual can quarrel. What is surprising is that Climacus seems unaware of its *communal* dimension. Surely an absolute relation to the absolute telos must be expressed not just

---

[3]Emanuel Hirsch, *Kierkegaard-Studien* (Gütersloh: C. Bertelsmann, 1933) 805.

in the life of the single individual but also in social and political institutions. Climacus, however, seems to be positively against such social engagement, for he argues that the individual's God-relationship should have *no* external manifestation whatsoever. The finite for him is a cloak which the religious individual should use to conceal his or her relationship to the absolute telos. This aspect of Climacus's thought must surely be rejected. It is not enough simply to bring the concept of God into relation to the finite, for surely the Christian position is that the concept of God should, through the humble agency of the religious individual, *transform* the finite.

There thus seems to be a contradiction in Climacus's thought. He wishes the God-relationship to permeate the finite but in a way that makes absolutely no difference to the finite, and yet the logical conclusion of his position is that the God-relationship should transform the finite.[4] If we wish to learn how to transform ourselves religiously, then Kierkegaard in the guise of Johannes Climacus is a guide of great profundity. If, however, we wish to aid the Church in its mission to facilitate the coming of the kingdom of God on earth, then we must seek another guide.

---

[4]It is not enough for Johannes Sløk to claim that Kierkegaard's "formidable attack on the church, on society, and on the establishment ought to make him immune to this sort of critique," for Kierkegaard is content only to knock down and not to build up. He does not address the question of what sort of institutions we are to put in their place. Johannes Sløk, *Christentum mit Leidenschaft* (Munich: Kaiser, 1990) 131-32.

15

Subjectivity Is (Un)Truth:
Climacus's Dialectically Sharpened Pathos

Lee C. Barrett

When Johannes Climacus, master of inactivity, lit up a new cigar in the cafe in Frederiksberg Gardens, he resolved to make things more difficult for humanity. His resolution bore fruit in this cryptic juxtaposition found in his discussion of "subjective truth" in *Concluding Unscientific Postscript*. On the one hand, subjectivity is truth, but, on the other hand, subjectivity is untruth (CUP, 1:207). This antinomy complicates life enormously for the reader. The puzzling passage cannot be ignored, for it occurs at an important juncture in the text. In the preceding section Climacus had been critiquing his era's dispassionate "objectivity" and presenting Socratic inwardness as an attractive alternative. Climacus concluded, "So, then, subjectivity, inwardness, is truth" (CUP, 1:207). Then, when the reader would expect Climacus to elaborate further the implications of the Socratic position, he disrupts the anticipated flow of his exposition with a consideration of the possibility of "going beyond" Socrates. According to Climacus, this advance beyond Socrates is indeed possible if the subjectivity which has already been declared to be truth "is in the predicament of being untruth" (CUP, 1:207).

By saying this, Climacus has achieved his espoused goal of making things difficult for the reader. Not only has Climacus abruptly changed the subject, but he has confronted the reader with an apparent contradiction concerning a matter of crucial importance. Moreover, Climacus is quick to rule out the obvious interpretation of his words. Whatever "subjectivity is untruth" may mean here, it is not a retraction of the earlier contention that, for existing individuals, subjectivity is "higher" than objectivity. The suggested untruth of subjectivity does not involve a regression to the view that objectivity is truth. The reader is forced to struggle to make sense of the seemingly contradictory assessments of subjectivity.

Interpreters of Kierkegaard have reached diverging conclusions concerning this passage's significance. According to some, one claim about subjectivity displaces the other in a dialectical development of authentic selfhood. According to others, the juxtaposition should be read as the free play of indeterminate signifiers, subverting the expectations of conventional reading. I shall employ an alternative approach which neither views the "truth" and "untruth" of subjectivity as having univocal meanings, nor regards them as so undetermined as to defy any particular interpretation. Without endorsing only one reading as valid, I will suggest that there are enough textual clues to support the claim that Climacus deliberately uses "subjectivity" in two different but complexly interconnected ways in order to pursue a coherent authorial strategy.

These different uses correspond to the two different dimensions of the comprehensive purpose of *Concluding Unscientific Postscript*. Throughout the book, Climacus seeks to restore the possibility of becoming a Christian in the midst of a Christendom which has forgotten what Christianity is. This task involves recovering what Climacus takes to be the simple meaning of Christianity: the conviction that the individual should respond to God's offer of an eternal blessedness. This simple proposal has two distinguishable dimensions. First, God is offering something which the individual does not already possess. Secondly, the individual should choose to receive it. In order to clarify Christianity, Climacus must elucidate both the "pathos-filled" aspects of the reception and the "dialectical" aspects of the offer. The "pathos-filled" project is to clarify "how" the individual should relate to the Christian option. The "dialectical" task is to clarify "what" that option, including its doctrinal concepts, involves. As we shall see, these two dimensions can be provisionally distinguished but never divorced. Because of the intricate interplay between these two dynamics, Climacus's use of concepts like "subjectivity" is fluid, varying from context to context. The unique challenges of his project lead him to modify language to suit his specific purposes. As we shall see, the differences between the two dynamics may help account for the opposed affirmations of the truth and untruth of subjectivity. In order to understand this juxtaposition, we will first examine how "subjectivity is truth" functions in the passional dimension, then explore how "subjectivity is untruth" functions in the dialectical (or conceptual/doctrinal) dimension, and then examine how they modify each other.

In order to respond rightly to the offered eternal happiness, the first requisite is a passionate interest in it. This sets the stage for Climacus's use of the dictum "truth is subjectivity." According to Climacus the problem is that contemporary people do not possess the sort of pathos suited for an interest in the eternal happiness which Christianity promises. They have forgotten what it is to exist, lacking a passionate concern for the shape of their own lives (CUP, 1:242). Climacus draws attention to this lack of self-concern through an analysis of different views of "truth," a seemingly unlikely vehicle to stimulate passion. He approaches the issue indirectly, via epistemology, because the age's sedating ideological self-delusion expresses itself in epistemological garb. The delusion is most effectively exposed from the inside.

According to Climacus, the lack of passionate self-concern is evident in the popular conviction that the highest good resides in conformity to external states of affairs, that is, "objectivity." Climacus seeks to discredit the notion that dispassionate thought is the primary path to human fulfillment.[1] The introduction sets the stage for this agenda by ridiculing the delusion of those who hope to "quantify" themselves into faith (CUP, 1:11). Similar condemnations of the salvific pretensions of "objectivity," particularly those of the fashionable idealism, recur throughout the text. Climacus's differentiation of objective truth and subjective truth is part of an exposé of the deadening effects of conformism, the dissolution of the individual in the spirit of the age. Confusions about "truth" must be dispelled in order to illumine what it is to exist truly.[2]

---

[1]See C. Stephen Evans, *Kierkegaard's "Fragments" and "Postscript": The Religious Philosophy of Johannes Climacus* (Atlantic Highlands NJ: Humanities Press, 1983) 119-23.

[2]See Robert L. Perkins, "Kierkegaard: A Kind of Epistemologist," *History of European Ideas* 12/1 (1990): 7-18.

Because of this polemical intent, the force of "subjectivity is truth" can only be appreciated by contrasting it with the rival claim that "objectivity is truth." Climacus emphasizes two characteristics of objectivity: the abstraction from the interests of the subject, and the desire for a certainty which precludes decision. Objectivity esteems detached, impersonal observation, free of the subject's idiosyncratic interests which might distort the pure perception of the object. The uniqueness of the subject's perspective is a potentially contaminating accident which must be transcended in order to attain a universal viewpoint, valid for all knowers (CUP, 1:193). Furthermore, the objective sensibility longs for the security of certainty and closure (CUP, 1:194). Certainty obviates the need to take risks by narrowing the range of candidates for truth to one option. From the objective point of view, no decisions, choices, or commitments are necessary (CUP, 1:203). Once truth is obtained, the appropriation of that truth should be an easy matter. One simply knows what is what and acts accordingly. For an objectivist, living truly should follow naturally from holding true beliefs. Consequently, there would be no need to be unduly concerned about the quality of the subject's own life.

Climacus's critique of the objectivist sensibility employs a twofold strategy. One attack questions the intelligibility of the ideal, and the other challenges the feasibility of the project. First, he debunks the notion of pure objectivity in general, showing that the ideal of neutral observation is self-defeating. This strategy is most evident in his reflections on the story of the lunatic who, in order to demonstrate his sanity, puts a ball in the tail of his coat, and exclaims "Boom! The world is round!" every time the ball bumps his rear (CUP, 1:195). Although the lunatic utters a proposition which is true in the abstract, his linguistic behavior loses intelligibility because of the absence of a specifying context. The lunatic's affirmation of the planet's roundness is so ill-suited to the situation that it is not even clear if he is talking about the shape of the earth. The tale points to the fact that language has meaning only when used in appropriate ways in appropriate situations. One crucial dimension of the meaning of any communicative act is the intelligibility of the interest motivating it. Another is the perspicuity of the purpose of the linguistic performance, which can only be construed by taking the author's relationship to the intended audience into account (CUP, 1:240). The nexus of concerns and purposes in which linguistic acts are embedded is constitutive of their meaning.[3]

Consequently, all intelligible claims to knowledge must occur against a background of particular human concerns, valuations, and commitments. These interests help constitute the intelligibility of any use of language. It is not the case that concepts or propositions possess objective, interest-neutral meanings which are only contingently related to human pathos. Affirmations devoid of all relation to specific human interests and purposes would lose determinate significance. When the champions of objectivity seek to eliminate all subjective interests, they inadvertently undercut the very concern for particular truths which their project presupposes. The objective spirit "absentmindedly" subverts itself. Pure objectivity, independent of passional contexts, would be indistinguishable from lunacy.

This appreciation of the interest-laden and contextual nature of meaning motivates Climacus's disquietude with the "speculation" of the idealist philosophers and theologians. Confusion inevitably results when a concept is uprooted from its typical passional context and transferred to another context governed by a different set of concerns. For example, the dogmatic concept "sin," with its mood of passionate self-criticism, is misconstrued if it is resituated in the detached mood of philosophical reflection (CUP, 1:269). A concept is evacuated of all meaning when it is translated into the abstract domain of speculation which possesses no defining interests or passions at all. The ersatz perspective of the "pure I-I," free of finite interests, would be the view from which nothing could be seen (CUP, 1:190).

Climacus's subversion of the intelligibility of pure objectivity is supplemented by his second strategy of raising doubts about the epistemological feasibility of the objectivist project. Even if the ideal of pure objectivity were intelligible, its attainment would still be empirically impossible. Absolute certainty is not possible for existing human beings. Because the knowing subject is situated in

---

[3]See Ronald L. Hall, *Word and Spirit: A Kierkegaardian Critique of the Modern Age* (Bloomington: Indiana University Press, 1993) 55-89.

a process of becoming, the subject's perspective, fund of experience, and interpretive community are always changing (CUP,
1:196). At most, "objective" truth is an approximation, subject to
revision in the light of further evidence and debate (CUP, 1:189).
In such matters as historical knowledge, probability is the most for
which one can hope. Certainty would require the occupation of a
transtemporal perspective which is not available to finite, temporal
beings (CUP, 1:212).

Climacus's bifocal critique of objectivity's intelligibility and
feasibility hints at a connection between the objectivist epistemological orientation and a particular set of disguised social and
personal interests.[4] If Climacus is right, epistemologies cannot
really be empty of all passional concerns. Their own protestations
to the contrary notwithstanding, epistemological proposals
incarnate the interests, usually unacknowledged, of the epistemologists. The articulated epistemology is symptomatic of deeper, more
pervasive hopes and fears. According to Climacus, the objective
spirit is really motivated by a fear of responsibility (CUP, 1:161).
The objectivity which claims to transcend idiosyncratic individual
interests serves the purposes of social conformity. Stripped of the
particularities of one's individual situation, one has no option but
to parrot the concerns and prejudices of the social environment,
the "present age." Such an attitude reflects the advice of a mother
who admonishes her child to mind its manners, watch the other
polite children, and behave as they do (CUP, 1:244). An age
devoted to objectivity is an age susceptible to ideology.

Climacus's strategy of exposing the failings of the objectivist
account of the general features of meaning and knowing is
pursued, not for its own sake, but in order to contrast it with the
sort of knowing appropriate to such life options as Christianity.
Here the theme "subjectivity is truth" has its proper home. In a
weak sense, "subjectivity," meaning the particular interests of the
subject, is a factor in all knowledge. However, it is a decisive factor
in certain kinds of knowledge according to the degree to which the
matter at hand requires the subject's passionate interest.

---

[4]See Merold Westphal, *Kierkegaard's Critique of Reason and Society* (Macon GA:
Mercer University Press, 1987) 105-25.

Interested passion is closely linked to the project of actualizing cognized possibilities in one's own life (CUP, 1:197). Profound subjectivity is a passionate interest in what one should become. Accordingly, subjectivity is also associated with the need to make a decision, to enact one of the possible options. Uncertainty about the life options makes a choice possible. If one option enjoyed compelling objective evidence to commend it over all rivals, the choice would be a charade. The need to live out some option makes the risk of choosing necessary. The paradoxical combination of uncertainty and resolution generates passion and becomes the central hallmark of a deepened inwardness. Climacus writes, "the less objective reliability, the deeper is the possible inwardness" (CUP, 1:209). Passion increases proportionately to the degree of risk. The interplay of self-concern, uncertainty, risk, and resolution gives an even stronger meaning to "subjectivity is truth."

This Socratic slogan takes on its richest meaning in regard to life options which maximize interest by requiring the transformation of all the individual's actions and passions. The Christian option shares this concern for scope and intensity with all forms of the ethical and religious life. Concepts pertaining to the comprehensive shape and direction of one's life as a whole cannot be made intelligible without the most passionate self-concern (CUP, 1:197). In regard to this "essential knowing," Climacus treats the "how," the passionately interested appropriation, as the formal condition for understanding the "what," the ideational content. For example, the presence of God in the created order, a "what," cannot be discerned without the appropriately passionate inwardness, the "how" (CUP, 1:243).

For essential knowing, direct access to the "what" would be fatal. For example, idolatry's promise of an immediate relation to the eternal has a natural tendency to subvert the appropriate "how." To view God as "a rare, enormously large green bird, with a red beak, that perched in a tree on the embankment and perhaps even whistled in an unprecedented manner" would invite the wrong sort of interest (CUP, 1:245). The appropriate response to such an immediately perceivable phenomenon would be amazement. The direct relationship with the ultimate promised by paganism misdirects the individual's attention outward (CUP, 1:243). This external focus would militate against the concern for the shape of one's own life, and the concomitant risk of committing oneself to the actualization of a possibility. In essential knowing, any alleged direct relation with the "what" must be broken in order to stimulate self-activity.

This consideration of "essential" knowing leads to the most rhetorically dramatic differentiation of the "truths" of subjectivity and objectivity. It is not merely the case that the "how," subjectivity, is the formal condition for the "what," objectivity. The "truth" of subjectivity is more than a question of epistemological emphasis. In essential knowing, subjective truth could be present even if the individual were entertaining objectively false beliefs. Climacus writes, "If only the how of this relation is in truth, the individual is in truth, even if he in this way were to relate himself to untruth" (CUP, 1:199). If someone living in an idolatrous land "prays with all the passion of infinity, although his eyes are resting on the image of an idol," he prays in truth even though he is worshiping something objectively untrue (CUP, 1:201). Conversely, to pray without passionate inwardness, even with the "true" definition of God, is to pray untruly.

Climacus is not proposing that the intensity with which a proposition is believed makes the proposition true, or that beliefs are validated by fervor. Rather, Climacus is suggesting that the genuine "what" of certain varieties of essential knowing can be defined through a description of the "how."[5] Although this is certainly not the case with the objects of most intentional acts, in this instance the highly specific manner of appropriation limns the contours of the content. The eternal happiness is definable solely in terms of its mode of acquisition. In a journal entry Kierkegaard himself interprets Climacus as suggesting that a scrupulous rendering of the "how" of faith will also produce a rendering of the "what" (JP, 4:4550).

Accordingly, Climacus never directly defines "God," "eternal happiness," or "the infinite" but rather describes the pathos in which they are rooted. For example, "God" is that without which every moment is wasted (CUP, 1:200), that which must be grasped

---

[5]See Andrew J. Burgess, *Passion, "Knowing How," and Understanding: An Essay on the Concept of Faith* (Missoula MT: Scholars Press, 1975) 47-52.

with "the infinite passion of need" (CUP, 1:201), and that which should be thanked at all times, not just once a year or on momentous occasions (CUP, 1:228). Climacus further elaborates this description of the determinate "how" appropriate to "God" and "eternal happiness" in his detailed portrayal of the resignation, suffering, and guilt which constitute the last third of the book. Most importantly, Climacus himself exemplifies some of the dimensions of the appropriate pathos, or at least those which are possible for a "humorist." Climacus's effusions about the "distant echo of stillness within oneself" and the "sublime tranquility of heaven" help delimit the meaning of "the eternal" (CUP, 1:235).

So far, Climacus's clarification of the "truth" of subjectivity does not require specific attention to Christian doctrines or any unique Christian pathos. He has been describing a general religiosity, later denominated "Religiousness A." This is a mode of pathos independent of the specific teachings of religious communities. This independence of Religiousness A from particular religious traditions does not mean that it is an "undialectical" mode of pathos. As we have seen, in Religiousness A, pathos is informed by thought, imagination, and will. Religiousness A does certainly involve the intentional appropriation of a way of life governed by such ideals as "resignation" and shaped by such concepts as "eternal happiness." However, these ideals and concepts can be developed in all cultural circumstances and can be articulated in a variety of historically particular conceptualities. Consequently, Climacus can describe Religiousness A as a possibility resident in all individuals, available through the self-concern which can arise in the course of any individual life (CUP, 1:584). The fact that it is an innate capacity of the human spirit, possible in all cultural circumstances, allows Climacus to associate it with the Socratic notion of "recollection." The development of this religious capacity does not require the mediation of particular communities of discourse, and certainly is not contingent upon specific claims about historical events. However, this "true" subjectivity is a precondition for living the religious or ethical life in any historical tradition, including Christianity.

As we have seen, Climacus's elaboration of truthful subjectivity is suddenly disrupted by the suggestion that subjectivity is untruth (CUP, 1:207). At this point the meaning of "subjectivity" shifts, in accord with a shift in Climacus's project. This same shift is repeated later in the transition from the section on "Pathos" to the section on "The Dialectical" (CUP, 1:555). Sorting out the features of his new purpose may clarify the ways in which "subjectivity" can be "untruth."

Even in the new context of the "untruth" of subjectivity, Climacus never retracts his contention that the appropriate subjectivity is a necessary formal condition for the apprehension of the sort of truth relevant to Christianity. He is proposing to "go beyond" the claim that subjectivity is truth, not backward into an objectivist sensibility. This advance continues to presuppose the "Socratic" attainment of inwardness. Passionate inwardness is just as much a prerequisite for understanding Christianity, as it is for any religiosity (CUP, 1:224). Climacus insists, "Every Christian has pathos as in Religiousness A" (CUP, 1:582). He warns that systematicians who, without inwardness, rearrange doctrines as if they were bits of objective information fail to grasp the very meaning of those doctrines (CUP, 1:15). Similarly, those speculators who attempt to "explain" Christianity by translating it into a passion-neutral conceptual medium destroy the passional conditions necessary for understanding it at all (CUP, 1:221). The aesthetic admiration of Christ's beauty would engender a mood of externality inimical to the inwardness necessary for truly understanding Christ (CUP, 1:248). In all these instances passionate subjectivity is as necessary for Christian faith as it is for any religious life (CUP, 1:249).

Although subjectivity in the sense of passionate concern for the quality of one's own life is a necessary condition for Christian pathos, it is not a sufficient condition. Subjectivity is "untrue" in the sense that a description of the "how" alone does not exhaustively specify the "what" of Christian faith. Climacus argues that the "dialectical" and "revealed" concepts of Christianity are not reducible without remainder to a description of the immanental pathos of general human religiosity. While Religiousness A is a permanent possibility of the human spirit, Christian pathos is only possible in response to a "revelation." Christian subjectivity does not naturally evolve out of the experience of humanity. Consequently, "direct" communication does have temporary validity within Christianity (CUP, 1:243). An "apostle" must proclaim the news directly so that it can be subjectively appropriated. In this instance there is a "what" which can be at least partly indicated without a description of the "how," even though it will not be fully understood. For example, the empirical claim that Jesus of Nazareth lived and died can be expressed in the historical language common to all humans. Direct language can also express the fact that a certain religious tradition regards this life as having absolute significance for the ultimate happiness of individuals.

These direct teachings concerning the salvific significance of specific historical events are not intended to disseminate intriguing information, but to make a new sort of subjectivity possible. As Climacus puts it, "the dialectical" should have a "retroactive" effect on pathos, sharpening it even further than the inwardness of Religiousness A (CUP, 1:581). For example, the doctrine of "incarnation " makes possible a unique gratitude for an "eternity" which comes as a gift to the individual from beyond the individual. "Atonement" makes possible a thankfulness for forgiveness and reconciliation unknown in Religiousness A. "Sin" makes possible a pervasive discontent with all that one has made of one's life, including the apparent spiritual accomplishments of Religiousness A.

Climacus's portrayal of the doctrinally refracted pathos of Christianity is disappointingly sketchy, particularly when compared to the exhaustive account of the three "expressions" of the pathos of Religiousness A. This is not due to any sense of its lesser importance, but to Climacus's own limitations. Climacus repeatedly confesses that he himself is not a Christian, and has "not fully understood the difficulty of Christianity" (CUP, 1:225). He cannot view Christian pathos from within, but only from the periphery. Climacus sees only what a humorist can discern. This largely restricts him to a descriptive *via negativa*. He can imagine how the concepts of Christianity would foster a pathos qualitatively different from his own or that of Religiousness A (which has similarities to a humorist's resigned sympathy), but he can only outline these new qualities by contrasting them to those with which he is familiar.

"Subjectivity is untruth" does more than point to the importance of doctrinal teachings as a necessary condition for the possibility of Christian pathos. For Climacus "subjectivity is untruth" has a stronger, more dramatic use. If the first use points to the ways in which doctrinal concepts make possible and require a new, more particularized pathos (and the insufficiency of generic religious pathos alone to produce Christian existence), the second use demands a critical assessment of one's religious capacities and passional development. Here the maxim "subjectivity is untruth" highlights the way in which specific Christian teachings authorize a new self-critique. The "untruth" of subjectivity is implied by the unique grammar of Christian concepts. The dialectically sharpened Christian pathos requires a suspicion of subjectivity itself. The problem is not merely that subjectivity is insufficient by itself to generate the Christian life; subjectivity is also positively dangerous to the individual's spiritual health.

"Subjectivity" in this context of Christian self-critique takes on a more precise meaning than it has elsewhere. Here it does not suggest the general "inwardness," "pathos," and "self-concern" ingredient to all "religiousness," including Christianity. Rather, this use of "subjectivity" refers to the cultivation of inwardness construed as one's own project. From its own perspective, Christianity discerns unexpected ways in which the project of cultivating religiosity can go awry. "Subjectivity is untruth" functions in part to generate critical concern about these tendencies in one's own religious life.

Christian teachings foster an intensified suspicion of one's own subjectivity in two different ways because "subjectivity is truth" could encourage two different subversions of Christian pathos. First, the valorization of subjectivity could lead to an identification of the divine with one's spiritual capacities. Climacus warns that the theme of Socratic recollection, if pushed in a certain direction, could promote reflective complacency (CUP, 1:205). Socrates himself, according to Climacus, had preserved a profound appreciation of the urgency and difficulty of actualizing religious pathos in temporal existence. Plato, however, transformed "recollection" into a speculative doctrine about the metaphysical attributes of the soul (CUP, 1:206). The soul enjoys a natural kinship with the eternal. In the Platonic elaboration of "recollection," the soul merely remembers in time that it is already eternal and changeless. Existence is only the medium in which the soul recalls its true identity. The root of this danger lies back in Socrates' original assumption that the capacity for religious pathos is still intact, enjoying uncorrupted innocence. This Socratic optimism is evident in Religiousness A's conviction of the soul's natural orientation to the eternal. This implies a kind of pantheistic attitude that "the eternal is continually hidden by it (existence) and in hiddenness is present" (CUP, 1:571). The celebration of the presence of the religious capacity could engender a disinclination to regard the actualization of the eternal in time as decisive. Climacus observes that Religiousness A "is oriented toward the purely human in such a way that it must be assumed that every human being, viewed essentially, participates in this eternal happiness and finally becomes eternally happy" (CUP, 1:581). Such a resigned sensibility would be offended by the proposal that eternal happiness is made possible by the eternal's entry into time at a particular historical moment. Religiousness A exhibits a "Platonic" dynamic which predisposes it to take offense at the incarnation and to disregard the summons to become a "new creature." In this context, to say "subjectivity is untruth" is to eliminate the very ground of the possibility of the Platonic slide into quiescence. "Subjectivity is untruth" here acquires a meaning as part of Climacus's polemic against a "backward relation" to eternity which the Christian concepts "incarnation" and "new birth" decisively rule out.

"Subjectivity is untruth," used for the purposes of Christian self-critique, warns of a second, potentially more serious danger resident in the project of nurturing one's subjectivity. The cultivation of passionate inwardness could contribute to a Pelagian self-congratulation for the profundity of one's own spirituality. Inwardness could be prized as the individual's own heroic achievement. As Climacus observes, even devout self-abnegation could be a paradoxical form of self-assertion. The attainment of an inwardness suffused with the resignation, suffering, and guilt which are essential "expressions" of Religiousness A could be treasured as a sort of religious "good work" performed by the individual. Ironically, the consciousness of guilt over the failure to relate one's life as a whole to the eternal (absolutely to the absolute, and relatively to relative ends) can be regarded as a primary indication that one is indeed related to the eternal (CUP, 1:531-33). The relation is expressed through the misrelation; the positive is expressed through the negative. The very agony of the guilt can be interpreted as the powerful lure of the eternal which already resides in one's soul. Consciousness of guilt can be taken as a sign of blessedness. One could even take comfort and pride in the strength of one's guilt.

According to the doctrine of sin, this sophisticated spiritual pride is not a mere possibility, but an actual tendency present in all individuals. Subjectivity is "untrue" in the sense that humans exhibit a predisposition to cherish the notion of a divine capacity within themselves and are prone to take profound offense at the thought that eternal happiness is not their own achievement. The ultimate offense to human subjectivity is the prospect that God freely bestows an eternal happiness which individuals could not win for themselves. The offer of eternal happiness made possible by the incarnation (the eternal in time) comes as an intrusion in one's typical way of experiencing one's self; it is not what reason or religious pathos would expect. The presence of the eternal in time, outside the individual, relativizes the significance of immanent human religiosity. It means that the eternal is not a perduring possession of the individual and that the self is not already divinely grounded. The concept of the incarnation prevents the individual from looking for an immanence of the eternal in subjectivity. Climacus writes, "There is no immanental underlying kinship between the temporal and the eternal, because the eternal itself has entered into time and wants to establish kinship there" (CUP, 1:573). According to Climacus, the doctrinal themes concerning the otherness of God, the specificity of the presence of God in Christ, and the gratuity of the offered eternal happiness all offend the basic dynamics of "immanent" religiosity.

In this context of self-critique, "subjectivity is untruth" has yet another nuance. The individual is exhorted to assume responsibility for this tendency to take offense. The tendency is not natural; there is nothing about subjectivity which necessitates that the individual must be inclined to take offense at the incarnation. Climacus writes, "Viewed eternally, he cannot be in sin or be presupposed to have been eternally in sin" (CUP, 1:208). Sin must be regarded as the individual's own fault, not as a defect in human nature (CUP, 1:208, 583). The doctrine of sin prevents the individual from construing the deformation of its subjectivity as a necessary tragedy which has befallen it.

This predisposition to take offense at the offer of an eternal happiness has profound epistemological consequences. "Sin" cannot be discovered through immanent religious inwardness; it must be authoritatively revealed. Sin cannot be understood apart from the offense which occurs when the individual recognizes that the concept of an historical incarnation of the eternal in time means that the eternal cannot be regarded as something which the individual already possesses. The meaning of the doctrine of sin is tied to the doctrine of incarnation. It cannot be reduced to "guilt," "ignorance," or any of the other concepts proper to religious immanence. In this sense, the meaning of "subjectivity is untruth" is dependent upon a nexus of logically primitive and foundational concepts of Christian discourse.

Even this strongest use of "subjectivity is untruth," with its condemnation of the individual's own inwardness, does not weaken subjectivity but rather promotes an intensified subjectivity. Here too the "dialectical" teachings rebound upon "pathos," producing a deepened subjectivity. Climacus even claims that existence can never be accentuated more sharply (CUP, 1:209). As with any religious concept, understanding "sin" requires a mutual fit of the "how" and the "what." The untruth of subjectivity is not a theory to be interpreted, but an "existence communication." Climacus insists, "The individual existing human being has to feel himself a sinner (not objectively, which is nonsense, but subjectively, and this is the deepest pain)" (CUP, 1:224). This "how" involves the pain which accompanies the recognition that one's own ostensibly noble quest for a deepened inwardness has been permeated with complacency and arrogance. It includes not only despair over one's own abilities, but also wonder at the mercy which could forgive such self-generated deformation (CUP, 1:228). Even when subjectivity (the predisposition to take offense) is most untrue, subjectivity (the appropriate passionate inwardness) is still truth.

To recapitulate, "subjectivity is truth" and "subjectivity is untruth" are not mutually exclusive assertions. The two claims are deployed in significantly different ways by Climacus. "Subjectivity is truth" is used to draw attention to the context of passionate concern which is constitutive for any meaningful religious discourse, Christian or otherwise. Climacus argues that all intelligible claims to know anything involve temporally situated interests. Talk of the "truth" relevant to the actualization of existential possibilities involves concern for the shape of one's own life, objective uncertainty, and risk to an intense degree. "Subjectivity is truth" points to the "how" which is necessary for any religious life. "Subjectivity is untruth," on the other hand, serves to draw attention to the insufficiency of inwardness by itself, without the "retroactive" impact of such doctrinal concepts as "incarnation," to generate a uniquely Christian pathos. Here a more particularized "how" emerges in response to a specific "what." Even more dramatically, "subjectivity is untruth" functions in the practice of Christian self-critique, exposing the covert tendencies to self-satisfaction and spiritual pride resident in the project of cultivating inwardness. In these diverse contexts, the concepts "subjectivity" and "truth" play significantly different roles. If these roles are distinguished, "subjectivity is truth" and "subjectivity is untruth" need not be mutually exclusive.

In light of the differences among these contexts, it may seem odd that Climacus chose to use the same concepts "subjectivity" and "truth" at all. Perhaps using different words, or at least adding appropriate qualifiers, would have prevented confusion. Was he merely trying to spread a veil of mystification over issues which could have been presented much more straightforwardly? Climacus's sensitivity to the importance of the form of a communicative act to its content would suggest that the ambiguity may be part of a rhetorical strategy. The ways in which the meanings of "subjectivity" in the text change and slip into one another reflect the ways in which the passionate inwardness essential for all forms of the religious life can change and slip into spiritual smugness and hubris. The concepts in the text may be unstable because human pathos is unstable. The possible confusion of the two uses of "subjectivity" may have an unfortunate analogue in the life of the reader. In sorting out the ambiguities, the inwardness of the reader becomes engaged. Text and reader begin to mutually illumine each other. The puzzlement concerning which meaning is operating in any given passage forces the reader to engage in the hard work of self-examination, just as Climacus, the indolent one who aspired to make life difficult, would have wanted.

16

Spiritual Trial in the Thought of Kierkegaard

Louise Carroll Keeley

In Johannes Climacus's account of religious development in *Concluding Unscientific Postscript*, suffering is its essential moment. Flanked by the preceding and subsequent accounts of resignation and guilt, identified in turn as the initial and decisive expressions of existential pathos, suffering figures as a central theme both structurally and conceptually. Nestled within Climacus's lengthy analysis of suffering, a brief but compelling account of spiritual trial (*Anfægtelse*) is found. Just as suffering is the essential coil in the process of religious development to the extent that it is implied by resignation and presumed by guilt, so too spiritual trial assumes a central position within his discussion of suffering as the essential category. One is reminded of Kierkegaard's strategy, practiced so often by his pseudonyms, of committing his most important insights to footnotes. Hiddenness and offhandedness are sometimes the ways through which he communicated his most serious thoughts. Though Climacus's discussion of *Anfægtelse* is prominently included in the body of the text and even afforded a central position there, his treatment of the topic is equally modest, unspectacular, and perhaps exceptionally earnest. It is, in effect, hidden in its very prominence.

The initial expression of existential pathos is resignation. It begins with the individual's decision to adopt an absolute relation to the absolute telos and a relative relation to all finite ends. This corollary—the assignment of relative significance to relative ends—entails resignation: the relativity of these subordinate ends "consists in the fact that they are subject to renunciation just in so

far as they may conflict with the demand of the highest good."[1]
Because the pathos of resignation is existential rather than merely
aesthetic, it must transform the individual's existence:

> If it does not *absolutely* transform his existence for him . . . if
> there is something he is not willing to give up for its sake, then
> he is not relating himself to an eternal happiness. . . . He needs
> only to allow resignation to inspect his entire immediacy with all
> its desires etc. If he finds a single fixed point, an obduracy, he is
> not relating himself to an eternal happiness.   (CUP, 1:393-94)

Hence resignation's sacrifice is ongoing and never complete, for no
inspection is ever final since immediacy can never be vanquished
once and for all. Suffering is the inevitable consequence for one
who is attempting to practice resignation but whose task is never
completely finished—in short, for anyone who takes up the task in
time. No one who pursues his religious development with earnestness can be exempt. Quite the opposite. Every religious deepening
entails a deeper immersion in suffering. In the long tradition of
spiritual direction and devotional literature, Climacus designates
the suffering which resignation entails as the "dying to immediacy" (CUP, 1:460-63). For Climacus, the suffering of dying to
immediacy is rare at least in part because it is prolonged; one instance of it hurls us headway toward another, then another, such
that the sufferer is prone toward exhaustion and regression. Whoever exhibits "the essential continuance of the suffering" (CUP,
1:460) has upgraded his suffering to the next, more exquisite level.

But this upgrading is presumably rare. Climacus contends that
the triumphant secularism of the nineteenth century is expressed
in the age's predilection for mediation. Here both/and dominates.
C. Stephen Evans underscores the fact that the process of mediation is appropriate when the competing claims of *relative* goods are
to be assessed: "the relative is the proper sphere of 'both/and,' and
the well-rounded person is the one who has broad interests, but
nevertheless keeps his responsibilities in proper perspective."[2] But

---

[1]David F. Swenson, *Something about Kierkegaard*, ed. Lillian Marvins Swenson,
rev. and enl. ed. (Minneapolis: Augsburg, 1945; ROSE ed.: Macon GA: Mercer
University Press, 1983) 179.

[2]C. Stephen Evans, *Kierkegaard's Fragments and Postscript: The Religious Philosophy of Johannes Climacus* (Atlantic Highlands NJ: Humanities Press, 1983) 164.

when mediation disregards the fact that "the absolute telos has the remarkable quality of wanting to be the absolute telos at every moment" (CUP, 1:401) and ranks it as one claim among others, it runs amok. Though relative ends must compete for their respective rankings, the absolute telos must remain precisely that—absolute.

It is in opposition to the age's mediating tendency that Climacus introduces his nuanced analysis of the monastic movement. While conceding that the movement has its eccentric features, Climacus's accent is on its passion which he commends highly: "the point is absolutely to venture everything, absolutely to stake everything, absolutely to desire the highest telos" (CUP, 1:404). But Climacus pronounces on the dubiousness of the movement for two reasons. First, to the extent that monasticism presumes that its renunciation is meritorious, it undoes itself; earnings, of any sort, imply a transaction rather than a decision. Second, and most importantly, Climacus criticizes the monastic movement because he believes that it seeks an external expression for what can only be accomplished inwardly: "The dubious character of the monastic movement . . . was that the absolute interiority, probably in order to demonstrate very energetically that it existed, acquired its obvious expression in a distinctive separate outwardness, whereby it nevertheless, however one twists and turns, became only relatively different from all other outwardness" (CUP, 1:405). The upshot is this: monasticism posits a commensurability of sorts between the internal and the external: "as soon as interiority is supposed to be decisively and commensurably expressed outwardly, we have the monastic movement" (CUP, 1:407). To the extent that the Middle Ages took up residence in the "little cubbyhole" (CUP, 1:408) of monasticism in order to attend to the absolute telos, it authorized an outward standard as commensurable with an inward decision. It is this tacit commensurability that Climacus finds so deeply objectionable.

Climacus has soundly rejected the tendency toward ethical mediation and, while praising the passion of monasticism, has judged it to be in error in its attempt to impose a finite external expression for its inwardness. Instead, he invites the individual to become absolutely oriented toward the absolute telos and to express this continually in one's life in hidden inwardness. This returns us to the individual who has undertaken the task of resignation: no outward determinants whatsoever can be correlated with his inmost life. Significantly, *it is this requirement which brings suffering*: "let us never forget that interiority without outwardness is the most difficult interiority, in which self-deception is easiest"(CUP, 1:406). With no distinguishing mark to identify him, and the threat of self-deception constant, his venture can only be undertaken with the strenuousness of inner resolve. The Middle Ages had concluded that God and the finite could not be thought together in existence, and urged the individual to break with the finite by fleeing to the monastery. Whoever undertakes the task of resignation does not flee from the finite but rather puts it together with the thought of God, producing "a combination that in existence is the very basis and meaning of suffering" (CUP, 1:483).

As religious interiority deepens a more potentiated form of suffering may appear: spiritual trial. It cannot appear until the individual has achieved some degree of religious inwardness. Since Climacus suggests that most people substitute relative ends for the absolute telos, or confer an equivalence upon all ends such that there is no telos identified as absolute, most people are effectively excluded from this trial. This is, of course, not meritorious. It is interesting to recall that throughout *Concluding Unscientific Postscript* Climacus has insisted that it is literally madness to devise such a strategy of avoidance: whoever exhibits an infinite, personal, passionate interest in an approximation or endows relative ends with absolute significance, is mad (CUP, 1:422). To be absolutely interested in something which is not the absolute is fanaticism or spiritual lunacy. By contrast, whoever does experience spiritual trial does so "only in the sphere of the religious proper, and there only in the final course" and hence has already realized some degree of spiritual health and maturity "in proportion to the religiousness" (CUP, 1:459) of his development:

> The moment the individual succeeds in practicing the absolute relation through the renunciation of relative ends (and it can indeed be this way at particular moments, although later the individual is again drawn into the conflict) and now is to relate himself absolutely to the absolute, he then discovers the boundary, spiritual trial then becomes the expression for the boundary.
> (CUP, 1:459)

Climacus concedes that this suffering is "probably terrible" (CUP, 1:459). But he denies that any form of dying to immediacy is self-torment since the self-tormentor remains impressed with his torment and hence has not achieved the requisite self-displacement which religious development demands (CUP, 1:463). Though spiritual trial can be agonizing, it is also educational. To be excluded from it means that one has not yet reached "the final course" (CUP, 1:459) of spiritual maturity.

Curiously, Climacus introduces the concept of spiritual trial within the context of the religious address. As "the organ of the religious life-view" in public worship, Climacus laments its failure to describe the intricacies or even the major features of spiritual trial in its very singular, and always private, expressions (CUP, 1:458). If it is mentioned, which it rarely is, it is given some undifferentiated status along with temptations, adversities, or obstacles. Climacus implies that leaving spiritual trial out of account does say something inadvertently about the age's spiritual disinclinations. Because the age declines to explore the depths of spiritual inwardness, those who *are* spiritually tried are effectively set adrift in inwardness and left to fend for themselves. One consequence of spiritual trial is a feeling of abandonment, and this solitariness only reinforces one's sense of being alone. Of course, those really in need of help are the ones "so complexly involved in the traffic of finitude" that the inwardness of the religious life is missed (CUP, 2:92). Climacus explains:

> The religious address should really be such that by hearing it one would gain the most accurate insight into the religious delusions of his era and into himself as belonging to the era. But what am I saying? This insight may be gained also by listening to a religious address that does not even hint at spiritual trials. One gains the insight, of course, but only indirectly by way of the address.   (CUP, 1:460)

Kierkegaard counsels the one undergoing spiritual trial to wait in faith, prayer, and silence. Alternatively, Vigilius Haufniensis humorously maintains in *The Concept of Anxiety*, "the most effective means of escaping spiritual trial is to become spiritless, and the sooner the better"(CA, 117).

Having contended that spiritual trial is rarely mentioned in contemporary religious addresses, Climacus offers his own, almost algebraic, account:

> In the sphere of the relationship with God, it [spiritual trial] is what temptation is in the sphere of the ethical relation. When the individual's maximum is the ethical relation to actuality, temptation is his highest danger. . . . But not only does spiritual trial differ from temptation in this way; the individual's position is also different. In temptation, it is the lower that tempts; in spiritual trial it is the higher. In temptation, it is the lower that wants to lure the individual; in spiritual trial, it is the higher that, seemingly envious of the individual, wants to frighten him back. . . . Temptation attacks the individual in his weak moments; spiritual trial is a nemesis upon the intense moments in the absolute relation. Therefore, temptation has a connection with the individual's ethical constitution, whereas spiritual trial is without continuity and is the absolute's own resistance. (CUP, 1:458-59)

Having complained that most religious addresses lump spiritual trial together with temptation, Climacus is careful to preserve their differences even as he asserts a kind of proportionality between them. The analogy consists in their positions and functions within their respective existence spheres: temptation is to the ethical sphere what spiritual trial is to the religious sphere. Moreover, because the ethical individual in temptation is positioned differently than his religious counterpart undergoing spiritual trial, they attend in different directions. The ethically minded individual is turned back toward something lower; the religious individual is turned forward toward something higher. This question of directionality is exceedingly important because conversion and spiritual development ultimately depend upon it. Temptation's lure is familiar: the individual is enticed to indulge himself in some lower vice to which he succumbs in weakness. In breaking through to higher ground the "trial" in *Anfægtelse* is less familiar and more fearful. The one undergoing spiritual trial can be undergoing it only because he seeks a deepened relationship with God. As the relationship deepens and intensifies, so too does the suffering which the contact with God brings. Though it is "the higher" which is testing him, the individual is repelled and wants to turn back. The person is "tempted to refrain from going on to realize the higher, and he gives in to the temptation by *failing to seek* the source of the temptation (which therefore should not really be called the *object* of temptation)."[3] The one who is so tried is tempted to retreat to the more familiar confines of the ethical, where duty and responsibility, though rigorous, do not require that one undergo the strenuousness of fear and trembling that spiritual trial always brings.

In addition to their contexts in competing existence-spheres and the fact that one is either attracted by something lower or repelled by something higher, temptation and spiritual trial are differentiated by inward determinants. The one who is tempted is tempted in his weakness; it succeeds, or not, in the degree to which it exploits that weakness. The one undergoing spiritual trial, on the other hand, can only do so after attaining a certain degree of spiritual strength or health: "the occurrence of spiritual trial is a healthy sign in a person's moral and religious development, in a way that is not true of moral temptation."[4] Similarly, the tempted one is guilty to the extent that it is his weakness which makes the temptation a temptation. To some degree a temptation is always a "self-temptation" to the extent that "we have created the very temptations we succumbed to."[5] Conversely, innocence qualifies the inwardness of the one undergoing spiritual trial. Though he is unlikely to have an affective experience of being innocent, he *is* innocent nonetheless.

Because Climacus clearly understood that spiritual trial was a solitary excursion, undergone alone and in inwardness, the public silence on this matter was especially problematic. Not speaking about it intensified the aloneness of the experience. Save for the experienced guides of the older devotional literature, one rarely met with any assistance.[6] In Kierkegaard's own case, the words of

---

[3]Evans, *Kierkegaard's Fragments and Postscript*, 175.

[4]Evans, *Kierkegaard's Fragments and Postscript*, 176.

[5]Jeremy Walker, *Kierkegaard: The Descent into God* (Montreal: McGill-Queen's University Press, 1985) 161.

[6]Two thinkers deserve particular mention. The first is Johann Arndt. Although Arndt is not mentioned in the text of CUP, the Hongs suggest in n. 722 (CUP, 2:261) that Kierkegaard "probably" has Arndt in mind when he refers to "one of the old devotional books" (CUP, 1:460) that does provide an apt description of spiritual trial. Arndt's treatise entitled *True Christianity* was first published as book I in 1605 in Jena, with additional books added later. In book II Arndt dis-

his *Journals and Papers* offer an especially poignant commentary on his own private experience with spiritual trial. The *Journal* entries substantiate Climacus's observations in addition to providing a kind of phenomenology of *Anfægtelse* that he was unable to find elsewhere: "Because religion is not taken seriously nowadays in Christendom, there is never a hint about spiritual trials" (JP, 4:4372). Though Kierkegaard never presumed to write a religious address on the matter or claimed to speak with religious authority, his private entries attest to his long acquaintance with spiritual trial and offer ready consolation to any fellow sufferer.

Kierkegaard's observations in his *Journals and Papers* confirm Climacus's broad perspective: "If one puts on the religious for everyday use, then spiritual trials are bound to come" (JP, 4:4364). But the real point of interest consists in the *Journals'* analysis of the complex inner workings of spiritual trial. Having pronounced it "dialectically complicated almost to the point of madness," Kierkegaard then delights in exploring its intricacies (JP, 4:4370). In so doing it becomes evident that Kierkegaard knew these depths because he lived there.

In a *Journal* entry penned on his thirty-fourth birthday, May 5, 1847, Kierkegaard differentiates between temptation and spiritual trial in a manner reminiscent of Climacus: "the temptation (Fristelse) to sin is in accord with inclination, (the temptation) of spiritual trial (is) contrary to inclination"(JP, 4:4367). The first attracts; the second repels. The enticing temptation needs little commentary, for the catalogue of sins to which it leads is all too

---

cusses the origins of spiritual affliction or disconsolateness, the reasons why God allows it, and the comforts or consolations available to those being spiritually tried. Though his analysis is complex and penetrating and his psychology subtle, it is the edifying aspect of his treatise which is particularly strong. The preface to the first book begins with a call to attention: "Christian Reader!" See John Arndt, *True Christianity* (Philadelphia: United Lutheran Publication House, 1868) 349-64. For a more readily available edition see Johann Arndt, *True Christianity*, trans. Peter Erb (New York: Paulist Press, 1979). However, in this edition the original volume has been reduced by two-thirds and the selections from the second to the sixth books are especially brief. The second thinker Kierkegaard mentions with reference to spiritual trial is Joseph von Gorres, author of *Mysticism*. Here Kierkegaard urges caution, calling *Mysticism* a work that is "so uncanny" with "such anxiety in it" that he has never read it completely through (CA, 143, 251n.45).

familiar. Nor is Kierkegaard's recommended strategy in the face of temptation surprising: "shun the danger" (JP, 4:4367), "flee the devil" (JP, 4:4378). In brief, "temptation is best fought by running away"(JP, 4:4382). The fact that one can be delivered through flight alleviates the weight of temptation by enabling the tempted one to exercise some free option against it, even if that option is merely to turn and run. Kierkegaard does not mean to minimize the difficulty of this (as anyone who attends to experience knows), but his accent rests on the freedom which the individual has to flee from and outrun the temptation.

It is more difficult to understand what Kierkegaard means by the repellant nature of temptation in the case of spiritual trial. The one who is being spiritually tried is not enticed by the object of temptation as something desirable. Instead, he feels ill at ease and deeply anxious about the possibility of coming into contact with it. Kierkegaard typically identifies the repellent danger as "thoughts which try the spirit" where these thoughts are what one seeks to avoid (JP, 4:4382-84).[7] Of course these thoughts may have, and often do, a corollary in actuality—some task that one is about to undertake, for example. An individual might fret about his worthiness to receive Communion.[8] If he is actually undergoing spiritual trial, the feeling of being held back or deterred from participation

---

[7]Johann Arndt's eloquent and stirring account of spiritual difficulty is compatible with Kierkegaard's perspective, despite the fact that he uses the language of temptation rather than spiritual trial, whereas Kierkegaard has gone to such great lengths to distinguish them. But when one examines the nature of these "temptations," as well as Arndt's advice to those who are afflicted, their meanings seem thoroughly compatible. "As in a tempestuous sea one wave is continually rolling over another, so do the various temptations of Satan pursue the afflicted soul; sometimes oppressing it with fearful and melancholy thoughts; at others, with impatience, unbelief, blasphemous and wicked thoughts. The terrors and miseries of such a soul are sometimes so great, that no creature can give it comfort . . . yea, even God himself appears dreadful to him. . . . " Arndt's advice to the dejected foreshadows Kierkegaard's: in these rare cases one must disregard "the reflections of our own hearts, the stings of our own consciences." For "if our heart condemns us, God is greater than our heart 1 John 3: 20." See John Arndt, *True Christianity*, 349-64.

[8]See CA, 143: "Thus a pious, believing Christian may fall into anxiety. He may become anxious about going to Communion. This is a spiritual trial, that is, whether or not it is a spiritual trial will show itself in his relation to anxiety."

in the Eucharist would function as the temptation which repels.[9]
Note that the temptation would keep him from sharing in the
Higher and it does so by insinuating that he has ventured too far,
presumed too much, and would be well advised to return to the
safely prescribed categories of the ethical. At the prospect of
drawing closer to God the person feels so agitated by anxiety that
he is tempted to abandon his desire for a deeper relationship with
God. Moreover, the anxiety is so successful in taking root that he
wants to give up his spiritual venture and is *almost* convinced that
God wants him to turn back as well. The "almost" is important
here, because certainty is never really established; some residue of
his original intention, however encrusted with doubt, urges him to
press on.[10] If he does so he has resisted the temptation which
repels and ventured to express his God-relationship, but he does
so in fear and trembling, without the felt consolation that others
not so tried enjoy. What others might do easily, with no threat to
their inward equilibrium, he does with great difficulty and
excruciating rounds of interior debate.

Abraham's predicament in *Fear and Trembling* might be classi-
fied as another example of spiritual trial.[11] Abraham believes that
he has been asked by God to sacrifice his beloved son Isaac. The
repellant force of the temptation is, in this case, all too obvious. To
begin with, Isaac's sacrifice entails the suspension of ethical
categories and a willingness to forego their seeming surety—just
at the moment when the relief that the ethical offers, with its
emphasis upon duty and responsibility, seems almost irresistibly

---

[9]See CA, 143: "Whoever is in a religious spiritual trial wants to go on to that
from which the spiritual trial would keep him away. . . . " That is, he had wanted
to undertake the spiritual venture and was attracted to the Good, but now feels
driven back or repelled by the temptation which cautions him against going
forward.

[10]See John Arndt, *True Christianity*, 359: "We ought to be comforted if we find
but one single aspiration of our hearts toward God."

[11]Evans, *Kierkegaard's Fragments and Postscript*, 176: "Another illustration of a
spiritual trial might be taken from Silentio's *Fear and Trembling*. Here again the
individual is repelled by the fearful uncertainty of the religious life and tempted
to take comfort in the security of the ethical. We cannot be sure, of course, that
Climacus would approve of every feature of this example, but it does seem to fit
his description of the concept."

attractive. Moreover, the repellant character of the temptation is especially strong: Abraham, after all, loves Isaac deeply. Besides, what if he is mistaken and this was not required of him at all? Abraham's victory through the repellant temptation was accomplished in fear and trembling made terrible by the fact that he could be completely wrong.

One can even find variants of spiritual trial in ancient stories, such as Apuleius's legend of Amor and Psyche (JP, 4:4381). In the fourth of a series of tests which Psyche is asked to undergo she is moved by an almost irresistible sympathy to put aside the task and turn back. Once again, what one is tempted to return to has sufficient credentials to make of itself a convincing bait—sympathy, after all, is usually a human good and hence comes well recommended by the ethical. Whoever holds out in this divine venture can do so only with a great deal of inward struggle, and a willingness to keep his attention fixed on what lies ahead. Other examples abound. Johann Arndt provides numerous examples from the Old and New Testaments, including Job, David, Jeremiah, the psalmists, Christ, and St. Paul: "the most holy and best beloved children of God are they that have passed through this furnace of affliction."[12]

On the one hand, Kierkegaard does not regard Anfægtelse as symptomatic of a spiritual disorder. He vigorously maintains that spiritual trial is a sign of religious health. It is only because one has ventured so far out in one's God-relationship that one can be tried. On the other hand, it is true that he does leave open the possibility of assigning spiritual trial to the category of a psychological disorder by identifying it as "in fact a kind of obsession" (JP, 4:4370). Moreover, his subtle analyses of the ways in which this obsession show itself suggest that he knew this territory from the inside out. This raises a fascinating series of questions on the relationship between spiritual and psychological health. First, certain questions might be raised about Kierkegaard's own mental health. [13]In his book *The Lonely Labyrinth: Kierkegaard's Pseudony-*

---

[12]John Arndt, *True Christianity*, 351.

[13]Someone might raise the question of the validity of a psychological interpretation of mental health based on one's writings (and the even more problematic instance of Kierkegaard's pseudonymous authorship). This has certainly been

mous Works Josiah Thompson does precisely that. Contending that Kierkegaard's authorship springs "from the very 'abscess' of his suffering as a man," his pseudonymous works turn out to be "successive moves in a complicated dialectic of therapy."[14] Henning Fenger reports that on the basis of an examination of the authorship rather than the man, the reputable psychiatrist Hjalmar Helweg suggested that Kierkegaard suffered from a familial form of manic depression.[15] Another with less clinical background, but

---

done in Kierkegaard's case. For example, Henning Fenger provides a brief account of the Danish psychoanalyst Sigurd Næsgaard's 1950 study *A Psychoanalysis of Soren Kierkegaard*. See Henning Fenger, *Kierkegaard. The Myths and Their Origins: Studies in the Kierkegaardian Papers and Letters*, trans. George C. Schoolfield (New Haven: Yale University Press, 1980) 69-71. Nevertheless, despite its not inconsiderable interest factor (where "interest" is a completely aesthetic category), I do not believe this qualifies as an act of *philosophical* inquiry. Kierkegaard's philosophy forbids such an interpretation, if not by anticipating psychoanalysis outright, by proposing as its task "to read through solo, if possible in a more inward way, the original text of individual human-existence relationships" (CUP, 1:629-30)—*each reader assigned to himself.* Besides, even if one refused to accommodate to Kierkegaard's criteria, as one might well do, the question still remains concerning its philosophical legitimacy. In an article in response to Josiah Thompson's *The Lonely Labyrinth*, Louis Mackey puts the matter succinctly: "Kierkegaard may have been a sick man. But he was also a more-than-usually self-conscious literary artist. His artistry deserves to be honored for itself, not merely as an incident in his therapy." See Louis Mackey, "Philosophy and Poetry in Kierkegaard," *Review of Metaphysics* 23 (1969–1970): 316-32.

[14]Josiah Thompson, *The Lonely Labyrinth: Kierkegaard's Pseudonymous Works* (Carbondale: Southern Illinois University Press, 1967) preface, 13. Thompson's study posed the provocative thesis that "Kierkegaard was a profoundly sick man and that the character of his sickness established a privileged perspective for the understanding of his work. Again and again Kierkegaard commented in his journals on the intimate connection between his work as an author and his life as a man" (13). Thompson, in effect, agrees with Camus's pronouncement that "Kierkegaard wants to be cured" (15). But if Kierkegaard is desperately searching for health, what illness is it that beset him? Thompson claims that "at the very nerve of his experience there was a single and most private laceration. . . . It was no less a sickness than *consciousness* itself—that characteristically *human* illness, that disease which made of man (in Nietzsche's words) 'the sick animal'—which afflicted Kierkegaard with such a virulent intensity" (209).

[15]Fenger, *Kierkegaard. The Myths and Their Origins*, 67-69. While noting that an outstanding psychiatrist, Ib Ostenfeld, disagreed with Helweg's analysis, Fenger—conceding his own nonmedical status—remains unconvinced by

with deep philosophical regard for Kierkegaard, muses that he might have suffered under an "abnormal psychosis" if certain passages in the authorship can be regarded as autobiographical."[16] In addition to these inquiries (which Kierkegaard would dismiss as a deceitful way to avoid inquiring about oneself, the only proper subject of inquiry), one might ask whether a relationship

---

Ostenfeld's position: "if one reads Kierkegaard's papers from the 1830s everything seems to support Helweg's hypothesis, and nothing seems to refute it" (68).

[16]*Stages On Life's Way*, ed. Walter Lowrie (New York: Schocken Books, 1967) 289n.91. But can the authorship be regarded as autobiographical? Kierkegaard strongly cautioned against this in "A First and Last Explanation" appended to the body of CUP: "What has been written, then, is mine, but only insofar as I, by means of audible lines, have placed the life-view of the crea*ting*, poetically actual individuality in his mouth. . . . Thus in the pseudonymous books there is not a single word by me. I have no opinion about them except as a third party, no knowledge of their meaning except as a reader, not the remotest private relation to them . . . therefore, if it should occur to anyone to want to quote a particular passage from the books, it is my wish, my prayer, that he will do me the kindness of citing the respective pseudonymous author's name, not mine" (CUP, 1:625-27). Confronted by this request, Josiah Thompson complains: "He implores us to forget about him and pay attention to his characters—but he *is* his characters in so many ways. . . . What is it that in spite of Kierkegaard's claim to the contrary makes the paternity of the pseudonymous works so clear?" See Josiah Thompson, *Kierkegaard* (New York: Alfred A. Knopf, 1973), 139. Nevertheless, Thompson refuses to identify the pseudonyms with Kierkegaard. "To point out the Kierkegaardian signature of the pseudonymous writings is not finally to refuse Kierkegaard's injunction to regard the pseudonyms as independent beings. On the contrary, it is only by scrupulously complying with his plea that we can be led to the central meaning of the works." See Thompson, *Kierkegaard*, 144-45. He argues that it is the essentially duplicitous character of the pseudonyms which is central to an understanding of them. Cf. Evans, *Kierkegaard's Fragments and Postscript*, 7-8: "Kierkegaard tells us we are to regard the pseudonymous authors as independent beings whose views are their own. However, it by no means follows from this that Kierkegaard does not hold some of their views, still less that he rejects their views. . . . As a matter of fact, it is not hard to show that a good many of the opinions expressed by the pseudonyms were held by Kierkegaard himself. The method whereby this can be done is simply to compare the pseudonymous works with works that Kierkegaard wrote under his own name and with his opinions as expressed in his *Journals and Papers*. . . . This identification is particularly tempting in the case of Johannes Climacus, who more than any other pseudonym (except Anti-Climacus), seems to express views that lie at the core of Kierkegaard's own thought" (7-8). For the record, Kierkegaard's analysis of spiritual trial in his *Journals* is perfectly compatible with Climacus's remarks in CUP.

exists between one's spiritual and one's psychological health. I think that in this context Kierkegaard would want to underscore one point. If it is indeed true that "with God everything is possible" (SUD, 38), then God can break through any psychological disorder and transform it into love of God. More pointedly, the disorder might be—though not necessarily—the means through which one gains access to a developed spirituality. Just as beauty might be a mode of access to the life of the spirit, so too can spiritual affliction.[17] In any case, the point to be underscored is this: the spirit can break through any given configuration of the self if one consents to and desires its emergence.

Kierkegaard's analysis of the thoughts that try the spirit begins with the observation that "such thoughts come from the individual himself, although innocently," arising from within rather than received from without (JP, 4:4384). "Humanly speaking, the sufferer is completely without guilt. He does not, as in sin, deliberately provoke these thoughts; it is just the opposite, these thoughts plague him" (JP, 4:4370). Additional details confirm the resemblance of this condition to obsession. The sufferer feels responsible for these thoughts even though he longs to be rid of them. While acknowledging that they originate in him, he must simultaneously decline to assign responsibility to himself—even as the promptings of the self intensify their claim that he *is* culpable. "The more anxious he becomes, the more power they get over him," immuring him more deeply in the thoughts and in the anxiety (JP, 4:4370). "In itself the suffering is perhaps the most tortuous of all sufferings for a free being," Kierkegaard observes, - *"thus to be as if unfree in the power of something else"* (JP, 4:4370; emphasis added). This tortured interplay between freedom and unfreedom produces the anxiety peculiar to obsession as well.

In the case of temptation the recommended strategy is flight. But whoever adopts this strategy in spiritual trial will only imperil himself more "for every time he thinks he is saving himself by shunning the danger, the danger becomes greater the next time"

---

[17]Simone Weil, *Waiting for God*, trans. Emma Craufurd (New York: Harper & Row, 1951) 117-36; 137-215.

(JP, 4:4367). To be trapped in or held by anxiety is the great terror. As the obsession escalates the horror intensifies:

> In his anxiety he flees from them in every way; he perhaps strains to the point of despair all his powers of ingenuity and concentration in order to avoid not only them but even the remotest contact with anything that could be related to them. It does not help; the anxiety becomes even greater. Neither does the usual advice help—to forget,to escape, for that is just what he is doing, but it merely nourishes the anxiety.   (JP, 4:4370)

Equipped with an almost "insane ingenuity"(JP, 4:4370) he struggles to outwit these all too intrusive thoughts only to find that their grip on him is tightened. The understanding is led to acknowledge that a collision exists: in other temptations (*Fristelse*) evil can be outrun by flight; in this case (*Anfægtelse*), flight always leads to the sufferer being overrun by these evil thoughts. If, in his anxiety, he retreats further and further from these thoughts on the lookout for a safehouse where they will not trouble him, he will find that his escape is sabotaged from the outset. To the extent that he has conceded that other interior places are *not* safe, he has emboldened these evil thoughts to endanger *this* one. By conceding so much inward territory to these thoughts, in a desperate attempt to carve out a small oasis of peace, the sufferer has unwittingly struck a bargain with these thoughts which they have never been known to keep. The more he *fears* being disturbed by them, the more he *will* be disturbed. Hence Church attendance may not offer a peaceful and solemn refuge from these thoughts but an occasion of an ever more excruciating torture. Moreover, once the association is made between *these* thoughts and *this* place, it is forever spoiled as a place of refuge. In this way, with many such linkages, the conditions that one needs to meet in order to realize some inward peace become increasingly difficult to arrange. If flight and concessions invariably fail how is one to hold out?

Kierkegaard recommends the tactic advised in James 4:7: "Resist the devil and he will flee from you" (JP, 4:4378). It is important to understand that resistance is altogether different than flight. To resist is to stand firm, hold out, concede nothing. Nevertheless, Kierkegaard does not want the sufferer's resistance to empower the enemy even more by evoking a show of strength. In fact, the most effective resistance turns out to be a display of calm indifference. Just as a parent might resist the clamorings of a child by remaining indifferent to them, confident and unperturbed in her resistance, so too the one who is subjected to thoughts that try the spirit can be victorious through a resolve of absolute indifference:

> Such thoughts want to make you anxious, want to worry you to the point where your spirit is so weak and cowardly that you imagine that you are responsible for them; they want to worry themselves into you, foist themselves on you so that you will listen to them, brood on them. . . . Therefore be absolutely indifferent; be more indifferent to them than you are to a little rumbling in your stomach.   (JP, 4:4382)

The other strategy that Kierkegaard recommends is anger—not the debilitating sort that imperils its possessor more than the one to whom it is directed, but rather the kind of anger that registers an annoyance with which one has had enough (JP, 4:4382). In either instance the indifference and/or the anger must not be a mere display: one must really *be* indifferent or angry. At first glance it might seem that these affective responses have nothing in common, for indifference remains composed and uninvolved—passive, almost—whereas anger lashes out and challenges. But in this context what they share is the key to understanding why Kierkegaard recommends them in tandem. Both indifference and anger can be ways to deny responsibility, to shift the focal point of responsibility away from the self to another. When one is indeed responsible for something these strategies only increase one's culpability. Indifference to public policy that one regards as morally evil, for example, is a common way to decline any responsibility for its existence or continuance. Indifference makes the eloquent but morally suspect statement: "That does not concern me." Similarly, in the case of anger, an individual might try to shift the responsibility for some mood or some outcome to another, on the assumption that, whatever it is, "It is not *my* fault." But in those circumstances, perhaps rare, where one is indeed not responsible for something, a show of indifference or anger might be perfectly appropriate. Whoever is beset by thoughts that try the spirit is in such a situation: "such thoughts come from the individual himself, *although innocently*" (JP, 4:4384; emphasis added). His moral innocence can be argued for two reasons: (1) he can control neither their appearance or their demise, and (2) he does not will them—indeed, he wills to be rid of them. But in underscoring the individual's innocence, Kierkegaard's focus rests elsewhere:

> The fact is that when God loves a man . . . this man *qua* selfish will has to be completely demolished. This is what it means to die to the world; it is the most intense agony. But even if the religious person in accord with his better will is willing enough to do this, he can neither promptly nor completely get his will, his subjectivity , into the power of the better will in him, and therefore, after first making a most desperate resistance, it still continues to watch for a chance to disorganize the whole revolution that dethroned it. No religious person, even the purest, has sheer, purified subjectivity or pure transparency in willing solely what God wills, so that there is no residue of his original subjectivity, a residue still not wholly penetrated, a remote portion of residue still uncaptured, perhaps as yet not even really discovered in the depths of his soul—*out of this come the reactions*. But as the old devotional literature rightly teaches, the individual is completely innocent in this. Far from being something to be charged against him, *these thoughts which try the spirit prove that he has really become thoroughly involved and engaged.*
> (JP, 4:4384; emphasis added)

Once these thoughts that try the spirit have made the sufferer believe that he *is* responsible for them, their victory is almost assured *for this leads to his giving up the movement toward transparency that produced them*. Though he has escaped the agony which these thoughts bring, he has also given up the essentially Christian task of striving to achieve transparency before God.

Given Kierkegaard's analysis of spiritual trial as making for acute anxiety, how can one achieve such transparency and what does it mean to do so? Kierkegaard answers through an act of faith: "In order to endure this agony, a specific kind of religiousness is needed, is required, which humbly and without breathing a word submits it to God" (JP, 4:4370). Though offering up one's trial to God sounds neither new or especially profound, Kierkegaard gives it an unexpected meaning. For Kierkegaard, complete submission to God entails the corresponding admission that "Before you, O God, I am nothing, do with me as you will" (JP, 4:4370). In our age which insists upon the development of self-esteem (whether the self is estimable or not), such a concession might sound harsh or even retrogressive. But for Kierkegaard such an acknowledgement made inwardly with passion, means the demise of "self-centered willfulness"—the dismantling of the selfish will whose very presence had kept God at bay (JP, 4:4370). Although "no religious person, even the purest, has sheer, purified subjectivity or pure transparency in willing solely what God wills, so that there is no residue of his original subjectivity" it is the task of holiness to undertake this arduous process (JP, 4:4384). Note that it is a process to which one must attend, not an accomplishment that can be finalized as complete.

This dismantling of the selfish self is also the upbuilding of the truest self which God has entrusted to each individual. Self-annihilation and self-development emerge in tandem, not unlike the way in which sacrificial love invariably leads to the augmenting, rather than the depletion, of love. In both cases, the giving up entails a gain. This leads us to the most fascinating point of Kierkegaard's analysis. Whoever succeeds in holding out by faithfully submitting these thoughts to God has undergone a kind of annihilation. He has, in effect, acknowledged himself to be the kind of being who can have such thoughts. That is, *the act of submission which hands these thoughts over to God is also a very powerful act of self-acceptance*—a consent to being the very self which God has launched despite that self's features which one would sooner do without. To the extent that the self consents to be itself altogether, not selecting only the most likeable or virtuous aspects of the self to affirm, it becomes thoroughly itself.

Kierkegaard gives some pastoral indication of this when he advises the sufferer to acquire *"the frankness to think these evil thoughts together with God before God—in order to dispose of them"* (JP, 4:4370; emphasis added). The failed strategy of flight has been replaced by a kind of deep honesty, the frankness before God which is willing to be altogether itself. The coupling which makes spiritual trial so difficult is the combination of the thought of God as love with the presence of one's agonizing thoughts. To hold these two fast together is the challenge. Curiously, the bold resolve to become thoroughly honest before God deprives these evil thoughts of their power to terrify to the extent that one has shifted the focus away from them to God. Previously, to the extent that one did not subject them to the scrutiny of God and oneself, they controlled the sufferer. Though he becomes inventive in avoidance and perhaps manages to suppress them for a time, the emphasis remains all the while on the thoughts, since their avoidance is the governing factor. These thoughts can only be defused by confronting them head on, without flinching, and with confidence that God's love can absorb and defeat them. Though Kierkegaard claims that one ought to become master of one's thoughts, he does not mean that one ought to govern them by suppression, denial, or forgetfulness. This is the sort of "mastery" that most clergymen might recommend and Kierkegaard is careful to distinguish his from theirs. The mastery which he advises begins with a deep acknowledgement of them as one's own, where one thinks them together with the thought of God and holds fast to them in inwardness. Though Kierkegaard does not think that preoccupation with such thoughts is spiritually healthy, he does think that one must first turn a steady gaze on them and appropriate them as one's own in order to be oneself in one's relationship to God. Whoever can manage such trust can do so only with a childlike confidence in God's all accepting love—the kind of confidence that accentuates God's love rather than one's own weakness. Previously, by focusing on this weakness he gave it an undue preeminence, even as he struggled to eradicate it. Now, by acknowledging it as one's own and thinking it together with God, the emphasis shifts back to God whose constant love never fails. In all of this one is reminded of Anti-Climacus's definition of faith in *The Sickness Unto Death*: "The formula that describes the state of the self when despair is completely rooted out is this: in relating itself to itself and in willing to be itself, the self rests transparently in the power that established it" (SUD, 14).

In his *Journals* Kierkegaard maintained that *"what is strenuous is the infinite transparency before God"* (JP, 4:4373; emphasis added). But this is exactly what the individual undergoing spiritual trial is asked to achieve. This strenuous transparency is "the *action* of becoming *passive* over against God,"[18] of submitting all to God such that the true self can shine forth as it is. In willing to be itself as constituted by God the self consents to be transparent before God. Here transparency indicates a deep willingness to show and

---

[18]Evans, *Kierkegaard's Fragments and Postscript*. 171.

to be oneself before God. To be transparent is to consent to God's looking through or scrutinizing the self, without flinching, hiding, or denying. Transparency then becomes the highest form of intimacy since it consents to the arrangement (already undertaken) of God's inspection of the self. It is strenuous because it requires constant vigilance. In Genesis 3, after Adam and Eve have eaten the forbidden fruit, the Lord's approach immediately prompts them to hide. When the Lord calls out, the man admits that he hid because his nakedness made him afraid. Though Kierkegaard does not cite this passage in these *Journal* sections, it provides a metaphor to elucidate the meaning of transparency. Certainly no one, on his own power, can go back to the innocent nakedness which predates sin: Adam and Eve did not even know that they were naked since they lived confidently under the gaze of God. But it is possible, to press the metaphor a bit further, *to assume one's nakedness before God* and self and to venture daily to achieve an increased transparency. This amounts to a willingness to live the truth about oneself before God, to dissemble nothing, and to believe that God's love will be sufficient to contain it all. This does not mean that Kierkegaard advises the sufferer to abandon hope that his thorn in the flesh might be removed someday. Quite the opposite. Faith waits in confidence and knows "grace too has its time" (JP, 4:4370). But in the meantime, and this meantime might be an extended one, the sufferer performs the religious work of continually renewing his transparency before God.

Whoever undertakes this bold venture of faith may feel "as if the relationship were stretched too tightly" (JP, 4:4372). The combination which makes spiritual trial so agonizing is the coupling of the thought of God as love with the presence of one's excruciating thoughts. To hold these two fast together while maintaining one's spiritual composure is the challenge of strenuous transparency. Though Kierkegaard is aware that living passably in the category of spirit is rare enough and that mediocrity is the norm, he concedes that some genuinely spiritual people may benefit from an occasional slackening. The temporary diversions which he would prescribe include recreation, physical activity, and other "innocent human aids" (JP, 4:4373). Someone undergoing spiritual trial would be a likely candidate here. Because these thoughts that try the spirit originate in the imagination and feed on possibility, *action* is the best remedy against them. However, because most people "use diversionary aids all too promiscuously" most people are more likely to be in need of *spiritual* aids (JP, 4:4373).

We return now to *Concluding Unscientific Postscript* and the dilemma which faces the religious individual who is deciding whether or not to take an outing to Deer Park. Climacus proposes "to copy and describe as concretely as possible everyday life": his emphasis falls upon a definite individual about to undertake an actual, particular action (CUP, 1:464). But it is the difficulty inherent in the proposed activity which interests him most. The difficulty consists in the fact that "the flimsiest expression of the finite", that is, amusement in the park, is held together with the thought of God (CUP, 1:473). The religious individual is religious because he expresses his relationship to God in the concretion of daily life. When the resolution to be made or the journey to be undertaken is serious, it is easier to couple the thought of God with it. But always to do so, even in relation to life's finite trivialities—this is the challenge of religiousness. "If no one else wants to try to present the absoluteness of the religious placed together with the specific, a combination that in existence is the very basis and meaning of suffering, then I will do it," Climacus complains (CUP, 1:483).

The suffering which such a combination effects is the suffering of dying to immediacy, maintaining a relative relation to relative ends and an absolute relation to the absolute. When this is raised to a higher potency, spiritual trial can and frequently does emerge. But it is interesting to observe that Climacus ends on a note of human cheer:

> Our religious person chooses the way to the amusement park, and why? Because he does not dare to choose the way to the monastery. And why does he not dare to do that? Because it is too exclusive. So he goes out there. . . . "But he does not enjoy himself," someone may say. Yes, he does indeed. And why does he enjoy himself? Because the humblest expression for the relationship with God is to acknowledge one's humanness, and it is human to enjoy oneself. (CUP, 1:493)

The religious individual enjoying his day in Deer Park and the religious individual in spiritual trial are not essentially different. Both express their relationship to God in daily life, and to the extent that they achieve the strenuous transparency to which the religious life leads, it does not matter if their experience is one of amusement or trial, since God is to be found in both.

17

The Bilateral Symmetry of Kierkegaard's Postscript

Andrew J. Burgess

An old Chinese story tells of a person who seeks a sage to learn how to paint. "Bring me a fish," instructs the sage. When the apprentice does this, the sage asks him to describe it. No sketching is done yet, since a Chinese artist paints not from appearances but from the essence—the "tigerishness of the tiger," as it is called. Thus when the apprentice insists on sketching the fishiness of the fish right away, the master rebuffs him. After many weeks the aspiring artist is finally struck by the fish's most obvious feature: its bilateral symmetry. For every fin on one side there is a fin on the other, for every scale a corresponding scale. "Now you understand the fish," says the sage. "It is in your mind's eye. Go and paint it."

Compared to *Concluding Unscientific Postscript*'s central role in the Kierkegaard corpus, its structure has received little attention. In his commentary on *Postscript*, for example, Niels Thulstrup omits any substantial outline of the book, although he had previously provided an elaborate account of that kind in his commentary on *Philosophical Fragments*.[1] Even the first English translators of *Postscript*, David Swenson and Walter Lowrie, who must have read the book as closely as anyone else in their generation, translate inconsistently a key word dealing with the structure.[2] More

---

[1]*Commentary on Kierkegaard's "Concluding Unscientific Postscript,"* trans. Robert Widenmann (Princeton: Princeton University Press, 1984) 139.

[2]Swenson/Lowrie translate the word *Deel* with the English word "book" when naming the two major divisions of the book, probably in order to reserve the word "part" for the subdivision, since English otherwise might lack enough words for the finer subdivisions. But then where Climacus refers to one of these "books" (as for example on 23 and 331 in their translation) Swenson/Lowrie translate the word *Deel* with the English word "part." *Kierkegaard's Concluding Unscientific Postscript* (Princeton: Princeton University Press, 1941).

recently there have been a few attempts to analyze the book's structure, notably two essays by Stephen Dunning,[3] yet many aspects of its intricately woven texture remain unexplored.

How can anyone paint such a strange work as *Concluding Unscientific Postscript*? No other book in Kierkegaard's corpus is quite like it. Nor are there any canons prescribed for the postscript as a literary genre, not at least for the kind of postscript that ranges more than 600 pages. The approach here will therefore be a roundabout one, following the advice of the Chinese sage: first, examine the book, looking for its overall pattern, its "postscriptness"; and then, with this pattern in mind, go on and paint it.

The Shape of the Postscript

The table of contents for *Concluding Unscientific Postscript* (CUP, 1:v-xi) is long and detailed, paying attention both to the "outer frame" (the prefatory and concluding material of the book) as well as to the main body of text. The table is more than just a list of contents. It gives a set of guidelines for reading the text, as if Kierkegaard feels the need to write a mini-essay warning the reader at the outset about the unusual outline of the work.

The Outer Frame

Surrounding the main body is a framework with three layers: an outer layer made up of the title page at the beginning and "A First and Last Explanation" at the end, a middle layer of the preface and the appendix, and an inner layer of the book's introductory and concluding chapters. The "authorial voice" varies with each layer; that is, the style and viewpoint of the voice in each layer differs from that of the voice in the next layer.

(a) Kierkegaard is represented in his own voice on the initial title page and in the concluding "Explanation," which together form an outer envelope for the book. The pages of the "Explanation" are separate from the rest of the book, and they were sent to

---

[3]"Rhetoric and Reality in Kierkegaard's *Postscript*," *International Journal for Philosophy of Religion* 15 (1984): 125-37; and "The Dialectic of Religious Inwardness," *Kierkegaard's Dialectic of Inwardness: A Structural Analysis of the Theory of Stages* (Princeton: Princeton University Press, 1985) 181-213.

the printer after the rest of the manuscript (CUP, 2:viii; JP, 5:5871) with instructions to be printed at the very end of the book and without any page numbers. On the title page he lists himself as the editor only, with Johannes Climacus as the author. Although this is not an outright statement of authorship, it is still the first time in the pseudonymous authorship that Kierkegaard goes this far in acknowledging responsibility for the works. Then in the "Explanation" Kierkegaard explicitly states that he is the author not only of *Postscript* but also of several other works preceding it. The reason for the pseudonymity is that he wants through these pseudonyms to represent various opinions that are not his own. Thus, although he is legally responsible for these books, he does not necessarily share the opinions of any of the pseudonymous authors (CUP, 1:625-27).

(b) Within the outer envelope is a second envelope, authored by the pseudonym Johannes Climacus (CUP, 1:8, 623; JP, 5:5884). These are Climacus's preface and his appendix ("An Understanding with the Reader"). The close tie between Climacus's preface and appendix is demonstrated by one of the changes Kierkegaard made in editing the book, when he moved a page from the end of the preface to the appendix (CUP, 2:107; JP, 1:1038). Moreover, Climacus's flippant style is different from Kierkegaard's own tone in the book. In his preface Climacus gives thanks for the meager reception of *Fragments*, since this response shows that it has been understood as being without authority, and the appendix echoes this same point. Anyone who reads what he says is on one's own and cannot call upon the authority of Climacus or anyone else. In the appendix Climacus goes so far as to "revoke" (call back, take back) all he has said in the book (CUP, 1:619).

(c) In addition, the introductory and concluding chapters of the main text together make up a third envelope in which the book is enclosed. The book ascribes these two chapters, and all the pages between them, to Climacus's authorship, but part of the text does not represent Climacus's own position. In the last two pages of the introductory chapter Climacus makes an important move by putting the decisive question of the book into the first person singular: "How can I, Johannes Climacus, share in the happiness that Christianity promises?" (CUP, 1:17) This is not Climacus's personal question, however. He is only "an outsider" (CUP, 1:16);

he merely presents the question and does not take an interest in it as decisive for his own happiness. At the same time, he insists that the only person for whom this can be an appropriate question is someone for whom it has an infinite interest. In order for Climacus to present the question, then, he has to pose it *as if* it were his own, even though it is not. As Climacus explains in his appendix, the question is asked as an experiment, "in the isolation of the imaginary construction" (CUP, 1:617).

What kind of person would it be who would personally ask this question about eternal happiness? In a moving passage near the center of the book Climacus tells the story of how he came to direct his studies toward defining the differences between Christianity and speculative philosophy (CUP, 1:234-42). Late one Sunday evening he overheard two people in a graveyard talking. They were a grandfather and his ten-year-old grandson, and they sat beside the fresh grave of the boy's father. The dead man had abandoned his faith in favor of Hegelian speculation, and the grandfather lacked the education to be able to warn the boy against following his father's path. Besides, the grandfather would be dead by the time the boy was old enough to understand the questions involved. Climacus resolved, then, to make it his task to investigate the issues, and this was the resolve from which *Postscript* arose.

Accordingly, if some person had to be picked to represent those for whom Climacus takes up his hypothetical question about eternal happiness, the best candidate might be the ten-year-old boy from the graveyard. In a few years this boy would be a young man, facing the same challenge his father had, and then he would need the dialectical clarification that *Postscript* sets out to provide.

The elements of the introductory and concluding matter thus surround the main body of the book in three envelopes or layers:

> Title page (presumably by Kierkegaard, the editor)
> Preface (by Climacus)
> Introduction (by Climacus,
> with the "young man's" question)
> [Main body of text]
> Conclusion (by Climacus)
> Appendix. "For an Understanding" (by Climacus)
> "A First and Last Declaration" (by Kierkegaard)

Each introductory element is matched by a corresponding final element to form a part of a simple but powerful frame.

However, the relationships among these three envelopes or layers are highly complex. At the first level, Kierkegaard invents an author called "Johannes Climacus" to present ideas in a detached mode that he does not fully share. Then at the second level this imaginary author Johannes Climacus poses a hypothetical question for the sake of the boy from the graveyard who is not yet in a position to ask it; and also, of course, for the sake of all other seekers after eternal happiness, whoever they may be. That question in turn sets the problematic for almost the entire *Postscript*. Yet at all times the discussion operates on three levels: as an answer to the passionate question of the earnest seeker of eternal happiness, as the observations of the personally disinterested Climacus himself, and finally as an indirect argument by Kierkegaard against putting the question in a disinterested way. It is small wonder that Kierkegaard was exasperated by people who took statements from the pseudonymous works out of context (CUP, 2:168; JP, 6:6786). Ignoring the levels of argument is as much a logical error as ignoring the parentheses in a formula of symbolic logic.

Chapter Divisions within the Main Body of Text

Within the outer framework lies the main body of the *Postscript*, formidable and immense—and very oddly structured. This structure is indeed an inherent part of the argument of the book, and it can be traced back to the earliest drafts from which the text arose.

What strikes someone immediately about the book's divisions is their unequal size. Part one is a chapter of a mere thirty pages, while the only other part, part two, is more than 500 pages long. Part two, in turn, is divided into two sections, of which the first is about fifty pages and the second comprises almost all the rest of the book. The fourth chapter of section two, part two, again, is divided into two divisions, one of about twenty pages and the other of about 350; and division two in turn is divided very unequally into an A and a B.

Yet the structure of the book is anything but haphazard. Except for the four chapters in section two, each primary subdivision of the book is cut into two, and only two, parts; and except for the last division, between A and B, each second part is much longer than the first. (The two chapters of part one are another exception, but this division does not matter, since the objective approach to the truth of Christianity turns out to be a dead end.) Thus with a few exceptions the same plan holds throughout: the second part of each division of part two includes all the rest of the text.

This table of contents nearly shouts a warning against approaching the book in the usual way. A reader naturally expects that, however problematic a book may be in other respects, it will consist of bite-sized paragraphs and meal-sized chapters, letting the reader simply chew through one piece after another. The normal pattern for a book is serial order. Each chapter takes up a topic and builds on what was discussed in the previous chapter or chapters. For this particular book, however, a serial reading is not enough. Climacus has overlaid the standard outline with a schema of his own, directing the reader to reread the ideas in a very particular way.

Nor is the book's arrangement a late or contrived restructuring of the material. Like the bilateral symmetry of the Chinese fish, *Postscript*'s two-sidedness can be discerned in its earliest, embryonic versions. The genesis of the book went through four main stages: a set of early sketches, a provisional draft, a final writing draft, and a corrected final draft going to the printer (CUP, 2:viii). (1) In a short entry from the earliest sketch of the shape of the book (CUP, 2:9-11; JP, 5:5788-89) the three main points of part one (labeled "A" in this sketch) are noted, but there is very little about part two ("B") except the title of the first chapter on Lessing. Other entries for the early sketch have full notes for the Lessing chapter and for the objectivity/subjectivity split (CUP, 2:11; JP, 5:5790-91), but only general ideas for later divisions. (2) The titles and content for the first chapters in section two begin to appear in the provisional draft (CUP, 2:12; JP, 4:4537). A sizable section of text on Grundtvig was also removed from part one of this draft, perhaps as part of a de-emphasis on the objective issue (CUP, 2:16-29). (3) The outline for the final writing draft has "B" (on Lessing) divided into two sections, 1 and 2; and 2 includes the first two chapter headings ("Becoming Subjective" and "Subjective Truth, Inwardness; Truth Is Subjectivity"), as well as a title for his survey of a contemporary effort in literature (CUP, 2:12-14). (4) The final draft going to the printer changes the "A" and "B" headings to what they are in the published version and also makes appropriate changes in subheadings (CUP, 2:15). In summary, the manuscript evidence shows that the book was originally envisioned in terms of a single division with two more or less equal parts, but that, as the issues were thought through, the "subjective" side was divided and then divided again, producing the unequally divided outline in the printed text.

Thus the whole *Postscript*, from start to finish, and from inception to publication, exhibits a lopsided bilateral symmetry, with matching parts at the beginning and ending, and with matching—though very unequal—parts on the two sides of the main text. No fish ever swam with such uneven symmetry, and no bird ever flew. But at least one book was written this way, and, if that book's table of contents is to be trusted, this is also the way the book is to be read. Bilateral symmetry is the "postscriptness" of *Postscript*, and any analysis of the book will have to take it into account.

Painting the Postscript

"Now you understand the fish," says the sage. "Go and paint it." Since there is no allowance for artistic reproductions in this essay, the accompanying "Chart of the *Postscript*" will stand in for whatever "paintings" are drawn of the *Postscript*. In fact, the chart is only a bare diagram of the book's structure, showing the prefatory and concluding material as a border, and the symmetry of the chapters as a kind of flow chart. The reader's imagination must supply any missing stormy skies of existential anxiety, chasm of choice, vista of eternal happiness, and the like.

In order to simplify things the chart makes several alterations: (1) it does not represent matters of scale; (2) it omits some early divisions, such as the division in part one into two chapters, and of the Lessing pages into two chapters; (3) it introduces a division between chapters three and four of part two, section two, thereby permitting the last half of the section, dealing with "the issue in *Fragments*," to be displayed as a separate unit; and (4) it does

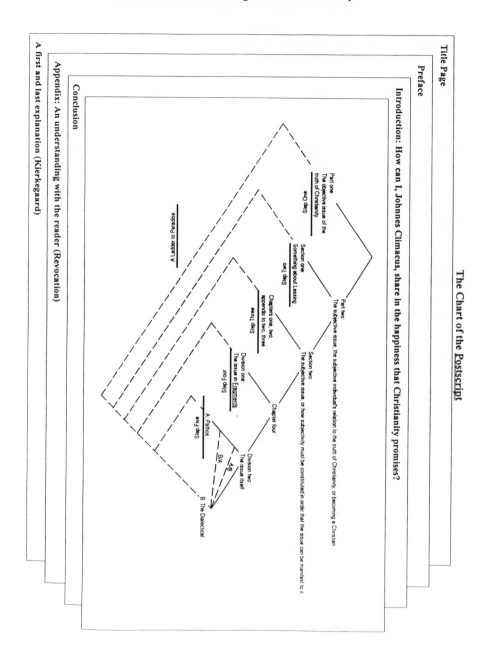

The Chart of the Postscript

Title Page

Preface

Introduction: How can I, Johnnes Climacus, share in the happiness that Christianity promises?

Part one:
The objective issue of the
truth of Christianity

Step One

Part two:
The subjective issue, the subjective individual's relation to the truth of Christianity, or becoming a Christian

Section one:
Something about Lessing

Step Two

Section two:
The subjective issue, or how subjectivity must be constituted in order that the issue can be manifest to it

Chapters one, two,
appendix to two, three

Step Three

Chapter four:

Division one:
The issue in Fragments

Division two:
The issue itself

Step Four

A. Pathos

Step Five

B/A

A/B

A Leap to Paradise

B. The Dialectical

Conclusion

Appendix: An understanding with the reader (Revocation)

A first and last explanation (Kierkegaard)

not show the intricate sub-subdivisions (for example, into initial, essential, and decisive expressions of existential pathos) of the last pages of the book.

The chart suggests at least three pictures of the *Postscript* text: a path with many branches, a set of nested boxes, and a ladder. These three pictures, in turn, interact with the three layers of the outer frame: the path with the introduction-conclusion layer, the boxes with Climacus's preface and appendix, and the ladder with Kierkegaard's title page and "first and last explanation."

Picture 1. The Branching Path

The most obvious way of making a picture from the chart is to envision a person standing at the top of the page and facing two choices, part one and part two. The option for the objective side (part one) is a broad path, short and easy, well marked by precedents in theological and philosophical tradition. On the other hand, the subjective option in part two (that is, the long, slanting right hand arm of the chart) leads along an increasingly dangerous path that a person would have to travel essentially alone. More- over, that subjective path has many further branches, and only by choosing each time the longer and more rigorous branch can the traveler find a way through. This person stands at a crossroads, with eternal happiness at stake. Either/or.

Climacus describes the two options sharply on the very first two pages of the book's main text (CUP, 1:21-22), only a few paragraphs after the place at the end of the introduction where the hypothetical question about eternal happiness is first raised. From the standpoint of the objective truth itself, he says, the question of eternal happiness cannot decisively arise. The "inquiring subject" who raises such a question objectively in history or philosophy "is indeed interested but is not infinitely, personally, impassionedly interested in his relation to this truth concerning his own eternal happiness" (CUP, 1:21). The path of the "inquiring subject" who raises the question of eternal happiness leads to a dead end, which Climacus describes briefly in *Postscript's* part one. The bulk of the book (part two) therefore pursues the other option, in which the question of eternal happiness is raised as a "subjective" issue, that is, by one who has an infinite personal interest in the outcome.

What kind of person would face this choice between two paths? It would be someone like the ten-year-old boy from the graveyard scene (CUP, 1:234-42), after he has grown up to be a young man and has to struggle with the difficulties of keeping the promise he made to his grandfather, that he would stay true to his faith.

Johannes Climacus, on the other hand, is confronted by no such alternative. His relation to the question is an objective, not a subjective, one; and, as he himself would be the first to say (for example, in CUP, 1:199), there is a world of difference between these two kinds of relations to the truth. In fact, as Kierkegaard remarks in later notes, the effort of *Postscript* to define Christian inwardness (subjectivity) distinctively is itself objectivity (JP, 4:4550). Climacus writes *about* the question of eternal happiness; he does not ask the question for himself. His investigation is "second order," that is, a philosophical and an historical inquiry. His role in *Postscript* is that of the "inquiring subject" (CUP, 1:21). Whether he also has another role as a religious thinker, and merely adopts the investigative role as a "humorous" *incognito* (CUP, 1:500-501), is something the reader is not told and does not need to know.

Although the picture of the path with many branches is helpful, it only partially charts *Postscript*'s intricacies, because it does not equally well represent all of the branches along the path. Following the first branch the chart shows a series of others, but the later turning points differ from the first one. One does not, for example, discover that a person is *either* somewhat like Lessing (part two, section one) *or* else is learning "how subjectivity must be constituted in order that the issue can be qualified in it" (part of the title of section two). Nor is there a choice presented between *either* Religiousness A *or* Religiousness B, although these two may indeed be legitimate alternatives in some other contexts. Much, though not all, of what these latter disjunctions provide is better characterized as an increasing clarification of the concepts on the subjective side of the initial either/or of the book, rather than as more and more new choices.

Picture 2. The Set of Nested Boxes

In order to bring out the role of *Postscript*'s structure as a series of progressively more precise clarifications, another picture is called for, a set of nested boxes. This pattern is not entirely new, but continues the arrangement found in the layers of the outer frame surrounding the main text. *Postscript* is like an elaborately wrapped present. First the reader finds three layers of wrappings and then the present itself, which is a set of boxes, one inside the other. Open the first box and another is inside; open that, and there is yet another. Each box has all the rest inside of it, just as each of the second halves of Climacus's divisions of the main text (except the pages on religiousness A and B) contain all the rest of the book.

To start making this picture in the chart, simply draw lines so that the disjunction between parts one and two of the text becomes a "box" framing the whole work. Further lines then make sections one and two into a "box" within the first box, and then more lines make the other divisions in the book into boxes nested within each other. The broken lines on the chart show where all these lines would have to be.

Postscript as a set of nested boxes is the picture of *Postscript* in which Johannes Climacus is most immediately involved. Clarification of Christian concepts is his first task. Everything is done patiently and in order. At each layer of analysis he takes up the conceptual confusions appropriate to that box, before going on to the more specific set of concepts of the box that lies within it.

Climacus borrows freely from the techniques of Hegelian dialectic in his analysis, particularly in the final sub-subdivisions at the end of the book dealing with the relations between religiousness A and religiousness B (represented by A/B and B/A on the chart). Sometimes it even appears as if he has taken over Hegelian structures without being conscious of them.[4] Yet Climacus is no blind follower of the Hegelian movement of his century. Henry Allison's suggestion that *Postscript* might be "a kind of perverse parody of Hegel"[5] has much to recommend it. *Postscript* delights in spoofing the structures of Hegel's *Phenomenology of Mind* as much as *Tristram Shandy* does the genre of the novel.

---

[4]Dunning, *Kierkegaard's Dialectic* 189-212.
[5]"Christianity and Nonsense," *Review of Metaphysics* 20 (March 1967): 456.

Postscript, however, is more than simply philosophy for its own sake. It is philosophy written for a purpose, and that purpose is to clarify the confusions that have arisen between speculative philosophy and Christianity. This was the pledge Climacus made to himself after the graveyard scene, and it is the key to understanding not only *Postscript*'s message but also its structure.

Picture 3. The Ladder and the "Revocation"

The most obvious, and at the same time the most potentially deceptive, of the three pictures treated here is that of a "ladder to paradise." The metaphor describes an important element in Climacus's strategy—but only after it is "revoked," or, in terms of the chart of the *Postscript*, turned upside down.

One reason the ladder picture is obvious is that it is implicit in the name of *Postscript*'s main author. Johannes Climacus's namesake is a sixth-century Greek abbot named "John of the Ladder," who developed a series of devotional exercises that he called his "ladder to paradise." In one of his notes Kierkegaard applies the name ironically to Hegel: "Hegel is a Johannes *Climacus* who does not storm the heavens as do the giants, by setting mountain upon mountain—but enters them by means of his syllogisms" (JP, 2:1575).

Many aspects of the book suggest the ladder motif. *Postscript*'s argument moves stepwise to greater and greater heights—of passion and inwardness, for example, and of difficulty. Toward the end of the work the upward dialectical movement is particularly plain, especially through the three stages of the expression of existential pathos.

Yet the ladder metaphor can also be deceptive, because Climacus is no standard Hegelian. His distrust of Danish Hegelian philosophy is foreshadowed in an earlier Kierkegaard work, the "Diapsalmata" of *Either/Or I*: "What philosophers say about actuality [*Virkelighed*] is often just as disappointing as it is when one reads on a sign in a secondhand shop: Pressing Done Here. If a person were to bring his clothes to be pressed, he would be duped, for the sign is merely for sale" (EO, 1:32). Philosophy can be *about* actuality; that is, it can deal with the concept of actuality. But even the most ingenious dialectic does not provide actuality itself, any more than a sign store provides pressed pants. Thus, just as philosophy will not deliver actuality, a philosophical ladder to paradise will not deliver paradise. To say this about philosophy and dialectic is not to denigrate philosophy as such, but only to warn against a certain brand of philosophy that has its notions of concept and actuality all mixed up.

The tragedy of the deceased father in the graveyard scene is that he had made a similar kind of philosophical mistake. He had exchanged his Christian faith for a supposed higher wisdom (CUP, 1:238) that, by being *about* Christian faith, claimed thereby to be a new philosophical faith that had gone beyond Christianity to a higher level. This was part of the confusion Climacus promised himself he would set out to untangle.

Climacus's task involves a subtle methodological danger. If he succeeds in portraying the error in speculative theology in philosophical terms, his portrayal of Christianity may itself be taken to be a ladder to paradise that can substitute for simple faith. *Postscript* would then replace Hegel's *Phenomenology*, with the result that his attempt to help the grandfather and his grandson would be in vain.

The way Climacus adopts to avoid this methodological trap is so startling that a commentator may easily overlook it: he writes his conceptual analysis of Christian faith and then, when he is almost through, he takes it all back. He provides not only an essay but also its "revocation." The first definite hint of this move comes at a critical point in the book, just as he is about to describe the distinctiveness of Christianity itself. No book can be the answer, since "one does not prepare oneself to become aware of Christianity by reading books or by world-historical surveys, but by immersing oneself in existing" (CUP, 1:560). But if no book can make a person aware of Christianity, what of *Postscript* itself? Can one do without Climacus's book as well? That prospect does not seem to worry Climacus here in the least. In any case, at the end of the book he takes back whatever the book has said. "Everything is to be understood in such a way that it is revoked" (CUP, 1:619).

This strange revocation at the end of the book is paralleled by an equally odd incompleteness in the execution of the book's structural plan. Just when someone might expect to receive the definitive description of distinctively Christian subjectivity, at the point where religiousness A and B are discussed together, the prose becomes abstract and programmatic and the pages on each topic fewer and fewer, until finally the text gives out altogether. The outline of *Postscript* itself shows that something is missing. For every other division in the main text the second part is several times longer than the first, but with the division between "Religiousness A" and "Religiousness B" the pattern is reversed. The symmetry of the book requires that the "B" section describing the "how" of the Christian life be much longer than the "A" section, but it is not. At the final step of the ladder, where the height of passion is called for, Climacus's personal detachment from the project leaves him unable to describe, beyond the barest sketch, what Christianity is about. According to the symmetry of the book there should have been several hundred pages describing the distinctive "how" of religiousness B, in order to match proportionately the pages Climacus devotes to religiousness A. If Kierkegaard or the publisher could have afforded it, Climacus might well have ended his book with hundreds of blank pages. As it is, *Postscript*'s missing pages are still mute testimony that the book has not reached the end that its overall structure promises.

But does this revocation of *Postscript*, and the incomplete working out of the structure, mean that *Postscript*'s conceptual analyses are wasted? No, says Climacus. "To write a book and to revoke it is not the same as refraining from writing it" (CUP, 1:621). For some people at least—for the young man from the graveyard scene, for example—reading *Postscript* and then "revoking" it might be just what they need. The clarifications in the book might warn the young man away from certain kinds of "nonsense" (CUP, 1:568) that could distract him from a genuine personal quest. Although this would be a negative function for the book, it would be a worthwhile function.

Still, is there no positive function for *Postscript*? Cannot the steps to faith it describes provide some kind of guidebook for the philosophically sophisticated believer?

To take up this question, a new picture can be extracted from the chart of the *Postscript*. "Revoke" the chart. Turn it upside down, so that the divisions of the book become like rungs. The result will be Climacus's ladder, the third "picture."

Viewed this way, the chart may provide some spiritual guidance for the philosophically trained reader, although only to a limited extent. The reader may, for example, recall what the chart looked like right-side up, and some points on the chart may even be readable upside down. But the chart could never be a very complete guide, especially since the markings on the chart become hardest to decipher toward the end of the book, just where direction is urgently needed.

Moreover, the philosophically astute reader who uses *Postscript* as a personal guide will always be in danger of thinking of the book as if it were a new speculative ladder. For this reason, and many others, then, Climacus encourages the person who wants to become aware of Christianity to start, not by following the steps in his book, or any other book, and instead by "immersing oneself in existing" (CUP, 1:560).

The key issue for Climacus is the equality of all believers before God. The "simple person" and the "simple wise person" need to be understood as having the same degree of difficulty in relating to God; for example, with respect to the forgiveness of sins (CUP, 1:228). In order that the grandfather at the grave side will not be at a disadvantage over against some more educated believer, perhaps a devout theology professor, each has to receive some advantage over the other. The devout professor gets a clearer understanding of the steps toward faith than the grandfather, but at the possible danger (which the grandfather does not face) that this understanding might become confused with faith.

In its concern for equality *Postscript* resembles its predecessor under Climacus's name, *Philosophical Fragments*. In that book the "contemporary follower" from the time of Jesus turns out to have no advantage over the "follower at second hand." The advantages and disadvantages of both kinds of followers cancel each other out (PF, 104-105), just as in the case with the "simple person" and the "simple wise person" in *Postscript*.

This issue of equality is also part of the reason why, at the end of *Postscript*, Kierkegaard writes an "Explanation" that he, and not Climacus, is the person ultimately responsible for publishing the book (CUP, 1:625-30). By calling attention in the "Explanation" to the fact that Climacus is only a pseudonym, Kierkegaard in effect places Climacus's philosophical project within a larger religious context, thereby helping to prevent the reader from imagining that the role of the "wise person" must be the highest a human can attain.

Painting Mars in the Armor That Makes Him Invisible

To complete the gallery of paintings for this essay one last picture is called for, this time a little masterpiece by Climacus himself. In an early chapter of *Postscript* Climacus takes up an ironical case of spectacular failure. Immortality, he says, is a subjective question (CUP, 1:174). As soon as someone tries to deal with the question of immortality objectively, however, the question itself changes. It becomes a different issue altogether, and it is not clear how a person could demonstrate it or even why one would want to demonstrate it.

Climacus compares the attempt to prove immortality to the attempt to paint Mars dressed in the armor that makes him invisible. Just when someone seems about to succeed, the project fails. "The point is the invisibility, and with immortality the point is the subjectivity and the subjective individual's subjective development" (CUP, 1:174).

The concept of immortality described on this page is in precisely the same situation as the concept of Christianity in *Postscript* as a whole. Climacus suggests that the only people who can know something about Christianity are those who passionately affirm or passionately reject it (CUP 1:52). But if this is true, then Climacus, who lacks that passion, cannot know anything about it, and one more painting should be added to the set described so far: Climacus's final painting of Christian faith at the end of *Postscript*. Any set of blank pages will do, since like the picture of the armor of Mars the point is the invisibility.

The stages by which Climacus works in *Postscript* do look as if he were setting out to do something as absurd as painting Mars in invisible armor. At the beginning and through the middle of the book, he makes many remarkable preliminary sketches of faith. Toward the end, however, as the brush work on the analysis becomes more intricate, the conceptual picture becomes harder and harder to make out, until finally it is no longer to be seen. Still, Climacus is an honest workman, and he does not promise more for his painting than he delivers. He merely points out that it is not the same to paint a picture and then erase it as not to paint it at all. He does not deny that it is possible to draw an objective picture of faith. How could he deny it? In large part he has done that sort of painting himself, before he erased it off the canvas. But he does not think that an objective picture of the nature of Christian faith is of much religious use, except in a highly indirect way. What he rejects above all is the idea that a disinterested philosophical inquiry could somehow substitute for a passionate lifelong struggle up the ladder to paradise—or even take someone halfway there. The notion that someone could actually succeed in painting Mars's invisible armor, or "what is even more curious . . . succeed halfway," he rejects with the contempt it deserves (CUP, 1:79n).

Conclusion

How does it happen that Climacus seems to fail miserably in his attempt at painting, producing nothing but a blank page, while my essay dares to try three pictures after only a short art lesson from a Chinese sage? The answer is simple: Climacus sets out to paint faith, which is subjective, while this essay merely paints *Postscript*, which is a book *about* subjectivity but itself an objective matter. *Postscript* is a second-order project, about subjectivity, while this essay is third order, about *Postscript*'s objective treatment of subjectivity. All I have attempted is to sketch *Postscript* in its post-scriptness, and thereby to encourage the reader to examine the book again in some different ways.

Contributors

International Kierkegaard Commentary 12
Concluding Unscientific Postscript to "Philosophical Fragments"

THOMAS C. ANDERSON is Professor of Philosophy at Marquette University.

LEE BARRETT is Professor of Theology at Lancaster Theological Seminary.

ANDREW J. BURGESS is Associate Professor of Philosophy at the University of New Mexico.

JOHN D. GLENN is Associate Professor of Philosophy at Tulane University.

ALASTAIR HANNAY is editor of *Inquiry* at the Institute for Philosophy, University of Oslo.

NERINA JANSEN is Professor of Communication Theory emeritus at the University of South Africa.

LOUISE CARROLL KEELEY is Associate Professor of Philosophy at Assumption College.

DAVID R. LAW is Lecturer in Christian Thought at the University of Manchester.

WILLIAM MCDONALD is Lecturer in Philosophy at the University of New England.

EDWARD F. MOONEY is Professor of Philosophy at Sonoma State University.

ROBERT L. PERKINS is Professor of Philosophy at Stetson University.

M. G. PIETY teaches at Denmark's International School.

HUGH S. PYPER is Lecturer in Biblical Studies at the University of Leeds.

ROBERT C. ROBERTS is Professor of Philosophical and Psychological Studies at Wheaton College.

SYLVIA WALSH is Adjunct Professor of Philosophy at Stetson University.

JULIA WATKIN is Lecturer in Philosophy at the University of Tasmania.

MEROLD WESTPHAL is Professor of Philosophy at Fordham University.

Advisory Board

Index

Abraham, 131-32, 139, 142-43, 165
absolute relation to the absolute,
absolute telos, 263-89
absurd, 184
acosmism, 7, 169-86
action, 74-75, 81, 84, 201
actuality, 22, 170-84, 340
aesthetic, the, 52
Allison, Henry, 46, 339
anabaptists, 47n23
Andersen, Hans Christian, 239
Anderson, Thomas C., 188n5,
    202n25
anxiety, 320-23
apologetics, 44-46, 51
Appleyard, Bryan, 109
appropriating, 36, 121
appropriation, 20, 40, 45, 118-19,
    121, 199, 203
Aquinas, Thomas, 80
Arendt, Hannah, 313-14n6, 315n7,
    316n10, 317
Aristotle, 21n26, 24-51, 71, 73-75,
    80, 102, 191, 198, 248-51
    Metaphysics, 57
aspect perception, 86
ataraxy, 79
Atkins, Peter, 5, 105, 106, 107, 109,
    110, 111, 112
Augustine, 80
authorial voice, 229, 301, 330
authoritarianism, 40, 44, 46
authority, 123-26, 205, 225-26, 331
authorship, 331

Baptist movement, 47-51

Barbour, Ian, 96n2
Barrow, John D., 103, 111
Barthes, Roland, 64
beatitudes, the, 260
Beauvoir, Simone de
    The Second Sex, 18
beginning, 97, 190, 192, 193, 197
Beidler, Devon K., 97, 97n3
Beiser, F., 131, 211n, 223-24
Benardete, Seth, 34
Bentham, Jeremy, 45
Bible, 44-45
    Gospel of John, 260-61
    New Testament, 73-74, 81, 86,
        249, 255, 255n21, 260-62
Big Bang, 104, 106, 108
    pre-Big Bang, 112
bilateral symmetry, 329, 334-35,
    335, 342
Billeskov-Jansen, F.J., 243n22
Boethius, 67
Boole, G., 103
Boslough, John, 104n20, 109n49,
    112n56
Bronowski, Joseph, 108n39
Brooks, P., 258
Buren, John van, 56n5
Burgess, Andrew, 298n5

Carroll, L., 155
categorical imperative, 180, 180, 257
certitude, 179, 187, 190-94, 196, 199,
    201, 295-96
chance, 102n10, 106, 107, 109, 112,
    118n5
character, 74, 76, 80-83

Concluding Unscientific Postscript to "Philosophical Fragments"
International Kierkegaard Commentary 12

Mercer University Press, 6316 Peake Road, Macon GA 31210-3960.
Isbn 0-86554-575-8. Catalog and warehouse pick number MUP/H430.
Original (1984) text, interior, cover, and dustjacket design
    by Margaret Jordan Brown; recast (1992) by Edmon L. Rowell, Jr.
Camera-ready pages, cover, and dustjacket
    composed by Edmon L. Rowell, Jr. on a Gateway 2000
        via WordPerfect wp/5.1 and wpwin/5.1/5.2/6.1/8.0
        and printed on a LaserMaster 1000
        and a Hewlett Packard LaserJet 4/4M (Postscript).
Text font: Palatino 11/13 and 10/12. Display font: Palatino italic.
Printed and bound by Cushing-Malloy, Inc., Ann Arbor MI 48107.
    Printed via offset lithography on 50# Glatfelter Natural, B-31.
    Smyth sewn with Rainbow Pearl A endsheets tipped.
    Casebound in Kivar 9 over .088 binders boards;
        stamped on c.1, spine, and c.4 in blue foil with one hit gold foil
        on c.1 from dies supplied by Cushing-Malloy, Inc.;
        with black and white headbands and footbands;
            wrapped in dustjackets printed 2 pms colors
            (427 gray, 202 blue) and layflat film laminated.
                                                    [October 1997]